FRANCO

Spain and Spanish Morocco

FRANCE

Bay of Biscay

ANDORRA

El Ferrol
Gijón
La Coruña
Santander
Guernica
San Sebastián
Oviedo
Bilbao
ASTURIAS
GALICIA
León
BASQUE PROVINCES
NAVARRE
Vigo
LEÓN
Burgos
Gerona
OLD CASTILE
ARAGON
CATALONIA
Valladolid
Saragossa
Lérida
Barcelona
Oporto
Salamanca
Belchite
Tarragona
Avila
Guadalajara
Teruel
Castellón de la Plana
Madrid
Jarama
Brunete
Cuenca
Toledo
Cáceres
NEW CASTILE
Valencia
VALENCIA
EXTREMADURA
Lisbon
Mérida
P O R T U G A L
Badajoz
Albacete
Balearic Islands
MURCIA
Córdoba
Murcia
Huelva
Cartagena
ANDALUSIA
Mediterranean Sea
Seville
Granada
Almería
Málaga
Cádiz
Tangier
Gibraltar
Ceuta
Atlantic Ocean
Tetuán
Alhucemas Bay
Melilla
Nador
SPANISH MOROCCO
Annual

AFRICA

0   50   100   150 Miles

FRANCO

A Concise Biography

Gabrielle Ashford Hodges

Weidenfeld & Nicolson
LONDON

First published in Great Britain in 2000
by Weidenfeld & Nicolson

A CIP catalogue record for this book is
available from the British Library.

ISBN 0 297 64304 5

Typeset by Selwood Systems, Midsomer Norton
Printed in Great Britain by
Butler & Tanner Ltd, Frome and London

Weidenfeld & Nicolson

The Orion Publishing Group Ltd
Orion House
5 Upper Saint Martin's Lane
London, WC2H 9EA

For Paul

Contents

Illustrations

Acknowledgements

This book has been both very easy and extremely difficult to write. It was easy because I had access to an unrivalled collection of books, papers and articles on modern Spain and the Franco regime, and was the lucky recipient of the unstinting support and guidance of the foremost authority on this period, Paul Preston. It was difficult because this bibliographic collection resides in my house, and Paul Preston is my husband. Having spent fifteen years listening to Paul pontificate on General Franco, I was delighted to be given the opportunity to put forward my own views. Although writing the book under the baleful eye of the renowned author of an internationally acclaimed biography of Franco was not an entirely stress-free process, Paul infected me with a passionate interest in the Candillo, the civil war and Spain. His willingness to trail through draft after draft, commenting on the text, guiding my thinking and sharing his encyclopaedic knowledge of the period, has astonished even me. The many mistakes and infelicities that have seeped through a finely meshed net are, of course, all mine: as his wife, I felt honour-bound to ignore *some* of his sage suggestions.

I would like to thank Rebecca Wilson at Weidenfeld & Nicolson for commissioning the book – probably against her better judgement – and Giles Gordon for persuading her to do so. I am indebted to my editor, Toby Mundy, for the understanding and insight he displayed during the entire process. His vigilant guidance and shrewd observations helped transform an initially brash interpretation of the Generalísimo into a more accessible overview. His assistant, Alice Hunt, has been very patient in dealing with the later stages of the process, gently but firmly prising the much-amended manuscript from fingers feverishly engaged in last-minute tinkering.

I am extremely grateful to my mother, Joan Ashford-Hodges, for commenting on some early ideas, and for her resolute support and encouragement, and to my father, Anthony Ashford-Hodges, for proving that it is possible to combine professional eminence with humility and human concern. I am indebted to Gillian Woodman-Smith for agreeing, in the midst of a stressful house move, to look through the psychological aspects of the book. My thanks also to Gillian Isaacs Hemmings for going through the manuscript at such very short notice. I am grateful to Helen Graham for commenting on some preliminary thoughts. I would especially like to thank Sally Barker, who provided considerable support, and recommended a number of helpful books on the psychology of dictatorship.

Over the years, I have been lucky enough to spend some time with many Spanish friends who share a wealth of knowledge about, and direct personal experiences of, the Franco regime. Nicolás Belmonte and Nines Alonso have inculcated me with some understanding of what it is like to grow up under a dictatorship. Balassi Abando and his wife Maripaz provided insights into the attitudes and expectations of the Basques both during and after the civil war, and the trauma of political exile. Carlos Herreros has extended the generosity, hospitality and eloquent opinions for which Spaniards are renowned. Carmen Chinnery has given me vivid descriptions of her early childhood in a defeated Republican family in the Basque country, and her educational experiences in a stifling convent in the 1960s. My particular thanks go to Jaime Salóm for sending me a copy of his wonderfully perceptive play about Franco's father.

I am grateful to those friends – particularly Luiza Machado, Nadia Marks and Sharon Miller – who have been so tolerant of my inaccessibility, and Harriet Griffey for her soothing insights into the publishing process. The less than reverential suggestions of Elisabeth Allmand and Amrit Dillon, from Australia and India respectively, revived my flagging sense of humour.

Finally, I would like to thank my two sons, James and Christopher. Having shared a substantial proportion of their early years with General Franco while their father was engaged in writing his vast biography, it must have been disheartening to discover that the Caudillo had once more invaded the family home. Although it was often difficult to get my mind around major military campaigns while the boys thundered around the house brandishing a bewildering array of weaponry, they certainly helped illuminate the military mentality.

*   *   *

The author and publishers gratefully acknowledge the assistance of the following agencies, archives and private collections in locating the photographs and illustrations used in this book: La Actualidad Española; Archivo Histórico del Ministerio de Información y Cultura; Archivo Ramón Serrano Suñer; Colección Bartolomé Ros; Centre for Contemporary Spanish Studies; Ediciones Actuales; Instituto de España.

Introduction

General Franco – Fact and Fantasy

> Franco ... is a man in the enviable position of believing everything that pleases him and forgetting or denying that which is disagreeable. He is, moreover, arrogant and intoxicated by adulation and drunk on applause. He is dizzy from height, sick with power, determined to hold on to it come what may, sacrificing whatever is necessary and defending his power with beak and claws. Many think he is perverse and evil but I don't. He is crafty and cunning but I believe that he operates in the conviction that his destiny and that of Spain are consubstantial and that God has placed him in the position he occupies for great things.
>
> General Kinderlan to Don Juan de Borbón[1]

General Franco was one of four dictators who changed the face of Europe during the twentieth century. Although he appeared to lack the evil genius of Hitler, the comic charisma of Mussolini and the ruthless paranoia of Stalin, he succeeded in retaining absolute power from the moment he won the civil war in 1939 until his death in 1975. Strutting the international stage throughout much of the twentieth century, he attended the funeral of George V, fraternised with Hitler and Mussolini, confronted Churchill, Roosevelt and Truman, and was wooed by Eisenhower, Nixon and Kissinger. And yet, of all the European dictators, Franco remains the most elusive.

Full of loathing for his critical, rancorous, authoritarian father and dependent upon his devout and devoted mother, he emerges as an effeminate, inadequate individual who determined to shroud his shortcomings behind a harsh and cold façade. As an awkward, skinny child with large ears and huge mournful eyes, he did not seem marked out for great things. Derisively referred to as *cerillito* (little match-stick) at school and *Franquito* at the Military Training Academy, he was sometimes even called *Generalito* after becoming a brigadier. He was extremely short (he would never grow taller than 5 foot 3 inches) and increasingly portly, his hands were 'like a woman's and always damp with perspiration' and his voice was 'shrill and pitched on a high note which is slightly disconcerting since he speaks very softly – almost in a whisper'.[2] Even as a grown man, his military commands would sometimes burst forth in an ignominious squeak. Compared with Hitler and Mussolini his public speeches were inhibited, lacklustre affairs.

And yet, after joining the army aged fifteen, this mediocre figure ascended the military hierarchy like a meteorite. A brave, impetuous and inspirational soldier in Africa, he became a general in 1926 at the age of thirty-three. A pivotal figure in the July 1936 uprising against the left-wing Second Republic, he succeeded, within two and a half months, in establishing himself as sole military commander and Head of State of the Nationalist zone. By April 1937 he had overcome all his military and political rivals through the forced unification of parties in Salamanca. During the Second World War, Franco was vigorously courted by both the Allies and the Axis powers. In the wake of the defeat of fascism, he stubbornly ignored the West's pressure for liberalisation of his authoritarian regime. Confident of the Catholic Church's approval for his 'Christian Crusade' against communism, he assumed – quite rightly – that he could sit tight 'while the world squabbles and leaves us in peace'.[3] The cold-war paranoia of the western powers vindicated his intransigence. By 1953 Hitler's one-time admirer had survived international ostracism, consolidated his power within Spain and won himself the right to present himself publicly as the valued ally of the United States. When the so-called technocrats in his government produced an economic stabilisation plan in the late 1950s and the eventual 'economic miracle' resulted in a surge in living standards in Spain, the people thanked Franco.

What was it about this cold, inhibited, physically unimpressive individual – in so many ways the antithesis of the stereotypical Spanish personality – that enabled him to impose his will on a traditionally anarchic and passionate people throughout much of the twentieth century? The massive propaganda machinery that ground into action during the civil war, and dominated Spanish lives for nearly four decades, created the myth of a *Caudillo* or warrior-King. He was projected as an all-seeing, saintly father-figure entrusted with God's mission to wipe out communism, separatism and Freemasonry. In fact his power derived from his ability to manipulate competing, greedy and ambitious groups, who recognised that by supporting him they would safeguard their own political supremacy. Terror that any move to remove him from power would result in another civil war did the rest. Much energy went into reminding the people of the dangers of such an eventuality. The vanquished would never be allowed to forget that they had been defeated in war. The victors had a powerful vested interest in keeping Franco in power. If he fell, they were left in no doubt that they would be abandoned to face an enemy bent on revenge.

Despite his ruthless obsession with his own survival, Franco remained convinced that he had adopted power out of a selfless concern for his people. In December 1966, just before the national referendum, the Caudillo would tell the Spanish people, 'I was never motivated by the ambition for power. From my youngest days, they placed on my shoulders responsibilities beyond my age and my rank. I would have liked to enjoy life like so many ordinary Spaniards, but the service of the *Patria* monopolised my every hour and took up my life.'[4]

This startling capacity for self-delusion permeates every aspect of Franco's life. Pompous, inflated with his own destiny and importance, convinced that his fate and that of Spain were entwined within some deified destiny, he could be shy, withdrawn and humble. Masterly at manipulating his supporters' weaknesses and greed, and at balancing competing political factions within his regime, he pronounced himself uninterested in politics. Harsh and unforgiving with the Spanish people, he was hopelessly indulgent with his family. Frighteningly cold and unemotional, he was easily moved to tears. Stern and moralistic, he turned a blind eye to corruption within his regime. An inveterate chatterbox, he was the master of the unnerving silence. Although he commended himself on his humility, and urged his protégé Juan Carlos to adopt a simple lifestyle, he was 'Aloof in the manner sometimes associated with royalty' and very keen on sitting on chairs hitherto reserved for kings.[5]

Dictatorial and intolerant, he often behaved like a deprived child. (As Chief of State, when provided with his favourite meal – a stew laden with meat – he would petulantly complain 'but I like potatoes as well'.[6] On another occasion, when commended on his hearty appetite after a day out hunting, he replied darkly, 'I eat well when they let me.')[7] Profoundly authoritarian and intolerant of opposition, Franco indignantly denied being a dictator. In 1947 he moaned, 'I am not free, as it is believed abroad, to do what I want.' In June 1958 he told a French journalist that 'to describe me as a dictator is just childish'. Nevertheless, terrified of being displaced, he fiercely resisted appointing his successor until he was nearing his death. His brother-in-law Serrano Suñer, author of his political power, wrote 'never, not for a single instant, did Franco consider letting an institution with a blood-and-flesh king overshadow the authority of his own position in which he had concentrated all the powers of the state'.[8]

Wracked with contradictions, Franco had himself been busy sowing the seeds of dissent from the moment he grasped power. The victorious Caudillo, who described the civil war as 'the struggle of the *Patria* against the anti-*Patria*, of unity against secession, of morality against crime, of spirit against materialism,'⁹ would preside over a Spain wracked by sect-arianism, swamped by materialism and steeped in corruption. The 'unifier and centralist was dividing Spain and fomenting separatism'.¹⁰ The man who in his autobiographical film-script, *Raza*, sentimentally announced 'how beautiful it is to be Spanish ... Spain is the nation most loved by God'¹¹ was the same man who vengefully proclaimed his intention to 'destroy Madrid rather than leave it to the Marxists'. Although in 1946 he claimed that 'Our justice could not be more serene or more noble, its generosity is based solely on the supreme interests of the *Patria*', his dic-tatorship was a harsh, partisan and corrupt affair.

One clue to the contradictions inherent within General Franco's per-sonality lies in the fact that – like the other European dictators – he displayed from an early age the sort of blinkered ideas and prejudices that Erich Fromm links to the sado-masochistic personality, and to 'the authoritarian personality' with which it is closely linked. Extensive research indicates that – like Franco – such people come from cold families who, anxious about their status in society, maintain rigid and prurient ideas about sexu-ality and aggression, and impose their values upon their children 'with a heavy hand'.¹² Their neurotic offspring often display symptoms of 'nar-cissistic personality disorders', which usually occur in 'persons who have suffered intense injuries to self-esteem in early life, compensate for this by developing a grandiose conception of themselves, and respond to attacks on their inflated self-image with rage'.¹³ They may experience the need to identify with an idealised group, and 'condemn, reject and punish' anyone who violates the values of that group. In the words of Norman Dixon, such a person is 'finding and persecuting in others what he has come to fear in himself'.¹⁴ Lacking in tenderness or empathy, they are preoccupied only with themselves, their thoughts, ideas and wishes. Resolutely unaware of their own shortcomings, they display a closed, rigid attitude to life, along with a hypersensitivity to any form of criticism. They believe in super-natural forces, Fate, Nature and God as the determinants of success. Imbued with an overwhelming sense of their own uniqueness, unencumbered by feelings of ambivalence and blessed with a breathtaking capacity to lie cynically without 'the friction of guilt', they free their followers of all inhib-itions on previously unacceptable behaviour. Driven by their own selfish needs rather than any concern for the society they control, poor at antici-pating the consequences of their actions and ruthless about safeguarding their power, they can seem utterly beguiling, plausible and compelling to more socially constrained individuals. Full of admiration for the powerful, and contempt for the powerless, they yearn to gain complete mastery over others. Certainly all four dictators 'felt uneasy with people who were [their] equals – or [their] superiors – in any respect, as is frequently the case with narcissistic and authoritarian characters'.[15]

According to Norman Dixon, such people often make very successful politicians and, given the opportunity to do so, will become dictators. It is, however, one thing to have dictatorial tendencies, quite another to become a dictator and yet another to remain one. This book is an investigation of the political, personal, psychological and social influences that enabled Franco, a deeply flawed individual, to suspend his own and other people's disbelief for over forty years.

CHAPTER 1

Small Acorns

Franco and his family, 1892–1910

Rather than the qualities which raised him from the masses, it was those qualities he shared with them and of which he was a representative example that laid the foundations for his success.

Joachim Fest[1] on Adolf Hitler

Francisco Franco Bahamonde was born in the early hours of 4 December 1892 in El Ferrol, a small port in Galicia, in north-western Spain. A tiny tight-knit naval community, it was geographically, and temperamentally, cut off from the rest of Spain: America was considered more accessible than Madrid. Spanish naval ships had sailed from the port of El Ferrol throughout the eighteenth and nineteenth centuries to fight against Spain's enemies, particularly the English. El Ferrol's fortunes had waxed and waned alongside Spain's imperial ventures. By the time Franco was born, it was once again enjoying a vicarious if short-lived importance as one of the three Atlantic bases from which Spain was waging war with its remaining Latin American colonies.

Franco's forebears on his father's side had first arrived in El Ferrol in 1737, where they established a tradition of service in the administrative branch of the navy. Franco's great-grandfather was nearing his thirtieth birthday when news of the 'mortal blow' delivered to the Spanish fleet at Trafalgar reached the shocked populace of El Ferrol, home of many of the thousands of sailors who were killed or wounded during the battle. Despite the seniority attained by Franco's ancestors, the virtual caste system that existed within the local naval hierarchy prevented the family from fraternising with the 'real' naval officers in the sea-going sector. What the family lacked in social status, they made up for in fertility and longevity. Franco's great-grandfather, Nicolás Manuel Teodoro Franco y Sánchéz, lived an extremely long life during which he married three times and had fifteen children. He too had entered the administrative branch after 'proving' in 1794 that he was of 'pure blood, of Hidalgo family and a man of property',[2] and rose to the equivalent rank of lieutenant-colonel in the army.

One of his sons, Franco's grandfather Francisco Franco Vietti, did even better. By the time he died in 1887, he had become a director of the Naval Administration in El Ferrol. He managed to buy a house in 'almost the best part of the town',[3] the Calle de Maria (where Franco was born), but even he could not shunt his family up the social scale. He had five sons and two daughters. The eldest, Nicolás Franco Salgado-Araujo, born in 1855, was to be Francisco Franco's father. Neither Nicolás nor one of his younger sisters, Hermenegilda, brought much credit to the family name. The former horrified the local populace with his zest for women, gambling and drink, while the latter scandalised both her parents and their narrow-minded neighbours by falling passionately in love with a cousin whom she was forbidden to marry. Moving to Corunna, she would, in due course, become godmother to her errant brother's middle son, Francisco, who would regularly visit her house during his childhood. Although 'extremely cultured and well connected with the high society of the city', like her older brother in El Ferrol she was 'very eccentric'.[4] Unlike him, she would never marry. Small, thin and spectacularly mean (as, indeed, was Nicolás), she darted through the streets of the town, with her little old servant walking several steps behind.[5] The family propensity for longevity did not abate over the years. 'Aunt Gilda' died in 1940 at the age of eighty-five. Her brother died two years later aged eighty-eight. Francisco himself would die in 1975 aged eighty-three.

Despite his wild tendencies, Nicolás Franco followed the family tradition and joined the Academy of Naval Administration when he was eighteen. While Nicolás seemed to hanker after a good time rather than professional glory, he was hard working and disciplined, and eventually attained the highest possible rank of intendente-general, or vice-admiral, although this was probably due to length of service rather than professional dynamism. As a young man of twenty-one, he was dispatched to Cuba, where he fully exploited the sexual and social diversions on offer, and then to the Philippines, where he fathered an illegitimate child, Eugenió Franco Puey, with a fourteen-year-old girl. (Years later Eugenió's son-in-law, Hipólito Escobar, would make contact with the Caudillo. To avoid any scandal, he was rapidly promoted from his job as a small-town librarian to become director of the Biblioteca Nacional.)[6] Don Nicolás returned to a parochial El Ferrol only with the greatest reluctance. Unable to fraternise with the elite, sea-faring naval officers and unwilling to share the local preoccupation with 'the arrival of the last ship and the fulfilment of duty and everyday gossip',[7] his capacity for boredom was stretched to snapping point. Nicolás was in need of a diversion.

Perhaps that was why, on 24 May 1890, aged thirty-five, he made the improbable decision to marry the deeply pious, 24-year-old Pilar Bahamonde y Pardo de Andrade, daughter of the commander in charge of naval equipment in the arsenal. To begin with, Nicolás was doubtless drawn to the young Pilar's 'transparent beauty ... oval, symmetrical face, and pensive melancholy eyes'.[8] He may also have hankered after a stern and critical figure to curtail his unfettered appetites. It was certainly a socially advantageous match, and winning the hand of 'one of the most beautiful and admired women in El Ferrol' 'satisfied his vanity and gratified his narcissism'.[9] However, the egotistical Nicolás could not have chosen somebody more likely to disapprove of his attitudes and lifestyle. He has been described as 'an easy-going man of the world, a rake even'[10] and 'a gay companion, a bibulous amorist with little taste for family life'[11] and with 'a reputation for fast living ... a free-thinking bon-viveur'.[12] In contrast, even as a young woman Pilar was 'conservative, extremely pious, almost a saint'.[13] In his biography of the Caudillo, the eminent psychiatrist Enrique González Duro claimed that Don Nicolás felt trapped in a relationship in which he felt 'insufficiently matched in affection by his wife who was not at all sensual, hardly spontaneous, excessively responsible and completely identified with the traditional role of wife and mother ... much more concerned with appearances than with realities'.[14] Rebelling against his wife's moralistic ways, Don Nicolás would prove to be neither a committed husband nor a devoted father.

The ill-suited couple were to have five children in quick succession: Nicolás was born on 1 July 1891, Francisco on 4 December 1892, Pilar on 27 February 1895, Ramón on 2 April 1896 and Paz, the younger daughter, on 12 November 1898. These five were not their only parental responsibilities. On 25 April 1894, Nicolás's aunt died, leaving her husband with ten children aged between two and sixteen. He named Nicolás, his nephew and a close neighbour, as their guardian. When the uncle died as well, the younger children leant upon Doña Pilar as a second mother.[15] The second youngest, Francisco Franco Salgado-Araujo, or Pacón as he was called, aged four at the time of his mother's death, was extremely fond of Doña Pilar. He would shadow his younger cousin Francisco throughout his long career. His memoirs and diaries, which chronicle their almost daily contact until 1971, provide valuable insights into Franco's early childhood, military achievements and political career.

The most profound influence upon the young Francisco was his relationship with his mother. On the basis of his own – and Pacón's – idealised

memories of her, Doña Pilar has been presented by most of Franco's biographers as an almost perfect Madonna-like figure. Franco's friend and first
biographer, Joaquín Arrarás, describes her as 'A mistress always of herself,
her moral courage strengthened by the intensive life of her spirit, she faced
life's problems with a serenity and a fortitude that might be called stoical
were they not more aptly described as Christian.'[16] González Duro claims
that 'her calmness before suffering was admirable as was her tranquil smile
in adversity'.[17] Paul Preston refers to her as 'a gentle, kindly serene woman
[who presented to] the world a façade of quiet dignity and religious piety',[18]
and Pacón solemnly proclaims that 'her example and her deep-rooted
religiosity were of the greatest value in our education'.[19]

In the early 1940s, Franco would write a fanciful account of his childhood,
producing an autobiographical film-script entitled *Raza*, which charts the
history of a Galician family from 1897 until the end of the civil war. Although
Raza exposes more about Franco's innermost fantasies than his actual
childhood, it unwittingly reveals his underlying psychological motivations,
his real attitude to his family and how this relationship fed into the prejudices that would underpin his entire political career.

In his film-script, Franco portrays Doña Pilar as the caring, warm and
devoted mother, Isabel de Andrade, and insists that 'there is no greater
wisdom than that of a good mother who looks to the care and concern of
her children'.[20] Given the religious and social constraints within which she
lived, the frustrations of her husband and the personality traits of her
middle son, it seems unlikely that Doña Pilar was a warm, affectionate or
spontaneous wife or mother. Even George Hills, one of Franco's more
fulsome biographers, concedes that 'the aloofness, the coldness of the adult
Franco, noted so often by men who served under him' must have had their
origins in his early family circumstances.[21]

On the surface however, Doña Pilar was the perfect mother. She spent a
lot of time praying. Her children were always beautifully attired. Her house
was spotless. Whether this was normal behaviour for diligent housewives
at that time or was more pathological in origin, it is noteworthy that
Francisco would obsessively echo these tendencies throughout his life. Even
as a small boy he displayed an unhealthy preoccupation with wearing the
correct clothes. Throughout his life, dressing-up would be an aid to his
different heroic poses.

Francisco's relationship with his father, although quite different, was
equally influential. According to Pacón, Don Nicolás was 'a man of great
intelligence' who, like his sister Gilda, had 'a strong character which led
him to do what he felt like without worrying what people would say'.[22] Like
his middle son, he was full of contradictions. Fun-loving and self-indulgent

in the world at large, he was a harsh disciplinarian at home. A political free-thinker with a marked sympathy for the freemasons and profound distaste for religion, he was a tyrannical authoritarian with his children. Although Pacón would fondly recall his guardian taking his sons and their young cousins for long walks and kite flying above the sea in El Ferrol, he acknowledges that he was 'an extremely severe and austere character' who 'never took pride in the merits of his children'.[23] Whether Don Nicolás's egocentric attitude and aggression towards his children was his way of venting the frustrations he felt within his marriage, or an attempt to compensate for his dissolute behaviour outside the home, there is no doubt that his behaviour was unpredictable and extreme.

Although the couple diverged on almost every issue, both Don Nicolás and his wife were determined that his sons should transcend their humble origins and join the 'real', sea-going, navy. Pacón particularly remembers Don Nicolás's 'magnificent teachings on the naval history of El Ferrol', his blow-by-blow account of 'the attack of the English and the landing of a fleet ... on 28 August 1800' and his determination to make 'sure that we learnt everything about naval terminology and technology'.[24] It is perhaps noteworthy that, despite the yearnings of Francisco – or Paquito as he was sometimes called – to impress his father by joining the navy, only his older brother Nicolás fulfilled his father's professional ambitions by becoming a naval engineer. Nevertheless Don Nicolás's passion for Spanish naval history, and his preoccupation with the sea and warships, would exert an enormous influence upon Francisco's life – as would his erratic disciplinary methods.

He regularly beat his three sons. Although he never dared to beat his daughter, Pilar, saying 'I must either kill her or ignore her, and since I could not kill her, I ignored her',[25] she later claimed that he ran 'the house like a general'.[26] In her memoirs Pilar oscillates between indignant protestations that her father's beatings were quite justified, dubious assertions that she had beaten her own children with no ill effect, and bitter memories of Don Nicolás's violence against her brothers. Even Pacón concedes that his guardian was 'always excessively demanding and severe' with his children, and easily lost his temper if contradicted. There were, he records, enough anecdotes about Don Nicolás's ill-tempered ways to fill a book.

In fact, a play was written about Don Nicolás in 1985 by the Spanish dramatist Jaime Salóm. Entitled *The Short Flight of the Cock*, it is based on the written and spoken testimonials of close friends and associates of the family. Although ostensibly a work of fiction, the play throws considerable light on Franco's father and on his tempestuous relationship with his wife and children. Don Nicolás emerges as a larger-than-life personality who bridled against living in a 'mediocre provincial city inhabited by dull people devoid of imagination' with a wife who was more inclined to 'say a rosary for the blessed souls in Purgatory and our departed loved ones' than spend time with her husband. His wife is portrayed as a cold, moralistic, petty-minded snob. Don Nicolás berates her for being 'still as a marble statue' in bed, protests that 'your virtue and your modesty are only a way of feeling superior to other people' and wistfully recalls that 'I would have given my life for a kiss … If you understood me just once…'[27]

Whatever the truth of the matter, it certainly seems to be the case that, far from trying to resolve her marital problems, Doña Pilar invested her energies in trying to shield the family's resolutely lower-middle-class credentials – they were allegedly forced to have lodgers to help out financially – from the probing eyes of provincial neighbours. Despite her Madonna-like reputation, there is, strangely, nothing to suggest that Doña Pilar protected any of her children from her abusive husband. Whether she believed that, tainted by original sin, they deserved everything they got, or simply felt powerless to intervene, her failure to protect her sons from Don Nicolás's wrath may well have been perceived by them as passive collusion, or a frightening symptom of her powerlessness.

While all the children suffered in one way or another, it was the timid, withdrawn and socially conscious Francisco who inspired their father's most overt loathing and derision. His inhibited and cautious personality did little to ignite the fervour of paternal pride or love and made it difficult for him to compete with his charismatic, extrovert, macho brothers. Perhaps his placing within the family compounded his difficulties in forging a role for himself. Nicolás was the oldest child, Ramón the youngest, and – until Francisco was five – Pilar the only daughter. Francisco was just another boy, and a rather unimpressive one at that. Extremely short, skinny and effeminate, with a high-pitched voice and huge reproachful eyes, he clearly unnerved his father. Don Nicolás was much more at ease with his other sons, who were so like him in many ways. On the basis of interviews with Franco's older cousins on both sides of the family, George Hill describes young Nicolás as a 'quick-witted but inattentive student'. He was an irrepressible, confident child who grew into a charismatic, fun-loving, unreliable man. Ramón – fondly remembered as 'naughty, a madcap' – was also blessed with a spontaneity and charm that contrasted strongly with Francisco's stilted personality. A neighbour later observed that 'Ramón got on very well with everyone else. The rest of the family didn't. They thought they were superior.' Another one recalls that Ramón was also 'the most daring, the most cheeky, the father loved him most'. Pilar, a forthright child, was also very like her father. Constantly announcing 'I always did what I wanted, I do what I want, and I'll always do what I want',[28] she was viewed as potentially 'an excellent commander-in-chief had she been a man'. Francisco, on the other hand was a strikingly unremarkable child, a plodder. 'He was meticulous; he was good at drawing but otherwise quite average, quite ordinary.'[29]

Of the three boys, Paquito was the closest to his mother, mirroring her deceptively gentle, but disapproving expression, rigid values and moralistic outlook, sharing her ready propensity to tears and her steely and unrelenting convictions. In Salóm's play, his exasperated father explodes that he's 'Always hanging on to her skirts! She'll end up turning him into a plaster saint like his grandfather, or something worse', and complains to his wife that 'with your pampering and priggishness you've made him into a strange, timid boy'. When Pilar accuses him of hating his middle son, he indignantly denies it, but concedes that 'he scares me sometimes. When he fixes me with those black eyes and that faraway look of his, I don't know whether he's showing me contempt or indifference.'[30] Whatever the reasons for Francisco's irritating ways, his father 'never let any opportunity pass to show the antipathy that he felt towards his second son who was so different from him in every respect'.[31] Francisco's inability to earn his father's admiration would rankle with him throughout his life.

Profound contradictions within Francisco's personality were evident from the start. Suspended between a subservient quest for invisibility from Don Nicolás's wrathful eye and an indignant determination to be seen and acknowledged, he was confusing and difficult from an early age. On the one hand, he is described as a happy little boy, fishing in the quiet waters of the *ria* of El Ferrol, mucking around in boats, and playing pirates on the gangplanks of the ferries. On the other, he emerges as isolated, undemonstrative and cold. Desperate to impress and frantic for approval, he displayed an obstinate refusal to please. Operating within a very tight emotional range, he showed few signs of pleasure or pain, anger or delight. Even as a child he was described as 'cold' and yet 'sentimental', as unemotional and yet always getting upset about everything.[32] Although he would never form close friendships, he was obsessed with playing wild childhood games with leaders and followers, goodies and baddies, during which he could resolve his feelings of powerlessness. While one of his teachers remembered him as a 'nice lad, of a happy disposition, thoughtful: he took time answering questions but he was a playful lad', his sister viewed him more as 'a little old man'.[33]

Physically frail and emotionally fragile, he had no compunction about flying at his significantly larger brothers when they annoyed him. Timid and vulnerable, he displayed an icy determination to avenge perceived injustices from an early age. In her memoirs, Pilar recalls the rage and bitterness with which the young Paquito nurtured a grievance after being unjustly punished by his father. But despite Francisco's burning sense of anger, it was in fact his older brother Nicolás who bore the brunt of his father's physical rage. Both Pilar and Pacón would recall an occasion when the young Nicolás was forced to spend an entire day under the sofa because of some transgression with his homework. As Francisco doubtless noticed, his father's brutality towards Nicolás was tempered by his regard and affection. Having watched the often abusive, occasionally affectionate, physical encounters between his father and Nicolás, Paquito displayed a detached attitude to violence from a very early stage. His sister Pilar recalled how, when he was only eight and a half and she was six, she heated a long needle until the tip was red-hot, and pressed it on to his wrist. Instead of screaming or robustly hitting his little sister, Francisco adopted a clinical interest in the pain he was suffering, commenting merely 'how shocking the way burnt flesh smells'.[34] Perhaps he learned such martyred restraint from his mother. The fastidious and fragile Paquito was undoubtedly Doña Pilar's favoured child. If Freud is right when he argues that 'a man who has been the indisputable favourite of his mother keeps for life the feelings of a conqueror',[35] then Franco's relationship with his mother clearly had a profound impact upon his subsequent career. Nevertheless, enraged by his father's favouritism for Ramón, Franco's attitude to his younger brother would be marked by a murderous rivalry throughout their lives.

And so the Franco children grew up in a profoundly unhappy household in which they were bullied physically by their liberal father, and morally by their religious mother. This would have had an enormous impact upon all their lives. Despite the fact that all three sons were very different, they would all grow into highly destructive, egotistical men who were driven by naked self-interest rather than personal responsibility. While Ramón vented his self-destructive tendencies in a number of wild and dangerous aeronautical adventures, Francisco flung himself into heroic and death-defying feats on the battlefield. Nicolás's risk taking was vented in his involvement in corrupt ventures of one sort or another. Politically, Ramón and Nicolás, like their father, were free-thinkers, close to Freemasonry; Francisco, like Doña Pilar, was profoundly conservative. Like their father, both Nicolás and Ramón were constantly 'chasing women' and generally sought out the good life. Francisco, like Doña Pilar, was sexually inhibited, austere and disapproving. However, all three brothers were extremely flexible and self-serving when it came to furthering their careers. Despite his unbending views on life, Francisco was endlessly adaptable when it came to safeguarding his political power. His brother Nicolás happily jettisoned his own political beliefs in order to pave his extremely right-wing younger brother's path to absolute power. Benefiting hugely from Franco's corrupt regime, he became embroiled in a number of financial scandals along the way. Ramón also changed his political spots once Francisco became supreme leader in the Nationalist zone during the civil war, albeit somewhat reluctantly. Although, once Francisco had left home, he always did his best to avoid Pilar,[36] she too exploited the Franco name to the full once he was in power. In her memoirs, she reluctantly concedes that her good fortune in business might have derived from the fact that 'my surname opened many doors for me'.[37] Only their intractable father refused to compromise his political – or personal – views in order to benefit from his son's power. An outspoken opponent of the Nationalists during the civil war, outraged by Francisco's close association with Hitler and appalled at the repression and widespread corruption of the regime, he was regularly arrested – and then shamefacedly released – in the 1940s for badmouthing the Caudillo in Madrid bars.

Politics had long since been a source of conflict in Franco's fateful difficulties with his father. Similarly, family tensions would influence Franco's politics. Back in the 1890s, while Don Nicolás was attempting to impose his authority upon his family, the Spanish government was itself fighting to keep control of the country's rebellious American colonies. These colonial wars, which had raged throughout much of the nineteenth century, culminated in the loss of Cuba to the United States in the great naval defeat of 3 July 1898. Although the whole of Spain suffered enormously from the loss of the last remnants of Spain's great empire, the blow to morale in El Ferrol was enormous. Thousands of the sailors who engaged in this disastrous venture came from Galicia. The loss of close relatives and the return of large numbers of dispirited, wounded and mutilated men to El Ferrol had a direct impact upon the lives of most of the town's inhabitants. Although he was only five years old at the time, it would exert enormous influence upon Francisco's subsequent political and military career, perhaps because some of the returning servicemen lodged at the house in the Calle de Maria. Long after he became Generalísimo, Franco could still 'remember their names perfectly.'[38]

The loss of Cuba and the stark exposure of Spain's vulnerability occurred at a crucial moment for a powerless young boy suffering at the hands of his liberal father. The dichotomy between Nicolás's egalitarian views and authoritarian attitudes would become enmeshed in Francisco's mind with Spain's doomed imperial venture against the Americans in Cuba, particularly after his own family broke up nine years later, just as he was entering the military academy. There he would encounter a culture that unquestioningly blamed the break-up of the national family on the weakness of liberal politicians. Although as a child he merely incorporated the '1898 disaster' into his childhood games, he would, in due course, seize upon the loss of Cuba to validate his conviction that he – like Spain itself – was under attack from everything he associated with his left-wing, anti-clerical, Freemason father.

In the years following 1898, while Franco's own family was being torn apart by his parents' diverging views, the rift in Spain between military and civil society, and within civil society itself, was widening dramatically. At the turn of the century, those elements that drove Spain inextricably towards the civil war in 1936 were firmly in place. The divisions in society had their origins deep in Spanish history. If the monarchy is taken, at some level, to be parent to the people, the Spanish were sadly lacking in this respect. Throughout the tempestuous nineteenth century, Spanish history became part comic opera, part Dickensian tragedy, with a series of corrupt and incompetent monarchs and regents being regularly swept off the throne by one set of aggrieved generals, and then swept back on again by another. As Caudillo, in 1946, Franco would give his version of what had gone wrong in the century preceding the ignominious loss of Cuba:

From March 1814 to September 1833, ... we lived in a constant struggle between absolutists and liberals: six years of absolutism with an anti-liberal repression, three of liberalism with a brutal persecution of the absolutists, ten of moderate absolutism until the Queen Regent, six years full of rebellions and continuous uprisings; a civil war which ends with a foreign armed intervention, the loss of virtually all our overseas possessions and the establishment of the causes of the Carlist war.

There were three Carlist wars in all. The first one, which lasted from 1834 to 1839, completed the economic ruin of Spain begun during the Napoleonic Wars, and established the army as the arbiter of political life. As Franco gleefully observed, things did not improve:

From the September 1833 to September 1868, the life of Spain could hardly have been more turbulent. In thirty-five years, forty-one governments, two civil wars, the first of which lasted six years; two regencies and a queen dethroned, three new constitutions, fifteen military coups, innumerable disturbances, repeated killings of monks, lootings, reprisals, persecutions, an attempt on the life of the Queen and two uprisings in Cuba. A real paradise!

From the overthrow of Isabel II to Alfonso XIII, a little more than thirty-four years, twenty-seven governments, a foreign king who lasts two years, a Republic which in eleven months has four presidents, a seven-year civil war [the last Carlist war], various revolutions of a republican character, cantonal uprisings; an external war against the United States and the loss of the last remnants of our colonial empire, two prime ministers assassinated and two new constitutions.[39]

This pithy if tendentious account of Spanish history leaves out the complexity of social problems. From the end of the Napoleonic Wars to the outbreak of the civil war in 1936, Spain was torn – like Franco's own family – between forces pushing for reform and reactionary elements determined to resist it, come what may. There was hostility between backward-looking conservatives determined to safeguard an absolutist regime with a monarch at its head, and those who wanted a more moderate form of government with a wider power base. There were clashes between Catalan and Basque federalists and Castilian centralists, and between the Catholic Church and liberals. The absence of a flexible political system capable of adjusting to social change resulted in periods of reactionary rule by a rampantly self-interested political elite being followed by explosions of violence among the urban working classes and dispossessed rural proletariat, which were then brutally repressed. As the century drew to a close, religion was clashing with competing political doctrines (liberalism, Marxism and anarchism) for the heart and soul of the people.

When, in 1876, Carlist insurrection was finally brought to an end and the restoration of Alfonso XII took place, the exhausted Spanish people hoped that this would provide some stability. While an increasingly retrograde Catholic Church, determined to fight a rearguard action against the onslaughts of the modern world, had associated itself closely with the Carlist movement, it was forced to recognise the validity of the restored Borbón monarch to secure Catholic supremacy in Spain. Although the idea of free elections was still considered far too radical to countenance, in 1885 the Liberal and Conservative parties took turns in power (*turnismo*) within a system of very limited suffrage. There was little to choose between the parties, both of which represented landed interests. Both parties opted for a repressive approach in the face of unrest, often with the use of the army. The entirely fraudulent 'elections' were ruthlessly managed by the traditional local bosses, known as *caciques*. Electoral falsification left the politically and socially excluded with the stark choice of violent resistance or apathy. By the turn of the century, they were increasingly inclined to opt for the former.

It was in this situation, in 1898, that Spain lost Cuba. This was the final straw for the army, leaving it with fewer opportunities to flex its military muscle at the very time that its numbers had been inflated by the absorption of extremely right-wing Carlist officers into its ranks after their defeat in the civil wars. Without overseas empires to defend or foreign wars to fight, the army's primary remit became the repression of social unrest within Spain and the defence of national unity against regionalism. Justifying their role in terms of an exaggerated rhetorical patriotism, and a hypersensitivity to civilian criticism, army officers flung themselves behind demands for a radical form of national revival or 'regeneration' to be found in Spain's glorious past. Such an idea would hold an enormous resonance for the adult Franco.

As a child, he must have been aware that many of his school friends – including his lifelong companion Alonso Vega – had lost their fathers and brothers in the humiliating naval defeat of 1898. He clearly wished that he had lost his own as well. He rectifies this situation in *Raza*, in which he creates a perfect family and then kills the whole lot off. Before doing so, he rectifies all the shortcomings of his own childhood. Far from living in a modest house in El Ferrol, the fictional family inhabit a *pazo*, an elegant mansion. The dissolute Don Nicolás is replaced by the dashing and heroic naval officer, devoted husband and doting father, Captain Pedro Churruca (the surname of one of the most celebrated admirals in Spanish history and a hero of Trafalgar). His wife, Isabel de Andrade – who is 'explicitly linked to the Virgin Mary'[40] – is gentle, warm and affectionate. At the beginning of the script, while awaiting their father's return from sea, she earnestly advises her four children that 'you don't know how lucky you are to have a father like yours'.[41] The hero José (the Franco figure) is fully aware of his father's merits. He is an honourable, respectful and scholarly child. Isabelita, the only daughter – in marked contrast with the opinionated Pilar – is a winning combination of her mother and St Theresa, while the youngest son, Jaime, is a muted echo of José. The eldest son, Pedro – who contains elements of Franco's real father and brothers, and denied elements of himself – is a sadistic child who is horrid to weak and fragile creatures, is obsessed with money, lies to his mother and displays a wanton disregard for his father's noble naval values. When his mother solemnly tells him that, as the eldest son, he is the one his father 'loves the most', he snorts, 'And I thought the reason we loved papa was because we wouldn't go to school today.' When Captain Churruca returns from sea laden with lofty gifts for his offspring, the evil Pedro displays a singular lack of interest in his tales of Spain's glorious past. He is offensively sceptical about the 'beautiful death' of an ancestor during the battle of Trafalgar, and is unable to understand his father's views on the importance of dying for one's country, preferably while wearing a full-dress uniform.

A gushing José, on the other hand, is transfixed by his father's stories, and is suitably appreciative when his father gives him a drawing pad. (In fact, Don Nicolás never showed any interest in Francisco's artistic skills.) The children crowd around their father to marvel at a book about Christopher Columbus. 'How beautiful,' cries José, 'I'll never forget it!' 'How young!' says Isabelita. 'How rich!' observes Pedro. In marked contrast with the sort of comments Don Nicolás actually made about Francisco, Captain Churruca lovingly predicts that José will become 'either a great soldier or a saint' and – wrongly as it turns out – that Pedro will become 'a great naval officer'. In *Raza*, Franco ensures that Churruca articulates his own fanciful prejudices and not his real father's political notions. Before embarking on his last fateful mission to Cuba, the captain bitterly denounces 'foreign intrigues and, what is worse, the invasion of Freemasonry' in Cuba and the Philippines, and announces that 'all we have left is our own self-respect, the concept of duty; but between dying of self-disgust and dying with glory there is no choice'.[42] Surrounded by hostile American ships in Cuba, Churruca urges his crew to fight heroically, and announces that 'Reasoning disappears when faced with duty', pointing out that 'There is no such thing as a pointless sacrifice.' Having ordered that the flag be nailed to the mast ('it will be victorious or go down with us'), he dies a hero's death. The victorious but humbled Americans are full of admiration for 'naval officers worthy of a better fate'.[43] Although in Franco's film-script, when the ship is hit Captain Churruca stands on the ship's bridge in his full-dress uniform saluting '¡España! ¡España! ¡España!' while it sinks, in the film itself he falls to the deck wounded, kissing the religious medal his wife gave him on his departure.

Back in El Ferrol, his sanguine wife expresses the daunting hope that 'the children will be worthy of his sacrifice.' Needless to say, Pedro fails dismally in this allotted task. That he is destined to betray his father's memory is made clear when José and his sister Isabelita berate him as a 'rebel' and a 'Mason' during impassioned re-enactments of Spanish loyalists versus rebels. The family then moves to Madrid, where Isabel de Andrade jealously guards their financial and social standing. She is not assisted in this laudable task by her eldest son. While, throughout the saga, José displays an unfaltering interest in 'spirituality and heroism', and – as his father had predicted – carves out an impressive career for himself in the army, the feckless Pedro goes from bad to worse. Not only does he get thrown out of the Naval Academy, but he goes to university – 'the centre where, according to his father, all the evils of Spain were fomented'[44] – and then becomes a lawyer, a liberal, a Freemason and a Republican sympathiser. Like Don Nicolás, he is a dissolute womaniser, whose anti-clerical, republican tendencies are deemed to have brought disgrace upon the *Patria*, and to have driven his mother to an early grave after she is attacked by a group of church-burning youths in May 1931 under the noses of the Republican guards. When civil war breaks out, her 'Christ-like son', José – keen to get his own back on the 'corrupt and materialist patriarchs who are ruling the Republic'[45] – sets out to avenge his mother's death. This is a fraught and heroic task. At the beginning of the war, José is trapped in one of the besieged rebel garrisons in Madrid. When he attempts to escape disguised as a workman to get a message to General Fanjul, he is shot from behind by the cowardly reds, taken prisoner, put on trial and 'executed' by a firing squad. Brought back to life by the kiss of his chaste girlfriend, he goes on to lead a battalion to victory in the battle for Bilbao. His miraculous revival has a biblical quality, which captures Franco's messianic sense of himself.

His brothers are not so lucky. Pedro – who betrays his mother by joining the Republicans at the beginning of the civil war – is shot by them for betraying their cause. But he manages to 'redeem' himself just before dying by conceding that the Nationalists 'will make an honourable Spain while we [the Republicans] will make a Spain of murderers'.[46] Jaime, after leaving the navy to become a monk, is shot by Republican militiamen. José's best friend and Isabelita's husband, the cowardly Luis, is killed off under ignominious circumstances during the civil war. José himself only just survives to console his sister and marvel at the omniscient Caudillo. Out of the entire family, only José and his unthreatening sister Isabel manage to defy death. As Ramón Gubern argues in his psychological analysis of the film-script, Raza highlights the split between Franco's sense of inferiority and his need for 'psychic over-compensation'.[47] (On the other hand, as his brother Ramón would caustically observe in 1931, 'To further his career, Paco would be perfectly capable of murdering our mother, and, just to show off, of killing our father.')[48]

This retrospective fantasy, written in the early 1940s, indicates that Franco never resolved what Freud called the 'Oedipus complex', whereby a boy's desire to emulate and be loved by his father clashes with an unconscious desire to displace and destroy him. Such an attitude informed Franco's attitude to authority figures throughout his life, during which his quest for paternal acknowledgement would be repeatedly undermined by the fact that anyone more powerful than him had to be displaced, and anybody less important was of no consequences. The rampant idealisation of Isabel de Andrade and her traumatic death indicates that he was suppressing underlying feelings of ambivalence and hatred towards Doña Pilar as well. Raza strongly suggests that Franco was driven by the need to 'split' everything and everyone – including himself – into perfect, if somewhat harsh, or irredeemably evil.[49]

This tendency may well have been exacerbated by another momentous event in Francisco's life which also took place in 1898. His baby sister Paz was born that November. Until her arrival, Francisco had always been his mother's favourite child, but Doña Pilar clearly doted on her new daughter. It seems that Nicolás did as well. That the five-year-old Francisco felt profoundly jealous and displaced by the birth of his baby sister is revealed in *Raza*, when he replaces her as the much loved baby in the family with Jaime, the pseudonym he adopts for himself as author of his film-script. His dreams of compensating for this displacement by forging a brilliant career for himself in the navy is indicated in *Raza* when Jaime – in many ways Franco's alter-ego – is the only son to follow in his father's footsteps and became a naval officer.

At the time, however, a career in the sea-going branch of the navy was highly unlikely. His aspirations must therefore have focused on following his father into the naval administration. However, in 1901 the Escuela de Administracion Naval was closed, partly because of the cost of the war. The Cuban disaster had ended the Franco family's traditional route into the administrative branch of the navy. (Had it remained open, perhaps in 1936 Francisco would have been a naval quartermaster.) Given Doña Pilar's profound suspicions about civilian professions and universities, which she feared might inculcate her sons with heathen notions and radical political views, it was decided that the family would attempt to transcend their social shortcomings by sending Nicolás and Francisco to the Naval Preparatory School. To prepare them, they attended a small private school in El Ferrol run by a local priest 'who believed in the clouting of heads as a means of energising brains'.[50] These harsh educational methods cannot have done much for the timid Francisco's confidence or softened his harsh notions of authority. Short and painfully thin, Paquito had still not grown into his large eyes, ears and nose. His diminutive physique and high-pitched voice were the source of much derision among his school-mates. One of them would later recall him as an isolated figure. 'He was always the first to arrive and he went to the front on his own. He avoided everyone else.'[51]

Although Pacón went to a different school in El Ferrol, an isolated Francisco still depended upon him for company. The two boys both sat their public examinations in Corunna, where they stayed with 'Aunt Gilda', sleeping on a mattress on the floor of her house. During this time they forged a close association, and discovered – or so Pacón later alleged – a mutual passion for religion and the monarchy. The former tendency was nurtured by Pacón's aunt, an abbess of a convent in the town, whom the boys visited almost every day for 'pious advice and tasty snacks'. Their commitment to the monarchy would be aroused in 1906 when they read news of an attempt on the life of King Alfonso XII and his Queen.[52] Both boys were horrified.

Back home in the Calle de Maria, things got much worse for the Franco family when, in 1903, Paz died after an undiagnosed four-month illness. Her premature death came as a terrible shock to both parents. Although a high infant mortality rate rendered this a not uncommon experience at the time, it clearly had a huge impact upon the family. In the wake of Paz's death, a distraught Doña Pilar appears to have withdrawn even further into herself and her religion. In a state of perpetual mourning, she sought to replace her beloved daughter by developing a cloying dependency upon the effeminate eleven-year-old Franco – 'so good, so silent, so attached to her'.[53] Nicolás too was badly affected by the loss of his favoured child. In Salóm's play, he protests, 'Of course I remember that angel ... she was the sweetest, most loving of my children, the only one who would never abandon me, who would have consoled me in my old age.'[54] After the death of his daughter, Nicolás tried to bury his own pain and escape his wife's rejecting despair in vigorous bouts of drinking, gambling and womanising. A neighbour recalled that he conducted a very public affair with a woman who ran a tobacco stall in El Ferrol, and was not averse to whoring.[55] Although Francisco was mortified that his father's behaviour should expose the family to public criticism, ridicule and shame, he may well have been secretly gratified by the removal of Paz as a potent revival for his mother's favours.

He would not have been unusual in this respect. According to the psychoanalyst Melanie Klein, children often hanker for the death of a sibling and then feel personally responsible if this occurs. If Klein is right, it is possible that after the death of his little sister, Francisco, feeling triumphant that he had survived, guilty at having 'killed' off his 'rival' and fearful that his distraught parents would punish him harshly, vigorously projected all the bad feelings on to others. Given that Franco's entire career was driven by a compulsion to 'project'[56] internal feelings of hatred on to the external world, and then feel persecuted by them, it seems likely that he got stuck in this defensive cycle at an early stage. Paz's death also seems to have provoked in Francisco another common psychological defence used by survivors: the manic conviction that his own survival meant that he had been specially selected by Fate or Destiny for some special purpose.[57] Just as it has been argued that Hitler's mother unconsciously 'delegated' him to come to her rescue, with oppressed Germany standing as a symbol for the mother,[58] so Franco's niece Pilar Jaraiz Franco would later claim that, during this time, Doña Pilar placed all her hopes in Francisco as the future saviour of the *Patria* (herself), praying 'for the salvation of a child-king who had poor health who might be able to give hope and save a fatherland in danger'.[59]

Such a lofty future looked extremely unlikely in 1903. However, given the gloom that shrouded the Franco household, it must have been a relief when, having passed their examinations, Francisco and Pacón were able to join Nicolás at the Naval Preparatory College in El Ferrol. At twelve, Francisco was the youngest pupil in the college. Although Pacón recalls that, because of his 'great memory', his young cousin was able to 'do well without killing himself',[60] Francisco was still experiencing difficulties carving out a social niche for himself. Exhibiting 'fits of melancholy or excessive seriousness he was withdrawn, deeply conscious of a supposed inferiority, yet liable, if challenged, to display an almost aggressive obstinacy'.[61] Just as he had never hesitated to fly at his significantly larger and stronger brothers, so at the Naval Prep School he would vigorously defend himself if he perceived himself to be under attack. Given his extreme sensitivity, this was a not uncommon experience.

Francisco's hopes of following his brother Nicolás into the Naval Academy itself suffered a setback in 1907 when the government, bankrupted, among other things, by its colonial wars, was forced to suspend admissions, consolidating the link, in Franco's mind, between the Cuban disaster and his personal fate. Taking it as a personal slight, Francisco would nurture a lifelong grievance against a civilian government which, he was firmly convinced, had spitefully and wantonly wrecked his chances of a career in the navy. A more philosophical Pacón accepted that 'those of us who aspired to join the navy had no other choice but to prepare to join the army'.[62]

Thus it was, in 1907, that an adolescent Francisco travelled to Toledo to sit the entrance examinations for the Military Academy. Although this distant, dusty, landlocked city was a long way from El Ferrol, according to Salóm, Don Nicolás was particularly keen for Francisco to move away from the family home. Concerned that 'he's always running to your skirts for protection', he told his wife, 'He'll be better away from us, believe me.'[63] Perhaps that is why he insisted on accompanying Francisco on the hot and dusty two-day journey all the way to Toledo and back. Francisco, who had grown from an unprepossessing child into an awkward, uncharismatic teenager, was no more engaging to his father at fourteen than he had been at four. Don Nicolás did not exploit the opportunity to forge closer links with his middle son, who would later recall that throughout the journey his father was 'rigid and up-tight, lacking the empathy and concern which would have made him a warm companion'. Despite his difficulties, Francisco's examinations 'went perfectly'. After receiving official notification of his success he spent the rest of the summer in El Ferrol, marching through the streets in the tunic, red trousers and sabre of the infantry ('what greater dream could there be for a fourteen-year-old boy'), working on 'his military bearing and perfecting his salute.'[64] He entered the Academy on 29 August 1907 along with 381 other applicants, including his childhood friend Alonso Vega. Pacón, who failed 'figure drawing', would join him a year later.[65]

Francisco's departure from the house in Calle de Maria coincided with a split in his family. It has always been assumed that around this time Don Nicolás was promoted and moved to Madrid. However, on the basis of various testimonies compiled by Francisco Martínez López, it seems that, in the first instance, Don Nicolás moved to Cadiz. Wherever Don Nicolás moved, his wife and children remained in El Ferrol. The orthodox view – propagated by Franco himself – was that he forbade his wife to accompany him. However, Pacón's wife, Pilar de la Rocha, whom he married in January 1942, would later record that 'the problem was created when [Don Nicolás] was posted to Cadiz and his wife didn't want to accompany him'.[66] In his play, Salóm also argues that Doña Pilar refused to leave El Ferrol on the grounds – as articulated by her indignant husband – that 'in any other place in the world you'd only be a poor ignorant provincial who goes around showing off her piety'.[67]

Whatever the truth of the matter, the entire family was appalled when Don Nicolás finally did move to Madrid and formed what would prove to be a lifelong and very shocking attachment to an attractive, sensual and warm young woman, Agustina Aldana. Liberated from the reproachful gaze of his disapproving wife, Don Nicolás seems to have left his more abusive self in El Ferrol, perhaps in part because his new companion – an open-minded 'girl of the people' – was different from Doña Pilar in every way. Although he still drank and would 'occasionally get angry and shout'[68] he remained totally faithful to Agustina until his death in 1942. The couple even had a child – Pacón's wife notes that 'she passed as their niece but everyone assumed she was their daughter' – to whom they were apparently both devoted. (Perhaps Nicolás viewed her as a replacement for Paz.)

Although Doña Pilar staunchly resisted the advice of friends to go to Madrid and confront his live-in lover, she milked the role of the abandoned wife for all she could. Dressed in black and permanently tearful, depressed and withdrawn, she subjected her children to 'whispered admonitions about [their] absent father'[69] and insisted that they visit him and 'pay their respects' whenever they were in Madrid, possibly to avoid further scandal. While Nicolás, Ramón and Pilar were all regular visitors to their father's house, an increasingly harsh and unforgiving Francisco – perhaps blaming his father for his own banishment from the family home – vigorously resisted this directive. His views on his father's unorthodox domestic arrangement can be deduced from his later diatribes about all liberals and free-thinkers being drunken philanderers.

Francisco's great rival Ramón remained at home with his embittered mother and teenage sister. Even Nicolás was a regular visitor to the family home from the Naval Engineering School, where he dazzled the neighbours with his splendid naval uniform. Only Francisco was dispatched from the family home to a 'strange, dark, almost ominous city ... a fortress if there ever was one',[70] symbolically pervaded by the gloomy religious paintings of El Greco. Hot and arid and miles from the sea, Toledo was very different from the green, sea-port of El Ferrol whose 'wide plains of dark sands furrowed by snaking streams of sweet water', 'incandescent summers' and 'blue curls of a light breeze' were sensuously described by Franco in *Raza*.[71]

The socially and emotionally shocking breakdown of Francisco's parents' marriage, and his departure to the all-male, anti-maternal environment in Toledo, could not have come at a worse time for this sensitive and shy young teenager. Wracked with profound feelings of homesickness, Francisco withdrew further into himself, and leant upon the Academy's profoundly right-wing tendencies to consolidate his hatred of his father and everything he stood for. Like his teachers at Toledo, Franco proved to be virulently hostile to, and uninterested in, the Spain of humanism, liberalism and tolerance, which he associated with Don Nicolás. In the same way that Franco blamed his father for the disasters and humiliations of his childhood, so right-wing officers blamed Spain's humiliating loss of empire on an incompetent civilian government that had abandoned traditional Spanish virtues: 'unity, hierarchy and militant Catholicism'.[72] In the wake of the split within his own family, the army's feverish commitment to maintaining the moral integrity of an undivided *Patria* had a powerful resonance for Francisco. Furthermore, the Military Academy promised the possibility of transforming Franco's childhood dreams of greatness into realistic ambitions. As an old man, he could still recall the 'inexpressible emotions' he had felt when he first walked into the 'grandiose' regimental square, dominated by a statue of Charles V inscribed within the words 'I will die in Africa or I will enter Tunis victorious.'[73] It would form a crucial bridge between the childhood games that had helped him compensate for his inadequacies in El Ferrol, and his role as a 'heroic soldier' in Morocco.

To begin with, however, his conduct in the Academy did not seem to mark him out for later glory. While all the young cadets were subjected to the 'hard Calvary of the *novatadas*' (harsh and humiliating initiation rites imposed upon the youthful newcomers by the older cadets) Francisco's inhibited and introspective ways and less than impressive physique earned him the ridicule of the other cadets. He would, years later, bitterly recall 'the sad welcome offered those of us who came full of illusions to join the great military family'.[74] His high-pitched voice was the source of particular derision. Especially erratic during his painful teens, it was always prone to erupt into a shrill falsetto when he was under stress. His problems were compounded when, because of his diminutive size, various adjustments were made to his training routine. Despite his indignant protestation that 'Whatever the strongest man in my section can do, so can I',[75] he was considered incapable of wielding the standard-size rifle and was forced to drill with a weapon that had 15 centimetres sawn off the barrel.

Irrespective of his difficulties, Francisco submitted stoically enough to the rigours of barrack life, subliminating the harsh realities of day-to-day existence in a fanciful determination to carve out an outstanding military future for himself. Perhaps he derived solace from the rigid structures of the military hierarchy and – like many young cadets at that time – was relieved to discover that 'for the first time in his life, he was not subject to arbitrary conditions but to a single law'.[76] The Academy's suppression of individual identity and strict sense of order, obedience and duty would at the very least have been familiar, probably even reassuring. Furthermore, in the army at least it was possible to earn respect, something he could never achieve with his own father.

Friendship, on the other hand, was no more a priority for Francisco in Toledo than it had been in El Ferrol, possibly because it required a spontaneity and mutual respect of which he was incapable. Stubbornly reluctant to seek out popularity, he kept a cool and disapproving distance from his peer group. Moralistically disinclined to join in wild sexual and alcoholic binges in the town, which were uncomfortably reminiscent of his father's behaviour, he sought out the approval of his superiors by immersing himself in military books. Although he emanated an aura of profound vulnerability, driven by underlying feelings of suspicion, resentment and mistrust towards others, he still responded aggressively when he perceived himself to be under attack or on the receiving end of injustice. When an older cadet got him into trouble by hiding his books on two separate occasions, an incandescent Francisco hurled a candlestick at his head, triggering a furious fight in the dark, during which books, pillows and punches were hurled. His intransigent refusal to divulge the names of the others involved when sternly ordered to do so by the commanding officer secured him the grudging admiration of some of his comrades, including Juan Yagüe and Emilio Esteban Infantes, who would later play a crucial role in the civil war. However, although the other cadets recognised that 'he had behaved in an exemplary way in refusing to disclose the identity of his tormentors',[77] he never inspired their warmth.

That Francisco's slavish quest for the admiration of his superior officers was not always successful was revealed on the day of Pacón's arrival in Toledo in 1908, where he discovered that his young cousin had been confined to barracks for 'talking in the ranks'. Blithely unaware of the harsh protocol imposed at the Academy, Pacón rushed to ask a commanding officer if Francisco's punishment could be deferred to another day as they had both been invited out to lunch by a civilian uncle who had travelled up from Madrid especially. Not only was this reprieve withheld, but Pacón was immediately arrested and confined to barracks by the ill-humoured commanding officer for daring 'to enter the flag-room wearing your black waterproof instead of folded over your arm as the regulations demanded'. 'It was', he records, 'the last time [his uncle] visited a military establishment.'[78]

While Pacón was driven mad by the Academy's petty preoccupation with 'which parts of uniform you had to wear on the basis of where you happened to be',[79] Franco eagerly soaked up the undiluted diet of harsh discipline and military history being vigorously peddled – primarily to compensate for the shortcomings of Spain's actual military might. However, even he conceded that the system was 'routine' and involved 'having to learn stuff by heart'. In a retrospective attempt to explain his poor showing at the academy, he recounted how a bold attempt to diverge from the regurgitation of the set text ended in further humiliation. When he attempted to dazzle the class with a detailed and original disquisition on fortifications, his teacher, far from marvelling at his erudition snapped 'you're not in the Ateneo!' (the great Madrid debating society) and gave him a 'poor mark'.[80]

Day after day, the impressionable young cadets were subjected to the nineteenth-century concept of the army's right to intervene in Spanish politics and to be ever ready to overthrow civilian governments according to its view of the national interests. Tales of the army's triumphant role in the battles of the past were presented in terms of innate qualities of bravery and resistance rather than acquired tactical or strategic skills. The training encouraged neither debate nor team-work: individual glory was seen to be of paramount importance. Proudly proclaiming that tales of individual bravery 'taught us more than all the other disciplines', Franco would later dwell lovingly on 'the glorious scars' left on the head of a member of the teaching staff after a hand-to-hand knife fight in Morocco. Heroism, a wild bravado and defiance of death were seen as the benchmark of a good soldier. As in German military academies, the importance of learning how to die was drummed into the young cadets from a very early stage.[81] This suited an omnipotent and self-destructive young Franco, who was desperate for a feeling of invulnerability or an early death.

Such an attitude was just as well, given the deficiencies of the military curriculum in Toledo. Although new technology and advances in naval strategy in the United States were responsible for the fiasco in Cuba, the officers in Toledo stubbornly clung to their belief in traditional military tactics. The importance of outmoded frontal assault with platoons in strict formation was emphasised, rather than skilful use of ground. While certain aspects of Spanish military training – dexterity in fencing, riding and rifle shooting – had some parallels with Sandhurst, there were striking differences. The relative youth of the cadets and their almost monastical segregation from civilians (except when they went on wild forays into the town) contrasted with the British military training. The Spanish cadets acquired a theoretical knowledge of topography, tactics and elementary field engineering in the classroom rather than in the field. General Mola, a key figure during the civil war, would later complain bitterly about a training which he claimed imbued the cadets with a Germanic rigidity of mind, and the rash assumption that they could move entire armies across the face of Europe without the slightest practical experience in handling a platoon.[82] An uncritical and encyclopaedic knowledge of major Spanish military engagements and a mindless acceptance of any decision taken by Spanish generals were emphasised. Franco would base his entire military and political career on a rigid faith in military regulations and the conviction that absolute obedience and loyalty to superior officers should be paramount – even for civilians.

During Franco's time in Toledo, deeply conservative forces in the army seized the opportunity to compensate for the humiliation in Cuba and re-establish Spanish greatness by expanding Spain's foothold in north Africa. The situation in Morocco was never straightforward. Until the beginning of the twentieth century, it had been ruled by an authoritarian Sultan. Two major rebellions against the Sultan opened the way for the British and French to expand their imperial influence in this area. As a side-effect of Anglo-French rivalry, Spain was allocated a protectorate in an anarchic region in northern Morocco that was virtually impossible to police. The Sultan retained nominal control within the extensive French zone, and one of his nominees, known as the Khalif, did so in the Spanish zone. This arrangement satisfied neither the indigenous population nor the Spanish occupiers. Although the fierce tribesmen loathed their Spanish overlords, the aggrieved army officers clung to their belief that all their problems in Morocco derived from the colonial ambitions of France and Britain and the weakness of Spanish politicians – a viewpoint that was energetically endorsed by the officers in Toledo. They were therefore extremely keen for the government to do so something 'bold' in Africa.

To the frustration of the army, however, bankrupted by Cuba, the Spanish government was displaying a total lack of interest in either safeguarding or extending the empire in Africa. Spanish businessmen who had managed to forge favourable mining terms in Morocco were therefore deeply concerned when a tribal rebellion against the Sultan began to threaten Spanish controlled mines outside Melilla.[83] They immediately joined forces with army officers close to Alfonso XIII to try and pressurise the government of Antonio Maura to safeguard their investments. In June 1909 Maura finally relented. The army was ordered to protect the Spanish mines in Morocco.

Despite its enthusiasm for this venture, the army was in fact wholly unprepared for a major military engagement. Reservists, many of them married men with children, had to be called up. Maura's decision to dispatch a ramshackle expeditionary force to expand Spanish territory as far as the mineral deposits of the mountains near Melilla resulted in massive casualties to the Spanish force. On 27 June alone, over 500 Spaniards were killed and many thousands wounded. The fact that working-class men were now forced to lose their lives in an unnecessary and bloody engagement launched by an incompetent government to protect the economic interests of the mining companies did little to ease social tensions within Spain. On 12 July 1909 a monarchist paper angrily declared that 'If the country knew that we were going to resolve some problem in Morocco, it would tolerate an imperialist policy. But since it sees that we are going to Morocco without knowing how or why, it does not support this venture ... we would only accomplish one thing: we would waste the soldiers' blood and the taxpayers' money.'[84] Spontaneous anti-war demonstrations broke out in those places where the hapless reservists and conscripts had been recruited, or were departing from, for this unpopular encounter. Spreading rapidly, these were inflamed by a general strike in Barcelona called by anarchists and socialists. A declaration of martial law by the captain-general of the region provoked an outburst of anti-clerical fervour and church burnings.

On 29 July 1909 the government of Antonio Maura ordered the trigger-happy army to restore order in Barcelona during what became known as the *semana trágica* (tragic week). Officers, convinced that social ferment and military humiliation in Morocco were the inevitable consequences of anti-militarism, anti-clericalism and Catalan separatism, had no inhibitions about firing point blank at the barricades with field artillery. Many rebels were arrested, 1725 were summarily tried and five were condemned to death. As the strike in Barcelona degenerated into violence, the Moroccans pushed forwards to the walls of Melilla. For the army these events compounded the view that an impotent and incompetent central government was incapable of containing anti-patriotic assaults on the *Patria*. In Toledo, where 'the burning topic ... was always the political and military events of the day', the young cadets 'were all burning with indignation at the way political and military events were unfolding'.[85] They considered it absolutely typical – not to say treasonable – that pacifists and revolutionaries should provoke civil unrest while the Spanish army was engaged in a noble imperial endeavour in Morocco.

It was during this time in Toledo that the youthful Franco seized upon the ignominy of 1898 and the war effort in Morocco to transpose his aggrieved feelings of social and personal inferiority into a laudable nationalistic resentment. His desire to avenge his own humiliations at the hands of his father now blended with a determination to preserve the *Patria* itself by carving out a glorious military career for himself in Africa. However, when he completed his studies at the Academy in June 1910, a heroic future looked unlikely: the eighteen-year-old cadet passed out 251st out of 312 cadets. In *Raza*, Franco attempts to explain away this less than auspicious start to his army career. At José's passing-out ceremony from the Academy, our hero pontificates at length on Spain's glorious past, Toledo's rich history and Cervantes' contribution to Spanish culture. José explains how he had spent a week's allowance buying six copies of Cervantes' minor work *La Ilustre Fregona* to try and educate his comrades. When they fell into the hands of a teacher, he had been arrested. His rapturous friend Luis, confirming that José had 'learned more from the stones [of Toledo] than from the books', cries, 'Have you ever seen anything madder? He could have come top for his ability and the way the teachers all liked him so much, and yet he sacrificed it all for this sort of vain gesture!' A sententious José insists, 'I would never change my concerns just to come top.'[86] In reality, Franco himself would be endlessly flexible in his quest for power.

Francisco's desire to compensate for the unimpressive start to his military career on the battlefield of Africa was, in any case, undermined by the fact that, as a second lieutenant, he was too junior to apply for postings to Morocco. He and Pacón were therefore commissioned into a small regiment based in their hometown of El Ferrol. Back in the Calle de Maria, things had not changed much. His unhappy mother still lived with her elderly father. Dressed perpetually in black, she spent her days praying and her nights weeping. Francisco dutifully slipped home from the barracks most days. Although, away from the family home, the adolescent Francisco had discovered a deep-rooted resistance to church – as a soldier in Africa he would become known as 'the man without fear, women or masses ... With no interests or vices other than his career'[87] – when in El Ferrol he tried to please his mother with displays of Catholic piety. He even went so far as to join a pious society known as the Adoración Nocturna. However, neither his presence nor his ostentatious displays of religious fervour could lift the cloud of despair hovering over Doña Pilar.

Garrison duty in a small provincial town was not a thrilling prospect for the young cadets, in heroic mode and full of military ardour. Both men were bitterly disappointed to discover that the company contained only fifty men as against the 240 which was normal in the African army. A hapless Pacón was still struggling to master the tedious intricacies of military protocol. When he first presented himself at regimental headquarters, his new commanding officer refused to receive him on the grounds that 'the black gloves that you are wearing are not authorised when you're on duty'. He was curtly advised to 'withdraw and present yourself again when you're wearing the hazel-coloured ones that you should have been wearing in the first place'. 'Was it for this', he would indignantly muse, 'that I spent three years studying the campaigns of Hannibal and Napoleon?'[88]

Although Franco doubtless approved of the regiment's pedantic preoccupation with correct dress, military life in El Ferrol was hardly the sort of lifestyle he had in mind. His days were spent in routine parading, drilling and riding. In the evenings, desperate to compete with his splendidly attired brother Nicolás, and put distance between himself and the thirteen-year-old Ramón, he would stroll up and down the Calle Real with his comrades, sporting his military uniform, spanking new moustache and rakishly angled regimental pill-box. Any hopes of winning admiring glances from the town's rigorously chaperoned young women were, however, seriously misplaced. A military uniform was nowhere near as impressive as a naval one, and the chances of him overcoming his physical shortcomings and the social reservations of the families of El Ferrol were limited. His transitory and painful passions for his sister's friends – particularly tall, slim brunettes, not unlike his mother – never developed beyond yearning glances and tortured outpourings of poetry, which a derisive Pilar showed her jeering friends.

It was therefore a huge relief for Franco when he, Camilo Alonso Vega and Pacón were finally dispatched to Morocco, where the prospect of rapid promotion or a speedy death was infinitely more compelling than the stultifying existence in El Ferrol. Although hundreds of officers and thousands of soldiers had already been killed during the war, there is no evidence that Doña Pilar attempted to dissuade either him or, later on, his brother Ramón from joining the conflict in Africa. (In Salóm's play, an incredulous Don Nicolás expresses disgust at her readiness to send 'our sons to conquer a few worthless rocks that don't even belong to us'.)[89]

On 17 February 1912 the three young men arrived in Melilla, a mal-
odorous, unhealthy shanty town with a run-down population who 'gather
like flies at the smell of war'.[90] Franco was just nineteen. Although an excited
Pacón records that they were 'absolutely thrilled with that city' and, even
more improbably, comments on 'the good military spirit' among the con-
scripted men,[91] the three young men soon discovered that the reality of war
was very different from the glamorous tales of military glory upon which
they had been fed in Toledo. The badly equipped Spanish army, weighed
down by a top-heavy bureaucracy and hampered by governmental confusion, was forced to use untrained, unmotivated Spanish conscripts in
what they perceived as a profligate and pointless encounter with an
extremely determined enemy, who knew the wild terrain backwards. Even
Franco later conceded that he was more anxious about his own men turning
on him than about fighting the Moroccans.

Franco was still incapable of joining in the camaraderie of military life,
but he latched on to a military ethos of absolute obedience and a shared
rhetoric of patriotism, heroism and honour like an infant to the breast.
In Africa, every aspect of his life was dictated by army protocol. Not only
was there little space for emotional or rational ambivalence, but the
war provided an explicable, noble and external explanation for feeling
threatened and debased. His anger at the shortcomings of an absent and
powerless liberal government echoed his childhood resentments of his
father.

Franco also enthusiastically espoused the virulently anti-female ethos
being peddled by other officers, many of whom – like him – were keen to
escape any reminder of their emotional dependency upon their mothers.
Such an attitude was not unusual for young soldiers with fascist tendencies
at that time. In his classic study of German fascism, *Male Fantasies*, Klaus
Theweleit analyses more than 250 of the novels and memoirs of members
of the German Freikorps after the First World War, many of whom would
join Hitler's shock troops. He identifies a number of themes that crop up
in Franco's *Raza*, including a marked tendency to idealise mothers and kill
off fathers. They usually kill off their mothers as well, and – as in *Raza* the
idealised *sister* becomes the love object. Theweleit therefore concludes that
such men are driven not so much by an Oedipal desire to kill their fathers
as by a compulsion to escape from the symbiotic relationship with their
mothers, in whom 'the protectress and sufferer are united in one and
the same person'. Like their sons, even these idealised mothers are split,
emerging as 'loving and protective' and yet 'mothers-of-iron, who don't
even bat an eye at the news of the death of the sons they have sacrificed so
much to raise'.[92]

Whatever Franco's underlying psychological motivations, operating under instructions from a higher authority, engaged in what he considered to be a historic mission, he would prove to be a startlingly effective soldier. This is hardly surprising, if Erich Fromm is right when he notes that 'The authoritarian character loves situations that limit human freedom, loves being submitted to fate. The soldier will gladly submit to the whim or will of his superior.'[93] As Norman Dixon observes, the army is 'an unusually good environment for men who lacked inner controls'. For such people, it is deeply reassuring when the alarming randomness of life is replaced by clearly delineated patterns and 'the anxiety of uncertainty is reduced'.[94] Certainly Franco appears to have found it liberating to hand over personal and moral responsibility to his military commanders. Profoundly reluctant to put himself in a position where he could be blamed for his actions, as political leader he would convince himself that he was operating under instructions from an even higher authority: God.

The brutalising conditions of war transformed profound predispositions into immutable character traits. Cut off from mainland Spain and the core of the Spanish army, detached from the culture in which he was living, and rigidly separate from the men who surrounded him, there was nothing to moderate Franco's tendency to brutality, his emotional withdrawal or his fanciful dreams. While Franco's aspirations and emotional shortcomings were hardly unique, the way in which they became enmeshed with his own private dreams was. As with Hitler, war turned 'the fantasy world of adolescence into reality'.[95] Like the Führer, he would use the ceremony and 'dressing-up' associated with war and the military life to 'conceal and glorify his personality'.[96] Leaving the gawky child, the timid schoolboy and the mediocre cadet far behind, a resolute Franco looked resolutely to a glorious future. However, although his head was in the clouds, his feet would remain firmly on the ground.

CHAPTER 2

The Emergent Hero

Africa, 1910–31

My years in Africa live in me with an inexpressible force. There was born the possibility of rescuing Spanish greatness. There was founded the set of ideals which today is redeeming us. Without Africa I can scarcely explain myself to myself, nor could I fully explain myself to my comrades in arms.

Francisco Franco[1]

The nineteen-year-old Franco was confirmed in his new rank as first lieutenant in June 1912, the only promotion he would ever receive as a matter of course. Upon his arrival in Morocco, he became part of inept and sterile military operations aimed at establishing defensive links between the larger towns. He soon applied for a transfer to the native police – or Regulares – recently established by Dámaso Berenguer. Manned by fierce Moorish mercenaries, the Regulares would provide him with endless opportunities for heroic exploits and fast promotion. Franco proved to be much more at ease commanding Moorish troops than Spaniards, presumably because as a white man he considered himself their social and intellectual superior: something of a father-figure, a role in which he emulated Don Nicolás's erratic style.

In December 1912, on leave for the first time, Franco spent Christmas in Melilla, where he fell passionately in love with Sofía Subirán, the daughter of Colonel Subirán, brother-in-law to the High Commissioner in Morocco. Franco's improbably sentimental notion of love was very much in evidence with the socially superior Sofía. Although she did not succumb to his charms, she would later confess that she had enjoyed being treated 'as if I were a supernatural being.'[2] Between 6 January and 5 June 1913, Franco wrote to her almost daily, sometimes in batches of four or five postcards at a time. The pictures he selected were a singularly bizarre assortment for a young soldier who prided himself on his masculinity. They range from photos of very young girls with their arms round each other's necks, to prepubescent virginal girls staring coyly but provocatively at the camera, their impending sexuality hinted at in the scandalous exposure of a shoulder. Occasionally, more stately, matronly young women sit by a lamp, reading a book, or young girls are wrapped around the neck of a horse, or play with a fluffy kitten. Franco's maternal fixation is revealed in a series of pictures in which a young girl gazes devotedly at what appears to be her baby son, who is lying in her arms looking sated. This strange if revealing selection of pictures – more the sort of thing a romantic young girl would send to a friend, than a brave soldier to his loved one – were accompanied by stilted protestations of Franco's devotion in his relentlessly uniform handwriting. A stiff, formal and remarkably persistent Franco refers only fleetingly to the tedium or terror of life in the battle zone. By 9 March, clearly dissatisfied at Sofía's response, Franco writes 'el que espera desespera, Sofía y yo espero' ('he who waits is in despair Sofía, and I am waiting'). By 5 June he is forced to acknowledge that 'you still don't love me, isn't that true Sofía', but complacently adds, 'though I believe that you are mistaken'.[3] The readiness with which Franco dismissed Sofía's reservations as nonsensical is a clear indication that his capacity for self-criticism or emotional reflection were already seriously flawed.

Blighted in love, Franco flung himself into soldiering with a self-destructive, almost suicidal fervour. Having helped reinforce the base at Ceuta, Franco was posted to the garrison of Tetuan, where he distinguished himself as an exceptional and courageous soldier. Between 14 August and 27 September 1913, he engaged in several operations, winning the Military Merit Cross first class for action in the field on 12 October 1913. On 1 February 1914, at the age of twenty-one, Franco was promoted to captain 'por méritos de guerra'. His high-pitched, often shrill commands and diminutive physique were now offset by wild bravery in the field and a total disregard for danger, which earned him, if not the affection, then at least the respect and loyalty of his men. His incredible nonchalance under fire soon became legendary. On one occasion it was alleged that the cup from the canteen he was drinking was shot from between his fingers: finishing his drink, he called out, 'Better shot next time!' Unable to differentiate between his heroic childhood fantasies and real life, he surged into battle on a white horse. He had finally become the boy's-own hero he had always dreamed of being. Perhaps he was filled with an omnipotent belief in his own immortality, or was attempting to defy his own mortality by killing others. Maybe he was convinced that the only way to get his parents' or Sofía's attention was to die. Either way, he was the beneficiary of extraordinary good luck. Within a mere thirty months, thirty-five of the forty-one officers of the Regulares whom Franco had joined were killed or wounded, but he was seriously wounded only once. The Moors were convinced that he was blessed with *Baraka* or 'the mystical quality of divine protection which kept him invulnerable'.[4] Whatever his motivation, the link in Franco's mind between sex and death is exposed in *Raza*. The only sexually charged physical encounter between José (Franco) and his beautiful and chaste girlfriend Marisol takes place when she comes to collect the 'martyr's corpse' after he has been shot by Republicans. Overcome with emotion, she lifts the cloth from José's face and in what Ramon Gubern, in his Adlerian analysis of *Raza*, calls 'skin contact with necrophiliac con-notations'[5] places her cheek next to the apparently dead soldier's face. For whatever reason, killing would become an integral part of his life. As Caudillo he would vent his destructive and sexual impulses hunting animals. Redemption through punishment and the nobility of death – such important themes in *Raza* – became lifelong obsessions.

Franco was not the only soldier intent on killing himself as well as others. One of Berenguer's hand-picked officers was also inspiring admiration for, among other things, his reckless habit of sitting exposed on parapets jeering at the enemy while bullets flew past his ears. Five years older than Franco and 6 feet tall, the gaunt Emilio Mola was strikingly different from the diminutive new arrival in the Regulares. However, the two men respected each other as soldiers and shared a profound hatred and mistrust of civilian politicians. Like the other committed Africanistas, both men believed that involvement in the glorious Moroccan venture qualified them, and them alone, to safeguard the motherland from the incompetence of the civilian government, and the treachery of left-wing pacifism. Anybody who opposed them, on whatever grounds, was considered to be a danger to the *Patria* and a challenge to the army. Both men would play a pivotal role in the military rebellion in 1936.

In 1916 Franco was seriously wounded for the first and only time in his life in a battle at El Biutz. Pacón, who had been posted back to Galicia on 30 October 1912, records, somewhat surprisingly, that after receiving 'the pessimistic news ... that he had been shot in the stomach, Don Nicolás hastened to Tetuan with his estranged wife to see him'.[6] In his play about Don Nicolás, Salóm claims, rather more plausibly, that they visited him in hospital after he was transferred to Seville. On the journey to visit their dying son, an implacable Doña Pilar commends Franco for heroically defending Spain. 'Which one,' demands her irate husband, 'yours ... or mine?', adding, 'I don't understand how you can accept with resignation and even pride that they kill your own son!'[7] The concern of both parents may have consolidated Franco's belief that an early death – like Paz's – was essential to earn their devotion. In fact, despite a deeply gloomy prognosis,

Franco did not die, although it was, as Pacón records, 'a real miracle that he did not suffer peritonitis and the bullet did not enter any important organ.'[8] Although this miraculous escape did little to curb Franco's burgeoning belief in his invulnerability, the fact that he was plagued thereafter by rumours that this injury had left him sexually impotent cannot have helped his underlying feelings of emasculation.

Perhaps that was why he responded so robustly when the High Commissioner's recommendations that he be promoted to major and be awarded the highest award for bravery, the Gran Cruz Laureada de San Fernando for his efforts at El Biutz, were opposed by the Ministry of War. The affronted 23-year-old did not hesitate to appeal direct to the Commander-in-Chief of the Army, King Alfonso XIII. This audacious ploy, a clear sign that he had already lost sight of his lowly position in the overall scheme of things, was perhaps a symptom of his frustration with politicians, who, like his father, would not acknowledge his achievements. It clearly startled the King and irritated the government. Although Alfonso XIII granted his appeal for promotion, the government refused to award him the Laureada. This rebuff so rankled with him that he awarded it to himself at the post-civil war victory parade on 19 May 1939. Franco became a major with effect from 29 June 1916. Although he was reputed, at the age of twenty-three, to be the youngest major in Europe, this seems unlikely. There were certainly younger majors in the British forces during the Great War.[9] Nevertheless, even in the extraordinary conditions of the African War, this was a dizzy ascent up the hierarchical ladder.

As there were no vacancies for a major in Morocco, Franco's promotion brought his heroics in Africa to an abrupt halt. In the spring of 1917 he was posted to Oviedo, where he was joined, a year later, by his cousin Pacón and Camilo Alonso Vega, and met up with Joaquín Arrarás, who would later write a somewhat fanciful account of Franco's life up until the end of the civil war. At the time, however, far from marvelling at his exploits, the local elite referred to him as El Comandantini (the little Major). Subjected to the snobbery and derision of the town-folk and cold-shouldered by other officers of the rank of captain and major, many of whom were twice his age, Franco might just as well have been back home. He was as withdrawn as ever. A colleague recalls that 'he never came out on the town with us, he would always go home. He isolated himself.' Nevertheless, although Oviedo was as socially divided as El Ferrol, as a young army officer Franco was in a slightly better position to court important local families. It was during this time that he transferred his passion from Sofía to a slim, dark-haired fifteen-year-old convent girl from a prominent local family. Like Sofía, Mariá del Carmen Polo y Martínez Valdés was attractive on three crucial counts: her physical similarity to his mother, her prestigious family name and her ostentatious commitment to Catholicism. Despite the social disparity between them, the young couple had undergone similar experiences as young children. While Franco had experienced the emotional loss of his mother to depression, Carmen's mother had actually died, leaving her to be brought up by her elitist and ambitious Aunt Isabel. A ruthless Doña Pilar had never left Francisco in any doubt about her social aspirations for her family.

Franco was as dogged in his pursuit of Carmen as he had been with Sofía. He hid messages for her in the hat-band of a mutual friend and left notes in her coat pocket in cafés. He even went so far as to attend daily mass – an activity towards which he had developed a profound aversion since leaving home – in order to catch a glimpse of her from behind a wrought-iron grill. Although his sheer determination finally sparked an interest in the youthful Carmen, her father was absolutely horrified at the idea of his daughter associating with an impecunious and socially inferior young officer, whose social standing and chances of survival were roughly comparable to those of a bull-fighter. The family's frosty opposition to this socially and economically unfavourable union brought out a stubborn streak in the would-be lovers.

In Oviedo itself, the staunch, unbending traditionalism encapsulated by Carmen's family was confronted by a militant local working class led by the Socialist Party, which was demonstrating against rapidly deteriorating living standards and the 'criminal war in Morocco'. The army, disgusted at the government's apparent impotence in the face of this unrest, was itself wracked by internal divisions. Officers who had not fought in Africa and bitterly resented the faster promotion, greater kudos and higher salaries enjoyed by the Africanistas formed the so-called Juntas de Defensa to protect a system of rigid seniority that firmly precluded promotion by merit.

This rancorous internal debate fed into a national crisis. The army had already clashed with the government over whether or not Spain should participate in the First World War. To the chagrin of some generals, Spain was forced, for economic reasons, to adopt a position of neutrality. Although the consequent ability to export to both sides resulted in an industrial boom in the northern provinces, the influence of the landed, agrarian sector remained paramount, primarily through unequal taxation devices. This provoked an increasingly confident and frustrated industrial bourgeoisie to push for political modernisation and reform. The army played an active but contradictory role in this increasingly volatile situation. Although middle-ranking officers in the army were also objecting to low pay, anachronistic promotion structures and political corruption, they were horrified when the Basque and Catalan industrialists, determined to hang on to their war profits, began to finance nationalist movements. Meanwhile, rural and urban working-class militancy was inflamed by wartime short-ages and inflation. In this situation the socialist trade union, the Unión General de Trabajadores (UGT), and its rival, the anarcho-syndicalist Con-federación Nacional del Trabajo (CNT), united in the hope that a joint general strike might bring about free elections and reform.

In 1917, army officers at the forefront of the apparently reformist Juntas de Defensa united, for a brief and improbable moment, with workers and capitalists in a bid to sweep away the corruption of *caciquismo*. In the wake of the 1898 disaster, support for some form of revival was also widespread among industrialists, intellectuals and the bourgeoisie. However, the left's notion of what was wrong – 'the backward ideology of the ruling order, the corruption and clientelism of the political system, the apathy of the masses' – and their solution, 'a full blown programme of modernization based on European models'[10] did not coincide with the military perspective. While, for the left, *regeneration* meant replacing the corruption of the *cacique* system with democratic reform, for the Right it meant using the Army as an 'iron surgeon' to crush it, and the industrialists favoured something in between. The left was committed to regional autonomy, the army was obsessed with safeguarding the unity of the *Patria* against further imperial losses or regional autonomy (castrations).[11] The idea of the nation as a 'diseased body' that had suffered from 'dismemberments' or loss of territory, such an important part of Francoist rhetoric, became an integral part of right-wing ideology at this time.

The 'regenerationist' rhetoric only fleetingly masked the mutually con-tradictory agendas. The Conservative Prime Minister, Eduardo Dato, moved swiftly to exploit the incompatible demands of the workers, indus-trialists and army officers, and consolidate the power of the entrenched landed oligarchy. He bought off the military with economic concessions, provoked the socialists into calling a premature general strike on 10 August 1917 before the CNT was ready, and then utilised the army to crush the strikers. This resulted in 80 dead, 150 wounded and the arrest of 2000 workers, many of whom were beaten and tortured. The youthful Major Franco was one of the men 'responsible for restoring order' among the peaceful strikers in the mines of Asturias, where an 'African hatred' was unleashed against the mining villages and resulted in an orgy of rape, looting, beatings and torture.[12] This was the first time Franco was personally involved in diverting the colonial brutality normally targeted at the tribes-men in Africa against the Spanish working classes. It would not be the last.

Despite the successful repression of protest, successive administrations began to acknowledge that public opinion could be mollified only by imposing a defensive strategy upon the army in Morocco, and reducing military costs. Although this strategy did not go down well with Africanistas, Franco – displaying a self-serving pragmatism for which he would become famous – was unwilling to jeopardise his standing among the military in Oviedo by publicly associating himself with the Africanistas' grievances. Keen to curry favour with his mainland colleagues, he therefore joined the Juntas de Defensa, even though its aspirations were hardly in his long-term interests.

He was not just flexible on the professional front. Uninhibited by his association with Carmen, during this time Franco formed a passionate attachment to another young girl while on leave in El Ferrol. The extremely pretty María de los Angeles Barcón y de Furundarena, named beauty queen in El Ferrol 1919, was the rebellious daughter of an extremely wealthy family with aristocratic connections. Impressed by the young officer's 'concentrated seriousness' and the delicacy with which he treated girls, she would later recall that Franco 'had an air of mystery as if a fixed higher idea made him concentrate his every thought on that idea. He spoke little and to the point. I noticed he never had warm hands.' This fleeting relationship came to a violent end when, upon discovering her relationship with the impecunious young officer, her father gave her 'the biggest slap in the face that I have ever received'.[13] She did not tell Franco what had happened, but reluctantly stopped seeing him. Although Franco reconciled himself to this emotional setback with customary equanimity, he continued to send her postcards. When he became Chief of State, he always ensured that if she ever needed anything doing it was done immediately.

The rejected but by no means desolate lover returned to Oviedo where, without pausing for breath, he renewed his efforts to win the hand of the young Carmen Polo, who, to the horror of her family, finally agreed to marry him. It was during this romantic interlude that Franco met up with a like-minded army officer, José Millán Astray. This would be a profoundly influential encounter. Although the surrealistically lunatic Millán Astray – who, because of his many injuries in battle, was allegedly 'rebuilt out of hooks, bits of wood, string and glass'[14] – was strikingly different from the cold and calculating young Major Franco, the two men formed a close attachment. They shared a propensity for manic displays of intemperate bravery in battle, a childhood obsession with heroic tales and a morbid fascination with death. Neither would betray their mothers, either by forming strong sexual relationships with their wives or by leaving them.

Indeed, when Millán Astray's wife made the startling proclamation on their wedding night that she had taken a lifelong vow of chastity, a remarkably sanguine Millán readily agreed that they adopt a 'fraternal' relationship. According to Paul Preston, the men's 'obsession with spit and polish [and] bravery' may also have constituted an attempt to wipe out their father's stain upon the family name.[15] Like Don Nicolás, Millán's easy-going father had brought shame and social opprobrium upon his family. As a prison governor, he had taken bribes from the inmates in return for letting them have home visits. When one of his charges committed a violent murder while out on one of these unofficial paroles, Millán's father had ended up in prison.

When Franco first met him, Millán was enthusiastically propounding the idea that Spain should organise a volunteer, mercenary force along the lines of the French Foreign Legion to counteract the hostility of public opinion towards conscription, which was having such an adverse impact on the war in Africa. On 28 January 1920, Millán was promoted to lieutenant-colonel and named head of the newly formed Spanish Foreign Legion. He offered the like-minded Major Franco the post of second-in-command. Although this meant that Franco had to leave his anxious and fraught young fiancée, Carmen Polo, at home, there was no contest between the violent appeal of war and his emotional attachments. He left for Africa without a backward glance.

Although Franco always made much of his time in Africa, and Arraras romantically described how 'The call of Africa echoed in his soul . . . ensnaring him within its deadly grip',[16] he never mastered Arabic, or showed the slightest interest in, or empathy with, the traditions or customs of the tribesmen. His conviction – articulated to Manuel Aznar on 31 December 1938 – that 'Spain is a country that really, really, understands the Moslems and knows how to reach an understanding with them' and his belief that the Moroccans 'love us' and 'are grateful to us for an attitude which they always sensed in us' proved to be as misguided as his fantasies about his own family.[17] The Moroccans loathed their Spanish overlords.

The Africa to which he returned was very different from the one he had left three years previously. In 1919 General Damaso Berenguer had been appointed High Commissioner for the Moroccan Protectorate in the hope that this would stabilise the situation there. However, personal and strategic differences soon emerged between him and General Manuel Fernández Silvestre, the military commander of Ceuta. Although both men were favourites of Alfonso XIII, Berenguer was inclined to work towards a peaceful domination of the tribes, while Silvestre was keen on provocative displays of military superiority and audacious advances into enemy ter-

ritory. This was the tense situation that greeted Franco upon his arrival
back in Africa on 10 October 1920.

As commander of the first battalion of the Legion, it was Franco's job to
forge an efficient fighting force out of the common criminals, misfits and
outcasts he brought with him. When Franco's hapless recruits first arrived
in Ceuta, they were greeted by a near hysterical Millán Astray wildly proclaiming, 'You have lifted yourselves from among the dead – for don't forget
that you were dead, that your lives were over. You have come here to live a
new life for which you must pay with death. You have come here to die.
¡Viva la muerte!' This less than optimistic greeting was followed by the
stern reminder that 'Since you crossed the Straits, you have no mother, no
girlfriend, no family; from today all that will be provided by the Legion.'[18]
Far from deterring the men, Millán's depressing prognosis seems to have
inflated their shrivelled souls with energy. That night his 'bridegrooms of
death' ran amok: by the morning a prostitute and a corporal of the guard
had been murdered.

Within a rapidly escalating frenzy of destructiveness, Millán and his
ruthless second-in-command implemented a routine of savage if erratic
discipline. Having released feelings of uncontrollable anger and aggression
in the Legionnaires, considerable energy was needed to ensure that it was
directed against the enemy, and not their superior officers. Millán engaged
in frenzied physical assaults on any Legionnaire who did not display the
required levels of deference. On the day of their arrival, he leapt upon an
insolent mulatto, 'lifted him off the ground, threw him into the centre of
the circle and beat his face horribly with both fists'.[19] In 1941 the writer
Arturo Barea, who served in the African army in the 1920s, described how,
when dealing with his men,

Millán's entire body underwent an hysterical transfiguration. His voice thundered
and sobbed and howled. He spat into the faces of these men all their misery, their
shame, their filth, their crimes, and then he dragged them along in a fanatical fury
to a sense of chivalry, to a renunciation of all hope, beyond that of dying a death
which would wash away the stains of their cowardice in the splendour of heroism.[20]

As Pacón blithely points out, 'perhaps the loss of his arm, of one of his eyes
and his many mutilations undermined his good humour'.[21]

It was, however, the icy Franco not the fiery Millán who insisted that the
death sentence be imposed to maintain discipline among the men. On
one occasion he coldly directed that a Legionnaire who had hurled his
unpalatable food in the face of an officer be shot on the spot, and ordered
his traumatised comrades to march past the corpse. When an officer who

had trained with Franco in Toledo questioned these extreme measures, Franco snapped, 'You don't realise what kind of people they are. If I didn't act with an iron hand, this would soon be chaos.'[22] Even the infamous Gonzalo Queipo de Llano, later renowned for his brutality during the civil war, was horrified at the equanimity with which Franco presided over the beatings of his Moorish troops.

Neither Millán nor Franco imposed any restrictions on the atrocities the Legionnaires carried out against the native population, including decapitating prisoners and wielding their heads as trophies. While Franco showed no overt physical enjoyment of the bestial extremes of his wild compatriots, he clearly derived a remote sadistic satisfaction from their savagery. His stilted record of his exploits in Africa written in 1922, *Morocco: The Diary of a Battalion* – similar in its literary style to the formal, turgid, fanciful prose of his postcards and *Raza* – captures the polarities of his psyche. Devoid of real feeling, it oscillates between sentimental testimonials to his men's heroics, unemotional but vicarious accounts of their depravity, and passionate diatribes about the indifference of the Spanish nation to the heroism and patriotism of the soldiers in Africa. In 1922 he inserted a fictitious account of a moving encounter between a brave young officer and a 'grizzled veteran soldier', who turns out to be the young officer's long-lost, but devoted and admiring father.[23] His fantasised yearnings for paternal acknowledgement were interspersed with chilling accounts of his men's violence. He proudly records an occasion when 'Little Charlot, the buglar boy brought in the severed ear of a Moor.'[24] The strange link between extreme violence and gross sentimentality was illustrated when in 1922 the Duquesa de la Victoria, who had organised a team of volunteer nurses, found two severed Moorish heads nestling among the roses sent to her by the Legion.

That the Franco who sent women pictures of coy young girls and kittens was capable of such markedly sadistic tendencies exposes profound splits within his personality. The harrowing conditions in Africa catered perfectly for his rapidly diverging emotional needs. Not only did they equip him with an acceptable, indeed by his standards justifiable and glorious, outlet for his own repressed sadism, but the war provided a heroic mask with which to disguise this aspect of his personality from himself and others. He was not unusual in this respect. As Erik Fromm points out, 'A person can be entirely dominated by his sadistic strivings and consciously believe that he is motivated only by his sense of duty.'[25] Furthermore, wracked since early childhood by feelings of inferiority, powerlessness and individual insignificance, it is hardly surprising that Franco was so keen to fuse his identity with that of the mighty Spanish army.

Franco's deluded beliefs in his and the Spanish army's noble prowess would be seriously put to the test when the differing military priorities of General Berenguer and General Silvestre culminated in disaster. On 21 July 1921 the aggressive Silvestre ordered an ambitious and ill-advised advance into the territory beyond the Spanish stronghold of Melilla. Here he encountered Abd-el-Krim, the fierce new leader of the Berber tribes of the Riff, who inflicted a monumental defeat upon the Spanish troops at the village of Annual. Tribal leaders seized the opportunity to drive the fleeing Spanish troops back to the walls of Melilla. Within a few hours, thousands were massacred and 5000 square kilometres of barren scrubland lost. Devastating massacres took place at various outposts, including Dar Drius and Nador.

Such a stark and costly exposure of the shortcomings of the invincible colonial Spanish army – with its echo of the 1898 disaster – must have shaken Franco's lofty notions of power and authority to the core. However, on this occasion he was in a position to avenge the humiliation himself. Franco's troops were dispatched by sea to support the defence of Melilla, arriving on 23 July 1921. Although his impassioned request that he be allowed to relieve the last remnants of the garrison at the village of Nador was, to his disgust, turned down, his courageous behaviour and willingness to use unorthodox military methods soon covered him with glory. The hapless military high command, on the other hand, was brought under close scrutiny by the government in August 1921 when it directed General José Picasso to report on the disaster at Annual.

Franco displayed particular skill during the ensuing campaign to defend Melilla from the marauding tribesmen. Pacón recalls an occasion when Franco angrily berated a superior officer for placing his men in danger, shouting, 'Can't you see that your unit is in dangerous terrain dominated by the heights occupied by the enemy? Don't you understand that they are causing casualties that could be avoided? Who ordered you to get into such a ridiculous position?' The startled Lieutenant-Colonel apologised profusely and followed Franco's brusque directions to 'get out of that position as quickly as possible'. When a 'gob-smacked' Pacón expressed astonishment at his insubordination, a nonchalant Franco commented, 'I didn't notice his two stars [but] his officers, NCOs and troops will have been extremely grateful for my flouting of regulations which avoided them losing their lives, being wounded or falling prisoners of the enemy.'[26]

On another occasion, Pacón records how Franco galloped from one side of the battlefield to the other, encouraging the men and directing operations. Having reassured Pacón that he had called for reinforcements, Franco urged him to remain in position, to 'cover your flanks well and do not be affected by the tenacity or bravery of the enemy' and to retreat when ordered to do so by himself 'calmly and with confidence of success ... As the Legion credo demands, not one single man will be left behind.'[27] Franco then raced off to a small rise some distance away, where he not only reversed a panic-stricken retreat by the native police, but also managed to persuade them to turn back and reconquer the position they had just relinquished. When an astonished Pacón later asked him how he was able to act so swiftly, Franco replied that he knew the men would flee because he had noticed through his binoculars that their superior officer had been wounded. Aware that this would result in a 'general and disordered retreat followed by the loss of the position and its occupation by the enemy', he launched himself into action.[28]

According to Pacón, although his men were terrified of Franco, they were profoundly reassured by the calm confidence with which he made military decisions in the midst of mayhem and bloodshed. The camp was always filled with relief when Franco returned from leave, because when he took charge of a military operation there was 'a great certainty of victory ... no long faces or questioning looks'.[29] Despite his histrionics on the battlefield, however, there was always much speculation about Franco's sexuality, both at the time and later. Colonel Vicente Guarner, who was with Franco in Africa, later commented that 'Since Franco was never known to show any attractions to girls nor have any amorous adventures, there used to be mutterings about a possible homosexuality.' He discussed this issue with the second adjutant to the Legion, Fermín Galán, who confessed that suspicions were aroused when Franco refused to share the tent occupied by all the officers of the corps. Instead he pitched two more – one for himself and a young German Legionnaire, the other for his two adjutants. Galán commented that 'He always felt an inclination for well-togged-out males. He was narcissistic and feminine in voice and attitudes, although there was no proof of homosexuality.'[30]

Whatever his underlying sexuality, Franco chose to punctuate his military exploits with occasional visits to see Carmen Polo in Oviedo, where growing press adulation ensured that he was assiduously courted by the local aristocracy. It is hardly surprising that Franco's confidence soared during this time. Usually so deferential with his superiors, he was now even prepared to stand up to his own terrifying commanding officer. On one occasion, when Millán, who had just promoted his own private secretary, turned down Franco's request that one of his NCOs be promoted, an ironic Franco asked whether this was because 'he isn't a good enough typist!'[31] Franco's men were delighted by this shot at Millán. As Franco ascended the hierarchical ladder, Pacón records that he 'always gave his subordinate officers initiative in how best to carry out his instructions. That is to say he did not overload us with unimportant details and was always serene.'[32] Although this approach was an advantage on the battlefields of Morocco, it would prove significantly less efficacious when Franco moved into the world of politics. As supreme military commander and political leader, Franco's diverse managerial style would be driven more by the need to scatter 'blame' as widely as possible than by the desire to inculcate responsibility in his underlings.

In September 1921, Millán Astray was seriously wounded in the chest during a counter-attack. Flung to the ground, bleeding copiously and near to death (a condition he had seemingly hankered after for some time), he rolled around on the ground screaming 'They've killed me, they've killed me', but recalled himself sufficiently to sit up and roar '¡Viva el Rey! ¡Viva España! ¡Viva la Legion!' before being borne away on a stretcher. He handed over command to Franco. Six weeks later, Franco and his men finally entered Nador, where they found, in Franco's words, 'an enormous cemetery' of the rotting corpses of their comrades. In Monte Arruit too, Franco bitterly describes 'the horrendous picture that presented itself. The majority of the corpses [of Spanish soldiers] have been profaned or barbarously mutilated ... We left feeling in our hearts a desire for revenge, for the most exemplary punishment ever seen down the generations.'[33]

It is not without significance that, when Franco had his film-script Raza printed in 1942, he created a publishing house, which he called Numancia after an historic Spanish siege. For ten years – between 143 and 133 BC – the occupants of this citadel were besieged by the Romans. When Numancia was finally laid to waste, the few defenders who had not been killed, or starved to death, killed themselves. Franco's preoccupation with relieving sieges was echoed by the men of the Freikorps for whom, Theweleit argues, a 'castle' (or besieged fortress) often carried the connotation of 'high-born mother' and is usually associated with the womb. Thus did a siege symbolise the body of the pure mother being laid waste by the attacking hordes.[34] Franco's and his men's attitude to native or 'low-born' women was less indulgent. When at one point an officer ordered his men to cease firing because their targets were women, a Legionnaire was heard to mutter, 'But they are factories for baby Moors'. 'We all laughed,' recalled Franco, 'and we remembered that during the disaster [at Melilla] the women were the most cruel, finishing off the wounded and stripping them of their clothes, in this way paying back the welfare that civilisation had brought them.'[35] These devastating experiences in Morocco had an enormous emotional resonance for Franco, fanning his blood-lust, his paranoia and his desire for vengeance, and triggering an obsession with the relief – and imposition –

of military and political sieges that would dog his conduct as military commander during the civil war. By the 1940s, an emotionally and politically withdrawn Franco would withdraw the whole of Spain into a besieged garrison.

Back in Africa, Franco was in a position to avenge these violations himself. Although by the beginning of 1922 Spain had managed to reappropriate much of its lost territory and stabilise the situation in Africa, when a blockhouse near Dar Drius came under attack by tribesmen the defending Legionnaires sent out a frantic appeal for help. Franco stormed off to assist with only twelve men. They returned some hours later covered in blood with the heads of twelve tribesmen strapped to their belts. This is the only recorded incident of Franco being directly involved in a physical atrocity.

However, while the press in Galicia jubilantly celebrated the 'sang froid, the fearlessness and the contempt for life' of 'our beloved Paco Franco', the wider picture was less clear-cut. The army's costly and disastrous exploits in Morocco had further inflamed opposition on the left and discredited the King, who was personally implicated in General Silvestre's ill-considered and disastrous advance. Denouncing the corruption that had contributed to the military rout, the socialist orator Indalacio Prieto demanded the closure of the military academies and the expulsion of senior officers from the African army.

The 'Picasso report' on the Annual disaster, commissioned by the government, resulted in the forced resignation of thirty-nine officers, including the High Commissioner Berenguer. The report was then submitted to the Responsibilities Commission in the Cortes to allocate political blame for the military disaster. Franco, on the other hand, was publicly commended for his role at Annual. In 1922 he met with Alfonso XIII, who embraced him warmly and commended his bravery after Millán Astray's injury. An unusually humble Franco protested to the press that 'What he has said about me is a bit exaggerated. I merely fulfil my duty.'[36] His commanding officer during the defence of Melilla, Brigadier General José Sanjurjo – who would be at the forefront of the military uprising in 1936 – requested that he be promoted to lieutenant-colonel. Because of the ongoing inquiry into the Annual disaster, the request was turned down. Although Millán Astray was promoted to full colonel, and Sanjurjo to major-general, Franco was awarded the military medal but remained a major.

Millán soon succeeded in tarnishing his own career when, on 7 November, he dispatched a petulant and public letter to the King threatening to resign his commission in protest at the influence of the Juntas de Defensa. To his dismay, the influential *Junteros* persuaded the reluctant King to accept his resignation: on 13 November 1922, Millán was relieved of his command of the Legion, ostensibly for health reasons. When it was decided that his second-in-command was not sufficiently senior to take his place, Lieutenant-Colonel Rafael de Valenzuela took over command of the Legion. Franco, bitterly commenting that 'There's no shooting ... Now all we do is vegetate', immediately requested a mainland posting. On 12 January 1923 he returned to Spain, where he received his Military Medal and was named as one of an elite group of military courtiers by the King.

Neither the terrifying Africanista he had been, nor the uncharismatic General or autocratic Caudillo he would become, was discernible in the relaxed and affable young officer on display back on the mainland. In an engaging profile written at the time, a Catalan novelist described the young Major as having a 'sunburnt face, his black brilliant eyes, his curly hair, a certain timidity in his speech and gestures and his quick and open smile make him seem like a child'. 'When praised', he commented, 'Franco blushes like a girl who has been flattered.' During the interview the self-effacing hero brushed aside favourable comment – 'I've done nothing really!' – rhapsodised about the bravery of his men – 'Even the wounded, dragging themselves along covered in blood, cried ¡Viva la Legion! ... so manly so brave, I felt an emotion that choked me' – and dismissed the suggestion that he was fearless with a puzzled smile. 'I don't know,' he commented. 'No one knows what courage and fear are. In a soldier, all this is summed up in something else: the concept of duty, of patriotism.' He jovially responded to the question 'Are you in love, Franco?' with the reply '¡Hombre! What do you think? I'm just off to Oviedo to get married.' Niceto Alcala Zamora, the Minister of War during the Primo years, and subsequently President of the Second Republic, would later comment how much he had liked Franco's air of modesty, 'the loss of which when he became a general damaged him significantly'.

Franco's dazzling career, early promotion and royal recognition stimulated an outbreak of feverish hero-worship in Oviedo when he returned there on 21 March 1923. Jubilant locals presented him with a gold key to the city, while the good and the great sought to out-do each in their glowing tributes to the romantic young hero. The readiness of people to perpetuate a reverent, almost mythological perception of Franco inevitably contributed to his distorted sense of self.

In Africa, bereft of Millán's invigorating lunacy and Franco's reign of terror, the Legionnaires soon lost their enthusiasm for blood and bravery. However, when Abd el Krim, who had imposed such ignominy upon the Spanish at Annual, launched a fresh attack against the defensive Spanish line outside Melilla and Lieutenant-Colonel Valenzuela was killed in action on 5 June 1923, it was agreed that Franco should take over as commander of the Legion. This required him to be promoted to lieutenant-colonel, back-dated to 31 January 1922. His new elevation provoked a fresh and frenzied outburst of accolades to the self-effacing hero in the press. Wined and dined at official banquets, he was widely commended for his bravery. Even the Legionnaires became embroiled in the fantasy. Franco's promotion meant that he would, once again, have to leave his distraught wife-to-be behind while he risked almost certain death in the battlefield. Franco's noble comment that his duty as a soldier would 'take precedence over any feelings, even those with roots deep in the soul' should be taken with a pinch of salt, but his protestation that 'When the *Patria* calls, we have only one rapid and concise response: *¡Presente!*' came from the heart. Carmen's feelings can only be guessed at.

In command in Ceuta, Franco was soon engaging in feats of fearlessness. Abd el Krim had followed his successes with a major push on Tifaruin, a Spanish outpost west of Melilla. On 22 August, two banderas of the Legion under Franco's command dislodged nearly 9000 men besieging Tifaruin. Back on the mainland, however, tension between the army and conscripts leaving for Africa erupted into violence in Malaga, resulting in the death of a non-commissioned officer. Corporal Sánchez Barroso was blamed for the killing, arrested and immediately sentenced to death by the army. Alarmed at a potential backlash from the public, the civilian government asked for and obtained a royal pardon. This, along with the investigation of 'responsibilities' for Annual, so enraged the army that on 13 September the somewhat volatile General Miguel Primo de Rivera, a close friend of General Sanjurjo, launched a military coup. The King, somewhat fatefully as it turned out, colluded in his role as constitutional monarch being superseded by Primo's military dictatorship. For the moment, however, a broad spectrum of Spaniards seemed inclined to give the new regime a chance.

Members of the Legion were rather more ambivalent. Most of the officers who supported Primo were members of the Juntas de Defensa, and Primo had himself expressed concern at the escalating social and economic price of maintaining Spain's Moroccan protectorate. Franco, on the other hand, comfortable with the idea that the army should take over power from an incompetent civilian government, and seriously disinclined to challenge a superior officer, kept his head down. In any case, his personal life, very briefly, took precedence. On 22 October 1923, he returned to Oviedo to marry the 21-year-old Maria del Carmen Polo, with Alfonso XIII acting, through the proxy of the military governor of Oviedo, as best man.

A public wedding is almost as efficacious as a foreign war to divert public discontent. With Franco the Spaniards had both. The inhabitants of Oviedo looked to the young couple to take their minds off their personal and national sense of inadequacy and impotence. Huge crowds gathered to see their great hero enter the church under a royal canopy, and emerge to wild applause. Franco's romantic young bride, overwhelmed by the publicity and inundated with telegrams from members of the Legion welcoming her as their new mother, was swept up in the fantasy of the occasion, commenting, 'I thought I was dreaming or reading a beautiful novel ... about me.' Although Franco's mother, glowing with pride, attended the ceremony, Franco's father did not. Whether Franco was reluctant to expose his family's eccentric living arrangements to the prurient gaze of Oviedo society, or whether Don Nicolás himself refused to attend, his absence highlighted the rift between the two men. Franco must have derived some solace when a journal in Madrid headed its commentary with an epoch-making headline, 'The Wedding of an heroic Caudillo'. This was the first time the title 'warrior-King' was bestowed upon the young Colonel. It would not be the last.

Despite the hopeful speculations of the local press that 'Those polite and gallant phrases whispered by the noble soldier in the ear of his beautiful beloved have had the divine epilogue of their consecration', Carmen's romantic notions cannot have lasted long. Although their marriage was more enduring than that of Franco's parents, it was devoid of any sign of passion or great love from the very start. Once his role as the gallant and knightly supplicant for her favours was removed, Franco was exposed as a cold and physically inhibited man. More at ease with wooing women than winning their favours, he clearly preferred the battlefield to the marital bed. The union became increasingly formal over the years, with Pacón commenting that Franco always became particularly morose and inhibited in his wife's company. Photographs of the couple seem to vindicate this opinion.

After their honeymoon the newlyweds travelled to Madrid to 'Kiss the hand' of the King, before moving to Ceuta to set up home. Although the Queen recalled Franco as a 'silent and timid young officer', he would later claim that during dinner with the King and a very merry Primo de Rivera, he had boldly outlined his treasured plans for safeguarding and reinforcing Spain's position in Morocco. Whether or not he mustered up the courage to do so, it was clearly a subject close to his heart. One of the many articles he contributed to a military journal was significantly entitled 'Passivity and Inaction', and in it he railed against 'the parody of the Protectorate', blaming rebellion among the indigenous tribes on Spanish weakness.

By the time Franco returned to Ceuta in 1924, an increasingly ebullient

Abd el Krim was calling himself the 'Emir of Riff', refusing to recognise the authority of the Sultan and seeking recognition for an independent Moroccan state by the League of Nations. Apart from a small area around Melilla, the Spanish were now confined to the towns of Ceuta, Tetuan, Larache and Xauen. Rumours that Primo de Rivera was considering a total Spanish withdrawal from Morocco generated desertions of Moroccan troops who did not wish to be left to face the vengeful tribesmen on their own. Many Legionnaires robustly stated that they would stay at their posts whatever happened. Franco was more ambivalent. Reluctant to rock the boat by engaging in insubordinate discussions with his comrades, he none-theless delivered a passionate speech against *abandonismo* when the Dic-tator himself decided to visit the Spanish base in 1924. Primo's gloomy assessment of the cost of maintaining or reinforcing the colony did not go down well with the officers. While discontent simmered on the edge of open rebellion, Franco, appalled by his own audacious challenge of the Dictator's authority, hastened after Primo as soon as the meeting was over to apologise and offer his resignation, which was, to his relief, airily brushed aside.

Military discontent largely fizzled out when, in October 1924, Primo changed his mind about abandoning Morocco, named himself High Com-missioner of Morocco in October, and courageously took responsibility for the evacuation of Xauen. In what would become a life-long pattern of behaviour, Franco now adopted two incompatible stances and oscillated between the two. Having loudly boasted that he would resign rather than accept the withdrawal of Spanish troops, he humbly acceded to Primo's directive that he command the Legionnaires covering the tortuous evacu-ation of the exhausted and dispirited civilian population of Xauen after a further offensive by Abd el Krim. Despite Franco's profound reluctance to relinquish an inch of territory to the enemy – a preoccupation that was much in evidence during the civil war – he covered the four-week evacu-ation with considerable bravery and skill. He was rewarded for his valour when he was awarded yet another Military Medal, promoted to full colonel on February 1925 with effect from twelve months earlier, and allowed to keep command of the Legion despite his seniority. In March 1925, Primo presented a delighted Franco with a glowing testimonial from the King, asserting that 'The beautiful history that you are writing with your lives and your blood is a constant example of what can be done by men who reckon everything in terms of the fulfilment of their duty.'[37]

In June 1925 an agreement between Primo de Rivera and the French commander in Africa, Philippe Pétain, resulted in a combined military operation, which involved landing 75,000 Spanish soldiers at Alhucemas under the overall command of General Sanjurjo. Colonel Franco was placed in command of the first party of troops to go ashore and establish a bridgehead. Poor organisation and inferior strategic planning by Sanjurjo resulted in a chaotic operation, which culminated in the Spanish troops being directed to withdraw. Franco, however, anxious that a retreat would demoralise his men, swiftly countermanded the order and managed, against all the odds, to get ashore and establish the bridgehead. Without his initiative it would have been impossible for the Spaniards to link up with the French moving up from the south. Although Franco nervously sought to justify his behaviour both to himself and his superior officers by citing military regulations that allowed officers some flexibility under fire, by ignoring orders he had displayed the sort of military imagination that would elude him as supreme commander during the civil war. Thanks, in some measure, to Franco's efforts, on 26 May 1926 Abd el Krim gave himself up to the French authorities.

Meanwhile, on 3 February 1926, at the age of thirty-four, Franco had been promoted to brigadier general. One of the most persistent minor myths about Franco is that he was the youngest general in Europe since Napoleon. In fact, in the 1880s, at least three Spanish officers were promoted to general at younger ages, and there were many young brigadier generals in the British army during the First World War.[38] Franco was, however, the first cadet from his time in Toledo to attain such dizzy heights. His seniority forced him to leave Africa and return to Spain, where he joined the most important, and socially prestigious, brigade in the army: the First Brigade of the First Division in Madrid. His father did not offer his congratulations on his promotion. His attitude to his son's achievements can be gleaned from a story related by his grandson, Nicolás Franco de Pobil. Apparently, during the course of a family meal that took place after Franco had become a general, 'as a result of a disagreement between them [Don Nicolás] beat the shit out of him, breaking a baton [or walking stick] on his back'. It was no wonder that Franco was so desperate for glory, celebrity and public acknowledgement.

He was not the only one. On 3 February 1926, the day of his promotion to brigadier general, his flamboyant younger brother Ramón crossed the South Atlantic in a Dornier DoJ Wal flying boat, built under licence in Spain. Relations between the two brothers had always been strained. The incautious Ramón, so different from his restrained and socially conscious older brother, had shadowed him throughout his military career. As a pilot in Africa, he had always proved to be, like Francisco, brave if 'precipitous'. He was, however, 'much wilder, more bohemian'. His flat-mate in Tetuan complained bitterly that the irrepressible Ramón used to steal his underpants ('I used to say to him "I don't mind you pinching my socks, but underpants makes me sick" ').[39] Ramón's disregard for personal hygiene and his propensity for enthusiastic whoring contrasted sharply with Franco's rigorous views on life. Franco was appalled when, in 1924, Ramón violated protocol by failing to ask the King's permission to get married to Carmen Díaz ('who was, well, "a woman from the life" ').[40] Nevertheless, Ramón's triumphant exploits as a latter-day Christopher Columbus, which boosted the fledgling Spanish aeronautical industry and brought prestige upon the King and nation, not to mention the Franco family, forced Francisco to suppress his disapproval and jealousy of his brother. Instead he adopted the patronising attitude of a proud father – a role that did not bring out the best in Ramón.

The brothers' rivalry was not helped when a plaque outlining their 'heroic deeds which constitute glorious pages of the nation's history' was unveiled on the family house in El Ferrol. How their father viewed the exhibitionist success of his less favoured son can only be guessed at, although Salóm indicates that he was extremely proud of Ramón. In El Ferrol, where firework displays, the continuous hooting of ships' horns in the bay and playing of bands ashore alerted the populace to the heady achievements of the Franco boys, Doña Pilar Bahamonde – despite gloomy contemporary photographic evidence to the contrary – must have been delighted. On 12 February 1926 a holiday was proclaimed in El Ferrol in honour of Francisco and Ramón.

Later that month, those cadets who had been at Toledo with Franco met to pay their tributes to the first of their intake to become a general. Their impetuous and reverential outpourings were enough to turn anybody's head, particularly one as inclined to self-congratulation as Franco. He was given a dress sword and a parchment claiming 'the glorious names of the important *caudillos* will be raised on high, and above them all will be lifted triumphantly that of General Francisco Franco Bahamonde'. Like obsequious courtiers competing for favour, the previously scornful cadets fell over themselves to display their 'admiration and affection to him in recognition of his patriotism, his intelligence and his bravery'.

The birth of Franco's daughter – and unusually for the fecund Franco family, only child – on 14 September 1926 in Oviedo brought a rare note of joyous reality into Franco's life. He would later recall that 'when Carmen was born, I thought that I would go mad with joy'. In the absence of any evidence that Doña Carmen was ever pregnant, it has been strongly suggested that the baby was the adopted product of one of the rapacious Ramón's sexual exploits.[41] Whatever her parentage, Carmen's birth unlocked an emotional door in the inhibited General, who spent more time with his 'extremely hairy' daughter than his wife ever did, leaning over the cradle endlessly singing her songs.[42] Perhaps he had finally found somebody else whom he could love, and who loved him without questions. Franco's rather beautiful Modigliani-like portrait of his daughter would, years later, stand out from the array of lifeless paintings he usually favoured, most of which were of dead animals.

Back in Madrid with his new regiment, the faithful Pacón at his side as his adjutant, Franco adopted the sort of schizophrenic managerial style that would bedevil his regime when he came to power. While harsh disciplinary measures were still very much the norm with the soldiers, he was happy to leave his colonels to run things pretty much as they liked. Away from the battlefield, his enthusiasm for hard work waned rapidly. Like Hitler and Stalin, he was more inclined to indulge his enthusiasm for cinema than monitor the day-to-day affairs of the regiment. He loved chatting with his military associates, and met up with other generals from the Madrid garrison in a select gentleman's club every day. He was, however, most at ease with like-minded Africanista colleagues like Generals Millán Astray, Varela, Orgaz and Mola, all of whom would play an important role during the civil war, and important associates from Toledo like Yagüe, Monasterio and Vincente Rojo (who would, to Franco's fury, later lead the Republican army against him in Madrid). During these encounters, Pacón records that Franco always spoke about military subjects, never commenting on the politicians of the day, and notes that 'He never, ever criticised his superior officers, not even when speaking about the disaster at Annual.'[43] Whenever Franco recounted anecdotes of his long stay in Morocco, like a child's bedtime story, 'he would always do it in exactly the same words as if he were reading it'.

In 1926 Franco had a revealing encounter with the artist Luis Quintanilla, a friend of Colonel Alfredo Kindelán, founder and head of the Spanish air force. Long after Franco had become Caudillo, the artist would recall a dispute between Franco and Kindelán about a French phrase. When this was resolved in favour of the latter, Franco continued to argue his interpretation in a restrained, boring and insistent manner until the exasperated artist sarcastically conceded that, given that Franco knew more than anybody else on the subject, he must be right. Failing to recognise the irony, Franco finally seemed satisfied.

That Franco was capable of shedding the rigid, tedious elements of his personality only when he was play-acting was revealed when he appeared fleetingly alongside Millán Astray in a film entitled La Malcasada, made by his friend Natalio Rivas during this time. Franco played an army officer recently returned from the African wars. The effervescent, jovial, sociable young general in the film, swigging wine and laughing uproariously at his comrades' jokes, has little in common with the profoundly pompous Franco described by Pacón and Luis Quintanilla. It is not surprising that, when in a position to do so, Franco would seize upon celluloid to project an idealised image of himself.

The reality of the military situation in Africa was somewhat different from Rivas's film. Although the success at Alhucemas had greatly improved relations between Primo's government and the Africanistas, not everybody in the military was content. The operation had resulted in a massive increase in the size and cost of the African army, and Primo's decision to reimpose the principle of promotion on merit did not go down well with the army in mainland Spain, where opportunities for this were few and far between. Primo's partisan approach provoked a lacklustre coup on 24 June 1926 and near-mutiny in artillery barracks all over the mainland. It is ironic that General Franco, so pivotal during the 1936 uprising, was enraged by the artillerymen's rebellion. According to Ramón Serrano Suñer, a brilliant young lawyer who would marry Carmen's beautiful younger sister Zita, and who would play a central role in the consolidation of Franco's political power, he was 'more than passionate, he was voracious, everything that was suggested seemed to him weak and any repression insufficient'. He claimed that the phrase Franco employed most often was 'They have to be shot!'[44]

Although Primo appeared to contain the situation, the crevice within the military lurched sickeningly towards an unbridgeable rift. Some members of the officer corps moved towards the Republican movement, while others – predominantly the Africanistas – remained loyal to the Dictatorship. The failure of the Republican officers to rally to either Primo or the King's defence would contribute to the coming of the Second Republic in April 1931. The refusal of the Africanistas to accept the Republic paved the way to civil war in 1936.

In public at least, Franco kept a characteristically low profile in the midst of these shifting fidelities, and was rewarded when Primo appointed him to the prestigious role of director of the General Military Academy in Saragossa. Established by Primo in 1928, it drew together the academies of the infantry in Toledo, the artillery in Segovia, the cavalry in Valladolid and the engineers in Guadalajara. Having attained a position of considerable professional responsibility, Franco seemed keen to devolve this to others as fast as possible. His propensity to turn a blind eye to the shortcomings of his officers would become a central device when, as Head of State, he presided over a regime which echoed that of the Third Reich: absolute power without moral or personal responsibility. His lackadaisical leniency did not extend to the young cadets, the first intake of whom arrived in October 1928. Franco's enthusiasm for dead, heroic fathers led him to insist that rules for the entrance examinations be relaxed for the orphans of officers who had died in battle. He rather spoilt the effect by notifying the candidates in question that their successful entry to the Academy owed more to the death of their father for Spain than to their own merits.[45]

General Franco's romantic belief in the efficacy of bravery rather than superior numbers or advanced technology meant that modern warfare techniques were as irrelevant in Saragossa as they had been in Toledo. His 'ten commandments', extrapolated from Millán Astray's notions of patriotism, loyalty to the King, military discipline, sacrifice and bravery, were drummed into the impressionable young cadets. The denigration of democratic politics was an integral part of the training. Cadets were also inculcated with notions that Franco learned at his mother's knee, such as 'he who suffers overcomes', and injunctions to 'Volunteer for every sacrifice at times of greatest risk and difficulty'. They were directed to display a 'jealous concern for [their] reputation'.[46] Keen to catch the young cadets out, the Director would lurk in shop doorways hoping that they would pass him unnoticed and therefore fail to salute him. He would then leap out, summon them back 'in that dreaded, soft, high voice' and berate them for their insubordination. The moralistic General seemed to derive a vicarious thrill out of monitoring the sex life of his young charges. Keen to eradicate syphilis among his troops, he terrorised the cadets with sporadic spot checks in the town to ensure that they carried a condom at all times and were always correctly attired. Failure to produce 'this armour' resulted in heavy penalties.[47]

A daily diet of romantic mythology, bullying discipline and ideological indoctrination would ensure that most of the officer cadets would join the Nationalists in 1936. Instructors were selected on the basis of their military prowess in Africa and an ability to mirror Franco and the Africanistas' rigid ideological views rather than their mastery of advanced technological or logistical skill. Almost all of them would play a crucial role in the military uprising of 1936. Many of them would join the fascist party, the Falange Española, which would be established by the Dictator's son, José Antonio Primo de Rivera, on 29 October 1933. Not surprisingly, Franco's time as director of the Academy was hailed as a triumph by the Africanistas and a total disaster by liberal and left-wing officers. His brother Ramón scornfully denounced it as 'troglodytic' and guaranteed to produce bad citizens.[48]

While Franco achieved in Saragossa the social acceptability he had been so desperate for in El Ferrol, he was ill at ease with the important civilian local families and dignitaries who now courted him. However, he did forge some historically important associations during this time. At the wedding of Ramón Serrano Suñer to Franco's sister-in-law, Zita, José Antonio Primo de Rivera acted as the groom's witness.

Years later, when seeking to impose a coherent rationale upon his career, Franco would pinpoint this as the moment he realised that as a 'result of my age and my prestige' I had been 'called to render the highest services to the nation'.[49] However, the path from establishment figure to rebel would prove to be long and convoluted. His volatile sense of self was revealed in May 1929 in an interview that he and Carmen gave to *Estampa*, a precursor of *Hello* magazine. Although his insistence that he was simply 'a soldier ... who wishes to pass unnoticed' seems laughably insincere, the interview exposes an underlying dilemma that would dog his entire political and military career. Torn between the desire for a 'father-figure' – be it his commanding officer, Dictator or King – to smile on his success, and a ruthless determination to seize all power for himself, his aspirations were never consistent. While Franco's statement that he hoped 'Spain should become as great again as she once was' and his priggish protestations that he was satisfied 'to have served my fatherland to the full' were the usual fare for an officer at that time, his statement that he had entered the Infantry Academy in Toledo 'against the will of my father' hints at a hidden agenda. (It was, in fact, Don Nicolás's idea that he attend the Academy.) Perhaps, by publicly challenging his father in 1929, in some way he had opened the way to rebelling against the legal government in 1936. His strange comment that 'All this is only with regard to my profession because my real inclination has always been towards painting' suggests that he was hiding his political ambitions from himself. He was not the only one. Doña Carmen, 'the beautiful companion of the general, hiding the supreme delicacy of her figure behind a subtle dress of black,' delivered a blushing account of their romantic courtship (both lied about their ages when they first met: Doña Carmen adding a year and Franco subtracting one), then coyly conceded that her husband's only defects – his greatest merits as far as his adoring public were concerned – were that 'he likes Africa too much and he studies books which I don't understand'. Like Franco's mother, Carmen's self-abnegating façade shrouded a steely determination and considerable ambition.

During this time Franco's ego and ambitions continued to expand alongside his girth. Shedding his skin as the lively, attractive and imaginative – if ruthless – soldier, he was beginning to metamorphose into the cautious, hesitant and unimaginative military commander of the civil war. He would never again lead units of assault troops in the field. Having forged a secure position for himself within the military hierarchy, he should have felt more secure. He did not. While the war in Africa had provided him with a plausible explanation for his feeling of being under attack, and an outlet for his aggression, his current existence did not. He needed a new external enemy to hate, revile and subdue. As a replacement for the Moroccan tribesmen, Franco latched on to the threat of the communist masses to justify his paranoid fears and espousal of increasingly authoritarian politics.

He was not unusual in this respect at that time. In her analysis of Spanish fascism, the cultural historian Jo Labanyi argues that from the end of the nineteenth century 'the male fear of woman and the bourgeois fear of the masses became indistinguishable'.[50] Certainly Hitler would repeatedly talk about the masses as if they were women, fickle and untrustworthy.[51] Whatever Franco's motivations, it seems clear that while his paranoid view on communism were hardly unique, they reveal more about his inner fears than about the real world. His subscription to the virulently anti-communist bulletin produced by the Geneva-based Entente Internationale Contre la Troisième Internationale fed his fears and hatred. This was further fanned when a bright-eyed Franco visited the German army's General Infantry Academy in Dresden. He returned to Spain filled with enthusiasm for German military efficiency and a burning sense of injustice at the insult of Versailles. This was the beginning of an infatuation with Germany that would not peter out until 1945.

The Primo Dictatorship fell on 30 January 1930. During his time in power, Primo had succeeded in alienating every section of society. Massive deficits, a poor harvest and the beginning of the Depression had taken their toll on the Spanish economy. The army was now bitterly divided. Alfonso XIII, who had alienated the old monarchist elite by throwing in his lot with Primo in 1923, now infuriated General Sanjurjo, Director-General of the Civil Guard, by withdrawing his confidence from Primo, who quietly withdrew to Paris where he died on 16 March 1930. Unable to return to the constitutional monarchy of 1923, which he so recklessly abandoned in favour of Primo, the King selected General Berenguer as the new Dictator. The short-lived dictatorship was confronted by hostile Catalan industrialists, a fatally split army and an increasingly radicalised working class.

Although in May 1946 Franco would romantically recall the Dictatorship as 'a unique parenthesis of peace, order and progress', he was, at the time, remarkably sanguine about Primo's fall from power. Perhaps he felt a subliminal satisfaction at the displacement of an authority figure, or wished to distance himself from the failures of the dictatorship. Either way, the King's selection of him as his personal favourite helped reconcile him to Primo's departure. On 4 June 1929, Alfonso XIII had personally bestowed upon Franco the Medalla Militar he had won in 1925. A year later, on 8 June

1930, General Franco headed a huge parade, including the entire body of cadets he had brought to the capital from Saragossa, to celebrate the swearing of the flag by the Madrid garrison. On 6 June he appeared on the balcony at the Royal Palace alongside Alfonso XIII.

Ramón, clearly exasperated by his brother's triumphalist behaviour and preferential association with the King, decided to compete for some attention of his own. During the summer of 1929, he had undertaken another flight across the North Atlantic. The trip was a disaster. Not only did it end in a massive and costly search for the pilot and his crew, but it transpired that Ramón had substituted the flying boat built in Spain for a German aircraft, possibly as the result of a bribe. The indignant head of Military Aviation, Colonel Alfredo Kindelán, immediately ejected him from the air force. His exploits not only undermined the credibility of Spanish aeronautics, and constituted an insult to both King and *Patria*, but also brought discredit on the family name. Franco's pained and moralistic determination to treat Ramón like a prodigal son, which echoed his mother's martyred attitude to his father's indiscretions, exasperated his younger brother to screaming point. His plaintive plea to Ramón to consider the 'great sorrow that such things cause Mama, a sorrow which the rest of us share' earned him a withering enjoinder to stop his 'vain bourgeois counsels', step down from his 'little general's throne' and cease inculcating poor values in the cadets at Saragossa. Ramón then veered rapidly to the left, got heavily involved in anarcho-syndicalist conspiracies aimed at bringing down the monarchy and, in the most provocative move of all, became a Freemason. Although Ramón's motivations seemed to derive more from frustration with Franco and a vengeful attitude to authority than sage political analysis, unlike Franco he was acutely aware of the very tenuous position of both General Berenguer's dictatorship and the King.

In mid-August 1930 a broad front of socialists, middle-class Republicans, Basque and Catalan regionalists and a number of influential monarchists who, alienated by Alfonso's XIII's mistakes, had become conservative republicans, united in a pact signed in San Sebastian. They established a provisional government-in-waiting to plot the downfall of the King. General Mola, as Director-General of Security, notified Franco that Ramón was closely involved in these developments, and directed that he ask him to desist. Franco's attempts to do so were not a success and the authorities were obliged to detain Ramón in a military prison. Franco visited him once more to alert him to the bewildering array of charges being brought against him, including gun-smuggling, attempting to organise the making of bombs, and the attempted murder of a monarchist. His blandishment were to no avail. Escaping from prison, Ramón became involved, alongside

Queipo de Llano, in a revolutionary plan for a combined general strike and military coup to bring down the monarchy and establish a Republic under the auspices of the provisional San Sebastian government. He then fled to Paris.

In November 1930, when Franco went to Versailles in France to attend a course for generals preparing for high command, he visited Ramón. Ignoring his brother's gloomy political predictions about the imminent collapse of the Dictatorship and the monarchy, Franco returned to Saragossa absolutely convinced – in the words of Pacón – that the Spanish people 'would not take this leap in the dark that would cost them rivers of blood.'[52] Franco, whom Queipo claimed had asked him to spearhead a coup in September 1924 – was himself approached by Alejandro Lerroux – the cynical leader of the Radical Party and the most prominent figure of the San Sebastian Pact – who invited him to join the Republican conspiracy. According to Serrano Suñer, he responded in a characteristically irresolute fashion, when invited to join them, he listened politely and hinted that he *might* do so if the *Patria* was in danger. 'Disgusted with himself for not throwing (the intermediaries) off the balcony' he soon reverted to wanting them shot again.[53] His ambivalence was resolved on 12 December when a Republican conspirator, Santiago Casares Quiroga, initiated a premature rebellion in the garrison of Jaca in northern Aragon, after which he intended to march south and spark off a pro-Republican movement in the garrisons of Huesca, Saragossa and Lerida. In fact, this precipitate action succeeded only in alerting the authorities to the plans and provoked the declaration of martial law in the entire Aragonese military region. When a sporadic general strike broke out in Saragossa, Franco nailed his colours to the King's mast by putting the Academy in a state of military readiness and arming the cadets.

The Jaca revolt was easily suppressed and the two alleged ringleaders, Captains Fermín Galán (who, as Franco's adjutant in the Legion had speculated about his homosexuality) and Angel García Herández, were shot on 14 December. Franco's conviction that 'my brother Ramón has to be shot'[54] notwithstanding, he and other senior officers were satisfied with this brisk and brutal response to the rebellion. However, the two officers were hailed as martyrs in the country. The public outcry damaged the monarchy in a way that the revolt had failed to do. On 15 December, the fugitive Ramón (who would dedicate his autobiography to 'the martyrs Galán and García Hernández), having apparently lost all sense of proportion, decided to fly over the royal Palacio de Oriente in Madrid with the intention of bombing it and, presumably, killing the king. Allegedly concerned by the sight of women and children strolling through the gardens, Ramón dropped leaflets calling for a general strike instead, after which he fled to France once more. His own leaflets were swiftly followed by others of unknown origin, denouncing Ramón as a 'bastard apparently drunk on your blood'. Franco, evidently more outraged at the implied slur on his mother than at Ramón's attempts to kill the King, rushed to Madrid to demand an official explanation from the primary suspects for this insult – General Berenguer (Head of Government), General Mola and General Federico Berenguer, the Captain-General of Madrid – all of whom nervously denied any involvement in this public defamation of the Franco family's name. Filled with aggrieved feelings of family solidarity, Franco immediately dispatched Ramón a large amount of money to Paris, and professed the hope that, severed from the 'hatred and passion of the people who surround you', he would see the light and 'rebuild your life far from these sterile struggles which fill Spain with misfortune'.

Franco was horrified when public outrage at the execution of Galán and García Hernández provoked the more liberal element in the government to withdraw their support, forcing General Berenguer to resign on 14 February. He was replaced by Admiral Juan Bautista Aznar. Municipal elections were scheduled for April 1931. The court-martial proceedings against officers involved in the uprising took place during an electoral campaign that was dominated by the furore following the executions of the two men. As a prominent member of the tribunal, an implacable Franco insisted that 'it is necessary that military crimes committed by soldiers be judged by soldiers who are accustomed to command'. Refusing to be swayed by public opinion, the court imposed a further death sentence, five life sentences and many other lesser sentences on the rebels, all of which were later commuted.

Up on his high military horse, Franco had seriously miscalculated the political situation. The municipal elections of 12 April 1931 went against the King and the Dictatorship. In order to avoid massive bloodshed, General Sanjurjo, Director-General of the Civil Guard, ordered them not to support the floundering monarchy. When General Berenguer also directed the captains-general to avoid acts of violence that might impede 'the logical course that the supreme national will imposes on the destinies of the fatherland', Alfonso XIII's fate was sealed. The King quietly withdrew from Spain, leaving it open to the establishment of the Second Republic. In a pivotal statement to his prime minister, Admiral Aznar – published in the newspaper *ABC* – he conceded that 'the elections celebrated on Sunday show me clearly that today I do not have the love of my people.' However, he made it clear that he had not abdicated, and hoped one day to return. Conceding that 'I made mistakes from time to time', he insisted that 'I am King of all Spaniards, and also a Spaniard. I will find ample means of maintaining my royal prerogatives and of resisting those who combat them. Nevertheless I am decided that I must distance myself from any course which might force compatriots to fight each other in a fratricidal war. I do not renounce my rights ... [but] until the nation speaks, I deliberately suspend the exercise of royal power and I leave Spain.'[55]

The King's flight came as a terrible shock for General Franco, who at some level seems to have equated it with his father's abandonment of the family when he was a child. It seriously tarnished his attitude to the monarchy thereafter. Once in power, he would do everything possible to prevent the return of a king to the Spanish throne. The coronation of Alfonso XIII's grandson, Juan Carlos, did not take place until 1975.

CHAPTER 3

Will You Won't You
Join the Dance?

The Road to Rebellion, 1931–6

General Franco is a crafty so-and-so who always looks out for himself
General Sanjurjo, 1933

Although the municipal elections of 12 April 1931 were a disaster for the monarchists, in the countryside the landed bosses or *caciques* remained unchallenged. Power was assumed by the Provisional Government, whose membership had been agreed in August in the Pact of Sebastian. Led by Niceto Alcalá Zamora, a conservative Catholic landowner who had once been a minister under the King, it was dominated by Socialists and centre and left Republicans committed to a sweeping programme of reform.

A bemused Franco monitored the situation from Saragossa. He bitterly blamed Benguerer, Sanjurjo and the Civil Guard for failing to defend the monarchy from 'historic republicans, Freemasons, separatists and social-ists'.[1] Nevertheless, he accepted orders to fly the Republican flag at the Academy, and reluctantly directed his cadets to maintain 'discipline and total obedience to orders [and to] sacrifice [their] thoughts and ideology for the good of the nation and the tranquillity of the Patria'. The reasonable view of Franco – and many other army officers – that the defence of the monarchy by the army in December 1930 was wholly legitimate clashed with the central premise of the new Republic, that the regime from 1923 to 1930 was unconstitutional and support for it was illegal. Franco was understandably resentful that officers who had treacherously plotted against the Dictator, including Generals Gonzalo Queipo de Llano, Eduardo López Ochoa and Miguel Cabanellas, were rewarded with pres-tigious posts, while courageous and competent officers who had simply been following orders were unjustly victimised. Unlike many others, however, Franco was not prepared to jeopardise his career, his social status – everything he had fought for since the Toledo Academy – with ill-conceived gestures of defiance.

However, neither his innate pragmatism nor his fluid personal style could disguise the personal animosity that now flared between him and Manuel Azaña, the brilliant new Minister of War. Although these solitary figures were on opposite sides of the social and political spectrum, they shared a profound reluctance to compromise and a tendency to be arrogant and insensitive. Azaña, however, looked to a hopeful future for the Spanish people, while Franco delved into a fantasised past. Azaña was motivated by a lofty if unrealistic desire to bring about a 'beautiful Republican utopia',[2] while Franco – for whom such notions were anathema – assumed that Azaña was driven by personal malice against him.

Azaña's determination to eradicate the problems of militarism in Spain, which he considered to be a 'noisy and disorderly obstacle to national politics',[3] would challenge everything that Franco and most of the Africanistas held dear. Most damaging of all, when Azaña became Prime Minister on 14 October 1931, and then President of the Republic in 1936, Franco would look to him as 'father of the Republic'[4] to give him the acknowledgement and respect he craved and felt he deserved. However, Azaña – who was as closely identified with the Republic as Franco was with the Patria – did no such thing. Neither sufficiently flexible nor calculating enough to exploit the General's hunger for flattery, his powerful sense of duty or his deeply rooted reluctance to challenge authority, he succeeded in creating an implacable personal enemy out of a potentially loyal officer. Franco was treated like a recalcitrant child. His military achievements would be snatched away and his loyalty discounted, while his irresponsible brother Ramón – who received a hero's welcome when he returned from exile in 1931, and was given the post of Director General de Aeronaútica by the new government – seemed to become the favoured son. Azaña, with his eyes on an idealistic horizon, unconcerned by petty rivalries or military sensibilities, would make a lot more enemies along the way. The cumulative impact of Azaña's military reforms would, in due course, result in the resignation of between half and two-thirds of members of the officer corps.

To begin with, however, Franco's indignation with the Republic was offset by a desire to carve out a role for himself within it. Ready as he was to relinquish conviction for a career, Franco's personal hostility to the regime was initially aroused when he was not, as had been widely rumoured, appointed as High Commissioner in Morocco. To his disgust, the post went to General Sanjurjo, whom Franco assumed was being rewarded for his refusal to use the Civil Guard to save the monarchy. Although a self-righteous Franco claimed in a letter to the right-wing paper *ABC* that he would not have accepted such a post if offered, since it would have constituted a betrayal of the monarchy, he was clearly deeply miffed. He would have loved the posting under any regime.

Personal resentment was transformed into high-minded political grievance when, on 17 April, Azaña had General Dámaso Berenguer and Emilio Mola arrested and put on trial for alleged offences in Africa, and their role in the trial and execution of Galán and García Hernández. This move – an integral part of the divisive 'Responsibilities' debate, which was seeking to establish whether royal interference, military incompetence or weak government had been responsible for the Annual disaster – appalled many members of the military. However, while Azaña's stipulation, on 22 April, that army officers must promise 'to serve the Republic well, obey its laws and defend it by arms' posed a genuine dilemma for some committed monarchists, Franco's pragmatism prevailed. While General Kindelán, a passionate supporter of the monarchy, went into exile rather than live under the Republic, Franco and many of his right-wing comrades – including Luis Orgaz, Manuel Goded, Joaquín Fanjul and Mola – accepted the directive. For many, it was an agonising decision. Fanjul would later describe the pain involved in offering up his 'humiliation to my *Patria*'. Franco, on the other hand, striving for the moral high ground, justified his decision to take the oath of loyalty to the Republic on the sanctimonious grounds that 'although those of us who have stayed on will have a bad time ... I believe that by staying we can do much more to avoid what neither you nor I want to happen than if we had just packed up and gone home'.[5]

A mere three days later, right-wing sensibilities were pummelled further when Azaña introduced a new law aimed at reducing the inflated officer corps. Known as the *Ley Azaña*, it offered retirement on full pay to those officers considered surplus to requirements. It stipulated that those who failed to take up the offer within thirty days would lose their commissions without any compensation. This attempt to stream-line the army provoked a virulent right-wing press to accuse the government of forcing noble officers into penniless unemployment or exile, simply because they did not support the Republic.

Clearly outraged at the way things were going, Franco visited Berenguer in his cell in Madrid on 1 May. Although he blamed Berenguer for not supporting the monarchy and, more importantly, for failing to promote him to major-general as promised in 1930, he agreed to act as defender in his court martial. Franco was profoundly offended when Azaña over-ruled this magnanimous offer on the grounds that he did not serve in the region where the trial was taking place. Professional insult was added to personal injury when Azaña replaced the eight historic military regions with 'organic divisions' under the command of major-generals who had no legal powers over civilians, and reinstated promotion on the basis of seniority alone.

Even Franco's self-serving flexibility was stretched to breaking point when, on 30 June 1931, Azaña decided to close down the Academy in Saragossa. Although the closure was part of Azaña's overall plan of modernisation, Franco was convinced that it was motivated by jealousy of his impressive military record, and a personal spite. Sanjurjo haughtily dismissed Franco's impassioned plea to intercede on his behalf with Azaña, commenting to the minister that he was behaving 'like a child who has had a toy taken away from him'. Franco would never forgive either man.

Nevertheless, he was in a state of emotional flux, full of rage towards the Republic, but desperate to find a place for himself within it. On 14 July, before packing his bags and travelling to his wife's country house in Oviedo, an emotional Franco made an impassioned farewell speech to the cadets in Saragossa. He railed against the difficulty of following orders 'when the heart struggles to rise in inward rebellion against the orders received, when one knows that higher authority is in error and acting out of hand' – a poignant description of his own childhood. His speech was punctuated with vicious asides against the 'pernicious' officers who had betrayed the monarchy and been rewarded with posts in Azaña's ministry. Perhaps the situation evoked a deep-rooted fury with his brothers, who had been favoured by his irresponsible father while he stood staunchly by his mother. Whatever his motivations, Azaña was not amused, noting in his diary that Franco's 'guarded attacks against his superiors' would constitute 'a case for immediate dismissal if it were not the case that today he ceased to hold that command'. On 23 July, Franco was informed that his spotless military record had been sullied with an official reprimand ordering him 'to temper his conduct to the elementary principles of discipline'. Although Franco dispatched his 'regret for the erroneous interpretation given to the ideas contained in the speech' to the Minister of War, and cited his willingness to fly the Republican flag and play the Republican national anthem as evidence of his loyalty to the regime, the rebuke remained in place. This, along with his eight-month banishment into semi-retirement, albeit on 80 per cent of his salary, sparked a sense of injustice that would, by 1936, be fanned into a vengeful inferno.

Franco's personal resentment was further fuelled by an outburst of church burnings perpetrated by anarchists who opposed the Church's close association with the corrupt caciquista system. Although he would later seize upon these fires to validate his belief that the Madre-Patria (his mother) was being systematically violated by the Republic, in the first instance his indignation may well have been fanned by rumours that his younger brother was providing anarchists with aviation spirit. Certainly

Ramón's jubilation at 'the expression of a people which wanted to free itself from clerical obscurantism'[6] did not go down well with his older brother. In *Raza*, Franco's virulent views on the Republic and Ramón are closely linked to these events. In May 1931, Isabel de Andrade – who like Doña Pilar is a devout Catholic – is attacked after remonstrating with a group of church-burning youths while Republican guards stand by and do nothing. When her eldest son, Pedro, finally deigns to visit his dying mother, he is told by the doctor that she is unlikely to survive 'the shocks and shame' being imposed on the *Patria* by the Republican regime. Only 'with peace and tranquillity' will she survive. However, the combination of Pedro's wayward political views and the Republic 'do not constitute the most favourable climate for Isabel's recovery' and as a result 'one autumn evening God granted her the consolation that she had prayed for so often of not seeing her *Patria* destroyed'.[7] Thirty years later Franco would still be raging about the church burnings, claiming that they captured the essence of the hated Republic. Ironically, although he bitterly blamed the Republic for the annihilation of the *Patria*, it was Franco himself who unleashed a frenzied assault upon the motherland in 1936, resulting in her virtual destruction.

Back in Oviedo, Franco's enforced leisure gave him plenty of time to feed his personal animosity towards Azaña and the world at large. Any satisfaction he might have derived from Ramón losing his post in the government because of his involvement in anarchist conspiracies against the Republic were dispelled when Ramón's Masonic colleagues saved him from another prison sentence, and helped secure his election as a parliamentary deputy for Barcelona. That the Freemasons – who rejected Franco's application to join on three separate occasions – should provide security for Ramón while he was turned out into the cold did little to ease his sense of injustice. Franco's hatred of the Freemasons and his brother surged, merging with his mounting fixation with the communists. While an embittered Doña Carmen dripped venom about the Republic into his receptive ears, Franco devoured the manically anti-communist propaganda being churned out in the bulletins of the Entente International, and daily reports in the right-wing press blaming the new regime for escalating violence and anti-clericalism.

That summer, outbreaks of violence and strikes organised by the anarcho-syndicalist CNT in Seville and Barcelona heightened the army's mounting sense of anarchy and crisis. Rumours about an impending coup abounded. Generals Emilio Barrera and Luis Orgaz were put under house arrest as the most likely leaders. Orgaz was then exiled to the Canary Islands. Convinced that Franco was 'the only one to be feared',[8] Azaña ordered that his movements be closely monitored. Animosity between the two men flared at a meeting on 20 August 1931, when a somewhat patronising Azaña warned Franco not to get carried away by his friends and admirers. His tentative suggestion that he would be happy to use Franco's services provoked the irritated General to snap 'and to use my services, they have me followed everywhere by a police car!' An apparently guileless Franco protested his general loyalty to the regime, but naively conceded that its monarchist enemies had been in touch with him. Azaña later described him as trying 'to seem frank but all rather hypocritically'. He did, however, have the surveillance lifted.

Franco's attitude to the Republic was not helped when, on 26 August, the remit of the Responsibilities Commission was widened to include the coup of 1923, the Dictatorship, and the Jaca court martial. Although Azaña had attempted in July 1931 to pacify the army by having Mola released and the warrant against Berenguer annulled, his efforts were sabotaged by the Commission's provocative decision to arrest a number of aged generals who had participated in the Dictatorship. Although ultimately very little action was taken against them, it was a disaster for the regime.

The rancorous debate over the new constitution, which took place between mid-August and the end of the year, sealed the hostility of Franco and many other officers to the Republic. Its attempts to break the overwhelming power of the Church in Spanish society, and particularly its monopoly in education, provoked the resignation of the conservative Prime Minister, Alcalá Zamora, and the Minister of the Interior, Miguel Maura. Azaña was forced to take on the role of Prime Minister on 14 October. Speaking for many on the right, the right-wing Spanish surrealist Giménez Caballero – one of the founding fathers of Spanish fascism – bitterly commented that the Republic 'had destroyed the very substance of our being. The very soul of us as Spaniards and as men ... The Catholic Spain had lost his God. The monarchist, his King. The aristocrat, his nobility. The soldier, his sword.'[9]

When Franco was called up as a witness by the Responsibilities Commission in December 1931, he was careful to shroud his statements with various declarations of respect for parliamentary law. Nevertheless, he made it clear that in his opinion, as a non-military body, the Commission was not entitled to make decisions about the military court martial in Jaca. While Ramón, and others like him, considered Galán and García Hernández to be 'martyrs for freedom',[10] Franco and his army comrades stubbornly insisted that the two men had committed a military offence for which they were justly punished.

Despite his tight-lipped differences with the regime, however, Franco was still a long way from joining open rebellion against the Republic. His personal hostility was in any case moderated in February 1932, when he was rehabilitated as commander of the XV Brigada de Infanteria de Galicia and military governor of Corunna. Pacón accompanied him as his aide-de-camp, a position he would retain for many years to come. The posting constituted a significant olive branch by Azaña, protecting Franco from a decree issued a month later requiring the resignation of any officer who had spent more than six months without a posting. However, if Azaña hoped to earn Franco's gratitude, he was disappointed. While Franco was clearly delighted to be back at the centre of local press adulation, which hailed the 'Caudillo of the Tercio',[11] he was not prepared to give Azaña any credit for the posting. Touchy and unbending, he was incapable of ever forgiving anybody who had offended him.

While Franco settled down in Corunna, the political temperature was rising fast. The right had launched an hysterical campaign against measures to facilitate agrarian reform and the much vilified move towards Catalonian autonomy, which were wending their laborious way through the Cortes. Many on the right, and particularly army officers, had long argued that any loss of 'Spanish' territory – be it the 1898 disaster, military setbacks in Morocco or regional autonomy – constituted not just an assault on the motherland, but, in the words of Gimenez Caballero, 'a castration and loss of potency' for both Spain and those who lived there. They therefore viewed the Republic's determination to grant autonomy to Catalonia as a moral outrage, tantamount to allowing it to become 'divorced from Spain'.[12] It was not, however, only the motherland that was perceived as being under attack from the Republic, but also the sanctity of marriage and manhood itself. The right was horrified when a new Republican divorce law meant that 'it was no longer just men separating from women [their mothers] but women separating from men'.[13] For General Franco the new legislation opened up the traumatic possibility (which was not in fact realised) that his father could now divorce his mother.

In fact, the huge abyss that was opening up was not so much between husband and wife as between the right and the left. The Civil Guard's violent propensity to suppress discontent and unrest among impoverished landless labourers in rural areas greatly consolidated the divide. On 31 December 1931 a peaceful demonstration and strike among the poverty-stricken landworkers in a small village called Castilbanco in Extremadura provoked a characteristically ruthless response. The Civil Guard shot into the crowds, killing one man and wounding two others. After decades of suppression, the angry villagers turned upon the four Civil Guards and beat them to death with stones and knives. The right-wing press attacked Azaña and the Socialist government for allegedly encouraging this outrage.

Sanjurjo, as Director-General of the Civil Guard, visited Castilblanco where, perpetuating the view that the working classes were somehow anti-*Patria*, he compared the killings to the atrocities perpetrated against Spanish soldiers by Moorish tribesmen, and blamed Margarita Nelken, an extreme left Socialist deputy for Badajoz, for the incident. Within the week, the Civil Guard exacted their revenge. A number of incidents in the south culminated in eight deaths and the wounding of many more. On 5 January 1932 they fired on a peaceful protest meeting in the village of Arnedo in northern Castille, killing four women, a child and a worker, and wounding thirty bystanders. Although rightly concerned that it would provoke a right-wing backlash, Azaña was persuaded to replace Sanjurjo with General Miguel Cabanellas. (Although many right-wing officers wrote to complain about his dismissal, Franco did not.) The right immediately adopted Sanjurjo as its hero. Alejandro Lerroux, founder of the Radical Party and a 'vulgarian with his hands permanently in the till',[14] who may well have persuaded Sanjurjo not to defend the King in 1931, now encouraged him to remove Azaña's Left Republican–Socialist coalition from power. Sanjurjo, who commented that General Franco 'is hardly a Napoleon, but given what the others are like . . .',[15] was aware that his support for a military uprising would be helpful.

Franco, however, was enjoying an easy-going lifestyle as military governor of Corunna. His busy social round and passion for sailing left little time for his laid-back regime of work, let alone military rebellion. He could visit his mother at weekends, presumably renewed his association with 'Aunt Gilda' and indulged his passion for fishing. It was during this time that he made his one and only civilian friend, Max Borrell, a businessman who had been kidnapped and brutally castrated while in South America. He became Franco's constant companion on his hunting and fishing trips after the war, and remained close to him until his final illness. It seems significant that Franco, who since leaving war-torn Morocco had been forced to sublimate his sexual needs and aggressive impulses by killing animals, should choose to do so alongside a man who had been so catastrophically emasculated.

Despite Franco's apparent lack of interest in plans for the impending coup, rebellious officers were very keen to know what position he would adopt. As always, he tried to have it both ways. Having insinuated to Sanjurjo that he would happily participate, he then angrily denied that he had said any such thing. His hesitancy derived from an innate reluctance to challenge authority, personal pique against Sanjurjo and a real concern about the inadequately prepared initiative, which he feared would 'open the doors to Communism'.[16] His lack of resolution was construed as enthusiasm for the coup, and when he visited Madrid to choose a new horse, he discovered that rumours of his participation were rife. Although he tartly told the officers concerned that if they 'continued to spread these calumnies' he would 'take energetic measures',[17] the nervous government directed that he should be followed constantly by the police, who were, according to Pacón, 'driven mad' by the General's inability to end a conversation and go to bed.[18]

On the day of the Sanjurjo uprising on 10 August 1932, Franco, back in Corunna, was due to go on leave. In fact, the Head of the Military Region, General Vera, asked him to delay this and stand in for him during a formal visit to the Admiral of the Spanish Fleet, which was anchored in the port of Corunna. While Sanjurjo supporters rose against the government, Franco was receiving full naval honours and a fifteen-gun salute aboard the Navy's flagship. When, in the wake of the coup, a frantic Azaña contacted General Vera to establish Franco's whereabouts, he was enormously 'reassured to hear that he was fulfilling a peaceful task at his post'.[19] Had Franco taken his holiday as planned, Azaña would have been somewhat less sanguine.

The Sanjurjo coup was, as Franco had predicted, a chaotic affair, but a helpful lesson. The right resolved never to rush into a *coup d'état* again without proper preparation or mustering the support of the armed urban police force and the Civil Guard. For many senior officers, Franco's refusal to participate was seen as a crucial factor in its failure. The self-righteous General notified Millán Astray that he would rise up against the Republic only if it tried to dissolve either the army or the Civil Guard, or 'if I could clearly see that the hour of communism had struck'. Furthermore, as he told his cousin Pacón, 'he never expected it to succeed because it did not include an important part of the Moroccan army'.[20] His 'labyrinthine ambiguity' throughout the proceedings had, however, stood him in good stead with both sides of the political spectrum. He secured his credibility with the right by assuring them that, although he did not feel the time was right for a rising, he respected those who did, and mollified the government by remaining at his post. An exasperated Sanjurjo, on the other hand, dismissed 'Little Franco' as 'a crafty so-and-so who always looks out for himself'.[21]

In the wake of the coup's failure, a conspiratorial committee was established to plan a future military rebellion more coherently. The moral legitimacy of a military uprising was vigorously peddled in *Acción Española*, a journal to which Franco had subscribed since its first issue in December 1931. The conspirators collected funds to buy arms, generated political instability and established 'subversive cells' within the army under the auspices of Lieutenant-Colonel Valentín Galarza, who had been closely involved in Sanjurjo's coup. Although Azaña was highly suspicious of the 'very intelligent' and dangerous Galarza, whom he viewed as 'Slimy and obedient but definitely on the other side',[22] the prosecution had nothing against him. There was nothing Azaña could do other than leave him without an active posting. Galarza would use his enforced leisure to secure the support of key generals for a future uprising. His friend Franco, so similar to him in many ways, was seen as a prime recruit.

For the moment, however, Franco was keeping his head down. He refused to join a clandestine monarchist organisation, the Unión Militar Española, which forged close links with Galarza, and coldly refused Sanjurjo's request to represent him at his trial, stating, 'I think in justice that by rebelling and failing, you have earned the right to die.'[23] Clearly it was not so much the rebelling as the failing he could not tolerate. Furthermore, he had not forgiven Sanjurjo for his various transgressions. Azaña was less vengeful. His reluctance to heed the Mexican President's advice 'to avoid widespread bloodshed and make the Republic live, shoot Sanjurjo'[24] would prove fateful. After a brief stint in prison, Sanjurjo escaped to Portugal, where he would become a crucial figure in the 1936 uprising.

Azaña's hopes that Franco's 'loyalty' during the coup would herald a change in their relations were soon dashed. In early 1933 Franco discovered that, because of Azaña's review of promotions, his placing within the army seniority list had been frozen and he had dropped from number one in the list of brigadier generals to twenty-four out of thirty-six. Years later he was still railing about having his rightful promotion 'pillaged' by the Republic. Given his ill-tempered attitude, Azaña decided that it would be a wise precaution to dispatch him to the Balearic Islands as commandante general, which he hoped would both gratify Franco and, or so he hoped, 'free him from any temptations'. Although Franco rashly boasted to his right-wing cronies that he would not accept this highly prestigious post, he could not resist its appeal. He tried to convince himself that he had retained the moral high ground by paying a childishly cool, and insultingly tardy, regulation farewell visit to Azaña on 1 March.

Although, in the wake of the failed coup, the Catalan Autonomy Statute and the Agrarian Reform Bill sailed through the Cortes, this triggered a particularly virulent backlash on the right, which succeeded, throughout 1933, in paralysing Azaña's government with a concerted campaign of obstruction. When, on 11 January, the forces of order massacred twenty-four anarcho-syndicalist villagers in Casas Viejas in the province of Cadiz, the right moved swiftly from delight at this repressive action to the most cynical exploitation of the situation. A smear campaign was launched in the press and in Parliament blaming the government for the atrocity and denouncing its policies as savage and unjust. The incident, which highlighted the Azaña government's failure to resolve the agrarian problem, alienated the Socialists who, convinced that the only chance for implementing reform was to form a government on their own, began to pull away from the Republican–Socialist coalition that had been brought to power in the elections 'of April 1931. As a result, Lerroux, the leader of the Radical Party, was called upon to form an all-Republican cabinet on 12 September 1933. Although Lerroux offered Franco the post of Minister of War, he turned it down, partly because of underlying suspicions of Lerroux's association with Ramón, but mainly because he knew that the cabinet would not last long. He was right. President Alcalá Zamora was forced to call a general election in November 1933.

Splits on the left and the abstention of the anarchists resulted in a victory for the right in the elections. Although the powerful Catholic authoritarian party, the Confederación Española de Derechas Autónomas (CEDA) – for whom Franco had voted – was the largest party in the Cortes, President Alcalá Zamora did not trust its leader José Maria Gil Robles, and so appointed the voracious Lerroux to lead the government. Dependent upon the votes of the CEDA, the increasingly corrupt Radicals, prepared to do anything to keep themselves in power, implemented the harsh social policies demanded by the CEDA's wealthy backers. The political situation polarised rapidly. While the government slashed wages, sacked union members, evicted tenants and raised rents, the Socialist leadership resorted to increasingly inflammatory revolutionary rhetoric in the misguided hope that this would alarm the right into moderating its actions and pressurise the President into calling new elections. In fact it simply provoked ever more repressive measures by the government, and convinced the army high command that a powerful authoritarian response was the only way to curb socialist anarchy.

Franco, however, had other things on his mind. At the end of 1933 he took his family to Madrid so that he could convalesce from the pain he was suffering from his war wound.[25] During this time he decided to seek out his own father. Maybe he was alarmed that his father was planning to divorce Doña Pilar. Perhaps, bereft of a king, dictator or president to marvel at his achievements, he was prepared to give Don Nicolás another chance. Either way, he seems to have impressed his father as little as a general as he had as a child. His sanctimonious please to Don Nicolás to abandon 'this life you are living and return to the family, the past will be forgotten' and his warning that 'If you don't, you will lose a son'[26] did not go down well with his irascible father. Franco swore – wrongly as it transpired – that he would never speak to him again.

In January 1934, a violent anarchist uprising in Aragon further inflamed anxieties on the right. It took the army, complete with tanks, four days to crush it, and resulted in a number of dismissals in the government. Diego Hidalgo took over as Minister of War on 23 January 1934. When Franco visited Madrid to pay his respects, the new minister was much taken with him. Shortly afterwards he promoted him from brigadier to major-general. Franco was forty-two years old. Franco considered this to be the least he could do after the humiliations he had suffered under the Republic. When Hidalgo visited the Balearic Islands, he was further impressed when Franco refused to release a prisoner – as was customary on such occasions – on the grounds that the only one available was an officer who had slapped a soldier. Briefly forgetting his willingness to beat and shoot his own soldiers for minor misdemeanours in Africa, Franco staunchly refused to release him unless ordered to do so, on the grounds that this was the worst crime possible. Awed by Franco's noble reasoning, Hidalgo invited him to be an adviser during forthcoming military manoeuvres on the mainland.

On 28 February 1934, at the age of sixty-six, Franco's mother caught pneumonia and died just as she was about to embark on a pilgrimage to Rome. Although Franco had put a lot of energy into placing an emotional and physical distance between himself and his mother, her death undoubtedly had a huge psychological impact upon him. However, although his distraught cousin Pacón records the sorrow with which he heard of the death of 'this wonderful lady I loved so much',[27] Franco showed no external signs of grief. Moving his family to a large apartment in Madrid, he immersed himself in a social whirl, entertaining important right-wing politicians, aristocrats and prestigious members of Oviedo society as they passed through the capital. Eschewing political and military pursuits, he escaped his distress in the cinema and helped Doña Carmen scour local flea markets for antiques.

Franco met with his father for the last time when the family assembled for the reading of the will. Don Nicolás arrived later, scruffily dressed, and refused to take off his hat throughout the proceedings. Determined to reappropriate the family home in El Ferrol, an aggressive Don Nicolás could hardly bring himself to speak to any of his children. Undaunted by his father's forbidding manner, a conciliatory Franco attempted to introduce him to his distinguished brother-in-law, Serrano Suñer, who was there in his capacity as a lawyer. To Franco's horror and Serrano Suñer's astonishment, Don Nicolás refused to proffer his hand and, barely moving his eyes in Serrano Suñer's direction, spat out 'Lawyer! Lawyer! Mischief-maker more like!'[28] Don Nicolás's defiant decision thereafter to spend his summers in the family home in Calle Maria with Agustina and their adopted 'daughter' provoked the sort of scandalised gossip among the neighbours that would have made his wife turn in her grave. As always, Don Nicolás responded with 'brusque gestures and the first words that came to mind'.[29] In the wake of his wife's death, under the new Republican laws, Franco's father underwent a civil marriage ceremony with Agustina. Franco's views on this arrangement can be gleaned from the fact that it was annulled under a Francoist decree of 1938, which invalidated all marriages carried out in the Republican period. This act of personal vengefulness might well explain the manifest aggression Don Nicolás always displayed towards the Caudillo. He would never see Francisco again.

Despite Franco's outer nonchalance, the loss of his mother and the difficult encounter with his father must have revived powerful childhood feelings in him. His paranoia about communism surged during this time. On 16 May 1934 he wrote to the Secretary of the Entente Internationale contre la Troisième Internationale commending 'the great work which you are carrying out for the defence of all nations against communism'. Although the Republic had paid for Franco's subscription to the organisation's bulletin for three years, reluctant to leave anything to chance he now took out a personal subscription to this virulently anti-communist publication. In the wake of his mother's death, the bulletin fed his conviction that he – and the *Patria* – were under attack from malignant, Marxist forces. These dark and entirely irrational anxieties about the red masses partly explain the vengefulness of his subsequent behaviour in the ruthless suppression first of the supposedly 'bolshevik' miners in Asturias, then of the Republicans during the civil war, and finally of the working classes after victory in the war.

Unfortunately, external reality reinforced Franco's neurotic views on life, with the left viewing everything the right did as evidence of their fascist ambitions, while the right viewed any left-wing initiative as tantamount to communist insurrection. While, under Lerroux's opportunistic guidance – with Gil Robles manipulating things from the wings – the Radical government swung further to the right, the despairing Socialists began to view the threat of a revolutionary uprising as the only way to safeguard the Republic. The situation polarised dramatically during the spring and summer of 1934 when the Radical Minister of the Interior, Rafael Salazar Alonso, provoked several socialist unions into a series of suicidal strikes. Aware that the left equated the CEDA with fascism, and would not countenance its participation in government, in September 1934 Gil Robles withdrew his party's tacit support completely, thereby forcing Lerroux to form a new cabinet, which included three CEDA ministers. As he had anticipated, this provoked the left to declare a revolutionary general strike all over Spain on 4 October, which was accompanied by a short-lived declaration of independence in Catalonia. Although most strikes were instantly suppressed, a more determined and better organised one, co-ordinated by the UGT, the CNT and the fledgling Communist Party, took place among the miners in Asturias. This provoked the replacement of the civil governor by a military commander, and the establishment of martial law.

Some weeks earlier, as arranged, Franco had returned to the mainland to join the Minister of War, Diego Hidalgo, in military manoeuvres. These took place under the direction of General Eduardo López Ochoa in León, terrain which was conveniently similar to that in Asturias. Whether Hidalgo's invitation to Franco was purely fortuitous – for the right at least – or a premeditated decision to ensure that he would be at his side in Madrid ready to help him suppress the anticipated revolutionary unrest, Franco would prove invaluable during the dramatic events to come.

President Alcalá Zamora dispatched General López Ochoa to lead the troops against the miners in the apparent hope that his reputation as a loyal Republican and Freemason would limit bloodshed. Although a request from Hidalgo and the CEDA ministers that he be replaced by Franco was turned down, the Minister for War put Franco in overall charge of the repression in Asturias and Catalonia on an informal basis anyway. The declaration of martial law gave General Franco virtual autonomy over civil and military law and order in the area, albeit under the loose authority of Hidalgo. This not only provided Franco with a timely outlet for the pent-up feelings of hatred and aggression evoked by his mother's death, but also gave him 'an intoxicating taste of unprecedented politico-military power'.[30]

Despite the fact that there were, at this stage, few Communists within Spain itself, Franco was easily persuaded by the Entente's paranoid bulletins that the uprising had been 'deliberately prepared by the agents of Moscow' and that the Socialists, operating 'with technical instructions from the Communists, thought they were going to be able to install a dictatorship'.[31] Having convinced himself that, as a danger to the *Patria*, left-wing Spaniards were not Spanish at all, Franco could unleash brutality against his fellow countrymen with the same ease with which he had unleashed it against the Moors. By describing the conflict in Asturias as 'a frontier war' against 'socialism, communism, and all "isms" that attack civilisation to replace it with barbarity',[32] Franco was applying Spain's colonial rhetoric to the Spanish people. In fact, as soon became clear, Franco was not so much inclined to defend civilisation from barbarism, as to utilise barbaric tactics to annihilate the demands of the miners to be treated like civilised beings. Fearing hesitancy on the part of some of the more liberal officers, Franco made sure that like-minded people ran the operation. He shipped in Moorish mercenaries because he knew that they would not hesitate to fire upon the Spanish workers. Colonel Juan Yagüe, an Africanista who had been in Toledo with Franco, took command of the African troops. Franco's cousin and childhood friend, Major Ricardo de La Puente Bahamonde, was replaced as commander of the Leon air base, because he was suspected of ordering pilots not to fire on the strikers in Oviedo. As in Morocco, Franco was able to distance himself from the actual violence – and his own sadistic impulses – by co-ordinating the huge operation from a telegraph room of the Ministry of War in Madrid. Assisted only by his cousin Pacón and two naval officers, Franco delivered unflinching orders to bomb and shell the working-class districts of the mining towns, and directed the army to fire on the miners at will. During lunches with Pacón and Hidalgo at the Ministry, Franco would chat animatedly about the news flowing in from the battlefront. When directed by the Minister of War to 'talk about women, theatre, anything but revolutionary movements', however, he fell silent.[33]

Franco's belief that the Peninsular army 'with its few and weakened units and very little battlefield preparation would have been unable to impose the law' against virtually unarmed revolutionaries reveals more about his state of mind than the reality of the situation.[34] His conviction that the suppression of civilians on mainland Spain was the same as the war in Morocco – albeit lacking the 'certain romantic air' of a *reconquista* – was not shared by everybody in the military. On one occasion Pacón was angrily harangued by a number of the Minister of War's generals and officers, who indicated 'with every sign of displeasure' that they considered 'that General of yours [to be] completely mad'[35] to have brought in troops from Africa. Nevertheless, Franco's military terror tactics – which mirrored ones he had used to good effect in Morocco, and foreshadowed ones he would use during the civil war – proved to be highly effective. The enormous number of deaths among women and children, and the atrocities committed by Yagüe's Moroccan units, totally demoralised the working-class rebels.

However, in a premonition of things to come, Franco determined that the task had not been finished until all those involved had been arrested and punished. He selected an erstwhile comrade from Toledo, the brutal Major Lisardo Doval, to take charge of this bloody and protracted business. Unencumbered by any judicial restrictions, the Major's reprisals provoked an immediate international outcry. In Spain, however, Franco – 'the man who had saved Spain from anarchy and bolshevism'[36] – was hailed in the right-wing press as the 'saviour of the Republic'. The highly aggrieved

Minister of War, on the other hand, was largely ignored. He would later complain bitterly that of 'all those who ... have given weight to the extremely meritorious and efficacious work of this General ... not one has had a single word of praise for the Minister who named him. If I hadn't made that appointment', the aggrieved Hidalgo continues, 'General Franco with his technical knowledge and his admirable bravery would have been far way in the Balearic Islands following the events in Asturias through the newspapers'.[37]

Despite the jubilant furore in the right-wing press, the wounds of 1934 were deep and little was done to heal them. A very reluctant Lerroux and Gil Robles, fearing that the issue of death penalties for the revolutionaries in Asturias and for the officers who had defended the short-lived Catalan Republic would provoke President Alcalá Zamora to dismiss them, reluctantly opted for clemency, but hinted that they would not be averse to a coup being launched to prevent this. Although Franco did not want a precipitate military uprising, like others in the military he felt that failure to implement 'exemplary punishments' immediately constituted 'trampling on the just rights of the military class'.[38] In fact it was Franco's vengeful behaviour itself which actively provoked what he feared the most: a surge in sympathy for communism. Furthermore, shattered and appalled by the brutality of the repression, the left resolved never again to be pushed into revolutionary or electoral disunity. Both moderates and extremists would fling themselves behind the Popular Front in the elections of 1936.

The uprising in Asturias fanned right-wing extremism and generated considerable anxiety among the middle and upper classes. The CEDA's timid and largely disingenuous attempts to undermine the need for social revolution by introducing extremely limited land reform was repeatedly blocked by the far right. Meanwhile, thousands of political prisoners remained in gaol, Catalan autonomy was suspended and a virulent right-wing campaign was launched against Azaña, who was illegally imprisoned. (He would never forgive President Alcalá Zamora for failing to prevent this.) While in prison, Azaña became the symbolic hero of the defeated left. Franco, on the other hand, awarded the Gran Cruz de Mérito Militar, became the darling of the right. When, in February 1935, a deeply suspicious President Alcalá Zamora refused Lerroux's request that Franco be made High Commissioner in Morocco, he seemed content with the post of Commander-in-Chief of the Spanish Armed Forces in Morocco. Franco was predictably unperturbed when his great patron, Hidalgo, was replaced as Minister for War by the Prime Minister, Lerroux, who held both posts from November 1934 until April 1935.

Not everybody in the military was so sanguine. When Jorge Vigón and

Colonel Valentín Galarza decided that the time was ripe to launch another coup led by Sanjurjo, they took care to find out Franco's opinion. His view that 'it was not the right time' was sufficient to deter them. That such prominent officers were now prepared to defer to Franco, as they had not in 1932, reveals the extent to which Asturias had heightened his standing with the right in the army. Although, with his taste for blood and power satiated, secure in his position as the government's favourite general, Franco had no compelling reasons to consider revolt against the Republic, others on the right were determined to pursue a more 'catastrophist' solution to 'conquer the state'. These extremists – who received financial support and arms from Mussolini – consisted of the Carlists, an extreme body of break-away royalists, the fascist Falange Española led by the beguiling José Antonio Primo de Rivera, and the influential and wealthy 'Alfonists', supporters of Alfonso XIII and General Primo de Rivera led by the charismatic José Calvo Sotelo, who had returned to Spain after the May 1934 amnesty from the 'responsibilities campaign' in 1931.

On 6 May 1935, five members of the CEDA, including Gil Robles himself as Minister of War, entered a new cabinet under Lerroux. Against the wishes of President Alcalá Zamora, who warned that 'young generals aspire to be fascist *caudillos*',[39] Franco was recalled to Madrid to take up the post of Chief of General Staff. Other rebellious officers were also brought in from the cold. Franco's arch-rival, Goded, became Inspector General and Director of the Air Force and Fanjul became Under-Secretary for War. Emilio Mola was made General in Command of Melilla. Franco's Africanista crony, José Enrique Varela, who had been prominent in the Sanjurjo coup, was promoted to general.

That military rebellion was, at this stage, the last thing on General Franco's mind was revealed in some unpublished notes written by Gil Robles in 1970.[40] The new Minister of War describes his Chief of Staff as a contained, cautious, circumspect man who was as keen to avoid military decisions that might provoke the President of the Republic, or cause unnecessary 'political battles in the Cortes', as he had been to avoid confrontation with his father as a child. He was clearly successful in this respect. Alcalá Zamora, who complained bitterly that 'Goded is out of his mind [and] Fanjul is an evil bastard who is pursuing to death Republican officers for the tiniest irregularities while promoting partisans of monarchy and dictatorship', considered Franco to be 'the most military and the most loyal'.[41] Despite his deferential ways, Franco was, however, keen to use his influential new position 'to correct the reforms of Azaña and return to the components of the armed forces the internal satisfaction which had been lost with the coming of the Republic'.[42] The two men reinstated promotion on the basis of merit within the army, and re-equipped it to help it cope with further left-wing unrest. According to Gil Robles (who by the 1970s was no great fan of the Caudillo), Franco was prepared to put in long hours at the Minister of War's side because 'he understood that the policies followed by me were in the interest of army and country'. Franco was clearly keen that they be in the interest of the family as well. He asked the Minister of War to appoint his older brother, Nicolás, a naval engineer, as a state delegate in the naval shipbuilding company where the Ministry of War was about to commission major works. In the light of Nicolás's shady dealings in the shipbuilding world, Gil Robles delicately declined, but Nicolás was awarded the job of Director-General of the Merchant Navy Fishing Fleet in October 1935 anyway, presumably with Franco's help. Franco was less indulgent with his younger brother. Ramón's appointment by Lerroux as the air force attaché to Washington DC, seems to have enraged his older brother, and fanned his suspicions of both men. Although Franco carefully purged his relationship with Gil Robles of any personal elements, he could not prevent himself from erupting into impassioned diatribes about Ramón's 'acts of indiscipline and political extremism'.

Ramón was not Franco's only problem. After being released from prison, Azaña was storming around the country delivering powerful speeches to huge crowds. These facilitated the formation of the Popular Front – essentially a revival of the Republican–Socialist coalition of 1931, with the addition of the tiny Spanish Communist Party. Thoroughly alarmed by this development, Franco finally contacted the Union Militar Española via Valentín Galarza in the summer of 1935. Henceforth he was kept closely informed of its plans for a military uprising, and – or so he claimed – used his influence to ensure that it did not launch 'a premature coup along the lines of a nineteenth century *pronunciamiento*'.[43]

Throughout this time, successive Radical cabinets were swamped by massive financial scandals, which resulted in President Alcalá Zamora sacking Lerroux as Prime Minister and replacing him with the austere conservative Joaquin Chapaprieta. Gil Robles provoked the new Prime Minister's resignation on 9 December in the hope that he would be called to form a government. However, the President, suspicious of the CEDA leader's propensity to further the career of anti-Republican officers, and alarmed by his attempt to transfer control of the Civil Guard and the police from the Ministry of the Interior to the Ministry of War, decided, on 11 December, to call new elections. Terrified that this would signal the end of the CEDA's political power, Gil Robles vigorously encouraged discontented generals to launch a coup to prevent the Cortes being dissolved. Although Generals Fanjul and Varela were amenable to this idea, Franco and others were concerned that, without the support of the Civil Guard and police, an uprising would fail. An interim cabinet under Manuel Portela Valladares was brought in on 12 December. Portela, a close friend of Alcalá Zamora, swiftly replaced Gil Robles as Minister for War with General Nicolás Molero. Although in his tearful farewell speech Franco proclaimed that 'the army has never felt itself better led than in this period', he was happy enough to stay on as Chief of General Staff.

The appointment of this somewhat more liberal cabinet provoked a fresh crop of plans for an uprising. While Calvo Sotelo urged Franco, Goded and Fanjul to launch a coup immediately, José Antonio de Rivera delivered a wildly ill-conceived proposal for an uprising to Franco's simplistic comrade Colonel José Moscardó, the military governor of Toledo. He suggested that Falangist militants and military cadets at Toledo emulate Mussolini's march on Rome, with a march on Madrid as the first step towards a full-blown Falangist rebellion. This absurd suggestion did not go down well with General Franco. Although, on the face of it, he was indignant that mere civilians were exploiting the 'most distinguished officers' for their own political ends, his reservations about the aristocratic and charismatic son of the late dictator seemed to derive as much from a kind of sibling rivalry as from ideological differences. As always, however, personal animosity and political pragmatism went hand in hand. He was rightly convinced that a precipitate uprising was doomed to failure, and hoped, for the moment at least, that it was unnecessary. If it did happen, however, he was determined that José Antonio should not get the credit. Despite Franco's caution, rumours that he was closely involved in plans for a coup continued to fly around the corridors of power. Although Franco staunchly reassured Portela that 'I will not conspire so long as there is no danger of communism in Spain', as far as he was concerned, the success of the Popular Front would be the equivalent of a communist revolution.

Plans for the election scheduled for February 1936 proceeded in an atmosphere of verbal violence and mutual distrust. The CEDA launched a massive propaganda campaign presenting it in terms of a life-and-death struggle between good and evil, survival and destruction. The Popular Front, in a dramatically less well-funded campaign, cited the threat of fascism and the need for an amnesty for the October prisoners. During a stormy campaign, Franco attempted to maintain contact with, but remain distant from, monarchist conspiracies and from the burgeoning fascist groups, which included Gil Robles' youth movement, the Juventud de Acción Popular (JAP), and the Falange.

After visiting Britain as the Spanish representative at the funeral of King George V, Franco returned to Spain on 5 February, and reluctantly agreed to meet up with José Antonio Primo de Rivera, who was pushing for an immediate uprising. Wracked by suspicion and dislike of the Falange leader, Franco was his usual elusive, non-committal self. The antipathy was mutual. After a less than productive meeting, an exasperated José Antonio observed, 'my father for all his defects, for all his political disorientation, was something else altogether. He had humanity, decisiveness and nobility, but these people . . .'.[44]

Franco's ambivalence about a military coup was partially resolved when, on 16 February, the Popular Front won a narrow victory in the elections, but gained a huge number of seats in the Cortes. For Franco, the jubilant crowds swarming through the streets signified the triumph of communism and anarchy in Spain. For the Director-General of the Civil Guard, General Sebastián Pozas – an old Africanista colleague who had, very unusually, remained loyal to the Republic – this was a 'legitimate expression of Republican joy'. Franco's attempts to persuade Portela either to stay in power and bring out the army, or place the Civil Guard and the crack police units under his personal jurisdiction should the army be called upon to reimpose 'order', were unsuccessful. However, at his frantic behest the Minister of War, General Nicolás Molero, persuaded the beleaguered Prime Minister to call a cabinet meeting to discuss the issue of martial law. Portela agreed that a State of Alert be issued for eight days. The President authorised decrees enabling Portela to suspend constitutional guarantees and to impose martial law and when he considered this to be necessary.

Within minutes of hearing of the cabinet's decision, Franco took the unprecedented and illegal step of trying to implement martial law himself without the agreement of either Portela or Pozas. This was the first time that he had ever directly gone against the law of the land. It would not be the last. Perhaps he was keen to re-experience the untrammelled powers he had enjoyed during the repression in Asturias. Perhaps he had convinced himself that the army was morally justified in doing anything to reverse the electoral results. Either way, his illegal action received the support of neither the Civil Guard nor the police, who refused to act without direct orders from Pozas. Franco's initiative came to nothing. He had, during this crisis, come closer to military rebellion than ever before. Torn between his conviction that the army had the God-given right to intervene in civil affairs, an innate reluctance to challenge a higher authority and a debilitating fear of failure, it would take a lot to persuade him to try again. Shaken by flying so close to disaster, Franco hastened to reassure Portela that he was not involved in any kind of military conspiracy because 'The army does not have the moral unity at this moment to undertake the task of saving Spain.' He slyly hinted that he would happily put the army entirely in the Prime Minister's hands should *he* wish to use the 'unlimited resources of the state [and] the police at your orders' to reverse the electoral results. Portela did not.

As the moment to hand over power to the Popular Front came nearer, a frenzied new crop of plans for military rebellions broke out. On 17 February, General Goded attempted to bring the troops out of the barracks in Madrid, but Pozas surrounded all the garrisons with the Civil Guard. On 18 February, José Calvo Sotelo visited Portela to try and persuade him to use Franco, the Madrid military garrison and the Civil Guard to impose order. However, despite desperate pleas from both Gil Robles and Franco to Portela to remain in power and use the army to reverse the election results, he and the interim cabinet resigned on the morning of 19 February. They handed power over to a characteristically reluctant Azaña that afternoon. Azaña's stirring belief that 'the hour has struck in which Spaniards stop shooting each other' struck a hollow chord with the aggrieved generals. Franco's instant dismissal as Chief of the General Staff reinforced his personal hatred of Azaña and helped transform his hesitant fear of rebellion into a burning desire to destroy the Popular Front at any cost.

The Popular Front government swiftly dispersed the rebellious officers far and wide. Goded became Commandante General of the Balearic Islands, Mola was made military governor of Pamplona, and Franco – despite his heated protestations that 'in Madrid I could be more useful to the army and for the tranquillity of Spain' – was dispatched as Commandante General of the Canary Islands. Although this was an important position, he considered it as banishment. When taking leave of the President, Alcalá Zamora, he promised that 'no matter what happens, wherever I am there will never be communism'.[45]

Franco's bitterness towards the Second Republic escalated still further when the Popular Front directed the army not to take military action to stem the church-and convent-burning activities being perpetrated by small groups of anti-clerical anarchists. 'Such orders,' he snapped, 'since they are unworthy, should never be obeyed by an officer of our army.' For Franco the assaults by left-wingers, whom he identified with his father, against the Catholic Church, which he associated with himself and his mother, were quite simply the battle of evil against good. He could not grasp the breadth, depth and variety of left-wing support for the Popular Front. For him they were all anti-clerical members of the Jewish-Bolshevik-Masonic conspiracy. For him they were all bad. The loathing was mutual. Upon his departure for the Canaries 'the butcher of Asturias'[46] was heckled in the port by an angry crowd.

After arriving in the Canaries, Franco swiftly formulated plans for the suppression of left-wing activity on the island, and then settled down to an easy-going existence. He was, as always, accompanied by Pacón, who notes that he never missed a single day playing a round of golf, or visiting the Yacht Club for a chat with his friends. He even started English lessons. He and Doña Carmen ensured that they were always present at high society functions on the island. Nonetheless, Franco's sense of rejection and his deep-rooted hatred of the Popular Front continued to smoulder. Irritated by the government's constant surveillance of his activities, he made uncharacteristically forthright and controversial remarks about the Republic. His unrestrained enthusiasm for Mussolini's Italy as a 'new, young, strong power which is imposing itself on the Mediterranean, which has hitherto been kept as a lake under British control' delighted the Italian Consul, and startled the British one. When he hosted a reception for the Admiral of the Fleet and his staff, Franco delivered heartfelt toasts to 'the greatness of Spain and the Spanish navy'. During an increasingly raucous affair, shouts of '¡Viva España!' and 'We must take our General to the mainland, we must save Spain from anarchy!' were heard. An attempt was even made to hoist a portly but delighted Franco on to the shoulders of the 'dangerously enthusiastic' young naval officers. The civilian authorities were horrified.[47]

Anxiety on the left about Franco's political intentions were not helped when Serrano Suñer put his name down – illegally as it happened – as a right-wing candidate in a rerun of the elections in Cuenca, where the election results had been annulled due to the falsification of votes. José Antonio Primo de Rivera, who was languishing in prison for his anti-Republican activities, was also a candidate in Cuenca, which he hoped would secure his release. Irritated at the sudden proliferation of right-wing candidates, which he feared would impact upon his own chances of success in the election, José Antonio angrily insisted that Franco's name be removed forthwith. An embarrassed Serrano Suñer was dispatched to the Canaries to explain the situation to a very touchy General Franco.

Although, as it happened, none of them could stand because the rules insisted on the original candidates standing, being forced to make way for his arch-rival would rankle with Franco throughout his life. Furious at José Antonio's high-handed treatment of him, and possibly concerned that his flirtation with politics would dent his credibility with the military, Franco set about trying to explain this failure to himself and to others. His sometimes strident, occasionally plaintive, often aggrieved explanations sounded increasingly like a little boy explaining to his angry father why he had not done his homework. In 1937 he staunchly claimed that *he* had 'publicly rejected' the right's request to be a candidate because he was busy organising 'the defence of Spain' and he would never have sullied his soul by becoming involved in a democratic government. In 1940, he patiently explained that he had stood down because he feared 'twisted interpretations' of his candidacy. At one stage he even protested that his name had got lost because the list had been 'burned' in an accident. In the end he veered back to the more impressive explanation that he had withdrawn 'because he preferred to attend to his military duties by which means he believed he could better serve the national interest'. His convoluted rewriting of this tale exposes his tendency to explain his personal shortcomings from the conflicting perspectives of the humiliated child, the critical father, the canny politician and the noble military man safeguarding the *Patria*. He would flit back and forth between these differing roles for the rest of his life.

Despite his increasingly intemperate criticisms of the Republic, Franco was still wracked with anxieties about flinging himself behind yet another military coup being hatched by disaffected generals, which they all agreed should be led by the exiled Sanjurjo. Unaware of his hesitancy, the left was convinced, in the words of Indalecio Prieto, that Franco was 'a man who could at a given moment be the Caudillo of a movement with the maximum chance of success'.[48] Whether or not this ill-advised piece of careers advice got back to Franco, mounting fears on the left that the Republic was doomed certainly helped inflate and focus his ambitions. After the impeachment of President Alcalá Zamora on 7 April for twice exceeding his constitutional powers in dissolving the Cortes before its term was up, Azaña himself became President. However, despite Azaña's hopeful belief that 'We govern with just cause and with laws. Ah! He who steps outside the law has lost all justification for what he does,'[49] the continued church burnings and attacks on right-wingers plunged him into a 'black despair' from which he would not emerge.

Unemployment soared alongside the rising expectations of rural and urban workers. The stubborn refusal of the Socialist leader, Largo Caballero, to allow members of the Socialist Party to join the Republican government, in the misguided hope that it would either collapse or trigger a fascist coup which could then be crushed by a popular uprising, undermined the government's strength and credibility. His policy of naïve obstructions resulted in the consumptive Santiago Casares Quiroga becoming Prime Minister rather than the dynamic Socialist, Indalecio Prieto. Despite well-publicised rumours about the impending coup, the ineffectual and ill Prime Minister left all the main conspirators in positions of power.

As Spain lurched sickeningly towards civil war, mounting hysteria on both sides of the political spectrum contributed to escalating instability and violence. On the right, inflammatory parliamentary speeches by Gil Robles and Calvo Sotelo, an hysterical press and the increasingly violent activities of the Falangist terror squads were fanning tensions. On the left, Largo Caballero – 'the Spanish Lenin' – riding on the crest of a wave of populism made wild and ill-considered speeches about the coming revolution to jubilant crowds of workers. May Day marches, clenched-fist salutes and vitriolic attacks on Prieto convinced the middle classes that only the army stood between Spain and a Godless communist revolution. Right-wing landowners, appalled by the new and determined spirit of radicalism among the hitherto subservient peasantry, openly encouraged right-wing plots against the Republic.

The military rebels now included a large proportion of colonels and majors throughout the army, as well as the paramilitary militias of both the Carlist movement and the Falange. They could not, as yet, rely upon General Franco. Although Galarza kept Franco closely informed of plans being formulated by General Mola, his involvement at this stage was minimal. It was General Mola, not Franco, who directed from his base in Pamplona in April 1936 that the imminent military action 'must be violent in the extreme in order to crush the strong and well-organised enemy as soon as possible'. It was Mola who promised that 'All leaders of political parties, societies or unions not committed to the Movement will be imprisoned and exemplary punishments administered . . . to strangle movements of rebellion or strikes.' Although Franco bitterly complained to Pacón that 'Orgaz is always pressuring me to rebel as soon as possible, and he says that victory is certain, a ripe fruit that some other general is going to eat', he was rightly convinced that 'it's going to be immensely difficult and very bloody'.[50] He was clearly concerned that it would also be unsuccessful. As he anxiously pointed out to Pacón, 'we've hardly got any army to speak of, the intervention of the Civil Guard looks doubtful and among the generals, majors and captains there are many who will be on the side of the government, some because it's the easiest option, others out of idealistic conviction.'[51]

Furthermore, rising up against the legally constituted government and Azaña – a much loathed but powerful parent figure – was not going to be easy for him. An increasingly distraught Franco wended his way through a psychological and political minefield. His entire status and authority were still dependent upon the government. Once it went, who would be in charge? Who would validate his military authority? In the aftermath of a successful coup, Sanjurjo would be Head of State, with Mola playing a crucial political role. The charismatic and popular José Antonio Primo de Rivera and Calvo Sotelo would be the main political protagonists. Where did he fit in? Although, when asked what reward he would expect if he joined the rebels, Franco somewhat meekly asked to be made High Commissioner in Morocco, was this sufficient to sacrifice everything he had? Although he despised the unruly 'rabble', he neither liked nor trusted any of the rebels. Furthermore, as he told Orgaz, 'Nobody should forget that the soldier who rebels against the constituted power can never turn back, never surrender, for he will be shot without a second thought.'[52]

Others were less coy. Some officers who, at different times, had enjoyed the favour of the Republic but had turned against it after the success of the Popular Front now agreed to take part in the uprising, including General Miguel Cabanellas, Fanjul, Goded and Queipo de Llano. While the tireless Colonel Yagüe prepared the Moroccan garrisons for the uprising, it was agreed that the rebel forces in Morocco must await the arrival of 'a prestigious general' before joining the rebels. Teetering on the edge of his terrible dilemma, Franco was still reluctant to dip more than a hesitant toe into the turbulent waters. He dispatched a frantic and convoluted letter to the Prime Minister in which he tried to resolve his ambivalence. He carefully explained that army discontent was not an act of disloyalty against the Republic but the consequence of its moral duty to safeguard public order and the welfare of the Patria. He hinted that if he were given the powers to deal with the mob as he had in Asturias, he would support the Republic and there would be no need for a military conspiracy. Casares' failure even to acknowledge the letter would prove to be a disaster.

Meanwhile, Africanista colleagues, exasperated about the daring hero's prudence, derisively dubbed him 'Miss Canary Islands 1936', while Yagüe bitterly criticised Franco's 'mean-minded carefulness and refusal to take risks'.[53] Although Sanjurjo announced that 'Franco will do nothing to commit himself; he will always be in the shadows because he is so crafty',[54] both he and Mola depended upon him, as 'the traffic light of military politics',[55] to provide the signal for other hesitant officers. When Franco began to sound out the attitude of other army colleagues, he discovered that, as he had feared, while some were responsive, others staunchly affirmed their loyalty to the Republic. This did not help focus his mind.

An exasperated Mola finally decided to pre-empt Franco's participation by arranging for a De Havilland Dragon Rapide – complete with a British pilot and 'holidaying tourists' – to be hired in England and dispatched on 11 July to the Canaries in order to fly Franco to Morocco to lead the rebellion there. As the plane set off on its secret mission, Franco, obsessing about the failed coup of 1932, oscillated ever more wildly. On 12 July he notified Mola that he would not join the rebels, and then two days later promised that he would. His desperate indecision was resolved by the assassination of Calvo Sotelo on 13 July in reprisal for the Falangist killing of a leftist officer. This response to an extreme and provocative campaign against pro-Republican

officers convinced many officers that the army must step in to save the
Patria from total anarchy. It was the signal Franco was waiting for. He
angrily proclaimed that 'The *Patria* has another martyr. We can wait no
longer.' It also, coincidentally, removed one of his most important political
rivals. Aware that the assassination would give the military the excuse they
needed for an uprising, Prieto frantically petitioned Casares to arm the
workers before a coup took place. He refused to do so.

While the British pilot of the Dragon Rapide, Captain William Bebb,
anxiously awaited instructions from an unknown messenger who would
identify himself with the passwords 'Mutt and Jeff' on the island of Gran
Canaria, Franco spent the night of 13 July in Tenerife battling with his inner
demons. The following morning he finally ordered Pacón to arrange a safe
passage for his wife and daughter from the Canaries to Le Havre for 19 July,
the day after the proposed uprising. According to his English teacher, this
act of decisiveness left him looking 'ten years older ... near to something
like losing his iron self-control and unutterable serenity'. Having finally
overcome the massive psychological barriers to joining the rebellion,
Franco was now confronted by the practicalities. How could he get from
his headquarters in Santa Cruz de Tenerife to the island of Gran Canaria
and so fly to Morocco in time for the uprising on 18 July? He could not visit
the island without the permission of the Ministry of War, which was, in the
circumstances, unlikely to be forthcoming. This problem was bizarrely
and suspiciously resolved when the military commander in Gran Canaria
managed to shoot himself in the stomach on 16 July. His fortuitous demise
gave Franco the excuse he needed. His family and a number of high-ranking
officers now had to go to Las Palmas on 17 July to attend the funeral.

Although co-ordinated uprisings were scheduled to take place all over
Spain on 18 July, this was brought forward to the evening of 17 July in
Morocco after an alert was issued that the conspirators were about to be
arrested. While Franco slept, the garrisons rose in Melilla, Tetuán and
Ceuta. He was notified of the successful uprising at 4 o'clock that morning.
This sense of crisis generated a surge of adrenalin that reaffirmed Franco's
sense of identity. He sent a rallying message to the other conspirators.
'Glory to the Army of Africa. Spain above all ... Blind faith in our triumph.
Long live Spain with honour. General Franco.' This triumphalist message
put Franco at the forefront of the uprising and brought many other officers
flocking to join the rebels. He immediately declared martial law in the
Canaries and issued a manifesto to be broadcast by radio in Las Palmas,
which included the handwritten postscript 'accursed be those who, instead
of doing their duty, betray Spain'. He neatly bypassed the issue of exactly
whose authority he was supporting by avoiding any mention of the Repub-

lic or the monarchy, stating simply that the army was defending the *Patria* itself from chaos, and announced that the coup was necessitated by the power vacuum in Madrid, where the government was failing to defend Spain's borders, or deal with 'foreign radio stations ... calling for the destruction and division of our soil'. Ironically, Franco promised to launch 'a war without quarter against those who use politics for their own ends, against those who deceive the honest worker, against foreigners and their Spanish toadies who openly or furtively try to destroy Spain.' He could have been describing himself.[56]

While Franco was busy trumpeting his reasons for usurping the authority of the legally constituted Republic, his personal situation was somewhat perilous. With the head of the local Civil Guard unsure whether to support the uprising, Franco and his fellow rebels were in considerable danger. Pacón was forced to use artillery fire to prevent a belligerent group of workers joining forces with the Civil Guard until such time as Franco's supporters on the island had been armed. When fighting broke out between the two groups, Franco handed over command to Orgaz, dispatched Carmen and Nenuca to the port to await their passage to Le Havre, and set off for the airport where his plane awaited him. It was a treacherous trip. With the roads commandeered by supporters of the Popular Front, he had to travel around the island in a naval tugboat. His plane finally took off at 14.05 hours on 18 July. Like so many aspects of his life, his journey would provoke an imaginative and romantic array of improbable accounts. He has been attired in a bewildering array of disguises, ranging from the dark grey suit of a diplomat to full Arabian dress, to which one inspired writer added a turban. Pacón's assertion that they both dressed in white summer suits and threw their military uniforms out of the window seems improbable, not least because both men were wearing them on arrival in Africa. There has also been vigorous speculation about exactly where and when Franco shaved off his famous moustache: the only thing, as Queipo caustically observed, that he ever sacrificed for Spain.

Whatever his choice of clothing, the tense and difficult journey, with a brief stop at Agadir for fuel, and an overnight stop-over in Casablanca because of a faulty landing light, generated an electrifying energy in the cautious General. Having hardly slept for days, an ebullient Franco resumed his unfaltering persona of hero of the Rif the moment he passed over the border into Africa. As it was unclear exactly who was in command at Tetuán, the plane flew in circles for some time, until Franco, spotting an old Africanista colleague, cried out, Biggles-like, 'We can land, I've just seen Blondy!' Upon landing he was enveloped in tearful eulogies from various comrades and Legionnaires. Handing over his command, an emotional

Lieutenant-Colonel Yagüe, forgetting his scornful comments about Franco, proclaimed, 'You ... who so many times led them to victory, lead them again for the honour of Spain', while Franco wept. Carried away by it all, Franco immediately raised the Legionnaires' pay by one peseta a day. However, he had his feet very much on the ground. Realising that the rebels were dramatically short of aircraft and other modern equipment, he dispatched Luis Bolín, the *ABC* correspondent who had hired the plane in London, and Bebb, to report to Sanjurjo in Lisbon, and then hasten on to Rome to seek Mussolini's support for the uprising.

Back in Africa, Franco was not answerable to any higher legal or military authority. The timely removal of Calvo Sotelo had paved the way to a much loftier political future than had previously seemed possible. The dizzying speed at which other rivals would now fall by the wayside consolidated his belief that providence and divine intervention were on his side. From the moment he threw in his lot with the rebels, Franco would countenance no opposition, from his supporters, his opponents or himself. His heartening cries that 'Spain is saved!' and demands for 'Blind faith, no doubts, firm energy without vacillations, because the *Patria* demands it' sound as much a warning to the hesitant aspect of himself as a message of hope to the rebels. It was the triumphant conclusion of a dialogue he had been having with himself throughout the spring of 1936, perhaps for all his life. In *Raza* he firmly projects all his ambivalence about the uprising on to Luis Echeverría, José's closest friend and Isabelita's husband. When Luis expresses doubts about the uprising, the hero José staunchly announces, 'You are not sure which is the road of honour. We must seek the road of honour and, if we cannot find it, we must do whatever mortifies us most in the certainty that that will be it. That is how I see it.'[57] Whether or not, as Gubern notes in his analysis of the film-script, 'this is a masochistic identification between pleasurable duty and the highest mortification', these sentiments capture the essence of Franco's tortured mind. When Hitler wrote about the Second World War, 'I am totally convinced that this struggle does not differ one hair's breadth from the battle which I once fought out within myself',[58] he might have been describing Franco and the civil war.

CHAPTER 4

Mine All Mine

Franco and the Civil War, July 1936–March 1937

In Morocco the war had gathered the scattered fragments of army morale in a fist clenched and raised for the punch.

Ortega y Gasset

A leader will be found in the individual who has the least resistance, the least sense of responsibility, and, because of his inferiority, the greatest will to power. He will let loose everything that is ready to burst forth, and the mob will follow with the irresistible force of an avalanche.

Carl Jung[1]

Stripped of his rank by the Republic on 19 July, at the time of the uprising, Franco was one of only four out of twenty-one major-generals on active service to declare against the government, the others being Queipo, Goded and Cabanellas. The rebels confronted the legitimate government, which had the support of some of the Civil Guard and much of the army (whose loyalty they dared not test against the rebels). Although many officers followed Franco's lead in the belief that 'Franco's with us. We've won',[2] other senior army officers were as reluctant to risk either their pensions or their lives as he had previously been. On the whole it was the middle ranks in the army who flung in their lot with the rebels. The majority of senior officers remained loyal to the government.[3] Not even all the Africanistas were enthusiastic rebels. As Raymond Carr points out, if *all* the officers had joined the rising, it would probably have been successful in a matter of days.[4] As it was, the rebels enjoyed only sporadic success. In the words of Ronald Fraser, 'The coup had fissured the Republic, not crushed it. In that sense it had failed.'[5]

Although in many ways Franco's worst fears had been realised, he adopted an attitude of absolute belief in the nobility and 'rightness' of the rebels' cause and total derision for the military capacity and moral determination of the enemy. (On the other hand, he cannot have been best pleased when the dismissive London *Times* described him as the 'brother of the well-known airman'.) He backed his morale-boosting speeches to the rebels with threats of 'exemplary punishment' for supporters of the Popular Front, and 'no pardon' for those who persisted in opposing the rebels. His 'iron will' and insouciant optimism – which contrasted with Mola's suicidal pessimism – put heart into the rebellion. Directing operations from his headquarters in the offices of the Spanish High Commission in Tetuán, he soon made it clear just how ruthless he was prepared to be. His first cousin, Major Ricardo de la Puente Bahamonde, had been arrested for trying to hold on to Tetuán airport for the Republicans. Unfortunately for Ricardo, he and Franco had, as children, been as close as brothers. But as with Franco and Ramón, their ideological views had diverged from an early age. One argument had culminated in Franco screaming, 'One day I'm going to have you shot!'[6] He kept his word. Franco refused to lift a finger to prevent his cousin being arrested, tried and shot by the rebels. His was not the only family torn apart by the uprising. Ostensibly keen to seize power in order to reverse the erosion of family life imposed by the Republic's reforms, the rebels would tear apart virtually every family in Spain.

In Madrid, Casares, the Prime Minister, was forced to resign. Although a despairing Azaña was convinced that 'It's too late', he and the government established a compromise cabinet under the moderate leadership of Diego Martínez Barrio. The new Prime Minister's attempt to pacify the rebels with promises of an immediate crackdown on left-wing militias and the prohibition of strikes simply inspired their derision and enhanced their confidence. With their blood up and their confidence surging, they were not going to accept tentative compromise solutions, or offers of high office by an emasculated government.

The beleaguered Martínez Barrio was replaced by Professor José Giral after only a few hours. A follower of Azaña, Giral reluctantly took the crucial step of arming the workers. The power vacuum at the centre meant that *ad hoc* revolutionary committees were able to seize the political initiative, leaving some extremist elements free to respond to decades of oppression, political exclusion and right-wing brutalities with atrocities of their own. The revolutionary zeal within the Republican zone gave the military rebels the retrospective justification they needed for their uprising. Bereft of any coherent political plan, other than a very hazy notion that they were restoring order and saving Spain from anarchy, they latched on to the spectre of 'communist revolution' – which had not, until they provoked it, taken place – to justify the uprising. But crushing the Republican militias would not prove as easy as Franco had hoped.

The raw, inexperienced left-wing militias, fired by sheer passion, experienced some unexpected early victories, which seriously impeded Mola's attempts to move down from the north towards Madrid. A below-decks mutiny against rebel officers in the Spanish fleet left the navy in the hands of the Republic, patrolling the Straits of Gibraltar. Although few small boats got sufficient African troops to Spain across the Straits to secure the success of the uprising in Cadiz, Algeciras and La Línea, Franco and the bulk of his African army remained ignominiously trapped in Morocco. Had the Republic succeeded in keeping them there, the rebels would have lost the war.

On the mainland, while traditional right-wing areas, ecclesiastical towns and deeply Catholic rural regions swung behind the rebels, in most of the Andalusian countryside the left seized power with the passionate support of the masses of landless labourers. With the Republican government helplessly wringing its hands, the popular forces also established individual power-bases in most of the important urban and industrial centres, including Madrid, Valencia, Barcelona, Malaga and Bilbao. Divisions in the officer corps in Madrid resulted in the capital being held by the Republic. General Fanjul was captured by militiamen. Encouraged by their success in the capital, hastily formed militia groups surged southwards towards Toledo and north-east towards Guadalajara, where the uprising had been temporarily successful. In Toledo, Colonel José Moscardó, along with a thousand Carlists and Falangists, barricaded himself in the Alcázar – a half-fortress, half-palace set high above the city and the river Tagus – taking the civil governor and the wives and children of some well known leftists as hostages. Guadalajara, on the other hand, was easily recaptured by militia groups.

In Granada, Franco's second-in-command at Saragossa, Colonel Miguel Campins, initially refused to declare martial law, and hesitated for a fateful two days before joining the rebels. Although he then placed himself under Franco's orders, he would be tried and executed for 'rebellion' on 16 August by a ruthless Queipo de Llano, who resolutely ignored Franco's impassioned pleas for clemency. Campins aside, to the horror of General Pozas, the entire officer corps of the garrison in Granada, the Civil Guards and the Assault Guards went with the rebels. After a few days of fighting, the city was easily occupied. While the Republicans just managed to hang on to Valencia, Seville was firmly taken by Queipo de Llano, who broadcast his determination 'to go on to the bitter end and continue our good work until not a single Marxist is left in Spain'.[7] Although the capture of the airport would prove invaluable to the rebel cause, Franco was not amused when

Queipo moved swiftly to establish a personal power-base in Seville, where his portrait soon bedecked the city.

In the Basque country, the role of the Civil Guard and the Assault Guards was, as Franco had predicted, crucial. In those areas where they remained loyal to the Republic, the rebellion was easily suppressed. Wherever they prevaricated, or actively supported the rebels, the Popular Front was easily crushed. In Galicia, Corunna was captured by the rebels on 20 July, after which they took the rest of the province. On the same day in El Ferrol, fighting between Republican seamen in warships and rebels on the land ended with the latter capturing a number of battleships and taking control of the crucial naval shipyard. Franco's father, who had been spending the summer in his family home with Agustina, would be trapped in El Ferrol for the duration of the war.

The province of Leon also fell to the rebels. However, by the time General Goded arrived in Barcelona, the uprising there had already been defeated by anarchists and those members of the Civil Guard who remained loyal to the Republic. Goded's defeat was a major blow to the rebellion and ensured that all of Catalonia would remain loyal to the Republic. In Barcelona, revolutionary crowds surged through the streets exposing, in the words of a young socialist, 'the power and strength of the masses'.[8] As John Whitaker of the Chicago *Daily News* bluntly put it: 'If I could sum up (the Nationalists') social policy it would be simple in the extreme – they were outnumbered by the masses, they feared the program to educate the masses and they proposed to thin down their numbers.'[9]

After three days of fighting, Spain was thus split by a line that meandered from half-way up the Portuguese–Spanish frontier in a north-easterly direction and met the Spanish–French border about 300 kilometres from the Mediterranean. Apart from a strip of coastline comprising Asturias, Santander and two Basque coastal provinces, all to the north and west of this line was in Nationalist hands (including Morocco, the Canaries and the Balearics, apart from Minorca). To the south and east, apart from Seville, Granada, Córdoba, Cádiz and Algeciras, the territory had been held by the Republic.

On the mainland, the rebels were keenly awaiting the arrival of General Sanjurjo from Portugal, where the Dragon Rapide was waiting to fly him over the border so that he could lead his troops in an assault on the capital. Sanjurjo – the 'lion of the Rif' – was entranced by the arrival in Portugal of the famous air ace Juan Antonio Ansaldo to pay his passionate respects to the new 'Spanish Chief of State'. Carried away with the excitement of it all, the portly General opted, in a misplaced bout of histrionics, to undertake the journey in Ansaldo's tiny Puss Moth instead.[10] On 20 July, the combination of the very large General and his extensive baggage, which was packed to capacity with full-dress uniforms and medals ready for his triumphant arrival in the capital, prevented the over-burdened plane from clearing the trees on take-off. General Sanjurjo was killed instantly. Only Mola, as 'Director' of the uprising, and José Antonio Primo de Rivera, confined in a prison in Alicante, remained as potential rivals to Franco. With Franco and his troops still stuck in Morocco, Mola was in effective charge of the coup.

Having established martial law in Pamplona, on 23 July Mola set up a seven-man Junta de Defensa Nacional in Burgos under the nominal presidency of General Cabanellas along with some civilian support from the monarchist Renovación Española group. Franco was named head of the Junta's forces on the southern front. With the moderate Cabanellas effectively a powerless figurehead, the remit of the Junta itself was extremely unclear and personal animosity between the major protagonists – particularly Franco and Queipo – soon flared.

A mere ten days after the rebels' illegal uprising, they designated defence of the Republic as a crime of 'military rebellion' punishable by death. To begin with, no form of trial at all was necessary to shoot a man, although in due course ad hoc military courts were established to try a bewildering array of 'offences'.[11] More than 50,000 Spaniards were killed in this way during the first six months alone.[12] The most notorious, and self-defeating, of all these executions was that of Garcia Lorca, then at the height of his reputation as a poet.

According to Hugh Thomas, this repression 'was an act of policy, decided upon by a group of desperate men who knew that their original plan had gone awry'.[13] 'It is necessary', trumpeted an increasingly nervous Mola, 'to spread an atmosphere of terror. We have to create the impression of mastery ... anyone who is overtly or secretly a supporter of the Popular Front must be shot.'[14] In villages across Spain, men were snatched from their houses, usually at night, by Falangist extremists – often a neighbour or a relative – shot in large groups and hurriedly buried in shallow mass graves. There was no going back. When, towards the end of July 1936, the French press reported on Prieto's peace initiative to end the slaughter, General Mola roared, 'Negotiate! Never! This war must end with the extermination of the enemies of Spain!'[15]

Franco's ability to carve out a political and military role for himself was, for the moment, seriously curtailed by his inability to transport his troops, past the Republican blockade, to the mainland. Although this problem was partially resolved when General Alfredo Kindelán – Ramón's erstwhile boss in the Spanish air force, whom Franco now appointed head of his own exiguous air forces – suggested that he fly them to Seville, with only four aircraft at his disposal this proved to be a slow and laborious business. He was aware that foreign aid was crucial if all of his troops were to be airlifted across the Straits.

While they both began to woo the fascist powers, Mola's request to the Germans for rifle cartridges struck a somewhat unimpressive note alongside Franco's audacious demands to both Italians and Germans for aeroplanes to transport the African army to the mainland. Once they were sure that the French were not going to support the Republic, the Italians responded by dispatching twelve bombers for Franco's use, two of which crashed along the way, and one of which was blown off course. Franco also made a bold bid for support from the Germans, sending emissaries who succeeded in gaining access to the Führer himself at Bayreuth on 25 July. They handed Hitler a terse letter asking for rifles, fighter and transport planes and anti-aircraft guns for the Nationalist cause. Fired by an evening of Wagner, and working himself into an anti-Bolshevik frenzy, the Führer flung diplomatic caution to the winds. Ignoring his advisers, who were concerned that the German involvement in Spain would bring them into conflict with Britain, he agreed to dispatch Franco twenty aircraft under a secret operation he called 'Magic Fire'. According to Hugh Thomas, nearly all the Germans who went to Spain, particularly the pilots, were young Nazis who believed 'Our foes are the reds, the bolshevisers of the world.'[16]

Heartened by Germany's positive response, on 27 July Franco blithely assured an American reporter that he would 'take the capital [and] save Spain from Marxism at whatever cost'. When the appalled reporter suggested that such an aspiration would require him 'to shoot half of Spain', Franco coldly reiterated, 'As I said, at any cost.'[17] There were, at this stage, thirteen million Spaniards in the Republican zone, eleven million with the insurgents.[18] The cost would be very high indeed.

Even with fascist assistance, the airlift of the African troops was still taking too long. To the horror of his advisers, on 5 August Franco decided to dispatch some of the Army of Africa by sea from Ceuta, with a makeshift air escort providing the 'victory convoy'. He was quite rightly convinced that, without trained officers, the Republican crews would be easily dispersed by air attacks. The Nationalists' domination of the Straits would henceforth facilitate a regular flow of ammunition and armaments from both Hitler and Mussolini to the rebels. Leaving Orgaz in command in Morocco, an ebullient Franco flew to Seville on 6 August, where he established his headquarters in a grandiose palace. He was joined by Pacón, General Kindelán and General Millán Astray, who had rushed back hotfoot from Argentina the moment he heard about the uprising. Having formed the basis for a general staff, Franco took stock of the military situation.

The Republic's military fortunes were seriously jeopardised by a communiqué issued on 9 August by the principal European powers, announcing that, under the declaration of 'non-intervention', all export of war material to Spain would be suspended. When the Republic's potential allies, France and the Soviet Union, placed their names alongside other European countries, including Britain and Portugal, the fate of the Republic was sealed. Although both Hitler and Mussolini signed the agreement, neither felt in the slightest bit circumscribed by its requirements. While the flow of aid from France to the Republic virtually dried up, Axis intervention would redress the flagging fortunes of the precarious *coup d'état* and transform the military rebellion into a protracted and devastating civil war.

Admiral Canaris, head of German Military Intelligence and a fluent Spanish speaker, and General Mario Roatta, head of Italian Military Intelligence, co-ordinated the provision of Italian and German aid to Spain. By the end of August, it was agreed that all assistance would be channelled exclusively to Franco. Emerging as the only Nationalist leader with international backing, Franco had successfully seized the political initiative from Mola. He also took overall direction of the military effort, occasionally visiting Mola and the battlefront in a Douglas DC-2. However, while Franco's success in Morocco and Carlist support for Mola in Navarre in northern Spain had opened up the possibility of marches converging on Madrid, the Nationalist war effort was fraught with difficulties from the outset.

It was soon clear that it was not just the long-term political views and the short-term military priorities of the rebel leaders that diverged; so did their personal styles. While Mola and Queipo de Llano presided over chaotic headquarters in Burgos and Seville, around which visitors happily milled, from the very start Franco surrounded himself with bodyguards who vetted all visitors closely. The more power he got, the more convinced he became that he was a major target for the murderous impulses of others. Although the executions, in early August, of his political opponents General Goded in Barcelona and Fanjul in Madrid by the Republicans may well have enhanced Franco's ambitions, they did little for his peace of mind. Even journalists were subjected to close scrutiny during interviews, which were monitored through an open door by a guard with a strategically placed mirror. Upon gaining access to the man himself, however, far from meeting a terrifying warlord, visitors encountered someone more akin to the Wizard of Oz: an extremely small, timid man who was lustrous of eye, large of stomach, strangely feminine and, in the words of John Whitaker, 'disconcertingly unimpressive'. According to the incredulous journalist:

his hand is like a woman's and always damp with perspiration. Excessively shy ...
his voice is shrill and pitched on a high note which is slightly disconcerting since
he speaks very softly – almost in a whisper. Although effusively flattering, he gave
me no frank answer to any question I put to him; I could see that he perfectly
understood the implications of even the most subtle query. A less straightforward
man I never met.[19]

Whatever Franco's personal shortcomings, the arrival in Spain of the
terrifying Army of Africa dealt a fateful blow to the Republic spirit and
generated a huge surge of confidence in the rebels. By using Moorish troops
against Spanish civilians in Asturias, Franco had, in his own mind, already
rendered the Spanish workers 'un-Spanish'. When he talked about the
Patria, he meant a partisan collection of well-to-do Catholic right-wingers.
He did not mean the liberal and working-class supporters of the Popular
Front. His attitudes did not bode well for the Spanish people. The 8,000-
strong African force was led by Lieutenant-Colonel Yagüe, under whom
individual banderas and units of the Regulares were led by Lieutenant-
Colonels Asensio, Delgado Serrano, Barrón and Tella along with Major
Castejón, all of whom were Moroccan veterans. Supported by Italian and
German air cover, the Moors and the Legionnaires swept north through
the Spanish countryside from Seville towards Madrid, in a bloodthirsty
rampage in which women were raped, prisoners killed and corpses sexually
mutilated by the Moors. Storming forward, they covered 200 kilometres in
under a week, a flood of terrorised refugees surging ahead of them.
Although Franco's brutal tactics may well have been driven by psychological
rather than military considerations, they proved highly effective. Not only
did they provide an outlet for the blood-lust of the African soldiers and
eliminate an enormous number of potential opponents and witnesses, but
they generated a crippling terror in the enemy. As John Whitaker wrote,
'The use of the Moors and the wholesale execution of prisoners and civilians
were the trump cards of the "best" elements in Spain.'[20]

Why Franco needed the Moroccans is clear. Why they were prepared to
fight for him is harder to grasp. It is difficult to accept the Nationalist myth
of Muslim troops eagerly volunteering their lives for the salvation of Spanish
Christianity. A much more likely explanation is that the Moroccan soldiers
were fighting neither for General Franco (who had killed a great many of
their Muslim brethren) nor for Christian ideals, but for money and loot
and – allegedly – 'rape' coupons. It has also been strongly suggested that
the promise of autonomy or some measure of home rule could have been
a major lure, an issue in which the Germans – keen for a foothold in the
Mediterranean – took a particularly lively interest. Ironically, it was the

Republic's failure to respond to overtures from Moroccan nationalists that inclined them to forge links with Franco.[21] Whatever their motivations, these Muslims would play a critical role in Franco's 'Christian crusade'.[22]

Although General Mola's Northern Army was brought to an unexpected halt in the north and north-west by workers' militias from the capital, nothing could stop the Army of Africa. On 10 August, Yagüe took Merida, an important communications centre between Seville and Portugal. Instead of ordering him to proceed on to Madrid, however, Franco directed him to turn south-west back towards Portugal to capture Badajoz, the principle town of Extremadura. Although Franco claimed this fateful diversion was necessitated by the need to link up with the forces of General Mola, unify the two sections of the Nationalist zone and open up the frontier to Salazar's Portugal, it simply gave the government more time to organise its defences in Madrid.

When the Nationalists arrived in the town on 14 August, the poorly organised workers who had fled to Badajoz and were defending the city with little more than scythes and hunting guns put up more of a fight than expected. Their resistance provoked a particularly frenzied outburst in the African troops. The Legionnaires and Regulares herded 2000 prisoners into a bull-ring where, in a 'paroxysm of war', they were all shot. The shooting went on for weeks afterwards, and the streets were littered with corpses. Asked by Whitaker why they had shot their prisoners, Yagüe briskly replied, 'Of course we shot them ... Was I supposed to take four thousand Reds with me as my column advanced racing against time? Was I expected to turn them loose in my rear and let them make Badajoz red again?'[23]

This costly diversion, which contributed little to the overall war effort, reveals as much about Franco's psychological defence mechanisms as his military priorities. Certainly his obsession with annihilating all resistance in the 'occupied zones', even though this resulted in him repeatedly diverting his troops away from Madrid and lengthening the war needlessly, hints at a neurotic rather than a political agenda. Perhaps, having projected hated aspects of himself – a feeling of impotence, vengefulness and hatred – on to the enemy, he was now attacking them. Perhaps Franco hated the weak and the dispossessed because they reminded him of that powerless part of himself he most wanted to forget. The more people he killed, the greater his fear of punishment and retribution, the more witnesses had to die. Whatever his motivations, there were practical benefits to his vengefulness. As Mussolini put it, 'Dead men tell no tales'.[24] Furthermore, the massacre at Badajoz – the first of many – sent a clear message to the people of Madrid about the consequences of resistance. It also earned Franco and the Nationalists great respect in Nazi Germany, where his patrons were keen for 'guarantees of victory not primarily in military successes, but in a systematic and thorough cleansing of the hinterland'.[25]

The Nationalists, like the Nazis, latched on to Darwinian arguments to justify their vengefulness, presenting it as a laudable desire to purge the motherland of the 'disease-ridden' Reds, who had introduced 'an influx of strains inimical to Spain ... of this taint in her bloodstream Spain must cleanse herself'. By killing ordinary Spanish people, they argued they would enable a purified Spain to 'rise up from this trial new and strong'. For Franco there were other benefits: such wanton destructiveness was 'a defence mechanism, a sign of wanting to live, of not wanting to die'.[26]

These biological imperatives could not, however, disguise the personal and political jealousies erupting in the Nationalist zone. Mola had already seriously blotted his political copybook with the monarchists by ordering the removal of Don Juan de Borbón – the third son of Alfonso XIII, who had become heir to the Spanish throne in June 1933, after his two elder brothers renounced their claims – from Spain, where he had turned up to fight on the Nationalist side. This arbitrary decision enraged monarchist officers, who immediately, and rather unwisely as it transpired, transferred the political allegiance to Franco. Franco moved swiftly to consolidate their support. In Seville, in an emotional address to the assembled crowds, he announced his personal decision to adopt the monarchist red–yellow–red flag, crying, 'This is our flag, the one on which we all swore, for which our fathers died ... the flag a hundred times covered in glory.' Although this gesture was driven as much by personal spite against Queipo, a committed republican, as by political acumen, it won Franco enormous support among conservatives and monarchists. The monarchist flag was adopted throughout the entire Nationalist zone two weeks later.

When, on 16 August, Franco flew to Burgos to discuss the progress of the war with Mola, he was greeted with manic fervour by the local population. Although it was clear to both men that a single overall military command, underpinned by a centralised diplomatic and political apparatus, was required, no decision was taken at this point. However, Franco's monopoly of foreign logistical supplies and the efforts of his energetic press office meant that he was already being described in the foreign press as 'Commander-in-Chief' and 'the supreme commander of the Spanish army'.

By late August 1936, an increasingly onerous workload, escalating responsibilities and a depressingly resilient Republic resulted in Franco looking and behaving less like a charismatic hero all the time. He aged dramatically. The absence of any legal, naturally ordained authority in the Nationalist zone meant that there was nobody whose orders he was prepared to follow, nobody to smile upon his success or commend his obedience. This clearly worried him. The arrival of his wife and daughter in Spain after their two-month exile in France did little to lift his spirits. To cheer himself up, and to escape from the sneering and superior Queipo de Llano, with whom he regularly engaged in ill-tempered, high-pitched arguments, he decided, on 26 August, to move his headquarters from Seville to an elegant sixteenth-century palace in Cáceres. His lofty and regal lifestyle contrasted sharply with the chaos and bloodshed of the battlefield.

Despite Franco's pessimism, the rebels had consolidated their position considerably. After the fall of Badajoz, Yagüe's three columns moved rapidly up the roads in the direction of Toledo and Madrid. By 27 August they had linked up to take the last town of importance on the way to the capital, Talavera de la Reina. After a week's bitter fighting, the town fell on 3 September and another appalling massacre was instigated. As John Whitaker would later recall: 'There seemed no end to the killing [of] simple peasants and workers ... It was sufficient to have carried a trade union card, to have been a Freemason, to have voted for the Republic.'[27] Verifying the enemy's exact political stance was not deemed to be necessary. As the notorious Captain Gonzalo de Aguilera put it, 'My dear fellow ... it only stands to reason! A chap who squats down on his knees to clean your boots at a café or in the street is bound to be a Communist, so why not shoot him right away and be done with it? No need for a trial – his guilt is self-evident in his profession.'[28]

In the south, General José Enrique Varela succeeded in establishing lines of communication between Seville, Granada, Cadiz and Algeciras, but had to abandon his attack on Malaga in order to defend Córdoba, while a newly equipped force under Lieutenant-Colonel Delgado Serrano swept north and established operational contact for the first time with the southernmost troops of Mola's Northern Army moving down from Avila. Meanwhile, Mola had attacked the Basque province of Guipuzcoa (a key agrarian and industrial area) in order to cut it off from France. The decision of the Italians and Germans to upgrade their assistance to the Nationalists via Franco led to the fall of Irun and San Sebastian in early September, cutting off the Basques from the French border at the western end of the Pyrenees. The Nationalist zone was now united in a single block from the Pyrenees through Castille and western Spain to the far south. These setbacks for the Republic resulted in the replacement of Giral's impotent Republican government by a more widely based, but scarcely more effective, cabinet led by Francisco Largo Caballero.

The Nationalist advance from Talavera was, however, impeded by Franco's laborious policy of purging every square inch of land of all leftists. Like Hitler, it seems, he considered retreat to be a sign of feminine weak-

ness.[29] Desperate counter-attacks by Republican militias provoked a particularly vicious response in the Army of Africa. It was during this time
that John Whitaker witnessed his first mass execution. Standing in the main
street of Santa Olalla in the Tagus valley, he watched the arrival of seven
trucks arrived carrying about 600 listless, exhausted militiamen, still clutching the filthy white flags with which they had signalled their surrender.
While Francoist officers handed their prisoners cigarettes, a couple of
Moorish troopers set up two machine guns. Whitaker chillingly recalls that
'The prisoners saw them. I saw them. The men seemed to tremble in one
big convulsion, as those in front, speechless with fright, rocked back on
their heels, the colour draining from their faces, their eyes wide with terror.'
In a nightmarish premonition of what would happen under the Nazis, a
cackling Moor feverishly peddled out 'San Francisco' on an ancient roll-
music piano while 'the two guns suddenly roared in staccato firing short
lazy bursts of ten or twelve rounds at a time punctuated by the silence'. The
appalled journalist could not understand either then or later 'why the
prisoners stood and took it. I always thought they might rush the machine
guns or do something – anything. I suppose all volition is beaten out of
them by the time they surrender.'[30]

In the wake of the massacre, Peter Kemp, a young Cambridge graduate
who had enlisted on the Nationalist side, was despatched to Santa Olalla to
report for duty. He too was shocked by the routine brutality of life in
the Africa army. Upon discovering that two of his men were drunk, the
commanding officer, Lieutenant Carlos Llancia (a 'strange mixture of kindliness and cruelty')[31] roared, ' "There has been enough drunkenness in this
Squadron. I will have no more of it, as you are going to see." Thereupon he
drove his fist into the face of one of them, knocking out most of his front
teeth and sending him spinning across the room to crash through two
ranks of men and collapse on the floor. Turning on the other he beat him
across the face with a riding crop until the man dropped half senseless to
the ground. He returned to his first victim, yanked him to his feet and laid
open his face with his crop, disregarding his screams, until he fell inert
beside his companion ... The two culprits were hauled, sobbing, to their
feet to have a half-pint of castor oil forced down their throats.'[32]

Maqueda, the adjoining town to Santa Olalla, fell to Yagüe's troops on
21 September. The road to Madrid lay before them to the north-east, Toledo
to the east. Although Mola's troops, experiencing difficulties on the Madrid
front, were anxiously awaiting the arrival of the African army, Franco
became obsessively preoccupied with the besieged garrisons of Toledo and
Santa María de la Cabeza. The emotional significance of sieges for General
Franco had been amply demonstrated during the Moroccan campaign.

Perhaps, as Theweleit suggests, at some level Franco may have associated Toledo (and indeed all castles) with a 'pure high-born woman'.[33] Such an association is indicated in *Raza* when José observes to his mother that the stones of Toledo 'don't just speak to us of war-like episodes and religious events but also of joy of feminine *dolores*' (which could be taken to mean menstrual pains). He tells a tale in which the terrified wife of Alfonso XI watches the approach of the Arab armies from a turret. Although there were 'very few knights guarding the lady', the Arab host saluted 'the defence-less lady' and passed on. José also refers to an incident in which the wife of Pedro I of Castilla (his mother) was trapped in one of the dungeons while 'the king [his father] was enjoying his impure love with Doña Maria de Padilla'.[34]

Whatever Franco's psychological motivations, politically he had his feet firmly on the ground. Although of logistical importance neither to the Nationalists nor to the Republicans, the siege of the Alcázar in Toledo had become a mighty symbol of Nationalist heroism. Against the impassioned advice of most of his officers, Franco therefore made the unexpected military decision to divert his troops away from the poorly defended capital in order to liberate the besieged garrison in Toledo. Before the assault began, Franco removed an allegedly sick and exhausted Yagüe from command, either because he anticipated his opposition to this untimely diversion or because he needed his political support in his forthcoming bid to become Generalísimo. The fact that Yagüe was promoted to full colonel and brought back to Franco's headquarters in Cáceres confirms the second explanation. Varela was brought in from Andalusia to take command.

Although Franco's unpredictable and confusing behaviour was causing considerable consternation on the military front – particularly in Germany – politically it seemed to pay off. For wildly contradictory reasons, Kindelán, Nicolás Franco, Orgaz, Yagüe and Millán Astray formed a kind of political campaign staff to push for Franco to become Commander-in-Chief and then Chief of State. Millán was committed to a military dictatorship, Yagüe was hoping for a fascist state, Kindelán expected the restoration of the monarchy, and Nicolás – hardly a disinterested participant – was being encouraged by the Germans to get his brother elected. On 21 September, as Maqueda was being captured, the Junta de Defensa Nacional and a number of senior officers held an historic meeting to discuss the organisation of the Nationalist zone. Although all the generals apart from Cabanellas were in favour of a single command, the most senior officers had gradually been eliminated from taking over. When it came to the vote for a Generalísimo, Kindelán proposed Franco, who was elected: Mola and Queipo de Llano foolishly assumed that his elevation was a stop-gap arrangement for the duration of the war only. The Junta's failure publicly to announce Franco's election revealed a general lack of enthusiasm for this arrangement.

Possibly hoping that a victory in Toledo would focus their minds, three days later Franco ordered the three columns of the Moroccan army under the command of General Varela to swing away from Madrid and move eastwards to Toledo. Having cut off the road to Madrid, they then moved south against the city under Asensio, Castejón and Barrón. Frustrated at being diverted from the capital and enraged at the resistance of the increasingly well-organised Republican militiamen, the soldiers of the African army were in a particularly vengeful frame of mind. The exclusion, during the final push on the Alcázar, of correspondents who had so far been allowed to witness the bloodiest battles of the war did not bode well for Toledo's Republican inhabitants. On 27 September a particularly appalling massacre took place which left the streets literally running with blood. Footprints could be seen trailing through the carnage. The streets were strewn with the beheaded corpses of militiamen. According to Whitaker, Nationalist troops 'boasted of how grenades were thrown in among two hundred screaming and helpless men'[35] in the San Juan Bautista hospital. Justifying the blood-crazed brutality to an appalled American journalist, Webb Miller, a Francoist officer blithely explained, 'We are fighting an idea. The idea is in the brain, and to kill it we have to kill the man. We must kill everyone who has that "red" idea.'[36] A lot more blood would flow to achieve this end.

Whether or not Franco's decision to relieve the symbolic fortress was motivated by emotional or political factors, it is difficult to understand in purely military terms. It resulted in a fateful two-week delay in the assault on Madrid, which enabled the Republicans to reorganise the capital's defences and transformed a straightforward military operation into a protracted and costly siege. Perhaps Franco was wracked by ambivalence about going for the heart and soul of the motherland in Madrid before every potentially vengeful leftist had been killed. Perhaps, like Hitler during the Second World War, he was permanently suspended between yearnings for victory and self-destructive flirtations with disaster. Whatever his emotional motivations, Franco had a political agenda as well. Although of little benefit to the Nationalists, the diversion bought him more time to resolve the thorny issue of a single authority in the Nationalist zone, and secured a major propaganda coup along the way.

On the evening of 27 September, Franco, Yagüe and Millán Astray greeted a euphoric crowd from the balcony of the Palacio de los Golfines in Caceres. Although Franco's high, fluting voice floated away on the wind, Yagüe and

Millán Astray excitedly proclaimed that 'Our people, our army, guided by Franco, are on the way to victory.' The jubilant crowds chanted, 'Franco! Franco! Franco!' These wild scenes, which were extensively reported in the Nationalist press, temporarily doused German irritation with the 'extraordinary' and 'incomprehensible' delays that had provided such a fateful breathing space to the Republican government. They stipulated that they wanted 'everything ... concentrated in Franco's hands so that there may be a leader who can hold everything together'.[37]

Close to seizing the crown, however, their protégé began to prevaricate wildly. On 27 September, an irritable Yagüe snapped that unless Franco was more vigorous about taking overall control, the Legion would seek another candidate. Franco lunged alarmingly between omnipotent proclamations to Berlin that he wished 'to be looked upon not only as the saviour of Spain but also as the saviour of Europe from the spread of communism' and humble assurances that he had no desire to get mixed up in politics. Desperate to curry favour with the Führer, he nevertheless regularly insulted Berlin by ignoring German communications entirely.

Luckily for him, his support team were more focused. When a second meeting was called in Salamanca on 28 September to confirm his appointment, Franco's supporters laid on a symbolic guard of honour for the prince in waiting. By this time the proposals for Generalísimo had become considerably more wide ranging. Not only did Kindelán want the army, navy and air force to be brought under a single command, but he insisted that the post should carry the function of Chief of State 'as long as the war lasts', thereby terminating the Junta de Defensa Nacional. The unwilling members of the Junta finally passed a formal decree stating that Franco would 'assume all the powers of the new state'. There was, at Franco's behest, no mention of any time limit. While a jubilant Franco happily hailed 'the most important moment of my life', an irritable Queipo snapping something 'unprintable' about him, wearily concluded that 'We've got to go along with his game until we can block it.'[38] A despairing Cabanellas, on the other hand, declared, 'You don't know what you've just done because you don't know him like I do since I had him under my command in the African army ... If, as you wish, you give him Spain, he is going to believe that it is his and he won't let anyone replace him either during the war or after until he is dead.' As Vicente Guarner, a fellow cadet at Toledo and Africanista explained many years later, 'The position occupied by Franco is the nation and since he has no superior officer, he will not move from there.'[39]

Unfortunately for the Nationalists, however, the qualities that had made Franco such an exceptional soldier and sent him soaring up the military hierarchy – obedience, flexibility under fire and a self-destructive physical bravery – rendered him a less than impressive overall military commander. According to Norman Dixon, an effective commander needs to display unconventional ideas, a minimal need for the approval of others, concern for the welfare of their own men and respect for the enemy.[40] General Franco proved to be bereft of each and every one of these qualities. As with many authoritarian personalities, inhibited by a fear of failure and the anxiety that he would be blamed for any mistakes, he was ill at ease with the huge responsibilities that accompanied absolute military power.

Politically, however, Franco was more acute. As he had doubtless anticipated, his decision to divert the troops to Alcázar had brought him huge dividends. Cinema audiences around the world watched a filmed restaging of Franco, posing as one of the great warrior heroes of medieval Spain, inspecting the site of this 'glorious liberation'. On 30 September the Bishop of Salamanca portrayed the Republican zone as an earthly city, full of hatred, anarchy and communism, and the Nationalist zone as a celestial place filled with the love of God, heroes and martyrdom. Although the defence of the Church was hardly a central objective of the rebels' initial declaration of their aims in 1936, from the moment it became clear that the war would be a protracted affair the espousal of Christian rhetoric was seen as crucial. The commendation of the Church now helped them transform a fratricidal war into a Christian crusade. Under the guidance of Pius XII,[41] the Vatican was more than happy to help on this issue. Having blessed those who were defending 'the rights and honour of God against a wild explosion of forces so savage and cruel as to be well nigh incredible',[42] he openly compared the Christian heroism of the Nationalists with the barbarous atheism of the Republic. This provided Franco with the higher authority he needed, and helped secure international support for the Nationalist cause. In Britain, convinced that the Catholic Franco was 'a gallant Christian gentleman', many Conservative MPs exerted considerable influence upon the government to shunt British policy towards favouring the Nationalists. Within Spain itself, the fact that 'priests appeared on balconies with generals and blessed flags' helped transform a chaotic uprising which had defined itself in terms of a fragmented assortment of negatives (it was against communism and against anti-Spain) into an ideological and political monolith.[43]

With Franco now masquerading as the defender not just of Spain, but of the universal faith, much thought had to go into organising his ceremonial investiture as the new Chief of State in Salamanca on 1 October 1936. Orchestrated by Falangists who were keen to emulate Nazi propaganda, and sycophants vying for political preferment, it was an extraordinarily triumphalist and lavish occasion to mount at the very beginning of a civil war, the outcome of which was uncertain, and which was tearing Spain apart. Guards of honour and a huge and cheering crowd lined the streets. In the presence of Italian, German and Portuguese diplomats, Cabanellas formally pronounced Franco 'Head of the Government of the Spanish State' and reluctantly handed over 'the absolute powers of the state'. Overlooking the fact that three-fifths of Spain was still in Republican hands, an impassioned Franco urged the crowds who greeted him with their arms jubilantly raised in the fascist salute to 'be proud, you received a broken Spain and now you deliver up to me a Spain united in a unanimous and grandiose ideal'. He assured them – somewhat fancifully given his subsequent behaviour – 'that the steadiness of my hand will not waver and will always be firm' and, even more mendaciously, that 'We will ensure that there is no home without light nor a Spaniard without bread.' Later the same day, he firmly declared that 'The business of government will be entrusted to experts, not to politicians.'

One of Franco's first political actions as Head of State was to consolidate his relationship with Hitler, who immediately dispatched an emissary to congratulate the Generalísimo on his elevation, and to explain his reluctance to recognise the Nationalist government until after they had captured Madrid. The excited German representative reported back to Berlin on 'the cordiality with which Franco expressed his veneration for the Führer and Chancellor and his sympathy for Germany and the decided friendliness of my reception'. However, without an actual state to run, the new Jefe did not seem entirely sure what to do with his new-found authority. Given that the external trappings of power were much easier to create than the fundamental structure of the state, Franco now moved his headquarters to the absurdly grand Episcopal Palace in Salamanca, where splendidly attired Moorish guards stood like Roman statues, vigilantly protecting their leader. Visitors were required to wear morning suits. A monumental fascist-type propaganda machine ground into action, which portrayed Franco as an all-seeing political and military genius, and the term Caudillo – designed to match Führer and Duce – was adopted. The Nationalist newspapers carried the slogan 'Una Patria, Un Estado, Un Caudillo' (which closely echoed Hitler's 'Ein Volk, ein Reich, ein Führer'). Franco's picture appeared everywhere, on cinema screens and on the walls of shops, offices and schools.

For Franco – as for other fascist leaders – this massive propaganda machine helped him achieve politically what he was striving for personally: the total repression of anxieties and doubts, the projection of omnipotence. If he could not adjust his inner self to the requirements of reality, then reality had to be rewritten to accord with his needs. The mass orchestration of public adulation – including the introduction of the fascist salute, one of the most extreme forms of abeyance towards the authority of the leader[44] – could only inflame his sense of his own destiny. As with Stalin, however, 'the hero-image of himself went hand-in-hand with the villain-image of the enemy'.[45] The loftier Franco's position became, the more vigorously he had to project his feelings of inferiority and hatred on to the enemy, the more ruthlessly they had to be punished. Like the Führer, Franco had plenty of collaborators willing to operate the repression on a daily basis, enabling him to distance himself from the slaughter. Their complicity tied them to his fate: if he fell from power, they would be left to face their accusers.

After his investiture, Franco's fellow generals were swiftly allocated more mundane, military roles. General Orgaz was made High Commissioner in Morocco, Mola was given command of the newly formed Army of the North, which had now amalgamated with the Army of Africa, while Queipo de Llano commanded the Army of the South. Cabanellas was given the meaningless role of Inspector of the Army. Franco was less successful in his choice of political collaborators during those early days. Like the man himself, underneath the pomp and ceremony and the superficial trappings of authority and efficiency, the Nationalist political machinery was totally chaotic.

Despite his apparently strong views on obedience and discipline, Franco was inclined from the very start to overlook the damaging antics of his appointees. This was hardly surprising: although there were extremists on both sides of the spectrum in the civil war, in the Nationalist Zone they were running the regime. Franco misguidedly entrusted his indolent brother Nicolás with the task of creating a state infrastructure and a Francoist political party, which was to be separate from the Falange. Nicolás's propensity to turn up late for work, to take protracted lunches and extended boozy dinners and to keep his visitors waiting for hours enraged the punctilious Germans. His laid-back regime contrasted dramatically with that favoured by Millán Astray, whom Franco unwisely appointed as head of Press and Propaganda. A bully and a show-off, Millán's less than sophisticated grasp of propaganda would be exposed in May 1938, when he made the infantile boast to Ciano, the Italian Foreign Minister, that 'Our Caudillo spends fourteen hours at his desk and doesn't get up even to piss.' He ran his office much as he had the Spanish Legion, summoning unfortunate journalists with a whistle, shrieking hysterically at any misdemeanours, and threatening with execution any foreign correspondent who criticised the regime. Millán's main qualifications for his new role were a slavering adulation for his boss Franco, 'the greatest strategist of the century', his awed advice to prospective visitors that they were about to enter 'the presence of the voice of God' and a much vaunted enthusiasm for '¡la muerte!'[46] His enchantment with death did not strike an unusual chord in Nationalist Spain where, according to John Whitaker, 'The Franco Spaniards talked lovingly of death, fondling the word as if it were a woman, repellent yet seductive.'[47]

Millán's less than inspired choice of assistants did not help matters. The journalist Bolín – who had been rewarded for his role in organising the Dragon Rapide in London with an honorary captaincy – was placed in charge of the foreign press corps. Strutting around in his breeches and high boots, tapping a rifle he did not know how to load, he snarled at the terrified journalists, spat on the corpses of executed Republican prisoners, and resolved to shoot anybody whose reporting was not up to scratch. One of his subordinates, Ignacio Rosales, helpfully explained to the appalled foreign press that 'the masses cannot be taught . . . they need a touch of the whip for they are like dogs and will mind only the whip'.[48]

Press liaison in the north was put in the hands of the notorious Captain Gonzalo de Aguilera, whose startling (if honest) statements that 'We're going to kill and kill and kill' did little to win the international press corps to the cause. Although the press assumed that his endlessly quotable diatribes, delivered in upper-class English (he had been educated at Stonyhurst), constituted an idiosyncratic personal viewpoint, he was echoing the beliefs of his leader. He intrigued foreign commentators with his widely propounded views that the war had been started by the existence of sewers, without which 'all these Red leaders would have died in their infancy instead of exciting the rabble and causing good Spanish blood to flow'. Aguilera advocated a return to a 'healthier time spiritually [when] plague and pestilence used to slaughter the masses' and articulated his conviction that the regeneration of Spain required the extermination 'of a third of the male population of Spain'. Such notions were not unusual in Francoist Spain, nor was his attitude to women. Clearly speaking from the heart, he insisted that 'we'll be done with this nonsense of equality for women . . . If a man's wife is unfaithful to him, why he'll shoot her like a dog.'[49] The bizarre and extreme nature of the regime was symbolised by the fact that the new office for Press and Propaganda shared a building with a Hindu alchemist who had turned up in Salamanca and promised to make all the gold that Franco needed to win the war. Exposed as a fraud, he would, in due course, be forced to flee the country.[50]

Even in such extreme and indulgent conditions, Millán Astray still managed to go too far. On 12 October 1936 a ceremony took place to mark the Día la Raza, the anniversary of Christopher Columbus's 'discovery' of

America. After the statutory church service, political, military and ecclesiastical dignitaries transferred to the University of Salamanca where, in Franco's absence, the Rector of the University, the elderly philosopher Miguel de Unamuno, took the chair. Deeply upset at the arrest and assassination of friends and acquaintances, Unamuno was horrified when a particularly vehement Nationalist speech inspired a Legionnaire to shout '¡Viva la muerte!' This induced a knee-jerk reaction in Millán who, leaping to his feet, orchestrated frenzied Legionnaire chants glorifying the war among his entourage, who had turned up to the occasion armed with machine guns. The venerable philosopher's passionate denunciation of the war as 'uncivil' and his proclamation that 'to win [vencer] is not to convince [convencer], and it is necessary to convince and that cannot be done by the hatred which has no place for compassion' did not go down with the demented Legionnaires.[51] An incandescent Millán turned upon him, shrieking 'Death to intellectuals!' Although, as Franco's representative, Doña Carmen bravely took it upon herself to escort Unamuno away from the murderous mob, the elderly philosopher was removed from his post at the university. He died in December, still protesting about the 'collective madness' and the 'moral suicide of Spain'. Despite the fact that Franco heartily approved Millán's interventions with Unamuno – he was now assisted by the surreal and eccentric Ernesto Giménez Caballero, 'one of the ideological founders of Falangism' – in 1937 censorship was quietly passed to the Press and Propaganda Delegation in Burgos, run by Falangists. Although Millán remained a roving, raving propagandist for the regime, he would immerse his energies in forming the Tercio de Mutilados, an organisation glorifying those like him, whose exploits on the battlefield had left them bereft of sundry limbs, eyes and organs.

With his political situation more or less secure, Franco now turned his attention back to family matters. To the astonishment of Kindelán and his officers, he decided to dispatch his brother Ramón to head the Nationalist air forces in Mallorca. Whether, from his position of supreme power, Franco could afford to be magnanimous, or was relying upon Ramón's suicidal impulses to lead him into mortal danger, can only be guessed at. However, as their sister Pilar would later observe, Ramón's enthusiasm for flying on the most dangerous missions soon overcame the reservations of the other officers to his appointment and would – perhaps as Franco hoped – lead to his early death.

The completion of the new cruiser *Canarias* in El Ferrol at the end of September had greatly boosted the rebel cause. Given that, with fascist support, the Nationalists dominated the air as well, the war seemed as good as over. On 6 October 1936 an optimistic Franco therefore notified journalists of an impending assault on the capital. Mola's two-part assault on the capital, devised in communication with Franco, began the following day. The four columns of the exhausted Army of Africa, under the command of the impeccably dressed Varela (who allegedly never removed his white gloves or medals, even when sleeping) assisted by Yagüe, began to move northwards ready to meet Mola's troops moving down to the south. Despite Franco's enthusiastic prognostications about the march on Madrid, he seemed to be preoccupied more with breaking the siege of Oviedo, where the Asturian miners had penetrated the town, than with the drive on the capital. Between 4 and 6 November the Nationalist advance on Madrid slowed down considerably. Franco's lack of decisiveness on the Madrid front – which might have arisen from his anxiety that Mola would get the glory, and an underlying anxiety that it was the home not only of the legally constituted government and the exiled King but also, when not in El Ferrol, of his father – did not go unnoticed in Germany. While Franco engaged in acrimonious discussions with his military advisers about how best to proceed, Admiral Canaris and General Hugo Sperrle were dispatched to Salamanca to advise him that German reinforcements would only be provided under the command of a German officer, and on condition that they were used in the 'more systematic and active conduct of the war' on the Madrid front.

Despite these problems, it was widely assumed even by the Republican government, which withdrew to Valencia on 6 November, that Madrid would fall rapidly under this onslaught. Indeed, some foreign journalists, looking forward to a night off, fabricated precipitate reports of Franco's victory parade scheduled to take place on 7 November. Aguilera buoyantly predicted that 'We are going to shoot 50,000 in Madrid. And no matter where Azaña and Largo Caballero and all that crowd try to escape, we'll catch them and kill every last man.'[52] However, the first shipment of arms and equipment from the Soviet Union to the Republicans, which had arrived in Spain on 15 October, ensured that a very different kind of war was about to begin. The arrival of Soviet tanks and aircraft proved to be highly effective against the Army of Africa.

Although Stalin had subscribed with not inconsiderable relief to the farcical international policy of 'non-intervention' in the Spanish conflict, his attitude had changed when the arrival of the Italian bombers in Spanish Morocco indicated that the fascist signatories did not feel remotely constrained by the agreement. Unwilling to see either a fascist Spain putting pressure on France, or a communist one provoking the British or the French right into open hostility, Stalin dispatched what he hoped would be sufficient aid to keep the Republic alive, but no more. Ever the cynic, he exacted a huge price. The 'revolution' within the Republican zone would be crushed, and the Republican government required to hand over virtually its entire gold reserves to pay for Soviet supplies. He even fiddled the exchange rates to ensure that the beleaguered Republic paid well over the odds for Soviet equipment, which was often shoddy and out of date.[53] Nonetheless, without the support of the Soviet Union, the Republic would have foundered during the early months of the war. Furthermore, the Comintern, cognisant of the fervour with which workers all over Europe and the United States viewed events in Spain, set about recruiting and shipping volunteers to fight the Nationalists. Fired by a passionate hatred of fascism and a willingness to risk their lives in the battle against it, these men and women began to pour into Spain from October 1936. Their fervour greatly boosted morale and galvanised the Republican war effort. As John Whitaker put it, 'The Republicans, mauled and butchered by Moorish mercenaries and foreign air corps, suddenly felt that the Republic was no longer alone ... they believed that to die now was not to die in vain.'[54]

The Nationalist advance on Madrid, combined with Mola's boasts that a 'fifth column' of Francoist supporters within the capital would link up with the four columns advancing on the city, triggered an outburst of atrocities against Nationalist prisoners, who were removed from Madrid gaols and slaughtered. Falangists panicked about the welfare of their leader, José Antonio Primo de Rivera, who was still confined in a Republican gaol in Alicante. Unable to share their concerns, the Generalísimo made a singularly lacklustre, not to say actively obstructive, contribution to Falangist attempts to jump him from prison. Despite the best efforts of his supporters, José Antonio was put on trial and then shot on 20 November 1936. Although Franco was understandably reluctant to share this news with party activists, he unwittingly revealed his deep-seated jealousy of the Falangist leader when in 1937 he notified Serrano Suñer that 'They've handed him over to the Russians and it is possible that they've castrated him' – perhaps as he himself wished to. Although politically Franco had a vested interest in perpetuating the mythological political heritage of José Antonio, he was profoundly jealous of the heartfelt support that the romantic and attractive Falangist leader inspired among the party faithful.

The removal of yet another rival did little to focus the Generalísimo's mind. Franco now compounded the error of diverting to Toledo, by hesitating for two fateful days to discuss tactics with General Wilhelm Faupel, the newly arrived German chargé d'affaires, and waiting for the arrival of guns, bombers and tanks. The Republicans used the time well. The defence of the capital was put in the hands of General José Miaja. Although Franco scornfully dismissed him as incompetent, and Queipo de Llano called him inept, stupid and cowardly, he surrounded himself with highly competent assistants, including his outstanding Chief of Staff, Lieutenant-Colonel Vicente Rojo, Franco's erstwhile colleague, who had – to Franco's fury – remained loyal to the Republic. Despite crippling concerns about how their random collection of arbitrarily armed irregulars would perform in battle, Varela's decision to rest his troops and further delay the assault on the capital gave Miaja and Rojo the chance they needed. Not only did they find Varela's detailed battle plan in a captured Nationalist tank – information they used to very good effect during the battle – but during the eerily silent night of 7 November they managed to pull the ordinary citizens of Madrid into a coherent fighting force.

Although the Army of Africa had experienced little difficulty in launching frontal attacks on largely undefended villages and towns in the countryside, they were not so well equipped to engage in urban warfare against a very different kind of enemy. Led by the highly organised Communist Fifth Regiment and the 1900 men of the Eleventh International Brigade, the people of Madrid fought a desperate battle for the capital. Fighting with their backs to its walls, armed with anything they could get hold of, the working-class militias managed to impose massive casualties on the Army of Africa. The arrival in Madrid of the legendary Durruti, a railway worker from Leon whose force of volunteer anarchists had helped safeguard Barcelona, further heartened the Republicans, even though he was killed in battle under suspicious circumstances on 20 November.

Although German and Italian recognition of the Nationalists on 18 November 1936 fleetingly lifted Franco's spirits, the military situation was far from happy. While Franco assured the cheering crowds that Nazi Germany and fascist Italy were 'the bulwarks of culture, civilisation and Christianity in Europe', a scornful Mussolini bemoaned the lack of spirit and bravery of the Spanish troops. The derisive Duce directed that reinforcements would be provided only if Spanish policy in the Mediterranean was 'in harmony with that of Italy'. He was keen for a fascist Spain to put pressure on France.

On the Madrid front, however, even the German Condor Legion – a force of 4000 men and a hundred aircraft supported by anti-aircraft and anti-tank units, under the command of Major-General von Sperrle and Colonel von Richthofen – failed to save the situation. Despite the systematic onslaught of these special units which were keen to experiment with terror bombing, and moderate success for Mola around the University City, by 22 November the Nationalist attack was repulsed. As John Whitaker starkly observed: 'The unyielding and unending Republican resistance took the starch out of Franco's troops ... the steam went out of Franco's punch ...

Lying in scooped-out ditches, Franco's Moors died by the thousands.' Franco had little army left. While Captain Roland von Strunk, Hitler's special agent in Spain, pronounced that 'Franco is finished', a dispirited Major Castejón announced, 'We who made this revolt, now we are beaten.'⁵⁵ Without a massive injection of foreign aid, and the arrival of thousands more Moorish troops, Franco would lose the war.

Given his terror of failure, Franco's feelings at having to abandon the assault on the capital can be surmised. His worst nightmares had come true. He had challenged the heart of the motherland, and he had failed. Enraged and humiliated by this setback, he refused to withdraw to easily defended lines a few kilometres outside the capital, and directed Asensio to fortify his positions in the University City. He would not countenance even small-scale retreats, even though they would release troops for other fronts.

Faupel dispatched a despairing telegram to Berlin stating 'We are now faced with the decision either to leave Spain to herself or to throw in additional forces.' As the American ambassador to Berlin pointed out, having 'recognised Franco as conqueror when this has yet to be proved, Mussolini and Hitler must see to it that he is successful or be associated with a failure'. The Axis powers decided to provide additional support, albeit with Italy bearing the brunt of the responsibility, since Berlin feared that German intervention might jeopardise its plans for rearmament. General Roatta was given command of all Italian and air forces already in Spain, and the ones about to arrive, and was directed to liaise with Franco and Faupel to create a joint headquarters.

The arrival of massive Italian aid in the form of officers, NCOs, specialist tank crews, radio operators, artillerymen and engineers, who were incorporated into mixed brigades of Spanish and Italian troops, was followed in December 1936 by two further contingents of 3000 Blackshirts, complete with their own officers, artillery and transport. Frustrated by Franco's outmoded military tactics, Mussolini insisted that the new arrivals be kept quite separate from the mixed brigades. Although the Caudillo was deeply offended by this directive, he was forced to swallow his pride in January 1937 and request a further 9000 Blackshirts. By mid-February 1937 he had received nearly 50,000 fascist militiamen and regular troops masquerading as volunteers. The Germans agreed to provide sufficient support in the form of aircraft, arms and equipment to ensure that Franco was not defeated. Ironically, it was this massive escalation in aid from the Axis powers, taken because of Franco's shortcomings as a military leader, which would help him win the war. There were other benefits. Convinced by the Germans that mass conscription was needed to expand the Nationalist forces into a large-scale modern army, Franco directed General Orgaz to organise this operation.

Seemingly impotent on the military front, and full of paranoid fears after the setback in Madrid, Franco moved to consolidate his political position. In Nationalist Spain rivalry emanated from the Falange, Carlists, monarchists and opponents within the army. With the Falange disorientated by the veil of secrecy with which Franco had shrouded their leader's death, Franco struck out at the Carlists who had, with Mola's permission, established a separate military academy for the technical and ideological training of Carlist officers. Claiming that this was the equivalent of a *coup d'état*, Franco gave their leader, Manuel Fal Conde, forty-eight hours to leave the Nationalist zone or face a court martial.

The biggest political threat, however, remained the monarchy. Although Franco was determined to prevent Don Juan becoming a replacement figurehead for the Alfonsine monarchists, his attitude to the Crown was always complicated. Just as Franco's political and military motivations drew on a bewildering array of conscious and unconscious impulses, so did his attitude to the Spanish monarch. He appears to have viewed King Alfonso XIII partly as an idealised father-figure, for whom he had briefly been the favoured son, and partly as an irresponsible parent, who had abandoned both him and the Spanish people. This split perception resulted in him delivering a stream of heartfelt but contradictory pronouncements on the monarchy. Suspended between a genuine commitment to the abstract notion of a king, and a virulent personal jealousy of his rival Don Juan, Franco was able to convince people in very different camps that he vigorously espoused their cause. He sought to persuade the monarchists that the restoration of the monarchy was a major priority, and the Falangists that as the champion of their revolution he was determined to prevent the reinstatement of a king at all costs. When, in December 1936, Don Juan renewed his attempt to join the Nationalist war effort, he therefore received a charming if cunningly ambiguous letter back from Franco stating that it was in the interests of neither the heir to the throne nor the *Patria* for him to risk his life. Franco then notified anxious monarchists that he only had the Prince's best interest at heart, and was determined to ensure that a returning monarch should 'come as a peace-maker and should not be found among the victors'.

In fact, Franco would far rather have the Pope validate his authority than a Spanish monarch who might win the hearts of the people and displace him as the alleged moral and spiritual leader of Spain. The return, on 22 December, of Cardinal Gomá from Rome as the Vatican's confidential chargé d'affaires – the first step towards full diplomatic recognition by the

Catholic Church – was a welcome diversion. Franco's efforts to consolidate his position on the battlefront were less successful. Madrid remained locked in a desperate stalemate. A frantic Franco directed Orgaz to take over the troops on the Madrid front, and Mola those in the north. Varela commanded in the field. Although the ravaged Republican forces were solidly dug in, luckily for the Generalísimo they were unable to launch a counter-attack against the seriously extended Nationalist front line. After much prevarication, and still refusing to allow a tactical retreat, Franco was finally persuaded to implement the proposal that General Saliquet had outlined the previous November for an encircling operation against the Madrid–Corunna road to the north-west, with a dual thrust from the south-west and the north-east. After some costly bloody encounters, and the replacement of the wounded Varela with Orgaz, this operation resulted in the Nationalists stabilising the fronts on 15 January 1937. Both sides lost around 15,000 men during this operation.

Meanwhile, Mussolini, frustrated by the deadlock in the capital and hungry for a bit of personal kudos, was pushing for a lightning advance on Malaga. Uneasy about the Duce's quest for personal glory, Franco hesitantly agreed to a combined assault upon Malaga, with Roatta advancing on land, and Queipo directing the bombardment of the city from the battleship *Canaris*. Marvelling at Franco's naivety about Mussolini's plans, Colonel Wolfram von Richthofen, Chief of Staff of the Condor Legion, noted in his diary that if Franco hoped 'for a share of the Malaga victory laurels', he should have informed himself of what the Italians were up to. Franco, who was keen for a triumph in Madrid, finally visited the front in early February. Reassured that Malaga would fall without much of a fight, he returned to Salamanca to oversee a new push on the capital. On 6 February 1937, an army of nearly 60,000 well-equipped men, under the direction of General Orgaz, had launched a huge attack through the Jarama valley towards the Madrid–Valencia highway to the east of the capital.

The battle for Malaga, launched three days earlier, was brief and brutal. Foreign journalists were, ominously, excluded. Arriving first on 8 February, the Italians flamboyantly ruled the city for a while before ostentatiously handing it over to Queipo. Keen to reinforce the idea that they arrived first, General Roatta dispatched a telegram to the Caudillo stating that 'Troops under my command have the honour to hand over the city of Malaga to Your Excellency.' In Malaga neither the Nationalists troops nor the Italians showed much mercy towards the demoralised and much depleted Republicans. Four thousand Republicans were shot in the first week alone. The killings continued on a large scale for months.

Franco was infuriated that the Italians were taking the credit for this great victory. He sharply reminded an insensitively jubilant Millán that 'a great deal remains to be conquered!' While Franco sulked about the Italian success, and Mussolini congratulated himself on the vast superiority of his troops, the Nationalist press implied that the victory was due neither to the Italians nor to Queipo, but to the direct intervention of St Teresa of Avila, whose hand – they mendaciously claimed – had been found in the luggage of the defeated military commander of Malaga. This was a much more palatable explanation for the Generalísimo, who thereafter never relinquished this particular holy relic. With St Teresa and the saints on his side, Franco's spirits soared once more. Determined to curtail the burgeoning ambitions of both the Italians and Queipo, he prohibited a further advance in Andalusia, claiming that he wished to concentrated on Madrid. According to Hugh Thomas, this was a major tactical error as the rest of eastern Andalusia, including Almería, would probably have fallen into the Nationalists hands fairly easily.[56]

Keen to eclipse the Italian triumph in Malaga with his own victory in the capital, Franco did not take at all kindly to the suggestion of Roatta's deputy, Colonel Emilio Faldella, that the Italians use their Corpo di Truppe Volontarie (CTV) to push for a rapid victory in Valencia. Fadella earned himself a protracted lecture from the Caudillo about how the 'systematic occupation of territory accompanied by the necessary purge is preferable to a rapid rout of the enemy armies which leaves the country still infested with enemies'. The unfortunate Italian officer was then coldly reminded by Franco's Chief of General Staff, Lieutenant-Colonel Antonio Barroso, that 'The Generalísimo's prestige is the most important thing in the war ... it is absolutely unacceptable that Valencia, the seat of the Republican Government, should be occupied by foreign troops.' When Faldella suggested that a major push be launched from Sigüenza to Guadalajara under General Roatta in order to close the circle around Madrid, a non-committal Franco airily notified him that he would use the Italian forces 'spread out over several fronts'. Determined to make his displeasure with the Italians crystal clear, Franco kept the new Italian ambassador, Roberto Cantalupo, waiting for several days before receiving him. On 17 February the incredulous ambassador reported to the Italian Foreign Minister, Count Galeazzo Ciano, that 'Here, the coin of gratitude circulates hardly at all.'

An extremely truculent Mussolini threatened to withdraw his support completely, but then contented himself with redirecting twenty fighter aircraft promised to Franco straight to the Italian command in Spain. Air force units that had previously flown under the Generalísimo's orders were now answerable direct to Rome. Meanwhile, the Nationalist advance ground to a bloody halt in the Jarama where the Republican troops, reinforced by the International Brigade, found themselves engaged in some of the most vicious fighting of the entire civil war. Ten thousand Republicans, including some of the most experienced British and American members of the Brigades, and about 7000 Nationalists lost their lives. Although Orgaz and Varela managed to hang on to the precarious line at the Jarama, the advance on Madrid had once more collapsed.

On 19 February, Franco was ignominiously forced to plead with a singularly unreceptive Faldella to launch his previously scorned offensive on Guadalajara in order to provide much needed distraction for his exhausted troops. By this stage, neither Faldalla nor Roatta was inclined to rush to the Generalísimo's support. With the Italians stalling, Franco felt it might be advisable to lay on a lavish ceremony for the new Italian ambassador. On 1 March he presided over an occasion in which military bands, splendid processions and a sumptuous reception amidst a court of army officers in full-dress uniform took place. However, the underwhelmed ambassador reported to Rome that when the Generalísimo greeted the wildly cheering crowd from the balcony, he 'was incapable of saying anything to the people that applauded and waited to be harangued; he had become cold, glassy and feminine again'.[57]

The split between the regal excesses on display in Salamanca and the relentless and unrestrained slaughter behind the lines seemed to mirror the tortured workings of Franco's mind. The Italians were horrified by the accounts they were receiving from the Italian Consul in Malaga, where the activities of Carlos Arias Navarro – who would, many years later, be reviled by Francoists as a dangerously moderate Prime Minister – had earned him the name of 'the butcher of Malaga'. After protesting to the Italians that the massacres were being carried out by 'uncontrolled elements', Franco directed that random killings be replaced by summary executions after *ad hoc* courts martial. Although Franco reluctantly agreed to comply with the code of military justice which demanded that all death sentences be signed by him personally, the numbers involved rendered this a less than meticulous operation. Indolently flicking through sheaves of paperwork, he displayed a chilling nonchalance, or a burning vengefulness, depending on his mood. Like Hitler, he was particularly inclined to specify execution by garrotte. (In July 1944 Hitler would order that the generals who had conspired against him be 'hung on a meathook and slowly strangled to death with piano wire, the pressure being periodically released to intensify his death agonies' – an event he had filmed and watched obsessively.) Having blithely assured Randolph Churchill that his policy was characterised by 'humane and equitable clemency', Franco turned his attention back to military matters.

After much prevarication and feet-dragging by the Italians, on 8 March,

Franco finally directed that three enormous, heavily equipped Italian divisions gather for the main attack on Guadalajara under the overall
command of Roatta, flanked by two smaller Spanish brigades under the
command of general Moscardó. Franco assured Roatta that they would be
supported by a north-eastern push headed by Orgaz from the Jarama. To
the astonishment of the over-confident Italians, their much vaunted
advance was fiercely repulsed by the Republicans, who had brought massive
reinforcements up from the strangely quiet Jarama front. Franco's failure
to give orders for the supporting attack under Orgaz and Varela from the
south until the Italians were well into the battle left the Italians' overextended lines seriously exposed. Even then it was not the full-scale assault
the Italians were expecting. Franco's refusal either to fulfil his promise for
the attack from Jarama or to relieve Roatta's troops, which were getting
battered in the front line, makes no military sense. Although it is possible
that he wanted the Italians to take the brunt of the action while his own
troops enjoyed a much needed respite, or that he assumed, after all their
boasting, that the Duce's invincible troops would have no trouble in wiping
out the Republicans, it is difficult to avoid the conclusion that he was
motivated by personal pique. This impression was consolidated when
Franco stonily refused to heed Roatta's desperate requests that he be allowed
to withdraw his freezing, battered and thoroughly dispirited troops from
the assault. Claiming that the Republic was 'militarily and politically
on the verge of defeat', an implacable Franco steadfastly insisted that the
Italians renew their attack on Guadalajara on 19 March.

   As the date drew near, an increasingly distraught Roatta travelled back
and forth between the battlefront and Salamanca to try and persuade the
Generalísimo to change his mind. The day before the proposed assault,
while the two men were engaged in a heated debate on the subject in
Salamanca, the Republicans launched an enormous counter-attack against
the poorly defended Italians on the battlefront. Franco and his Nationalist
forces received news of this military setback with mixed emotions. Clearly
delighted at the humiliation of the swaggering Italian troops, they could
not ignore the fact that this was a monumental disaster. General Roatta,
reluctant to acknowledge his own deficiencies during this military engagement, held Franco entirely responsible for the setback. While the shortcomings of the Italian troops played a significant role, the main problem
seemed to lie with Franco. Despite his complacent conviction that 'success,
after all, is found where there is the intelligent expertise of the commander,
the bravery of the troops and faith', his defects as a general were seriously
exposed during this campaign. He under-estimated the enemy, failed to
implement a pre-agreed plan of action, displayed no concern for loss of life

among his supposed allies and then, in an attempt to scatter blame far and wide, sought out scapegoats among his subordinates. According to Norman Dixon, such behaviour is a text-book display of military incompetence.[58] No wonder, as John Whitaker notes, 'Among the officers who commanded his columns in the field Franco was neither popular nor trusted.'[59]

Pondering his military options, the Generalísimo was not in a particularly receptive frame of mind when a news item in the *Daily Express* entitled 'Another Italian rout in Spain' was brought to his attention. Noel Monks, the unfortunate journalist responsible for violating strict Nationalist censorship rules prohibiting the mention of Italian or German troops in Spain, let alone military routs, was ominously extracted from a cinema by a member of the Civil Guard, and frog-marched to account for his actions to the Caudillo himself. He later recalled that General Franco was

paunchy even then, on this day in March 1937, when I stood before him. For the leader of a military revolt that had now been going on for nearly nine months, he was the most unmilitary figure I have ever seen. He seemed dominated by the massive desk he was sitting at. His face was flabby, and the eyes that glared into mine would have made good tors for a game of marbles, they seemed so hard.[60]

Having threatened to put Noel Monks in front of a firing squad, suspecting that this might provoke an international backlash, Franco expelled him from the Nationalist zone instead. This was a decision Franco would bitterly regret. Monks ended up reporting from the Republican zone, and was one of four foreign journalists who arrived in a still burning Guernica immediately after the assault, where they talked to the survivors.[61]

There were, however, some personal benefits for Franco out of the Guadalajara fiasco (or, as Ciano later put it 'my worst day').[62] Although Mussolini remained unconvinced by the Caudillo's feeble excuses, he was forced to acknowledge that his fascist troops were not the unbeatable force he had assumed. Determined not to leave Spain until he had re-established his military credentials and reversed the humiliation, Mussolini reluctantly conceded that henceforth Italian forces would be distributed in Spanish units and subject to the command of Franco's generals. 'Freed from a nightmare', a euphoric General Franco delivered a grovelling message to the Duce at his 'joy at being understood and appreciated'.

Meanwhile, Mola's Chief of General Staff, Colonel Juan Vigón Suerodiaz, had written to Kindelán begging him to persuade Franco to turn his attentions to the north, where the seizure of the coal, iron and steel reserves and the armaments factories of the Basque provinces would be a huge boost to the Nationalists. This argument was backed by the commander of the

Condor Legion, General Hugo Sperrle, who was pushing for a co-ordinated ground/air operation in this area. This shift in emphasis 'represented a stern realisation that Madrid could not be immediately taken, and that the war could not be won quickly'.[63] It was beginning to look as though Franco did not want it to finish before he had killed every 'Red' in Spain.

CHAPTER 5

Mental Fragmentation, Physical Annihilation, Political Unification

March 1937–March 1939

all Nationalist Spaniards would rather die than place the fate of Spain once more in the hands of a Red or a democratic government

Franco, to Faupel[1]

Men believe in the truth of all that is seen to be strongly believed ... all great deceivers ... are overcome by their belief in themselves, and it is this belief which then speaks so persuasively, so miracle-like to the audience.

Alan Bullock

On 23 March 1937, Franco summoned Mola to Salamanca to hammer out the operational details of the assault on Bilbao. These were based in large part on the proposals put forward by Mola's Chief of General Staff, Colonel Juan Vigón Suerodiaz and General Hugo Sperrle, commander of the German Condor Legion. It was agreed that attacks would proceed 'without taking into account the civilian population'. Back-up air support for Mola's large army would be provided by the Condor Legion and the Italian CTV, which would be successfully integrated into the Spanish units once Roatta and Faldella were replaced by General Ettore Bastico and Colonel Gastone Gambara in April. Although the Condor Legion was directly responsible to Franco, he was sufficiently impressed with Sperrle's deferential manner to allow him to liaise directly with Mola and Vigón. Continuous and rapid liaison would be maintained between the headquarters of Mola's ground forces and the Condor Legion.

Mola's offensive began on 31 March. Driven by the conviction that Spain was dominated by the 'totally sick' industries of Catalonia and the Basque country, Mola determined to destroy these and eliminate as many rebellious and difficult industrial workers as he could along the way. He bombarded the traumatised local population with leaflets and broadcasts threatening to 'raze Vizcaya to the ground, beginning with the industries of war'.[2] Such threats perplexed the Germans, who had assumed that the main objective of the operation was to gain the northern industrial capacity for Nationalist use. An incredulous Condor Legion's Chief of Staff, Wolfram von Richthofen – rather misguidedly, given Hitler's subsequent and self-defeating policy of annihilation – protested that 'I have never in my life heard such lunacy.'³

Franco and Mola's confidence that the entire north of Spain would fall within three weeks proved to be wholly misplaced: they had seriously under-estimated the determination of the retreating Basques, who imposed high casualties on the attacking forces. The Germans, keen to display their military superiority to the Italians, and anxious to develop their new techniques of co-ordinated ground and air attack, were, as always, deeply frustrated by the slow progress of the Nationalist troops. However, in due course the terror provoked by the artillery and aerial bombardment, and the chaos induced by political divisions within the Republican zone, began to erode Basque resistance.

Back in Salamanca, during the early days of the attack Franco, swinging back and forth on an increasingly wide emotional continuum, attempted to combat internal anxieties about possible failure in the war with increasingly extravagant displays of pomp and power. His convoluted attempts to justify the Nationalists' slow and cumbersome advance to the Italian ambassador, Cantalupo, reveal more about his own mental state than about military matters. In a neurotic dialogue with himself, he assured the frankly astonished ambassador that his concern for the well-being of the *Patria* meant that 'I must not exterminate an enemy nor destroy cities, nor fields, nor industries nor production. That is why I cannot hurry.' He then unwittingly revealed his neurotic sub-agenda by admitting that, although it slowed down the military operation, 'the slow task of redemption and pacification' was essential, for it 'will bring me less glory but greater internal peace'. In a nervous attempt to justify his war of annihilation against the Catholic Basques, he insisted that 'Franco does not make war on Spain but is merely carrying out the liberation of Spain.' His erratic homily to himself concluded with the statement that 'in sum, I must not conquer but liberate and liberating also means redeeming'. Unfortunately for the Basques, the Generalísimo's idea of redemption arose from hatred and destruction, and not through Christian love and forgiveness: he knew they could never forgive him. That was why he had to kill them.

As was so often the case, the tortuous workings of Franco's psyche ran alongside an apparently clear-headed political agenda. He needed to curb the Italians' enthusiasm for a swift victory so that he could buy time to perpetuate his power after the war. Thus he determined to 'occupy Spain town by town, village by village, railway by railway', and would not 'shorten the war by even one day'. Apparently thinking out loud, he openly acknowledged that 'It could be dangerous for me to reach Madrid with a stylish military operation ... first I must have the certainty of being able to found a regime.'[4]

During this encounter with Cantalupo, Franco exposed profound feelings of guilt and a real terror of punishment. Perhaps these derived from anxieties about attacking Catholics: after all, his mother had been one. Perhaps he was afraid of divine retribution. His strenuous attempts to convince himself and others that, with God and the Pope on his side, he could not possibly be guilty of anything would be put under significant strain in the Basque country.

If – as seems to be the case – at some level Franco associated the *Patria* (or, as it is more formally known, the *Madre-Patria*) with his mother, his desire to be physically fused with her, and yet to destroy her, was never more starkly exposed. Just as Hitler seems to have confused the German nation with his mother's cancerous body and himself with a surgeon who had to 'burn down to the raw flesh the ulcers of this poisoning of the well of our domestic life',[5] so did Franco. Many of Franco's collaborators were caught up in this incestuous fantasy. Giménez Caballero (a propagandist for the Nationalists) viewed Franco as 'the phallus that will penetrate Spain', who 'placed himself into Spain's insides ... to the point that it is impossible to know today whether Spain is Franco or Franco is Spain'.[6] In 1938 he wrote 'We've seen [Franco] leaning over a map of Spain operating on the living body of Spain with the urgency and tragedy of a surgeon who operates on his own daughter, on his own mother, on his own beloved wife.' He lovingly described how 'Franco's tears fall on the body of this mother ... that is Spain while over his hands runs the blood and the sorrow of the sacred body in spasms.'[7] The consequences of his surgery were devastating.

The Germans were clearly keen on a bit of surgery of their own. Having established a blockade at sea, the Condor Legion dropped a deluge of bombs in the town of Durango on the road between Bilbao and the front. By 24 April the merciless air bombardment and artillery pounding began to drive the Basques back in some disarray. In constant communication with each other, Colonel Wolfram von Richthofen and Vigón agreed that the retreating Basque forces should be bottled up around Guernica and Marquina. Franco was kept closely informed of the co-ordinated advance. Richthofen then organised a series of bombing attacks against the retreating Basque forces, which culminated in a massive bombardment of the small town of Guernica, where an influx of refugees and peasants for market day had swelled the local population to over 10,000 people. Between 4.40 and

7.45 in the late afternoon of 26 April, the tiny, defenceless town was virtually razed to the ground. One thousand six hundred and forty-five people were killed, and nearly a thousand wounded. The total destruction of this ancient capital of the Basque country by German bombers was later immortalised in Picasso's painting.

In the wake of international outrage, a highly defensive Franco delivered particularly fragmented and contradictory accounts of what had taken place. None of them accorded with those of the townspeople or foreign journalists who arrived shortly after the bombing took place. In the first instance, he directed his foreign press service heatedly to deny that the bombing had taken place at all, and to insist that there were no German planes operating in Spain. Having conceded that Guernica had indeed been destroyed, he then claimed that 'The Reds took advantage of the [Italian and German] bombing to set fire to the town.' Finally, having accepted that the town had been laid to waste by the Germans, he implied that they had been operating without his knowledge. His vigorous commendation of the actions of Sperrle and Richthofen, his refusal to instigate a detailed investigation of the atrocity, and his failure to insist that the German commanders be recalled to Berlin, as he would have done had he really suspected insubordination, all imply total complicity.

With Guernica reduced to a pile of rubble and his international reputation in shreds, Franco turned his attention back to safeguarding his political position in Spain. Although politically the Nationalist zone did not match the chaotic divisiveness of the Republican zone, the situation was by no means straightforward. The optimistic assumptions of Franco and his brother Nicolás that the passage of time and a military victory – which was, at that stage, by no means certain – would be sufficient to consolidate the Generalísimo's power were beginning to look somewhat naive. While Nicolás was taking somewhat haphazard responsibility for foreign matters, the south remained a virtually independent fiefdom under Queipo, and there were rumours that Mola aspired to be head of government and leave the running of the war to Franco. Furthermore, political rivalries between the main parties – the Falange, *Renovación Española*, the Carlists and the CEDA – were now bursting to the fore. Although they had all collaborated in the military conspiracy, had a powerful vested interest in victory and aspired to the construction of an authoritarian corporatist state, they all nurtured differing and competing ambitions about the exact nature of the regime. The monarchists wanted the restoration of a military monarchy similar to that which had operated under Primo de Rivera, the Carlists wanted a virtual theocracy under their own pretender, and the Falangists were keen for a Spanish equivalent of the Third Reich. With the bulk of militias pouring into the new mass army being fed by differing and competing political groups whose primary allegiance was not necessarily to Franco, something needed to be done to streamline his power-base.

Uniting the various political forces in the Nationalist zones into a fascist-style, single party, with Franco as its sole leader, was now a priority. Diffusing the political power of the different parties and absorbing them into a monolothic state party under Franco's leadership without triggering a popular backlash among their supporters was clearly going to be difficult. The combination of Franco's chameleon-like qualities and Serrano Suñer's sharp legal mind would greatly facilitate a complex political process.

The unification of the Nationalist coalition had already been abetted by the timely death or political emasculation of the leaders of all the main political parties. Calvo Sotelo, the influential monarchist politician, had been assassinated five days before the uprising. José Antonio Primo de Rivera, the charismatic leader of the Falange, was executed by the Republic on 20 November 1936. Gil Robles, leader of the CEDA, blamed for his legalist tactic before the rebellion – and unacceptable to Franco because he had once been the Caudillo's boss – was increasingly cold-shouldered in Nationalist Spain. As Franco had already dealt with the Carlists by expelling their leader, Manuel Fal Conde, the biggest popular and political threat to Franco's plans was now the Falange.

After the death of its leader, the Falange had split into two groups: those who supported the party's designated successor, Manuel Hedilla, and those who followed the *legitimista* group, primarily friends and associates of José Antonio Primo de Rivera, led by Augustín Aznar and Sancho Dávila. Hedilla's provocative pronouncement that he preferred 'repentant Marxists' to 'cunning rightists corrupted by politics and *caquismo*' did not endear him to his critics. His brash boast to the Germans and the Italians that the Falange would only tolerate Franco being Head of State for the duration of the war soon reached the Caudillo's ears. If there was one thing the Generalísimo would not tolerate, it was implied slurs on his omnipotence.

Serrano Suñer and Franco easily outmanoeuvred the guileless Hedilla, the new leader of the Carlists, the languid and moderate Conde de Rodezno and numerous leading monarchists, convincing each of them that they would play a pivotal role within a single party, but only if they supported him. After preliminary talks with the various elements in the Nationalist camp, Franco withdrew from direct negotiations, leaving everybody to try and gauge what was going on, and nervously adapt their positions accordingly. Although Franco remained closely involved in political developments, he was happy to allow Serrano Suñer to be the main architect of the single party and later of the Francoist state, and to use him as 'the lightning conductor'[8] for jealousies and discontent. Recognising that Franco's personal power had to be underpinned by a formal state structure fed by popular political support, Serrano Suñer immediately set about mobilising this. He attempted, along the way, to educate his politically instinctive but largely unsophisticated brother-in-law in the finer art of politics. In fact, Franco's peasant cunning and psychopathic tendencies were much more in tune with the Nationalist mentality than his intellectual brother-in-law, who inspired considerable political and personal mistrust among many of Franco's supporters.

Although, for the moment, Franco sensed that he would need his articulate brother-in-law to safeguard his power, and perhaps looked to him for support and guidance, personal suspicion would soon impinge upon the 'dream ticket' itself. Profoundly jealous of his upper-class background, good looks and urbane ways, Franco would turn upon Serrano Suñer once he had outgrown his political usefulness. He had to move carefully, however. Doña Carmen was delighted when the feckless Nicolás Franco was displaced as her husband's favourite by her charming brother-in-law. However, although she was content to have his wife – her younger sister Zita – live a subordinate lifestyle in a tiny apartment in the attic of her own lavish residence in Salamanca after her traumatic escape from Madrid, this would later change.

On the political front, an internal civil war in the Falange, in which both sides armed their supporters in a bid to take over the party by force, provided Franco's headquarters with the perfect justification for a military intervention and take-over by the Generalísimo. In Salamanca on 16 April the *legitimistas*, under Aznar, made the first move, deposing Hedilla from the leadership. Hedilla retaliated by sending a group of his men to seize the party headquarters and arrest Aznar and his followers. During the ensuing battle, two Falangists were shot dead. Although, when Hedilla was elected Jefe Nacional of the Falange on 18 April, he considered himself to be the victor, his jubilation was short-lived. When he rushed to tell Franco the joyous news, the Generalísimo bundled him on to a balcony, where he triumphantly announced the fusion of the Falange and the Carlists to a conveniently awaiting crowd and array of radio microphones. Clasping the leader of the Falange in a warm embrace, he gave the crowds the overwhelming impression that Hedilla was handing over his powers of leadership to Franco.

On 19 April, Franco's political triumph was enshrined in the formal decree of unification, in which the Falange, the Carlists, the CEDA and the *Renovación Española* were merged in a single, if not economically titled, party, the Falange Española Tradicionalista y de las Juntas de Ofensiva Nacional Sindicalista (FET y de las JONS). Sometimes known as the Falange, the new single party also came to be called the Movimiento. Franco was named as sole leader. Army officers made it quite clear that all political parties had now fallen under military control, and that the FET y de las JONS was subject to the political authority of the Generalísimo. The local sections of both the Falange and the Carlists were ordered 'to orient their current propaganda towards the integration of the Movimiento and the exaltation of the Caudillo'.[9] As Generalísimo of all the armed forces, Head of State, Head of Government and Jefe Nacional of the newly united party of the Falange, Franco's powers were comparable to those of Hitler, and greatly exceeded those of Mussolini.

Recognising too late what was going on, Hedilla refused the meaningless consolation prize of simple membership of the new executive committee, the Junta Política, and attempted to mobilise his rapidly dwindling forces in the provinces against the Caudillo. Franco responded swiftly. He had Hedilla arrested on 25 April 1937, tried for a number of selective and contradictory crimes, and sentenced to death. When a committed Falange supporter, Dionisio Ridruejo, visited him to object to the imposition of the death sentence, an astonished Generalísimo commented, 'But have they arrested Hedilla? I have still not been informed ... Doubtless, they found something incriminating against him.'[10] Whether this was pure political guile, or derived from a genuine ability to convince himself that the dispensation of justice derived from some lofty, irrefutable military authority over which he had no direct personal control, it would prove a very helpful strategy over the years. At one stage during the war, when his childhood friend Alonso Vega asked him what had happened to a mutual associate, Franco replied, 'The Nationalists had him shot' as if it was nothing to do with him.[11] When Pilar Primo de Rivera (sister of José Antonio) begged Doña Carmen to intercede on Hedilla's behalf, a stony-faced Franco snapped that 'he was determined to nip in the bud any action directed against him and his government by shooting the guilty party'. It was only when his brother Nicolás pointed out that it would be politically damaging to 'make a martyr out of a nonentity' that Franco finally agreed to commute the sentence. Kept in prison for four years, Hedilla was not formally pardoned for his supposed misdeed until May 1947. Franco's harsh response to Hedilla's insubordination effectively ended resistance to his plans to become absolute ruler of the Nationalist zone. Although ideological arguments continued to rage, the rank and file, fed up with the endless squabbles and rivalries between the various political groups, welcomed unification. Even the Carlists, who gained a very advantageous tax regime for Navarre, were prepared to bow to the inevitable, rather than risk dissension in the war effort or lose a preferential arrangement.

In the wake of unification, an excessive, corrupt and expensive court rapidly evolved, with a huge and well-paid party bureaucracy at its centre. Franco now played a masterly game, drawing out the jealousies of the principal groups within the Movimiento, and allowing them to neutralise each other in their bid to gain the upper hand. His instinctive awareness of his own inadequacies and insatiable greed gave him an extraordinary intuitive ability to gauge and exploit the weakness and avarice of others. Like a Mafia godfather, he bought off potential opponents with offers of a job, a gift or a favour – whatever it took to secure their loyalty – thereby weaving them into the very fabric of his regime. It did not take long for hardcore Falangists to recognise that displays of loyalty to Franco brought considerable benefits.

Franco would bring his family and military experiences in Africa to bear within Nationalist Spain. Once he had established himself as an authoritarian father-figure in the Nationalist zone, the differing groups formed a sort of argumentative and competitive brotherhood. Not only did an individual or a group have to challenge Franco's power as a father-figure, but also they had to risk the rage of their brothers as well.[12] Subsuming their individual frailties and sense of powerlessness within the security of a wider group, many of his supporters happily subscribed to their leader's confusing fantasies. Others cynically recognised the benefits of pretending to do so. Dispensing favours with one hand and disapproval with the other, he managed to keep them all at each other's throats and off his back.

Furthermore, like the Nazis in Germany, Nationalist Spain thus provided many perfectly ordinary people with a legal outlet for fundamentally criminal behaviour. Franco facilitated a thrilling release for previously repressed impulses, either by suspending an individual sense of morality – supposedly for the 'good' of the wider group – or, for those without an ethical code, removing the anxieties related to being caught. Murder, torture, rape and looting became acceptable because they were carried out on behalf of an idealised higher 'authority'. Franco also facilitated an outlet for the sort of burning hatred and terror of women that had been on display in Africa. That Franco's political collaborators felt desperately threatened by powerful, politicised women was made clear in a poisonous Nationalist press, which condemned the Socialist Margarita Nelken as 'not a woman, but a repulsive mixture, an almost androgynous item' and a whore who exploited her 'femininity for remunerative affections'.[13] The Communist leader, Dolores Ibarruri (Pasionaria), who exemplified what these men feared and hated, was denounced as 'An ex-nun [who became] famous when she hurled herself upon an unfortunate priest and ripped open his jugular vein with her bare teeth.'[14] Although in 1938 Franco expressed outrage that 'When you go to Asturias you will find girls of fifteen or sixteen years, if not younger, abused and pregnant. You will find constant examples of free love, of hateful abuses, girls who were requisitioned for this or that Russian officer and infinite proofs of barbarity',[15] the rape of women and girls was considered not only acceptable, but an essential part of the dehumanising process. According to Arthur Koestler, General Queipo de Llano 'described scenes of rape with a coarse relish that is an indirect incitement to a repetition of such scenes'.[16] As would be starkly revealed in the post-war era, this hatred of women and this perverted 'sexual psychothology'[17] was not confined to the war years.

As so often, Franco's neurotically driven fears brought significant political dividends. By encouraging his supporters to terrorise and eradicate the left, he would lay the foundations of a regime that would never be challenged. This mission required Franco to dismiss a number of international peace initiatives and to fight for unconditional surrender of the Republicans. In reality, the only person who might still challenge Franco's position of untrammelled authority within the Nationalist zone was Mola. Although his junior in terms of rank, Franco was bitterly jealous of Mola's pivotal role in preparing the uprising, which contrasted so sharply with his own tortured ambivalence. Although the military priorities of both men often diverged dramatically, their main differences were political rather than psychological. The austere, if manic, General Mola was horrified by the billowing net of corruption within which Franco had ensnared his subordinates. Furthermore, he had envisaged a Republican regime that would restore parliamentary government, not an authoritarian state. It was therefore somewhat fortuitous – for Franco at least – when on 3 June 1937 Mola's plane crashed *en route* from Pamplona to Vitoria, killing everybody on board. A very nervous Chief of the Naval General Staff was dispatched to give the Caudillo the terrible news. When, after many distraught hesitations and digressions he finally blurted out that Mola was dead, a very cool Franco replied, 'At last, so that's all it is. I thought you were going to tell me that they'd sunk the cruiser *Canarias*.' Greeting the arrival of Mola's body as it was brought down the steps of the plane at divisional military headquarters, the now very portly Generalísimo flung his arm out in a fascist salute, causing his uniform to split at the armpit and generating much suppressed merriment among his entourage. On the other hand, he displayed no emotions at the funeral. Although a monument to Mola was unveiled soon after, Franco was keen for his memory to be buried with his body. Mola's private papers were swiftly seized, and his leading part in the rising and the war was diligently downplayed to accommodate Franco's insatiable need for pre-eminence. His efforts did not prevent Hitler, years later, commenting that 'The real tragedy for Spain was the death of Mola; there was the real brain, the real leader, Franco came to the top like Pontius to the Creed.'[18] While the removal of yet another rival did little to diminish Franco's triumphant belief in his own immortality, he was not prepared to leave anything to chance. Hereafter he stopped visiting the front in a plane and travelled everywhere by car.

Imbued with a greater sense of political – if not psychological – security, his interest in the war greatly enlivened by Mola's demise, Franco engaged directly in tactical discussions with Colonel Antonio Barroso, his chief of operations, and General Kindelán. On 11 June, the Army of the North, now under the command of the diminutive but devoted General Fidel Dávila, renewed its march upon Bilbao, breaking through the city's defences on 12 June. The demoralised Basques, terrorised by the bombings of Durango and Guernica and convinced that they had been forgotten by the Republican government, fled the city, leaving the heavy industries still intact. Keen to avoid another international backlash, Franco ordered that only a small number of troops enter Bilbao. On 13 June he broadcast an ambiguous message to the inhabitants of the city warning them:

What you call the iron ring has been broken by our troops. Nothing can contain the victorious steam roller advance of the nationalist army. From one minute to the next Bilbao will be under the fire of our guns and all resistance is useless. If you want to avoid the destruction of the rest of Vizcaya and to prevent the war entering the capital and the zone that you still hold, surrender your arms.

His statement that 'You've got nothing to fear if you've committed nothing serious' was less than reassuring for supporters of the Republic, who knew only too well that simply to have opposed the rebels was deemed sufficient grounds for execution. His warning that 'If you surrender, take advantage of the moments you still have left. If you persist in rebellion, only death and destruction await you' made it quite clear that whatever they did, the Basques were doomed.[19]

The Nationalists entered Bilbao virtually unopposed on 19 June. Despite the fact that they had, as advised, surrendered, many thousands of Basques were executed or imprisoned. Franco's 'enthusiastic greeting' to Hitler, thanking him for his support, and his letter commending General Sperrle on his 'effective and splendid' air forces put his views on Guernica firmly in perspective. The Caudillo's fulsome outpourings contrasted sharply with

General Wilhelm Faupel's withering report to Berlin on his protracted conduct of the campaign.

That Mola's death – and German derision – may have induced a surge in Franco's anxieties, as well as in his sense of omnipotence, is revealed in his autobiographical film-script *Raza*. In a scene from his original script – omitted from the actual film – José's close friend and brother-in-law Luis gets into a defeatist frame of mind on the Bilbao front when a Nationalist warship is sunk. An officer's assurances, 'We must have faith. The Generalísimo was here this morning with us and he was tranquil', do not have the required effect. While a brave old man (not unlike the 'grizzled veteran' in Franco's Moroccan diary) insists on joining up because his two sons have died, Luis deserts and returns to his wife and family. A disgusted Isabel throws him out of the house for being a traitor. Franco then kills off Luis (who possibly represented his ambivalent and guilty self) when he tries to get back over the line into Bilbao. A heroic José, on the other hand, using an assumed name leads a *bandera* of the Legion in the attack on the city. Consoling his distraught sister, José urges her to remember only Luis' heroism and not his 'treachery'.

After the fall of Bilbao, possibly keen to quash 'treacherous' or 'defeatist' anxieties of his own, Franco moved his headquarters from Salamanca into the aristocratic Palacio Muguiro in Burgos, where he hoped to celebrate victory. He would remain here for a further two years. The campaign against the Catholics in the Basque country further inflamed Franco's need for formal recognition by the Pope. Not only did he crave the Pope's personal approval – and perhaps forgiveness – for neurotic reasons, but he also needed the Vatican to validate his political authority and to mobilise Catholic opinion in democratic countries in order to assuage international hostility to his regime aroused by the bombing of Guernica. Cardinal Gomá helped Franco and the Vatican resolve the potentially conflictive issue of the Catholic Basques being killed in their thousands by tainting them as communists and heathens. His collective letter 'To the Bishops of the Whole World', published on 1 July 1937, legitimised the military uprising and defended the Nationalists from accusations of fascism. Although two Spanish bishops refused to sign this, fearing it would provoke reprisals against Catholics in the Republican zone, it proved to be a huge boost to Franco's cause. Nonetheless, the Vatican's continuing hesitancy about according Franco full recognition, and its insistence that Rome retain the right to name bishops, rankled with their prodigal son. Apparently unable to differentiate between himself and the warrior-kings from Spain's glorious past – and perhaps confusing the Pope with his mean-spirited father – Franco stubbornly insisted that he be accorded the sort of medieval regal privileges that had been the source of such conflict between king and Church in the past.

Meanwhile, to Kindelán's dismay, it took the Nationalist forces three weeks to regroup for the next stage of the advance through Vizcaya into Santander. In 1941 he would write 'the enemy was defeated but was not pursued; the success was not exploited, the withdrawal was not turned into disaster'.[20] This breathing space enabled Rojo to launch a surprise offensive at the village of Brunete, 25 kilometres west of Madrid, which nearly succeeded in cutting the Nationalists off from Madrid. Franco was frantic. Gasping 'They've smashed down the Madrid front', Franco diverted two bridges, along with the Condor Legion and the Italian Aviazione Legionaria, to Madrid under the overall charge of Varela, as Rojo had hoped he would. In the unbearable heat and chaos of the Madrid front, with both sides regularly shelling their own troops, the Nationalists slowly drove the Republicans back to their starting point. As the Republicans retreated, so Franco's spirits soared. During this campaign, one of the bloodiest of the entire war, the Republicans lost more than 20,000 of their best troops. Totally unconcerned by the devastation and loss of life on the battlefront, an increasingly buoyant Generalísimo immersed himself in the day-to-day decision making from temporary headquarters outside Madrid.

On 18 July a desolate Azaña declared, 'It is not possible to base any political system on the decision to exterminate the adversary.'[21] An insensitively jubilant Franco, who had no such concerns, rhapsodised about his many victories over 'rabbles of murderers' and 'assassins and thieves'. In the midst of the slaughter on the Madrid front, he found time to return to Salamanca for the celebration of the first year of his Movimiento. Firmly placing himself on the side of God, History and Justice, he commended the fact that he had saved 'Imperial Spain which fathered nations and gave laws to the world' from anarchy. When the hellish devastation of the battle outside Madrid ended on 25 July, the feast day of St James, patron saint of Spain, the Generalísimo, taking it as a personal commendation, announced, 'The Apostle has granted me victory on his feast day.'

Rather than pursue the Republicans back to Madrid, Franco now made the perplexing decision to transport the Navarrese brigades back north in order to relaunch the attack on Santander. Whether he was reluctant for the capital to fall before he had wholly crushed the Basques, or felt a deep-rooted anxiety about challenging the heart of the *Patria*, his decision extended the war unnecessarily. By 14 August, General Dávila's troops were surging westwards towards Santander. Fearing another massacre, Mussolini hastily attempted to persuade Franco that it would be a great propaganda victory in the Catholic world if, for the first time in the war, he agreed to negotiate a surrender. In the light of Nicolás Franco's extremely surprising assurance that military and political leaders would be evacuated to safety on 23 August, the Basques surrendered to the Italians at Santoña, between Bilbao and Santander. Thrilled by the victory, the delighted Italians surged through the streets of Santander brandishing giant portraits of Mussolini. As agreed, Basque political personalities were placed on two British ships ready to be transported to safety under Italian protection. This was more than the Caudillo could bear. Deeply affronted by the Italians' triumphant behaviour, and appalled at the idea that his enemies were escaping unpunished, a vengeful Franco immediately imposed a Nationalist blockade on the port and demanded that the Italians hand over the Basque refugees. Fearing the worst, they refused to do so for four days, and then reluctantly complied on the understanding that the surrender conditions would be respected. Franco immediately instigated summary trials resulting in hundreds of death sentences. He was less than concerned by complaints that his dishonourable behaviour had compromised the Italians.

Although Franco viewed the collapse of the Basques as a great military triumph, his frenzied ideological hatred of the enemy had seriously clouded his political judgement. Just as Hitler's unfettered vengefulness on the eastern front transformed potential Nazi sympathisers into implacable enemies, and helped ensure his defeat in the Second World War, so Franco was driven by a self-defeating brutality. Had he behaved differently, he might have won the Catholic Basques – many of whom were fundamentally conservative – over to the Nationalist cause, and thereby reconciled many opponents to his regime. Furthermore, the Generalísimo, so vocal in his commendations of bravery, so dismissive of the need for numerical or technical superiority in battle, neither acknowledged nor commended them – or indeed any Republicans – for their bravery in battle and nobility in defeat. By failing to do so, he wantonly threw away the opportunity to lure thousands of Catholic Basques into the Nationalist army, and ensured that the Basques would be his fiercest and most effective enemies in the later years of his dictatorship.

On 24 August, while Santander was still tottering on the edge of defeat, the focus of the war moved westwards when the Republicans launched another diversionary offensive at Belchite aimed at encircling Saragossa. Although Franco dispatched a few extra troops from Madrid, he was persuaded not to fall for Rojo's diversionary tactics and postpone his proposed assault on Asturias. This was the first and only time during the civil war that, bowing to military pressure from his advisers, he was prepared to countenance a Republican advance into Nationalist territory. Although his decision was entirely vindicated in purely military terms, it clashed with

Franco's emotional priorities. Henceforth he would resolutely refuse to countenance any further loss of territory, whatever the cost to the overall Nationalist war effort.

The agreed military plans proceeded smoothly enough. Moving easily through the remainder of the north, by 2 September 1937 the Nationalists were ready to launch a three-pronged assault on Asturias. Blockaded by sea, assaulted from the air and shattered by the new German co-ordinated ground–air attack techniques, the morale of the desperate defenders collapsed. Gijón and Avilés fell to the Nationalists on 21 October. The Republic had now lost its coal industry and its northern army. The Nationalists could link the iron-ore production of the Basque country with the coal mines of Asturias. With all the ports of northern Spain in Franco's hands, the Nationalist fleet was free to concentrate on the Mediterranean, the Republic's only maritime supply route for food and arms imports. Meanwhile, the Nationalist army was released for use in the centre and the east. The ignominious retreat of the unfortunate Republican government from Valencia to Barcelona – ostensibly to oversee the mobilisation of Catalonian resources for the war industry, but also to be nearer the French border in the event of defeat – did little to dampen Nationalist confidence.

In the wake of these military successes, Franco turned his attention back to consolidating his position within the Nationalist zone. The massive propaganda machinery that had ground into action was used to project Franco as latter-day warrior-King. Side-stepping the corruption, extravagance and unfettered destructiveness with which his regime was wracked – not to mention the noticeable shortcomings of the heroic leader – this campaign succeeded in convincing Franco, and many others, that he headed a highly moral and austere crusade against the Godless hordes. Not only did the incessant propaganda help brainwash the Spanish people, but it enabled the Generalísimo to access massive displays of adulation whenever his ego showed signs of flagging. This massive generation of misinformation enabled external reality and factual evidence to be constantly modified to accommodate the Caudillo's private fantasies and fears, and the political requirements of the Nationalists, which were now wholly enmeshed. Thus did the political structures of Franco's regime come to reflect the inner workings of his psyche.

The statutes of the Falange, drawn up by Serrano Suñer and signed by Franco on 4 August 1937, had given the Caudillo absolute power. The supreme body of the single party, the Consejo Nacional, which was established in a carefully choreographed ceremony on 19 October 1937, became the primary outlet for the expression of the differing aspirations of the various groups in the Nationalist coalition. Members of its executive organ, the Junta Politica, were to be designated by Franco himself. As Franco had doubtless intended, the size and the ideological range of its members rendered the *Consejo Nacional* an impotent focus for potential discontent. What it lacked in political bite, it made up for with traditional pomp and well-paid sinecures for its members.

Franco's posturing as a medieval king was making it increasingly difficult for him to countenance the return of Alfonso XIII, Don Juan or anybody else to the throne of Spain. Although he had secured the continued support of the monarchists by promising a restoration, this was becoming less acceptable to him by the day. Clearly forgetting his erstwhile fury with those officers who had failed to support the deposed King in 1931, on 4 December 1937, Franco dispatched a letter to Alfonso XIII berating him for his involvement with 'the liberal and constitutional Spain' over which he had ruled, and which, he claimed, rendered the King entirely unacceptable to the 'new Spain'. He haughtily directed him to prepare his heir for a 'goal we can sense but which is so distant that we cannot make it out yet'. It would take several decades for it to become any clearer.

Imbued with a sense of his own omnipotence after openly challenging the King's authority, the Generalísimo adopted a confrontational attitude towards his fascist friends. Encouraged by military successes in the north, but enraged at the Italians' efforts on behalf of the Basque refugees, the Caudillo wrote a 'nasty letter' to Mussolini, demanding that General Bastico be immediately replaced, which he was by General Mario Berti.[22] Tensions between Burgos and Berlin also burst into the open in October 1937. These had been festering for some time due to Franco's resentment at Hitler's acquisitiveness with regard to Spanish mineral resources. For Franco, the Führer's demands for payment constituted an insulting refusal to acknowledge that, as Caudillo, he was fighting a mutually beneficial war on behalf of fascism. Irritated by the implication that he was a subservient party in the relationship, Franco decided – contrary to the terms of the preferential trade agreement sealed with the Germans in July 1937 to pay for their support to Nationalist Spain – to announce that all foreign titles to mines and mining rights were null and void. He soon regretted his defiance and nervously tried to persuade the new German ambassador, Baron Eberhard von Stohrer, that this move was not aimed at the Germans. But this did not prevent him, in early November 1937, from directing the Nationalist press to modify its assaults on Britain and its corrupt democracy. The Germans were appalled. Although Franco's burst of even-handedness was driven more by personal pique towards the Axis than by sympathy towards Britain, it brought him some diplomatic benefits. On 16 November, Britain announced a *de facto* recognition of Franco by appointing Sir Robert Hodgson as British agent to Nationalist Spain.

Having challenged the King and the Führer and consolidated his political position, Franco turned his attention back to the war. Full of confidence, he again decided – against the advice of his officers, who had hoped for an attack on Valencia or a sweep through Catalonia – to go for the capital. Becoming less deferential with his Axis allies by the minute, he planned to achieve on the Guadalajara front what the Italians had signally failed to do nine months earlier. Meanwhile, the Republican government desperately urged General Rojo to distract him by launching a diversionary attack on Teruel, the capital of one of the harshest Aragonese provinces. This he did, with considerable success, on 15 December. Taking the Nationalists completely by surprise, the Republicans entered an enemy-held provincial capital for the first time during the entire war.

Although Franco was urgently advised by his Italian and German advisers and members of his general staff not to take the bait, the fact that the Nationalist military governor was under close siege was a red rag to the bullish Generalísimo. On 20 December he transferred an entire army corps under Varela to what he called 'the witches' cauldron of Teruel'.[23] The Republicans fought desperately, street by street, against Nationalists who were forced, until reinforcements moved up from the Madrid front, to use petrol and hand-grenades. The battle took place in the midst of a bleak and bitter winter, in which temperatures dropped to minus 20°C. Soldiers on both sides died from exposure. Many more had to have their frost-bitten limbs amputated. The Nationalist garrison fell to the Republic on 8 January 1938. Flying into an uncontrollable rage, Franco bitterly denounced the military governor as a vile traitor who was solely responsible for the defeat. In fact, his own shortcomings as a commander were once more in evidence: he had relinquished a tactical advantage in Madrid, displayed a startling but characteristic profligacy with his own troops and, as usual, blamed a subordinate. Like Hitler, his inability 'to retreat for any reason' resulted in him repeatedly wasting 'elite units in the wrong place at the wrong time, so that on other fronts objectives could not be obtained'.[24]

By 18 January, reinforcements arrived under the command of Aranda, along with a corps from the Moroccan army, under Yagüe. Veering backwards and forwards, the desperate battle continued until, on 7 February, the Nationalists finally broke through, seizing great tracts of land, thousands of prisoners and tons of valuable equipment. Within two weeks, they had recaptured Teruel along with nearly 15,000 prisoners. Overlooking the loss of life to his own men and the bravery of his opponents, the Generalísimo displayed unseemly delight that the costly battle had seen the physical annihilation of the best units of the Republican army. Although, as Norman Dixon writes, 'The aspects of authoritarianism which constitutes a lack of humanity makes for military incompetence',[25] luckily for Franco his military deficiencies were continuously cushioned by the support of his Axis allies and the policy of 'non-intervention'. The Republicans could not rebuild their shattered army while the French frontier remained closed. The defeat marked a turning point in the war.

Franco's victory at Teruel induced a further surge in his megalomaniac tendencies. Despite the Duce's feverish communications urging him to launch a major and definitive offensive against the Republic, or to suffer the removal of Italian troops, he could hardly bring himself to communicate with Rome at all. In the end Franco sent a languid letter to Mussolini pointing out that a major victory was, of course, a priority, hinting that the withdrawal of Italian aid might be construed as sheer cowardice, and audaciously asking for more supplies. Although Ciano complained, 'We are giving our blood for Spain – do they want more?'[26] this sinuous and confusing missive left a bewildered Mussolini agreeing that the CTV be used in 'one good decisive battle'.

Despite Franco's sporadic bouts of ill-tempered insubordination, he remained keen to impress Hitler and Mussolini with the fascist credentials of his regime. When the governmental infrastructure of his power was completed on 30 January 1938 with the formation of his first regular cabinet, Franco claimed it would organise Spain along totalitarian lines and eliminate the class struggle, political parties and the electoral practices of liberal democracy. As Minister of the Interior, Serrano Suñer took total charge of the Press and Propaganda Delegation, now extended to cover radio. The 1938 Press Law (in force until 1966) firmly put the press 'at the service of the state'. All printed, visual and broadcast material had to be submitted to the censors prior to publication. German correspondents were exempted.[27]

Only generals who were sufficiently old, or sufficiently loyal to Franco, were countenanced in his cabinet: Queipo de Llano fell into neither category. General Francisco Gómez Jordana became the Minister of Foreign Affairs and General Fidel Dávila, Minister of Defence. The new Minister of Public Order, the aged General Severiano Martínez Anido, intensified the purge of leftists in captured territory. Other appointments reflected a shrewd balancing of competing forces within the Nationalist zone. Monarchists, Carlists and Falangists were all rewarded on the basis of loyalty to Franco, rather than skill in any particular area. Although he did not trust any of them, Franco managed to imply to each that they were the favoured one. The veteran Falangist, Raimundo Fernández Cuesta, became Secretary-General of the FET y de las JONS, and then Minister of Agriculture.

Serrano Suñer persuaded a reluctant Franco not to appoint his increasingly corrupt brother, Nicolás, as Minister of Industry and Commerce on the grounds that it was 'too much family'. Instead, Nicolás was dispatched as ambassador to Lisbon, where he eventually became a useful intermediary between Franco and Don Juan de Borbón.

The day after announcing his new government, Franco began to welcome foreign diplomats in Salamanca. Clearly expecting some sort of pathological lunatic, many of them were surprised and impressed by his constrained manner. His ability to appear as being the exact opposite of what he was, may well have been the result of a 'reaction formation', whereby a 'a person develops the traits which are the exact opposite of his real yearnings'.[28] It seemed to work. The French press raved about the Caudillo's 'glance which is unforgettable like that of all rare beings. A troubled and trembling glance full of sweetness; the man is delicious and mysterious. He is a miracle of tenderness and energy ... the ravishing thing about Franco is his purity.'[29] Just as the French ambassador would commend Hitler for being 'well balanced, filled with experience and wisdom,'[30] so the British representative, Sir Robert Hodgson, was very taken with the Generalísimo's modesty. Commenting on his 'soft voice' and gentle if rapid delivery, he was particularly taken by Franco's compelling eyes, 'which are of a yellowy brown, intelligent, vivacious and have a marked kindliness of expression.'[31] (In fact, as Erich Fromm points out, with extremely narcissistic people 'it is sometimes not easy to distinguish between the expression in the eyes of an extremely devoted, almost saintly man and those of a highly narcissistic, sometimes even half crazy man'.)[32]

Relations with Hodgson were so warm that, in marked contrast with the pro-fascist philosophy he had outlined only the previous day, Franco proclaimed that his new government would 'harmonise with English ideas'. This did not inhibit him from immediately reiterating his determination to cement Spain's relationship with 'those who were her friends in the days of trial during the communist menace': his Axis allies. The *Fuero del Trabajo*, a rather vague 'constitution' based on the Italian *Carta del Lavoro*, was implemented to do just this. Intended as a sop to the Falange, it claimed to represent a middle way between 'liberal capitalism' and 'Marxist materialism' and professed hazy revolutionary ideas that Spaniards be granted '*Patria*, bread and justice in a military and in a gravely religious fashion'. As became startlingly clear in the 1940s, Franco would not feel remotely constrained by these ideals, particularly with regard to 'bread and justice'.

Back on the military front, the collapse of the Republicans at Teruel had opened the way to a Nationalist victory. On 9 March 1938, Franco launched a massive Nationalist advance based on plans drawn up by General Juan

Vigón. Spanning a 260-kilometre wide front, it moved east towards the Ebro valley, with forays into northern Aragon towards the Pyrenees and south towards Valencia. The Nationalist forces encountered little opposition from their exhausted and depleted Republican opponents who, underestimating the scale of Franco's push, had been unwilling to divert troops away from Madrid. Under the overall direction of General Dávila, 200,000 men – which included the Army Corps of Morocco under Yagüe and the CTV under General Mario Berti, backed by the Condor Legion armed with massively superior equipment – punched its way through the fragile, overextended Republican lines. Although the Caudillo was temporarily dismayed at the sinking of the *Baleares* on 6 March 1938, his spirits were greatly buoyed by the swift and successful Nationalist advance.

However, unilateral instructions emanating from Italy and Berlin generated characteristic outbursts of ill-temper and confusion over military strategies. Mussolini's direction to Italian aviators to undertake massive and damaging bombing raids on residential areas in Barcelona provoked indignant orders to desist from an incandescent Caudillo. More than happy to order such bombing himself, he would not countenance the Duce's infraction of his sovereignty. On 10 March the irrepressible Yagüe recaptured the symbolic ruins of Belchite. By 23 March he had crossed the river Ebro near Quinto, the Navarrese army under Solchaga had reached the Pyrenees, while the Italian and Spanish forces swept into the south of Aragon. By early April, the Catalan town of Lerida had fallen to Yagüe. It was beginning to look as though the Nationalists would decimate the remaining Republican forces and occupy all of Catalonia.

Franco, concerned that a massive Nationalist triumph in Catalonia might provoke the French into joining the war on the Republican side, decided, to the astonishment of his advisers, to divert his troops to the south for an assault on Valencia instead. His ponderous conduct of the war generated a customary howl of derision in Italy. As Vincente Rojo would later write, 'with less effort and in less time, he would have had in May 1938 the triumph of February 1939'.[33] An exhausted Yagüe, enraged by the unnecessary diversion and disgusted by the repression, burst into a wide-ranging tirade about Franco's conduct of the war. For good measure, he then flung in some controversial opinions on the need to heal wounds, the bravery of the Republicans, and demands that Hedilla and his followers be pardoned. Under normal circumstances this would have earned him the direst of punishments, but as the heroic leader of the African army, a helpful acolyte in Franco's rise to power and a crucial source of support in the military, Franco could not dispense with him. Choosing to interpret his digression as a temporary blip resulting from wartime tensions rather than political ambitions, Franco brought Yagüe back to Salamanca long enough to redirect his thinking, and then restored him to the command of the Moroccan Army Corps.

Meanwhile Franco's forces advanced down the Ebro valley, cutting off Catalonia from the rest of the Republic and reaching the sea at Vinaroz to the north of Castellón on Good Friday, 15 April 1938. While the Nationalist press jubilantly announced 'The Sword of Franco has divided in two Spain still held by the Reds', to avoid the Italians and Germans staking a claim in the final victory a euphoric Franco broached the possibility that they could both withdraw their troops. His confidence was short-lived. The brief opening of the French border brought a much needed resurgence in Republican energy and equipment. The Nationalist advance towards Valencia, intended to widen the drive to the Mediterranean, met with fierce opposition and drew to an ignominious halt. Mussolini was forced to dispatch substantial reinforcements to Spain in June and July, while Franco, cap-in-hand, reinstated Germany's mining rights in Spain to secure its continued support.

The advance on Valencia was also proving slow and costly in terms of Nationalist troops. Franco therefore directed that the Germans and Italians launch a ferocious bombing campaign against the Republic's coastal towns and merchant shipping in the area. This resulted in a number of British ships being sunk. The Germans, fearing a British backlash, tried to persuade Franco to call off the attacks, while the wide-eyed Italians vigorously protested that the attacks had nothing to do with them. The Caudillo was persuaded to call them off only when it began to look as though Chamberlain might fall. He did not want to see him replaced by the resolutely anti-fascist Anthony Eden, who had resigned as Foreign Secretary in February in protest at the Conservative government's policy of appeasement.

The breathing space for the Republic proved all too brief. On 13 June the new French government closed the border with Spain while Chamberlain, endlessly ready to appease the Axis powers, was happy to accept Franco's view that he was fighting a Christian war against the anti-Christ. On 18 July 1938, the second anniversary of the military uprising, the Nationalist government paid a singularly long-winded tribute

to the man who, by divine plan, and assuming the greatest responsibility before his people and before History, had the inspiration and the wisdom and the courage to lift the authentic Spain against the *antipatria*; and then, as the inimitable architect of our entire Movement, personally and in unequalled fashion directs one of the most difficult campaigns known to History.[34]

In a somewhat discordant ceremony, flamboyant fascist displays by torch-bearing Falangists merged with the pageantry of a medieval coronation. Franco was confirmed in his role of the 'dignity of Captain-General of the Army and the Navy, the Chief of State, Generalísimo of the Armies of Land, Sea and Air, and Jefe Nacional of the Falange Española Tradicionalista y de las Jons'. Captain-General was a rank previously reserved for the kings of Spain. Franco thus fulfilled two fantasies, attaining regal ranking and winning the right to sport the uniform of the admiral of the fleet, a privilege he exploited wherever possible thereafter. (If he hoped this would impress his father, he would be sorely disappointed.)

While all these victorious celebrations were taking place, the Popular Army rallied its troops and, taking Yagüe completely by surprise, successfully established a bridgehead across the Ebro on the night of the 24–5 July. A week later they had moved 40 kilometres, but became bogged down in Gandesa. To the horror of his general staff, rather than moving forward on other, more important and relatively undefended fronts, including Barcelona, the Generalísimo immediately ordered a massive and costly counter-attack. While an uncomprehending Mussolini bitterly denounced Franco's 'flabby conduct of the war' and complained that 'I prophesy the defeat of Franco. Either the man doesn't know how to make war or he doesn't want to',[35] festering disagreements between Franco's own generals burst into open conflict for the first and only time. Pacón records that Franco's advisers literally shouted with frustration, while he screamed that his orders were not being followed.

On 28 August 1938 Franco received with predictable equanimity news that his younger brother Ramón was missing in action – presumed dead – while allegedly on a mission to bomb the docks in Valencia. After coldly commenting that it was an honour for him 'to give a life joyfully for the Patria', Franco ordered a hero's funeral for Ramón in Mallorca, which he did not attend. Nicolás was dispatched to represent him. Despite Franco's apparent lack of interest in the demise of his younger brother, it gave rise to a welter of improbable explanations. It has been suggested that his plane was sabotaged either by an indignant Nationalist colleague, or – his sister Pilar's favoured notion – by Freemasons on the grounds that he was writing a book exposing their highest order, of which, she alleged, he was a member. She clearly considered this view to be entirely vindicated by Franco's strange decision to have Ramón's house sealed immediately after his death, by which time, or so she claimed, the manuscript was already missing.[36] The Republicans, on the other hand, insisted that Ramón was shot down by an Italian plane because he was flying to join their cause. Whatever the truth of the matter, it seems probable that at some level Franco viewed Ramón's death as a satisfactory resolution of their lifelong rivalry. According to Melanie Klein, infantile death wishes against parents and siblings are fulfilled when one of them dies. The death may be viewed as a victory, leading to a surge of triumph, heightened fears of punishment and a general tendency for all the aggressive feelings to be 'manically subjugated, immobilised, denied and projected onto the external world'.[37] Given that this vicious cycle had been apparent throughout Franco's life, Ramón's death did not bode well for the Spanish people.

When, in late September, Hitler invaded Czechoslovakia, a beleaguered Franco was forced to accept that it was possible the Nationalist cause was not his main priority. It also raised Negrín's flagging hopes that the western democracies might now realise that they were on the same side as the Republicans in a war against fascism. An international realignment at this stage would have isolated Nationalist Spain, facilitated the flow of support to the Republicans and terminated any hope of a victory for Franco.

Although Franco's dependency upon the good will of wholly conflicting blocs of influence was clearly problematic, his split psyche came in very useful in his diplomatic dealings in Europe. After Munich, Franco hastened to commend Chamberlain for his 'magnificent efforts for the preservation of peace in Europe', and Hitler for his favourable settlement of the 'Sudeten German question'. He told the British that, although his sympathies were entirely with them, he would be forced to adopt a strictly neutral approach in the event of a general war, and indicated to the Germans his intention to align himself with them after the civil war was over. His dextrous diplomatic footwork was greatly aided by Chamberlain, who was hardly the best person to engage in negotiations with the European dictators. His childhood experiences were not dissimilar to those of all of them. He had lost his mother aged six and been brought up by an authoritarian father who preferred his older brother. Immature, ultra-sensitive, cold, secretive and depressed, he was, in the words of Norman Dixon, 'uniquely ill-equipped to cope with the Nazis'. Like the Caudillo, Chamberlain, desperate for acknowledgement and approval from Hitler, managed to convince himself that the Führer was utterly trustworthy, and had indeed taken a particular shine to him. His decision to surrender Czechoslovakia to Hitler in Munich on 29 September and thereby, in the words of Winston Churchill, to sustain 'a defeat without a war' not only rendered a wider European war inevitable, but drove the final nails into the Republican coffin. Chamberlain's accommodating attitude impressed Franco as little as it did the Führer. While an indignant Hitler, deprived of an excuse for a war, bitterly berated 'The cowards! They yielded to all our demands', Franco launched a virulently anti-American campaign and granted the Germans ever more favourable concessions in Spanish mainland and Moroccan mining enterprises.

The devastating battle of the Ebro pounded on through the burning summer and into the autumn. By opening the dams on the Pyrenean tributaries of the Ebro, the Nationalists managed to cut off the Republican forces from reinforcements and supplies. Nonetheless, literally clawing their way into the earth to escape the punishing air and artillery bombardment, they still refused to give way. On 30 November 1938 the Caudillo ordered a massive counter-offensive fronted by 30,000 fresh Nationalist troops armed with new German equipment. After four gruelling months, Franco's forces finally recovered the territory that had been gained by the Republicans in just one week in July. Although the level of bloodshed among the Nationalist forces horrified his generals, Franco was not concerned. He was even less concerned about the massive loss of life on the Republican side. In what might be construed as a Freudian slip, he dismissed amnesty or negotiation because 'the criminal and their victims cannot live side by side'.[38] Perhaps he feared that, if allowed to live, the surviving Republicans would punish him – the real criminal – for his vengefulness. Although Franco agreed to an exchange of a hundred British prisoners held by the Nationalists in return for a hundred Italian prisoners held by the Republicans, his attitude to the Republican prisoners was characteristically harsh. The British head of the commission established to oversee the process reported that he 'is worse than the Reds and I could not stop him executing his unfortunate prisoners'.[39] The departure of the International Brigades on 29 October 1938, after a moving ceremony in Barcelona in which the Communist leader, Dolores Ibárruri – La Pasionaria – commended them as 'the heroic example of the solidarity and the universality of democracy', consolidated the sense that defeat was imminent. However, the shattered Republicans had no alternative but to fight on: they had no illusions about what would happen to them if Franco won.

With victory at his fingertips, the Generalísimo was wracked by indecision. While a massive army gathered along an extended line in Catalonia, he avoided major military decisions by visiting Corunna to take possession of a large country house bought with money from a subscription organised by the authorities. The population had thus been obliged to demonstrate their loyalty to Franco in financial terms. The civil governor of the town was rewarded with a number of highly lucrative posts. Franco was less magnanimous when his niece and her very ill baby were finally released from a Republican prison, where she had been trapped for two years because of her close relationship to the Generalísimo. Rushing to Burgos to be reunited with her beloved aunt and uncle, she was hurt and astonished when they greeted her very coldly and made her feel 'like a beetle', presumably because she was now tainted with Republican diseases and poisons.[40]

Undecided whether to renew his attack on Madrid, try and knock Valencia out of the war or deliver a definitive blow to the Republic in Catalonia, on 23 December Franco was persuaded by the Italian General Gastone Gambara to opt for the latter. Five Spanish army corps and four divisions of the CTV, equipped with spanking new German equipment, smashed their way through the shattered Republican forces. Characteristically keen for an absolute victory in Catalonia, the highly competitive Italians surged ahead of the Spanish forces, whom Franco had directed to move forward cautiously so as not to trigger the French to support the Republic. Although the speedy Italian advance did provoke a timid reopening of the French border, Mussolini's belligerent statement that he would not hesitate to go to war with France on Spanish territory virtually ended the supply of aid to the Republicans.

Deeply impressed by Mussolini's magnificent display of might over morality, and full of derision for France, Franco gave vent to his own megalomaniac tendencies in an interview with Manuel Aznar on 31 December. Keen to emphasise his association with the bully-boys of Europe rather than the woolly-minded democracies, he allowed his expansionist fantasies to flow freely, claiming – somewhat ambitiously – that victory in the civil war was merely the first step to re-establishing Spain's imperial power. Recklessly jettisoning delicate diplomatic negotiations with Britain, he asserted that 'efforts to reduce Spain to slavery in the Mediterranean would impel him to go to war' and fancifully linked himself with Axis imperialism by insisting that Spain's great new military ambitions would be underpinned by 'an enormous industrial base'. His ability to adopt opposing viewpoints without noticing any contradiction was revealed when he complacently proclaimed that 'Our justice could not be more serene or more noble, its generosity is based solely on the supreme interests of the *Patria*. There is no kind of meditation which could make it more benign', then added that 'It is not possible without taking precautions to return to society or as we might say social circulation, politically and morally damaged perverted and poisonous elements because their re-entry into the normal and free community of Spaniards, just like that, would represent a danger of corruption and contagion.'[41] Although he insisted that 'it is not just my intention to win, but to convince',[42] to his mind both required high levels of brutality and needless verbosity. When the English student Peter Kemp was summoned to bid his farewells to the Caudillo at the end of November 1938, he encountered 'a small, tubby figure dwarfed by the broad scarlet sash and pendulant gold tassels of a full general' who 'spoke in one of the quietest voices I have ever heard' for 'half-an-hour, practically without intermission'.[43]

On 26 January 1939, the Nationalist troops entered Barcelona. While Luis Bolín, expressing horror at the 'accumulated filth which the Reds bequeathed to every town that they occupied',[44] mobilised a band of char-ladies to remove the dust from the Ritz hotel, half a million refugees fled north towards France. By 10 February all of Catalonia had fallen. The surrealist sycophant Gimenéz Caballero gave an insight into the Francoist mentality when he ominously assured the Catalans that the Nationalists loved them 'with the same passion with which one loves a woman. And passion, as you know, goes as far as murder, which is why it's called "a crime of passion"'.[45] Viewing their victorious occupation of Catalonia as tantamount to 'a jealous husband punishing his unfaithful wife',[46] the Nationalists determined to punish Catalonia harshly before bringing her back to the 'yoke' of marriage with Spain.

The Republican government fled northwards, first to Gerona and then to Figueras near the French border. The President of the Republic, Manuel Anaña, went into exile on 6 February. He was followed three days later by Negrín and General Rojo. His designated successor, Diego Martínez Barrio, would not return to Spain. General Miaja was left to command the remaining Republican troops. Although about 30 per cent of Spanish territory remained in Republican hands, military resistance was now impossible. Faint hopes for a negotiated settlement were dashed when Franco's Law of Responsibilities, made retroactive to October 1934, declared his opponents guilty of the blanket crime of supporting the 'illegitimate' Republic, being members of left-wing political parties or Masonic lodges, or displaying 'serious passivity'. This covered the full spectrum of Republican citizens. As in Nazi Germany and fascist Italy, the repression in the Nationalist zone became 'state directed violence',[47] which required the terrorising and liquidation of any group that could not be reconciled with the Nationalist vision of the *Patria*. This would continue long after the war was won.

British and French recognition of the Franco government left the legal validity of the Republican government in doubt, and unleashed a bitter internal battle in which the Republicans tore themselves to pieces. While the Communists, determined to exploit the 'desertion' of their political rivals to the full, refused to give in until the last second, the non-communist members desperately sought out a peace settlement to end the senseless slaughter. When the virulently anti-communist National Defence Junta established by Colonel Casado persuaded a reluctant General Miaja to join their ranks and arrest Communists in Madrid, fierce fighting between the Republicans themselves broke out in the capital. This civil war within a civil war achieved what Franco had been unable to do himself. It ended the political dominance of the Communist Party and left Madrid ready for the taking. However, Casado's hopes that his attempts to 'save Spain from communism' would facilitate a negotiated peace with Franco were soon dashed. Franco simply despised the Junta for being conciliatory. In any case, as Serrano Suñer pointed out, after so much bloodshed, a compromise peace was unacceptable.

After the desperate in-fighting had ended in the capital, the despairing Republican troops fled to the ports, surrendered or went home. A few took to the hills, from where they launched a bitter guerrilla resistance. On 26 March a gigantic Nationalist advance was launched through virtually deserted Republican territory, arriving the next day in an 'eerily silent Madrid', which a scathing Luis Bolín denounced as 'evil-smelling and dirty'. Anti-typhoid shots were designated a compulsory precaution for all officers about to enter the disease-ridden Red territory.[48] As Ciano, the Italian Foreign Minister, noted in his diary, 'Madrid has fallen and with the capital all the other cities of Red Spain ... The war is over. It is a new, formidable victory for fascism, perhaps the greatest one so far.'[49]

Franco's ambivalence about grasping the core of Spain, the home of his father, the centre of the legitimate Republican government and the base of the rightful King of Spain, was never clearer. He was violently ill. Confined to his bed with a severe bout of flu and very high temperatures, he could only hear about the bloodless fall of city after city. By 31 March, all of Spain was in Nationalist hands. Although Franco had dispatched a telegram to Alfonso XIII after each victory, he did not do so after the fall of Madrid. The indignant King construed this as a clear indication that a restoration was not a priority for the Generalísimo. The King bitterly protested that 'I picked Franco out when he was a nobody. He has deceived and double-crossed me at every turn. In him you see what we Spaniards mean when we are suspicious of the type which comes from Galicia.'[50] The Pope, on the other hand, wrote to Franco thanking him for Spain's 'Catholic Victory'.

The victory provoked a panic-stricken flight for the French border, where the Republicans assumed they would be welcomed with open arms. Instead, they discovered – in the words of a German Communist commissar – that 'The dirty road on which [they] stood was not merely the frontier between two countries, it was an abyss between two worlds.' Far from being heralded as heroes, they were treated like tramps. Their battered rifles and personal belongings were forcibly removed and emptied into ditches filled with chloride of lime. The same commissar comments, 'I have never seen eyes of such anger and helplessness as those of the Spaniards.'[51]

In Spain itself, things could only get much, much worse for everybody.

A despairing La Pasionaria had written, 'We have shouted until we were hoarse at the doors of the so-called democratic countries, telling them what our struggle meant for them; and they did not listen.' The European powers would soon be forced to pay for their refusal to heed her chilling warning 'that if today it is our turn to resist fascist aggression, the struggle will not end in Spain. Today it's us, but if the Spanish people is crushed, you will be next. All of Europe will have to face aggression and war.'[52]

Don Nicolás and Doña Pilar, at
the christening of Francisco
Franco, 17 December 1892.

Francisco in the cadet's uniform of the Military
Academy in Toledo. His brother, Nicolás
(sitting), wears his even more impressive Naval
Cadet's uniform (1907).

Ramón, Pilar and Francisco (sitting), *c.* 1906.

A haughty Second
Lieutenant Francisco
Franco looks to a glorious
future, September 1910.

One of the hundred or so
ambiguous and disturbing
postcards that Franco sent to
Sofía Subirán in Morocco
between 6 January and 5 June
1913.

Ever the Military Man. Lieutenant-Colonel Franco marries his youthful bride in Oviedo, 22 October 1923.

The human face of General Franco: with his daughter, Nenuca, *c*. 1937.

Comrades-in-arms: Francisco
Franco and Millan Astray in Dar
Riffien, Morocco, February 1926.

Plotting war: General Franco ponders his
military options in Teruel, December 1937.

Madrid, 1938. To save his beloved motherland from anarchy, Franco reduces it to rubble.

Right Franco's victory parade sweeps through a ravaged Madrid, August 1939.

Left The Church hierarchy rejoices in Franco's 'Catholic victory'. The Caudillo stands under the canopy hitherto enjoyed only by Spanish kings.

Top left Major Franco joins the Foreign Legion, Morocco, 1920.

Above Colonel Franco, after securing the successful Spanish landing at Alhucemas, Morocco, June 1925.

Left General Franco, Chief of the General Staff, on military manoeuvres, 1935.

Franco and an exasperated Führer during their famous encounter at Hendaye, France, 23 October 1940.

A suave Serrano Suñer with Franco and Mussolini, in Bordighera, Italy, February 1941.

'The Godfather'. The Caudillo, surrounded by a menacing, military hierarchy, accompanied (from the left) by a bejewelled Doña Carmen, a belligerent-looking General Moscardó, a devout Nenuca, and Pacón (in dark glasses), October 1949.

A tight-lipped Doña Carmen looks on as Franco greets Evita, June 1947.

The past and the future. The Caudillo with
Doña Carmen, Juan Carlos, and Princess
Sofia, celebrating the 36th anniversary of
the military uprising, 18 July 1972.

The beginning of the end. The Generalísimo, shortly after
the assassination of Carrero Blanco, December 1973.

CHAPTER 6

Do you Wanna be in
My Gang?

Franco in Victory, April 1939–December 1940

I find him besotted with state power and with personal power. Of everyone
in the Spanish government, he is the one who says the strangest things to me
and who speaks in language closest to the Axis.

The Portuguese ambassador, Pedro Theotonio Pereira

They say that General Franco, in one of his famous speeches ... actually
declared 'Spaniards! In 1939 our country was at the brink of an abyss. But now,
thanks to my courageous leadership, we have taken a giant step forwards!'

Uxio Valentín[1]

Paradoxically, victory in the civil war neither increased Franco's inner
security nor diminished his sense of destiny. It did nothing for his humanity.
His conviction that 'there is no redemption without blood, and a thousand
times blessed be the blood that has brought our redemption'[2] enabled him
to perpetuate the violence and terror of the war long after his victory.
Azaña's hopeful message to 'think of the dead and hear their warning ...
have no more hatred, have no more resentment ... the message of the
eternal fatherland which says to all its children: Peace, Pity and Forgiveness'[3]
could not be further from Franco's thoughts. For the Caudillo and his
supporters, success in the civil war was viewed as 'the triumph of the pure
over bastard anti-Spanish principles'.[4] It filled them with a pathological
desire to purge the motherland (or themselves) of the 'worthless', 'foreign'
and 'disease-ridden' Other[5] – by which they meant any person or ideal
associated with the Republic. (It is perhaps noteworthy that a large print-
run of Joaquín Arrarás's biography of Franco was issued at this time,
entitled *Franco. Edicion especial destinada exclusivamente a la venta en las
prisiones* (Special edition exclusively for sale in prisons).[6]

In order to maintain the tenuous notion that the victors represented the
noble aspects of the *Patria* – and were therefore without guilt – Franco had

to foist the dark, animal, evil side of his psyche on to the vanquished. He therefore had a vested interest in maintaining a degrading sub-culture of desperation among his opponents. Treating those on the left as he had the tribesmen in Morocco, Franco would reduce the working-class areas of cities across Spain to the sort of disease-ridden shanty towns he had encountered in Melilla. While starving Spaniards scrabbled for food in the gutter, he and his supporters enjoyed a lavish life of plenty. Franco had a political as well as a psychological agenda. By focusing upon Republicans as a scapegoat for all of Spain's ills, he provided his supporters with a coherent, discernible and largely defenceless enemy upon whom to project their hatred and aggression. Perhaps, as has been suggested of other para-noid despots, Franco was seeking 'to externalise guilt feelings in the form of an unending number of enemies whose death [he exulted] in surviving'. Like Hitler, perhaps he 'externalised guilt feelings by displacing them onto others and then killing them – by the millions – thereby demonstrating his special dispensation from death and his power over it'.[7]

The consequences of his attitude were appalling for the working classes of Spain. Many tens of thousands of executions took place after the war. Loyalty to the Republic, formally designated as 'military rebellion', was dealt with by savage military tribunals. Even Ciano was appalled at the conditions in which Republican prisoners were forced to work. Bitterly commenting that 'they are not prisoners of war, they are slaves of war', he denounced '[t]hat queer fish of a Caudillo, there in his Ayete palace, in the midst of his Moorish Guard, surrounded by mountains of files of prisoners condemned to death. With his work timetable, he will see about three a day, because that fellow enjoys his siestas.'[8] The suicide rate soared. Between 1939 and 1942, 200,000 people over and above the pre-war death rate would die from malnutrition. There was a surge in child mortality. In 1940 alone, 100,000 children under the age of nine died from starvation and contagious diseases associated with poor living conditions – tuberculosis, typhus and malaria. Staggering numbers died from diarrhoea and enteritis. In August 1941 even the regime's own medical commissioners predicted that between 1,700,000 and 2,000,000 would die from hunger and disease during the forthcoming winter.

Franco's vicious repression of his opponents did little to alleviate his paranoia. His latent suspicions of the Freemasons had, by now, developed into a passionate hatred, which had some parallels with Hitler's anti-Sem-itism. In the same way that Hitler's hatred of the Jews derived, in part, from his suspicion that his father had Jewish blood, so Franco's irrational hatred of Freemasons was probably exacerbated by his father's sympathy for their cause. The fact that his brother Ramón had been a member of this mutually supportive, highly selective secret sect, which had thrice turned down his own application to join, did not help matters. Like Hitler with the Jews, Franco's petty jealousy of the Freemasons developed into a pathological hatred, which he justified in lofty political terms. For Franco, the Freemasons were at the root of everything he despised: the moral decadence of Spain and its imperial decline. He blamed Freemasonry for everything from Napoleon's invasion of Spain to the disaster of 1898, from international efforts to impede his victory during the civil war to international ostracism in its aftermath. He was convinced that the liberal democracies of Britain and France were riddled with Masonic ideas. Most crucial of all, he believed that the Freemasons were involved in devious plots to bring down the Catholic Church. Although it was the retrograde political power of the Church, not religion itself, which the Masons objected to, Franco made no such distinction. As far as Franco was concerned, for Catholicism to reign supreme in Spain, anti-Catholic sects, whether masonry or Judaism, had to be annihilated.[9]

He was not entirely alone in his hatred of the Freemasons, a secret sect that had, since its arrival in Gibraltar in 1726, been associated with a fraternal and idealistic spirit. Since that time, membership of the Freemasons had been an increasingly divisive issue within the army, particularly during the nineteenth century. In 1936 most, but by no means all, Masonic officers joined the Republican side during the civil war. In 1937 Franco, convinced that his fall from favour during the Republic was part of a Masonic conspiracy, expelled all the remaining members of Masons from the Nationalist army. His neurotic agenda was clearly in evidence during the civil war. In Burgos on 12 October 1937, he would trumpet that 'Freemasonry and the [left-wing] Internationals are not children of the Patria. Those who support them are not legitimate sons of Spain.'[10] As bastards, they had no place in Franco's Spain.

The demented outpourings of Father Juan Tusquets, whom Franco directed to launch a major witch-hunt against the Freemasons, fanned his fears. Before the war had ended, a directory of Spaniards suspected of being Masons had been compiled. Despite the fact that of the 10,000 Freemasons who lived in Spain before the war, only 1000 had survived, more than 80,000 names were placed in the Caudillo's files. This inflamed Franco's anxieties and provided the basis of the purges that were carried out in the 1940s under the infamous Law for the Repression of Freemasonry and Communism. This did little to alleviate his fears. On 18 July 1943, he would proclaim that 'Since the end of the eighteenth century . . . there hasn't been a single rebellion or attempt at treachery against the Patria that was not forged in the shadow of Masonic lodges.' By 11 September 1945, he was convinced that 'Above states, above the life itself of governments there exists a super-state, a Masonic super-state, which imposes its laws on the affiliates to whom it sends its orders and instructions.'[11] Having established a virtual grotto packed with Masonic artefacts and publications, in the early 1950s Franco published a collection of his paranoid musings in a book under the pseudonym Jakim Boor.

It seems to be the case that while Franco's irrational attitude to Freemasonry was linked with his father and brothers, his passionate hatred of communism was, at some level, rooted in his faulty relationship with his mother. As a rallying cry against communism, his regime relied heavily upon the cult of the Assumption – the notion that the Virgin Mary's body, having *assumed* a state of glory, was taken straight to heaven, where she sits as queen above all the angels and saints.[12] The Nationalists' subliminal desire to protect the Virgin Mary – the 'perfect' mother – from the 'red hordes' (a projection of their distorted view of womanhood, which evoked their own vengefulness and need) is highly revealing. It seems to vindicate Theweleit's argument that soldiers who latched on to the fascist crusade against communism equated the external Bolshevic 'masses' with uncontrollable eruptions of feelings and fears from within, which, like their need for their mother, threatened to invade and engulf them.[13] No wonder Franco determined to transform 'the masses into a herd of mutilated beings'.[14]

Whatever the source of Franco's hatred of communism, it is certainly the case that, in the wake of victory, his need to divide women into good and evil – so clearly illustrated in *Raza* – became entrenched within the policies adopted by his regime. Within Nationalist Spain, women were deemed to be either whores, who provided an outlet for men's innate depravity, or unblemished, Madonna-like figures like Doña Pilar, who were 'passive, born to suffer and sacrifice and to be active only as guardians of the moral order'.[15] The regime's puritanical notions of womanhood were energetically propagated by Acción Católica, a secular organisation dependent upon the Church, and by the women's section of the Falange, the Sección Femenina. Established in June 1934, the latter was run by José Antonio Primo de Rivera's sister, Pilar. Both Pilar herself and the Sección Femenina closely mirrored Franco's own mother's sexually repressed, moralistic attitude to life. Unfortunately for Spanish women, this organisation was given the task of 'educating' – or indoctrinating – the women of Spain. A number of harsh laws against abortion, adultery and divorce, and for 'the protection of the birth rate', were introduced to safeguard the purity of the idealised mother.

Inevitably with Franco, the good mother had to be punished as well. 'Without her husband's agreement, a wife could not embark on any sort of activity outside the home. She could not take a job, start a business or open a bank account [or] undertake any journey of any length without her husband's approval.' Spanish women had no real rights over their children. Actively discouraged from enjoying sex with her husband, the Spanish wife was vigorously dissuaded from seeking pleasure elsewhere. Although adultery could result in a prison sentence of between six months and six years for both men and women, the law for women was always harsher. 'Men were only culpable if adultery took place in the family home or if he was living with his mistress or if his adulterous behaviour was public knowledge.'[16] It was no coincidence that Franco's father, Nicolás, fell into all three categories. On the other hand, the policies implemented by Franco's regime actively encouraged Spanish men to behave as Don Nicolás had, drinking and whoring while their submissive wives – like Doña Pilar – waited passively and uncomplainingly at home. (Ironically, in Salóm's play Don Nicolás bitterly comments, 'I was always the whoring member of the family, and now I'm the only one who has enough sense of shame not to screw everyone in sight. I may not exactly be a saint, but I have enough decency left to see the difference between right and wrong.')[17]

Having rendered marriage an utterly miserable business, the regime did its best to ensure there was no way out. The Republican law legalising divorce had been revoked in 1938. The only way to get out of an unhappy marriage was to have it annulled in accordance with the laws of the Catholic Church. Needless to say, a large donation to the Vatican would usually do the trick. Those without money or influence were trapped.

In order to maintain the viability of the good mother, Franco had to find an outlet for his hatred of 'bad' women as a source of contamination and evil. The myth of the traditional Francoist 'family' did not extend to working-class women. As the historian Helen Graham points out, 'no amount of persuasion on the part of the Sección Femenina cadres could persuade them of the joys of prolific motherhood'.[18] Desperate working-class women whose husbands had been killed or imprisoned by the Nationalists were driven out on to the streets in order to feed their families. Ironically, one of the consequences of Franco's 'Catholic victory' was a huge surge in prostitution and abortion. These women were prevented from seeking out solace in religion, as Franco's mother had. Unable to pay priest's fees, many of them were unable to get married or baptise their babies. (In 1949 it cost 200 pesetas to get married.) Dressed in rags and therefore unable to cover their bodies appropriately, they kept away from church. 'How', asked one woman, 'can I go to Mass in these clothes?'[19] Forced to behave in ways that were wholly at odds with their religious beliefs and moral convictions, many Republican women must have been demoralised to a point where they probably began to believe that they were, indeed, wicked.

Having crushed his opponents back home, Franco adopted a keen political and military interest in developments in Europe. Determined to join a mighty fascist triumvirate in Europe, but anxious to avoid provoking the much vaunted French army and British navy into hostile action, he would have to play a very careful hand. Although he was convinced that 'For me there is no moment for oscillation, I have chosen a path and I must follow it resolutely',[20] a volatile mixture of emotional vulnerability, shrewd pragmatism and escalating hubris would buffet him along a highly erratic diplomatic path. Unable to disguise the absolute contempt he felt for the western democracies, he would repeatedly throw away hard-won political advantages with the Allies in ill-considered acts of defiance and arrogance. His dealings with the Axis powers were not much better. Stirring statements of solidarity for his fascist heroes were punctuated with avaricious requests for financial support to bring Spain into the war, demands that Hitler and Mussolini acknowledge his imperial claims, and aggrieved outbursts at Germany's determination to exact payment for the assistance provided during the civil war.

To begin with, however, forgetting his anxiety to secure formal recognition of his regime from Britain and France, Franco hesitated only briefly before signing the Anti-Comintern Pact alongside Hitler and Mussolini on 27 March 1939. Blaming the delay on his Foreign Minister, Jordana, he hastened to assure his Axis allies that his participation in this anti-Soviet, anti-communist initiative 'came from the heart'. Lest the implications of this 'clear statement of future policy'[21] be lost on anybody, Franco then signed an Hispano-German Treaty of Friendship on 31 March, pulled Spain out of the League of Nations on 8 May and, in a flagrant act of defiance towards the British and the French, dispatched troops to Gibraltar and along the French border when Hitler and Mussolini signed the Pact of Steel at the end of May 1939. This did not prevent him, on 11 April, from delivering a warm and cordial speech to the new British ambassador, Sir Maurice Drummond Peterson, who succeeded in putting the diminutive dictator's nose firmly out of joint by using his towering military attaché as an interpreter. When – despite protestations from Leon Blum that 'it rated the apprentice dictator altogether too high' – the venerable Marshal Philippe Pétain was dispatched to Madrid to try and curtail the Caudillo's fascist fervour, it merely confirmed his derision for the French.

Although Franco's fascist posturings generated considerable concern among the Allies, they did not impede relations with the Church. On 19 March, Pius XII had sent his blessings to Franco, commending his 'Catholic victory'. On 1 April, clearly forgetting two major precepts of the Catholic Church – 'Love they neighbour' and 'Thou shalt not kill' – he hailed 'the most noble and Christian sentiments' of the Caudillo, and broadcast his apostolic blessings to the victory with 'immense joy'. Given that half a million people had been slaughtered, many of them Basque Catholics, as a direct consequence of the uprising in 1936, it is difficult to gauge what particular Christian values the Pope had in mind. This was a question that Cardinal Gomá would, in due course, begin to ask himself. In August, appalled at Franco's continuing vengefulness towards the vanquished, the Cardinal would issue a pastoral letter calling for forgiveness for the defeated. It was harshly censored. For the moment, however, relations between Franco and the Church could not have been warmer.

Dealings with Berlin had suffered a temporary blip in early May when Field Marshal Göring's proposed visit to Spain was bungled. Franco swiftly put them back on track when he instituted a series of celebrations designed to highlight the fascist colours of his regime, stress his links with Spain's imperial past and pummel the sensibilities of the ravaged Republicans. Spectacular events were held in all the major provincial capitals, culminating in Franco's state entry into Madrid on 18 May. As an embittered conservative Catalan politician pointed out, 'as if he did not feel or understand the miserable, desperate situation in which Spain finds itself ... he indulges the need to do a lap of honour around the country just like a bullfighter [strutting] around the ring collecting the applause'.[22] A 25-kilometre victory parade took place on 19 May. In a torrent of triumphalism, 200,000 troops – including Italian tanks and cavalry, Hitler's Condor Legion, Falangists, Carlists, Foreign Legionnaires, Moorish mercenaries, Portuguese volunteers and the landowners' mounted militia of Andalusia – surged through the war-torn streets of Madrid and past the Caudillo. In his speech Franco swore he would stamp out the political forces that had been defeated, and remain ever vigilant against 'the Jewish spirit which permitted the alliance of capital with Marxism'.

On 28 May, Franco attended a *Te Deum* to give thanks for his victory. It was an extravagant piece of religious theatre which evoked the close relationship that had existed between the medieval Church and the great warrior-kings of the past. He was even keener to forge an intimate association with his Axis allies. On 23 May an emotional Franco conveyed 'the imperishable gratitude of Spain' to the departing Condor Legion. Serrano Suñer accompanied the Italian troops back to Rome for a huge victory celebration, where he optimistically proclaimed that within two or three years 'Spain will be at the side of the Axis.'

Franco's victory did not, however, inculcate a magnanimous attitude towards his father. In Salóm's play, Don Nicolás notes that Francisco was 'Always surrounded by bishops, posing in every cathedral ... without ever mentioning that he has a family ...' Observing his son's victory parade, Don Nicolás, who had returned to Madrid at the end of the war, bitterly commented, 'Today is your day. The great day you've been waiting for since you were a child, the one your dark empty eyes always saw in the future ... they're all obeying you and applauding you ... they're all afraid of you, but not me!'[23]

In fact, no amount of swaggering could disguise the fact that Spain was hardly in a position to face a European war, much less pursue an expensive expansionist policy. The economy was in ruins, and the much reduced (if disproportionately large) army was not equipped to play a major role in Europe. Uninhibited by such considerations, Franco made the diplomatically dangerous, but psychologically useful connection between the 'false democracies' and Freemasonry and international communism. With the Republicans largely crushed, he needed new enemies upon whom to focus. He therefore directed his venom at 'perfidious Albion'. Even Hitler, who did not think it would be 'expedient either for Spain or for us if the Spanish government were to show their cards in advance over the attitude they would adopt in a possible war',[24] was startled by Franco's belligerent behaviour. The Führer certainly did not want Spain causing trouble when he was doing his best to keep the British and the French out of 'problems which were of no concern of theirs'.[25]

By 5 July, even the bullish Caudillo had been obliged to concede that, while he recognised the 'difficulties for Spain of remaining aloof from the conflict', the country needed 'a period of tranquillity to devote herself to internal reconstruction'. Nevertheless, he hastened to reassure Berlin that Spain would retain a large army to counter the 'impositions' of the British and the French. The Germans, reassured by Franco's attitude, thankfully concluded that he would adopt a 'vigilant neutrality'.[26]

Despite his aspirations in Europe, Franco was forced to admit that the situation was not entirely under control within Spain itself. A guerrilla war between the Republican stragglers and the Spanish army raged on in the mountains of Asturias, friction between Falangists and Carlists had burst into the open and General Queipo de Llano, still reigning over his semi-independent fiefdom in Andalusia, was openly disparaging 'fatty Francine'. Although unprepared to tolerate such insubordination, Franco was as reluctant to engage in personal confrontations with military colleagues as he had been to challenge his father. Perhaps he feared that bringing differences into the open would provoke military rebellion. Driven by his underlying instinct for survival, in late July he succeeded in side-stepping the issue by luring Queipo to Burgos for 'consultations'. He then detained him in a hotel for a few days until such time as he could be dispatched to Italy as head of a military mission. Although Ciano commended 'a clever move in order to ... get rid of Queipo de Llano and at the same time put him in his place,'[27] even Franco was surprised at the ease with which he defused this particular problem, which heightened his confidence in handling political problems on other fronts.

During this time, the Falange seized upon the Caudillo's enthusiasm for fascism, the volatile situation in Europe and mounting friction at home to stake their claim to ascendancy within the single party. Keen to consolidate his fascist credentials, this suited Franco fine, as long as he retained overall control in his own hands. On 31 July he therefore reasserted the Falange's position as the only political party in Spain. Members of all the armed services had to join the party and were directed to use the fascist salute on political occasions. Franco's power was greatly reinforced by the *Ley de la Jefatura del Estado* issued on 8 August 1939, which gave him 'the supreme power to issue laws of a general nature' and to issue specific decrees and laws without discussing them first with the cabinet. The press's hopeful statement that this signified the 'supreme chief's willingness to assume the powers necessary for him to take on the historic role of national construction'[28] was entirely misplaced. Ill-at-ease in the world of politics, Franco swiftly compressed his regime into the lackadaisical military mould he had favoured in Morocco and Saragossa: delegating 'responsibility' for day-to-day affairs as much as possible, he kept the real power in his own hands.

Franco would impose a simple military philosophy – or omnipotent psychology – on to the realm of economics and politics. Believing that his personal confidence was quite sufficient to maintain a buoyant economy, he gave his ministers free rein to do pretty much as they pleased, as long as they did not challenge his overall policy aims or espouse political ambitions of their own. Presiding over his cabinet's rancorous squabbles like an oriental despot, he gave his ministers the erroneous impression that they were participating in the formulation of policy, while making all major decisions himself. He neutralised potential opponents by severing them from their established power-bases, drawing them into posts for which they were uniquely ill-equipped and ensuring that no particular group or individual had too much power. Behaving sometimes like an autocratic parent, sometimes like a manipulative child, he engendered venomous sibling rivalry between his supporters. Harshly repressing even moderate opponents, he also played a masterly game of divide and rule with politicians, foreign leaders and ambassadors.

As with all authoritarian regimes, however, beneath a thin veneer of harsh efficiency – generated by military marches and fascist rallies – lay a deeply corrupt and inefficient structure which, like the Third Reich, was 'a chaos of competing and overlapping jurisdictions jealously guarded by leaders who did not trust their colleagues'.[29] As Robert Waite points out, 'A political leader who creates conflicting agencies, who sets forth irreconcilable policies, who thinks he conquers when he divides is a person who is externalising profound splits and conflicts in his psychological makeup.' There were, as always, political advantages to Franco's neurotic tendencies. His inscrutable refusal to commit himself to any one group, and his apparent inability to choose between competing elements within the regime, would create rivalry and confusion that reduced the possibility of coherent opposition.[30]

He contained it in other ways. If, within a totalitarian state, censorship and repression are taken, at some level, to be an external expression of a leader's internal defence mechanisms, Franco was clearly a seriously flawed individual. He depended upon the press, newsreels and radio to project his internal heroic fantasies and distorted dreams on to the external world. He relied upon them to shield himself – and everybody else – from any reminders of his shortcomings. Given the rigour with which restrictions were imposed, he clearly anticipated quite a lot. Certainly the regime felt the people needed constant reminders of their leader's prowess.

Censorship, propaganda and education went hand in hand. Although the Falange, the military and the Catholic Church played a pivotal role in all these areas, fanatical clerics held sway at the Ministry of Education. The social consequence of this was the proliferation of private education run by religious orders, from which those who had lost the war were largely excluded. Education was thus used to consolidate rigid divisions within society along class lines. Illiteracy was rife.

The defeated were excluded not just from education, but also from every aspect of Spain's political, cultural, intellectual and social existence. In 1939, the Law of Political Responsibilities set about purging 'cultural' workers – particularly journalists – from the workforce. All newspaper and magazine editors were state appointees and had to be Falangists. The state press agency, EFE, held a complete monopoly on all news coverage. It determined – in the words of the Falange's paper *Arriba* – to eradicate 'putrid liberal topics, sentimentalism, blasphemous liberal voice'.[31] Article 12 of the 1938 Military Press Law (in force until 1966), which directed that 'All Spaniards may express their ideas freely provided they do not contravene the fundamental principles of the state', remained a catch-all directive. If all else failed, civil rights could be suspended by military decree. Still nothing was left to chance. An exhaustive list of prescribed topics – endlessly extended to incorporate new dangers – was issued to all editors. These ranged from 'individuals associated with the Republic; arrests, trials, executions; guerrilla activity; strike action; the royal family; crimes and suicides' to 'food and housing shortages; price rises; industrial and traffic accidents; epidemics.' Even reporting on adverse weather conditions was unacceptable, perhaps because they indicated that the Caudillo's relationship with God was less than perfect. Most unmentionable of all, however, was the existence of censorship itself.

Determined to purge Spain of unacceptable foreign influences and consolidate the regime's fascist image, a decree based on Mussolini's Defence of the Language Law banned 'minority dialects' (Basque, Galician and Catalan) and 'foreign barbarisms'. The names of people, hotels and places had to be 'Castilianised'. Even the dead were not exempt. Tombstones with inscriptions in Basque had to be replaced by their distressed families. Comics in regional dialects were banned, and children's literature was closely monitored. *Little Red Riding Hood* was changed to *Little Blue Riding Hood*, Russian salad became 'imperial' or 'national' salad.[32] Although much creativity was channelled into inventive ways of circumventing censorship, as the regime doubtless hoped, the stifling of all creative expression had a deadening effect upon the Spanish people that would last for many years. It mirrored the emotional 'deadness' of their leader.

Vicious with Spaniards back home, Franco was, however, prepared to be endlessly flexible and accommodating with his fascist allies in Europe, even when their behaviour violated his most treasured convictions. In August 1939, Stalin, who had been an enthusiastic participant in the western alliance against Hitler, but who was profoundly concerned by the western powers' total indifference to the anti-Comintern Pact, decided to deflect German aggression towards the Soviet Union by signing a non-aggression pact with Hitler. Although Franco was fleetingly nonplussed by the Nazi–Soviet Pact, commenting that 'it's odd that now we're allies of the Russians',[33] he managed to reconcile his enthusiasm for Hitler with his own rampantly anti-Bolshevik stance by making the extraordinary claim that communism was dead in the Soviet Union. His supporters within Spain were less understanding. Serrano Suñer sought to defuse popular hostility to the Germans' unholy alliance with the hated Bolsheviks by allowing the Falangist press to project Nazi propaganda as news items.

It was somewhat paradoxical, as the British ambassador, Sir Samuel Hoare, would comment in the 1940s, that the Generalísimo – so keen to safeguard Spanish autonomy and wracked with abiding hatred of foreigners – should have allowed his country to be subjected to foreign control.

Hoare records how Franco's blind fixation with the Nazis resulted in a situation where

The Spanish people, the least submissive of all European peoples to foreign dictators, had once again been subjected to the rule of foreigners. The Nazis who helped to organise the party, the press and the police were the direct successors of the foreigners who had corrupted Spain in the eighteenth century, bolstered Ferdinand VII's regime in the nineteenth century and imported totalitarian methods in the twentieth century. Franco, the Nationalist leader, had by a strange perversion of policy denationalised his country.[34]

While Franco's dealings with his Axis allies left much to be desired, he proved to be masterly when safeguarding his authority within Spain. His cabinet of 9 August 1939 was a reflection of his instinct for offsetting competing forces within the regime. Two veteran pro-Axis Falangists were brought in: Colonel Juan Biegbeder replaced the Anglophile monarchist Count Jordana at the Foreign Ministry, while the troublesome Yagüe became Minister for the Air Force. The disgruntled monarchist Kindelán was given the humiliating post of military commander to the Balearic Islands. Serrano Suñer remained the most powerful minister, but Franco retained overall control of both foreign and domestic politics. His dealings with his ministers – even close friends – were characterised by a profound formality. He latched on to the deferential Jordana's advice to 'impose a rigorous etiquette around the chief thereby excluding the "tu" [informal form of address] and friendly and familiar manners and ensuring distance in all relationships'.[35] This tendency was evident from as early as 1933. When his childhood friend Admiral Nieto Antúnez, who had always addressed him with the informal 'tuteo', became his adjutant, he had felt obliged to address Franco as 'usted'. Franco did not respond by saying 'Don't be ridiculous!' When in the 1960s Franco's frequent hunting companion José Sánchez commented that maybe the time had come to use the informal form of address, Franco snapped, 'The correct mode of address for me is "Your Excellency".'[36] Even his great crony Max Borrell was required to address him as *Excelencia*. Serrano Suñer would later comment that given his 'purely instrumental idea of men it was logical that Franco wound soon adopt the strategy of a statue on a pedestal'.[37]

Franco's lofty placing was somewhat more precarious when dealing with his fascist allies in Europe. His aptitude for foreign politics was severely put to the test with the outbreak of war on 3 September 1939 after Hitler's invasion of Poland. The diplomatic dealings between Franco and Hitler about whether or not Spain should join the conflict in Europe would prove to be as volatile and thorny as those of any teenage courtship. Whenever Franco's enthusiasm to join the war soared, so Hitler's would wane. Like an excited child who wants more and more and fears that he will lose out if he settles for less, so Franco's conditions for Spanish entry on the Axis side expanded alongside Germany's need of him. The oscillations, obfuscations and arguments that characterised the dealings between the two men resulted as much from their volatile sense of self as from their changing military and political priorities. The fact that both men appeared to suffer from 'borderline personalities', in which somebody has 'two distinct selves ... equally strong, completely separate from each other',[38] complicated their dealings.

However, in the first instance, despite his claim to the Allies that Spain would observe 'the most strict neutrality', Franco simply could not contain his enthusiasm for the mighty German army. He immediately notified the German ambassador of his profound 'gratification over Germany's brilliant military successes' and boasted that 'he had foreseen the swift annihilation of the Polish army', but expressed some concern about 'the western advance of Russian influence'.[39]

Although Franco hoped the impending war would enable him to throw his weight around the international arena, he was for the moment powerless. Impotent on the military front, he strove not just for political omnipotence, but for economic self-sufficiency as well. Moving fluidly within a kaleidoscope of shifting ideologies, Franco blamed free trade for the humiliating loss of empire, and on 8 October 1939 launched his simplistic ten-year plan for 'the Reorganisation of our Economy in Harmony with our National Reconstruction'. This proposed that Spain rely entirely on its own raw materials without any foreign investments. For the 'other Spain', the cost of these irrational and ideologically blinkered fascist-style policies was high. Torn between a vengeful desire to punish his opponents and an omnipotent conviction that he could resolve Spain's problems all on his own, Franco's policy generated terrible suffering throughout the hungry 1940s, when 'bureaucratic interference with legitimate business combined in the worst possible way with the *laisser faire* economy of the Black Market'.[40]

Rationing became an integral part of political repression. Many essential foods could be purchased only at inflated prices on the black market. The fractured food supply within Spain was now dependent not only on social class, but also on political inclinations. While the primary beneficiaries of Franco's regime were in a position to buy pretty much what they wanted on the black market, for the less fortunate even bread and potatoes would become luxury items. Although the regime commended itself on maintaining law and order, corruption was rife. Francoist officials stood idly by while the black market strangled the flow of food and other goods to the ordinary Spanish people. While it was well known that the military actively profited from the sale of goods on the black market, any 'Reds' caught dealing in it were severely punished.[41] Any working-class woman caught with illegal goods was purged with castor oil and her head shaved in a sinister precursor of the chilling 'hygienised' programme that Hitler would implement at Dachau. Doubtless Franco and his supporters were gratified by a return, as Gonzalo de Aguilera had put it, 'to healthier times spiritually [when] plague and pestilence could be counted on to thin down the Spanish masses. Held them down to proper proportions, you understand . . . it's our programme [to] purge the country and we will be rid of the proletariat.'[42]

There were, as always, practical benefits to Franco's vengeful tendencies. By behaving like an omnipotent parent withholding food from his bad children, Franco sapped the will or energy for political opposition. As Bruno Bettelheim points out in his poignant account of Hitler's concentration camps, it is difficult to engage in radical thought or action when food – or the lack of it – becomes an all-consuming obsession.[43] Furthermore, the money and power accumulated both during and after the civil war not only rewarded Franco's supporters and tied them to his regime, but provided the bedrock for the prosperity (and mythology) of his later years.

As more and more people got their hands dirty, so the need for moralistic rhetoric mounted. Steeped in corruption, Franco's collaborators engaged in strident self-justifications and fed Franco's apparently bottomless need for adulation. On 18 October, when he decided to move his headquarters to Madrid, the mayor of Burgos declared, 'The city says with all its heart . . . glory to God on high and all praise to you, saviour of Spain.' Such protestations did little to encourage Franco's humility. Luckily for him, Serrano Suñer's feet were rooted more firmly on the ground. He dissuaded Franco from setting up his new headquarters in the King's residence in Madrid, pointing out that this might seem just a tad provocative to his monarchist supporters, who were hoping, against all the odds, for a restoration. Instead Franco selected the regal hunting lodge of El Pardo, just outside Madrid. While extensive restorations were undertaken, he and Doña Carmen moved to the Castle of Viñuelas, where they remained until March 1940.

On 20 November 1939, the third anniversary of the execution of José Primo de Rivera, Franco – cognisant of the huge political benefits that would accrue, and doubtless hoping to wrest his rival's heroic heritage for himself – ordered that the Falangist leader's body be exhumed in Alicante and brought to Madrid. After a ten-day and ten-night, 500-kilometre torch-lit procession, punctuated throughout by bonfires, church services, artillery salutes and bell ringing, he was buried alongside the kings and queens of Spain in El Escorial. The cortège was greeted in Madrid by the high commands of the armed services and representatives from Nazi Germany and fascist Italy. This massively divisive public ceremony ground fresh salt into the wounds of those who had lost the civil war and crushed any flickering hopes for reconciliation among the defeated. It provoked a frenzied outburst of hatred among the victors. Republican prisoners in Alicante were beaten and murdered.

José Antonio's reburial and Hitler's successes in Norway and Denmark seemed to unleash a particularly megalomanic bout of behaviour in the Caudillo. In a blinding piece of projection, Franco blithely informed the British Colonial Secretary, Lord Lloyd, that to his certain knowledge the best British ships had all been sunk, England was on the point of starvation and India was in the throes of revolution. Ignoring the avarice of his entourage, on 31 December 1939, in a rampantly anti-Semitic, anti-imperialist diatribe, Franco denounced 'those races marked by the stigma of their greed and self-interest'. In deference to the Nazi–Soviet Pact, he delivered somewhat startling attacks on the imperialists' 'persecution and extermination' of the Communist Party. He snubbed the British ambassador at a New Year dinner the same night. An appreciative Führer immediately dispatched several gifts, including a six-wheeled Mercedes just like his own.

Although, on 23 April 1940, a confident Franco assured the Portuguese ambassador that the Luftwaffe was about to wipe out the British navy, his pro-Axis ardour was not shared by all his senior officers. Unlike those of Mussolini, the Generalísimo's military ambitions were severely curtailed by members of his battle-hardened General Staff who, appalled at the idea of engaging in military action in Europe, were determined to moderate Franco's dreams with a cold dose of reality. In his saner moments, even Franco – an experienced soldier – recognised that Spain was not equipped for a major military engagement.

He sought to prove his invincibility in other ways. Unperturbed by Spain's plummeting economy, he calmly assured the people that massive gold deposits in Extremadura would form the basis of a flourishing economic future. When the gold failed to materialise, a roving Austrian opportunist convinced the Caudillo that Spain's future lay in a secret potion – a combination of water, plant extracts and other secret ingredients – which, he claimed, was superior to natural gasoline. Convinced that this would solve Spain's energy crisis at a stroke, Franco ordered that the necessary and extremely costly arrangements be made for its production, and happily predicted to the nation that Spain would soon become a petroleum-exporting country. His confidence was short-lived. When it emerged that the entire thing was a massive fraud, he was forced to have the perpetrators arrested. He was not the only gullible dictator. Hitler too (in the words of Alan Bullock) 'was full of clever ideas for making his fortune and fame from water divining to designing an aeroplane'.[44]

In early 1940, with his enthusiasm for the Axis powers still in the ascendant, Franco attacked England and the Jews in a radio speech. (A gratified Goebbels recorded 'Something, at least, for our money, our aircraft and our blood.')[45] Franco then directed that German U-boats be proffered crucial facilities in Spain's territorial waters, and kept the German Embassy informed of developments in countries where Germany had no diplomatic relations. Some members of the Church, however, were becoming increasingly uncomfortable with Franco's pro-Nazi stance. Latent tensions between the Falange and the Church flared into the open in March 1940 when the Cardinal-Archbishop of Seville, Pedro Segura, refused to attend a high-profile religious procession alongside the Caudillo and re-iterated Cardinal Goma's call for reconciliation. Although Franco authorised a campaign of harassment by Falangist thugs to silence him, the Cardinal bravely denounced *caudillos* as 'captains of thieves' and a synonym for the devil. It took all of Serrano Suñer's skill to dissuade Franco from jeopardising relations with the Vatican by having Segura expelled from Spain. His attempt to persuade Rome to withdraw Segura proved unsuccessful.

To his evident frustration, Franco was forced to watch from the sidelines while Hitler roved through Europe like a psychotic toddler, wantonly seizing, destroying and discarding everything in his grasp. On 10 May 1940, while the Spanish press heralded the German invasion of Holland as a 'defensive action', an appreciative Franco commended Hitler's 'good eye' and ability 'always to pick the right place and time'. The Allies were understandably extremely nervous about the Caudillo's intentions. Before returning to Paris to become Vice-President, Pétain sought to secure Franco's neutrality by reassuring him that the Republicans were being vigorously repressed in France, while the British replaced their prickly ambassador Peterson with Sir Samuel Hoare, whose primary remit was to dissuade Franco from joining the war. Although highly skilled and sensitive in his dealings with the Caudillo, the new ambassador was singularly unimpressed by his 'small, rather corpulent, bourgeois figure'. Marvelling that 'he could ever have been the brilliant young officer in Morocco and the Commander-in-Chief in a savage Civil War', Hoare was particularly underwhelmed by

Franco's voice which, unlike 'the uncontrolled shrieks of Hitler or the theatrically modulated bass of Mussolini', was like that 'of a doctor with a big family practice and an assured income'. He was even less impressed with Franco's public speeches, describing how 'he would read his annual oration in a low, monotonous voice with no sign of emotion and with little physical movement except for an occasional raising of the arm. It was the technique of a man who had been given a long dissertation to read for the first time.'[46]

His oratorial defects notwithstanding, Franco had no trouble brushing aside Hoare's tentative offers of British aid, airily declaring that Spain needed nothing from the British Empire and that any imports that were required would come from North Africa. This was the first, but by no means the last time that the British ambassador would be astonished by 'the cotton-wool entanglements of [Franco's] amazing complacency ... and his evident conviction that he had been marked out by Providence to save his country and take a leading part in the reconstruction of a new world'.[47]

To Hoare's dismay, the collapse of the French army and Britain's retreat at Dunkirk further boosted Franco's fascist fervour and inflamed his greed. He wanted Gibraltar. Nursing his dreams of a mighty Spanish empire displacing the imperial powers in Africa, Franco immediately despatched his Chief of the General Staff, General Juan Vigón, to the Führer with a letter expressing his 'admiration and enthusiasm and that of my people, who are watching with deep emotion the glorious course of a struggle which they regard as their own'.[48] Bemoaning the need to shield his support behind a curtain of neutrality, he expressed his hope that Germany would provide the necessary equipment to bring Spain into the war. Although Hitler, convinced that Britain was on the verge of defeat, had no intention of paying Franco's price for Spanish participation, he was soon in the grip of the sort of self-defeating doubts that had afflicted Franco during the civil war. The Führer's inexplicable failure to push home his military advantage and invade Britain after his success at Dunkirk had echoes of Franco's many digressions during the march on Madrid.

Mussolini's decision to join the war in June 1940 – which Franco's Foreign Minister, Beigbeder, told the US ambassador was 'madness' – and his ill-advised promise to Franco that 'in the new reorganisation of the Mediterranean which will result from the war, Gibraltar will be returned to Spain' heartened Franco once more. Two days later he decided, in the words of an agitated Hoare, to up-grade Spanish neutrality to 'the equivocal and ill-omened status of non-belligerency'.[49] Fears that this heralded an imminent declaration of war on the side of the Axis powers were, however, misplaced. Franco was reluctant to move without the promise of considerable support from the Germans.

Instead, in early 1940, while thousands of Spaniards were dying of starvation, Franco calmly spent his time learning how to paint. Like Hitler, who vented much of his creative energies both before and during his time in power designing improbably massive Freudian monuments to his own greatness, Franco immersed himself in drawing up plans for the location, design and building of an enormous mausoleum to Nationalists who had fallen to his cause during the civil war. The Valle de los Caídos, which was to 'have the grandeur of the monuments of old, which defy time and forgetfulness', did much to keep the hatreds of the civil war burning. On the one hand, it helped maintain Franco's tenuous notions of immortality; on the other, it may have reflected his deep-rooted fear that the people would need a very significant reminder of him after his death. Costing almost as much as Philip II's Escorial, its construction (which spanned two decades) was undertaken by the forced labour of 20,000 Republicans, whom Franco venomously determined must 'redeem' themselves for their crimes through hard labour. Many were injured, became ill or actually died during this huge and ruinously expensive operation.

Powerless in the military engagement unfurling in Europe, Franco decided to wage a diplomatic war in Spain, adopting an icy distance from the British and American ambassadors while warmly receiving the German ambassador, Eberhardt von Stohrer, at El Pardo. He also extended further concessions to Hitler, allowing German submarines to be provisioned and repaired in Spanish ports, German reconnaissance aircraft to fly with Spanish markings, and German planes to operate from Spanish airfields against Allied shipping. On 14 June, the day that the Germans poured into Paris, Spain occupied Tangier in what Franco hoped would be the first step to recovering a full-scale African empire.

Understandably suspicious of Franco's motives, the fleeing French government headed by Pétain sought to prevent him declaring war on France by calling upon him to act as an intermediary with the Germans and to request a cessation of hostilities. Although Franco accepted this supposedly impartial role, he immediately dispatched Vigón to Germany to make a formal offer to the Germans to go to war in return for 'war materials ... aircraft for the attack on Gibraltar ... perhaps the co-operation of German submarines in the defence of the Canary Islands'.[50] During a 45-minute meeting, the Führer expressed his delight that Franco had 'acted without talking' and 'his gratefulness for the attitude of the Spanish press'. He also exposed the somewhat self-interested hope that Spain's 'close relations with South America might help in the enlightenment of South America as a counter-balance to the bad influence exercised by North America'.[51] He did not, however, respond to Franco's offer to join the conflict.

On the morning of the armistice, Franco directed his ambassador in Paris, José Felix de Lequerica, to demand French territories in southern and eastern Morocco. Ignoring Franco's dubious insistence that this was necessary to curb outbursts of tribal unrest, and to prevent the Germans from seizing these territories themselves, the French military commander briskly notified the Spanish High Commissioner in Morocco that any Spanish incursion into French territory would be dealt with rigorously.

Undaunted by this setback, on 22 June, Franco curtly told the British ambassador that Britain should end the war because 'You can never win it', adding that failure to do so would result in 'the destruction of European civilisation'.[52] Dismissing American offers of aid dependent upon Spanish neutrality, Franco renewed his offer to Berlin to join the war. His offers of belligerence were, however, falling on deaf ears. Already weighed down with what he called his 'harvest helpers' (the Italians),[53] Hitler was reluctant to further Spanish claims in French Morocco, which he feared might provoke a British landing there. Keen for his own bases in Morocco and the Canary Islands, the Führer briskly notified Franco that he was unlikely to prevail upon Spain for assistance in a war he was confident of winning on his own. The loss of the maniacally pro-German General Yagüe – whom Franco was forced to dismiss as Minister of the Air Force for his policy of reinstating Republican officers and his involvement in a plot to overthrow him – delivered another blow to the Caudillo's pro-Axis stance. This did not prevent Franco, Beigbeder and Serrano Suñer involving themselves in a mad-cap scheme to help the Germans 'detain' the Duke of Windsor in Portugal and use him to oppose 'the Churchill clique' in peace negotiations.

Sir Samuel Hoare continued to work hard to secure Spanish neutrality. Having vigorously lined the pockets of senior Spanish army officers and proffered British assistance to help alleviate the conditions of near-famine in Spain, Hoare even hinted to Beigbeder that if Franco behaved himself Gibraltar and Spain's other 'aspirations' would be discussed at a later date. However, fearing that a successful attempt to overthrow Franco would provoke a German invasion of Spain, the British did nothing to encourage Republican hopes that as part of their war against fascism the Allies would turn against the Caudillo. The arrival in Spain from Berlin of Admiral Canaris, an admirer of Franco, sent the Caudillo's enthusiasm for Germany soaring. Although, on 6 July, Canaris made it clear that, for the moment at least, Germany was not interested in Spanish belligerence, he did ask that German troops be allowed to cross Spanish soil if the British invaded Portugal, or if Portugal joined the war on the side of the Allies. The Caudillo – keen to get Portugal for himself – notified him that Spanish troops would be quite sufficient for the task if the Germans provided artillery and aircraft.

Anxious to consolidate his own position in the peninsula, Franco met up with the Portuguese ambassador the same day. Gushing about Hitler as 'an extraordinary man, moderate, sensitive, full of the spirit of humanity and with great ideas', Franco suggested that the Portuguese extricate themselves from their friendship with the British as soon as possible. The Portuguese dictator, Salazar, rightly concerned at Franco's agenda, directed his ambassador to suggest that Spain and Portugal consolidate their 1930 Treaty of Friendship to defend each other's neutrality in the event of an attack, wherever it came from. While Salazar had the Germans in mind, Franco was keen to repel 'any demand or abuse by the English'. Soon after this meeting, mistakenly reassured by Hitler's armistice with France (which would in fact impinge upon his aspirations in French Morocco), Franco delivered a passionately fascist, aggressively imperialist speech on the fourth anniversary of the Nationalist uprising, 17 July 1940. Proclaiming that 'We have a duty and a mission, the command of Gibraltar [and] African expansion', he reiterated his belief that the key to Spanish ambitions – and the secret of Hitler's 'fantastic victories on the fields of Europe' – was discipline and unity.[54]

The cold wind of reality was, however, blowing hard. Allied pressure on Spanish fuel supplies was disrupting Spain's internal trade and on 24 July Franco was forced to sign an agreement with Britain and Portugal for the exchange of goods through the sterling area. Franco signed the Treaty of Friendship and Non-Aggression with Portugal five days later. These diplomatic niceties would be undermined from mid-August 1940, when the RAF's unexpected repulse of the German Luftwaffe during the battle of Britain boosted Spain's strategic importance to Germany. On 2 August, Ribbentrop notified the German ambassador in Spain, von Stohrer, that 'what we want to achieve now is Spain's early entry into the war'.[55] While the Germans considered how best this could be achieved, Franco, like an excited child, dispatched a personal letter to both Hitler and Mussolini containing a map of his 'African empire'.[56] This included 'Gibraltar, French Morocco . . . Oran and the colonies in the Gulf of Guinea'.[57] Having assured the Germans that the Friendship Treaty had resulted in Portugal being 'partially extracted from the British orbit and brought into ours', he implied that a declaration of war was imminent, pending German deliveries of gasoline, grain bread and 'military and other assistance required for carrying on the war'.[58] Undaunted by Mussolini's non-committal reply (he too was beginning to get cold feet, lest Franco press claims to parts of north

Africa that he had his eye on), the Caudillo expressed his 'profound, devoted admiration for the Duce'.[59]

In fact, German enthusiasm for Spanish participation in the war waned rapidly after a pessimistic assessment of the Spanish high command. Observing that 'too much individualism often leads to lack of discipline' among the soldiers and that the 'command is usually sluggish and doctrinaire', it concluded that 'without foreign help Spain can wage war of only very short duration'.[60] Hitler was in any case much more anxious to retain the goodwill of Vichy France than to fulfil Franco's ambitions in French Morocco. It was clearly easier to give the Caudillo less tangible assets. On 6 September von Stohrer bestowed the highly prestigious Grand Cross of Gold of the Order of the German Eagle upon a euphoric Caudillo. But despite Franco's jubilant expressions of faith in 'the triumph of our common ideals', the rapidly deteriorating economic situation in Spain was beginning to have an impact upon his expansionist aspirations. He was reluctantly forced to ask the United States for economic assistance. A very suspicious State Department indicated that it would only be prepared to channel aid to Spain via the politically neutral Red Cross, in the hope that this would buy the goodwill of the Spaniards, but not encourage Franco's war plans.

Both Britain and France were extremely concerned when repeated attempts by the Spanish to get an invitation for Serrano Suñer to visit Berlin finally came to fruition on 16 September 1940. In fact, the Spanish minister and his Falangist entourage received a less than fulsome welcome from a brash and boastful Ribbentrop, whose diplomatic shortcomings had earned him the title 'Brickendrop' when he was ambassador to Britain. Although, the very next day, the Germans would abandon Operation Sealion for the invasion of Britain, and turn their attentions to Britain's imperial nerve-centres at Gibraltar and Suez, Ribbentrop blithely assured the Spaniards that the situation in London was deteriorating rapidly and soon there would 'be nothing left but rubble and ashes'.[61] Hitler responded to the Caudillo's extensive shopping list, which incorporated a desire 'to get all of French Morocco' in his hands,[62] with an even longer one of his own. It included, to Franco's disgust, demands for a base in the Canary Islands, and the transfer to Germany of English and French business assets in Spain as compensation for German support during the civil war. Although Serrano Suñer's meeting with the Führer was more cordial, it proved to be equally unproductive.

While Franco tried to convince himself that unpalatable German demands emanated from 'the inflated self-regard of [Hitler's] underlings', and he continued to slaver over 'the sublimity and good sense of the

Führer',[63] he was deeply offended. On 24 September, Serrano Suñer and Ribbentrop met again in Berlin to discuss Mussolini's suggestion that Spain join Italy and Germany in a secret Tripartite Pact. Franco directed Serrano Suñer to notify Ribbentrop that he 'had been distressed in a friendly way' at German demands, which were 'incompatible with the grandeur and independence of a nation'.[64] At the end of a rancorous discussion between the two foreign ministers, it was agreed that the details for a secret pact should be resolved in a personal meeting between Franco and Hitler.

An aggrieved Hitler, pointing out to the Italians that without German and Italian support 'there would today be no Franco', was beginning to question whether Spain 'had the same intensity of will for giving as for taking'.[65] He notified the Italian Foreign Minister, Ciano, and then Mussolini himself, that he was opposed to Spanish intervention 'because it would cost more than it's worth'.[66] Hardly devoid of an acquisitive spirit himself, the Führer bitterly complained that 'As a German, one feels towards the Spanish almost like a Jew, who wants to make business out of the holiest possessions of mankind.'[67] In fact, with opposition to Spanish belligerence spiralling in the army and hostility breaking out between pro-British monarchists and pro-Axis Falangists, Franco's price was going up. Although he assured the German ambassador that 'his attitude towards Germany was not a momentary opportunism, but an eternal reality', the exasperated German ambassador pointed out that 'Spain could not expect us to provide her with a new colonial empire through our victories and not get anything for it.'[68] Although Franco was determined that he would enter the war – which he now realised was likely to be a protracted affair – only if the Germans paid him in advance, he hinted to the British that they had promised 'economic stability, Gibraltar and French Morocco' in return for Spanish participation.

Throughout this time, the relentless execution of Republicans snatched from the overflowing prisons continued unabated. Franco's insouciant attitude to the signing of death sentences was exposed when a number of high-ranking Republicans were executed in October and November 1940, including the Catalan President, Lluis Companys, who had been extradited from France by the Gestapo. This provoked an international outcry and generated considerable embarrassment for the regime. It was, however, in the nervous Allies' interest to overlook the regime's transgressions. None-theless, neither Churchill's indication that 'we shall be no obstacle to their Moroccan ambitions, provided they preserve their neutrality in the war' nor the Americans' offer of massive supplies of wheat in return for Spanish neutrality could douse Franco's pro-Axis tendencies. On 16 October 1940 he dismissed two of his most pro-Allied ministers from the cabinet, including

Beigbeder, whose beautiful English lover Rosalinda Powell Fox had persuaded him to abandon his pro-German sympathies.[69] Hereafter he venomously referred to Franco as 'the dwarf in the Pardo'. A Falangist engineer,
Demetrio Carceller Segura, was brought in as Minister of Industry and
Commerce, and Serrano Suñer took over as Minister for Foreign Affairs,
while retaining his role as Minister of the Interior. Although Franco took
nominal charge, day-to-day decision making was increasingly undertaken
by Serrano Suñer, who was now referred to as the *cuñadísimo*: the Generalísimo's 'brother-in-law of brothers-in-law'. While a delighted Mussolini
notified Hitler that 'the tendencies hostile to the Axis are eliminated or at
least neutralised', a high-profile visit by Heinrich Himmler consolidated
the impression that Spain was on the verge of joining the conflict.

Hitler, against the wishes of his own advisers, wanted to investigate
whether Spain could be brought into the war at some future stage without
jeopardising his own ambitions. A meeting between the two men was
therefore arranged. Franco finally encountered the Führer himself at the
famous Hendaye meeting on 23 October 1940. To the evident contempt of
the Germans, Franco's train pulled into the station eight minutes late,
disgorging as Admiral Canaris had predicted 'not a hero but a little pip-
squeak'. Unable to strike an appropriate attitude to the Führer, Franco
lunged wildly between extreme obsequiousness and stubborn inflexibility.
Given the profoundly narcissistic personalities of both men, they were
never destined to see eye to eye. The fact that they both believed that at the
very least they had been selected by God to carry out His mission on earth,
and were quite possibly a reincarnation of the Messiah Himself, rendered
the adoption of an open-minded or accommodating attitude by either man
extremely improbable. With Hitler's ego as closely identified with the
Third Reich as Franco's was with the *Patria*, they clashed on almost every
point.

Having, as he later put it, failed 'to prevent Italy flying to rescue our
victory'[70] a few weeks earlier, Hitler was unlikely to make any imperial
concessions to the Spaniards in the wake of German military success. Nor
did he welcome the Caudillo's presumption of equal status when Spain was
in a state of economic and military collapse. Franco's conviction that, as
far as the Moroccan empire was concerned, 'France had some withdrawing
to do' clashed with Hitler's determination not to jeopardise his relationship
with the Vichy government. Franco's unwise decision to lecture Hitler
about Spain's historical and moral rights in Morocco in a 'monotonous
sing-song reminiscent of a muezzin calling the faithful to prayer' did not
go down well with the Führer, who was neither accustomed nor inclined to
listen to other's people's tedious ramblings. Under the Caudillo's numbing

onslaught, Hitler could not even muster the energy to lie and simply offer French Morocco to the Caudillo. His inhibitions derived less from the fact that it was not in fact his to give than from his fear that 'with these chattering Latins, the French are sure to hear something about it sooner or later'.[71] Apparently unaware of the impression he was carving, Franco tactlessly assured Hitler that Spain could take Gibraltar whenever he liked, and pointed out that even if Britain were conquered, the British government and fleet would continue the war from Canada with American support. Leaping to his feet, an enraged Hitler shouted that he did not wish to continue the discussion. (He would later complain to Mussolini that 'rather than go through that again, I would prefer to have three or four teeth taken out'.)[72]

Despite Hitler's exasperated belief that 'with this fellow there is nothing to be done',[73] he was finally persuaded to continue the meeting. After a tense dinner, it was left to the two foreign ministers, Serrano Suñer and Ribbentrop, to draw up the secret protocol, while Hitler and Franco continued discussions alone. Franco's parting shot that 'Despite what I've said, if the day ever arrived when Germany really needed me, she would have me unconditionally at her side without any demands on my part' was fortunately not translated by the interpreter, who took this to be a formal courtesy. The Generalísimo's standing with the German high command was not enhanced when, waving his farewells from the rear of the train, he was only prevented from being precipitated head-first on to the platform as it lurched out of the station by the rapid intervention of General Moscardó. As it was, the aged train leaked so badly in the downpour which now ensued that both Franco and Serrano Suñer arrived back in San Sebastián soaked to the skin. The only firm commitment made by Hitler concerned Gibraltar. Muttering invectives about the Germans, Franco and Serrano Suñer worked on the secret protocol most of the night, then dispatched it back to Berlin with a number of adjustments that the Germans immediately removed. Meanwhile, a thoroughly aggrieved Franco complained to Serrano Suñer that 'These people are intolerable. They want us to come into the war in exchange for nothing', while Hitler ranted about 'the Jesuit swine' and 'misplaced Spanish pride',[74] and complained bitterly about the 'cowardly and irresolute' Franco.[75] Serrano Suñer, on the other hand, later explained to the Italian ambassador that the problems were due to the fact that 'Franco who has more a military than political mentality was ill-prepared for the tight dialectical game to which the Germans subjected him.'[76] For all the ill-will of the meeting, its rancorous aftermath and the vagueness of the protocol, it constituted a formal undertaking by Spain to join war on the Axis side at a date to be decided by the 'common agreement

of the Three Powers'.[77] However, by November 1940 a damning German
report on the situation with Spain, which had 'grown considerably more
critical' concluded that 'Spain may become a heavy burden to us.'[78] As a
withering Goebbels observed, 'The Führer's opinion of Spain and Franco
is not high. A lot of noise but very little action.'[79]

Clearly shaken by his encounter with the Führer, in the late winter of
1940 Franco seized upon a new and absurd idea for economic autonomy.
The extremist Falangist Civil Governor of Malaga (an erstwhile supporter
of Hedilla), José Luis Arrese, claimed that the famine could be solved at a
stroke by feeding the people dolphin sandwiches, with bread made from fish
meal. These improbable, not to say unpalatable, suggestions so impressed
Franco that the obsequious but ambitious Arrese soared up the political
hierarchy. In fact, Spain – as a German report put it – would remain 'in a
wild, almost anarchic state of disorder' for some time to come. Commenting on the famine conditions within Spain, David Eccles – the British
economic negotiator who had been sent to help Hoare secure Franco's
neutrality – described men, women and 'children picking over the dustbins
and the slop pails standing on the kerb'. Eccles, convinced that 'The Spaniards are up for sale and it is our job to see that the auctioneer knocks them
to our bid',[80] decided that it was a good moment for the British to step up
their policy of offering economic aid to Spain to secure its neutrality.
Smarting from German intransigence, and aware that his regime itself
would begin to suffer if Spain did not receive additional wheat from the
Americans, even Franco felt that the time had come to accept foreign
aid. Blithely assuring the American ambassador that he had not signed a
Tripartite Agreement with the Axis powers, Franco hinted darkly that the
only thing preventing him from issuing a public commitment to neutrality
was his anxiety about a 'Germany at the frontier crouched ready to spring'.[81]
Perhaps Franco was simply playing political games. Perhaps, in the immediate aftermath of Hendaye, his attitude to his great hero had been somewhat tarnished. As a like-minded personality, he knew better than anybody
how unreliable Hitler could be. Even Göring would later claim that the
Führer's failure to take Spain was his greatest mistake. Whatever Franco's
real motives, he was swift to reassure the Germans that all his agreements
and discussions with the Allies were 'vague and non-binding', and that
rumours that Spain had promised neutrality in return for the delivery of
American foodstuffs had been invented.[82]

Mussolini's misguided decision to launch his 'idiotic campaign in
Greece'[83] on 28 October (which led to the Yugoslav revolt and the British
expedition) forced a tight-lipped Hitler to change his war plans in order to
rescue him, and persuaded the Führer that he might need Spain to join the

war after all. However, the Caudillo's abiding horror of associating himself with failure, along with his apparent reluctance to join any club that would countenance his membership, resulted in a particularly stubborn, inscrutable and exasperating bout of behaviour. When, on 7 December 1940, Admiral Canaris formally requested that Franco enter the war by allowing a German army corps with artillery to cross Spain and attack Gibraltar, the Caudillo unwittingly revealed his hand when he stated that 'Spain could enter the war only when England was about ready to collapse.'[84] He then denied that he had said any such thing, and nervously cited an unexpected deterioration in the food supply as the main obstacle to Spanish entry into the war.[85] However, Hitler's offer of Gibraltar at the end of the war (until which time he needed it as a German base) was not sufficient to tempt Franco. Although in the bunker in 1945 Hitler was still protesting that 'with our Commandos [and] Franco's connivance'[86] he could have easily taken Gibraltar, the Spanish high command had determined that no Spanish initiative would be taken against Gibraltar while the British still had Suez. As the Germans waded through Franco's 'equivocal and vacillating' responses and his 'many digressions into details and non-essentials,'[87] tempers on both sides frayed.

CHAPTER 7

Franco for Sale

Franco and the Second World War, January 1941–December 1945

In all of the relations of this government with the most backward and ignorant
governments in the world, this government has not experienced such a lack
of ordinary courtesy or consideration.

> Secretary of State Cordell Hull to the Spanish ambassador,
> Juan Francisco de Cardenas, 13 September 1941

Although Franco's enthusiasm to join the war ebbed and flowed alongside
German fortunes, his price was creeping up. Not entirely convinced that
the Germans would win, he now not only wanted material aid and major
territorial concessions, but hinted that Spanish participation was dependent upon the Axis closing the Straits of Gibraltar and the Suez Canal.
Although his spirits soared in the wake of German successes in Yugoslavia,
Greece and north Africa, news of the British annihilation of Italian forces
six times the size of the Allied army at Benghazi in January 1941 sent them
tumbling once more. Hitler, feeling 'duty bound to afford relief to my
Italian friend and ally'[1] and forced to revise his overall military plans in the
Balkans, was beginning to suspect that he might need Franco's help after
all. However, while Berlin pointed out 'with comradely candor' that, with
the war all but won, 'for Spain the historical hour had now struck,'[2] Franco
dragged his feet. When the Germans crisply pointed out that 'without the
Führer and the Duce there would not today be any Nationalist Spain or
Caudillo', Franco indignantly protested that 'Spain intended to participate
in the war fully and not obtain anything as a gift.'[3] However, increasingly
strident demands from Berlin for 'a clear yes or no whether he was prepared
to enter the war immediately'[4] produced only 'thoroughly unsatisfactory'
communications from the Caudillo.

Mussolini, despite his conviction that it would prove a 'perfectly useless'[5]
enterprise, was asked by the Germans to try and get some sense out of
Franco. A meeting was arranged at Bordighera in northern Italy, early

February 1941. It was, as the Duce anticipated, a sterile encounter. While Franco rhapsodised about the Duce as 'the greatest political figure in the world ... a true Latin genius', the Italians viewed him as a 'chatterbox, disordered in his exposition, getting lost in minor details and giving rein to long digressions on military matters'.[6] Cognisant of Spain's increasingly desperate economic plight, Mussolini notified the Germans that the best that could be hoped for was to keep Franco inside the Axis camp. Aware of his plummeting importance, Franco stopped off at Montpellier on his way back to Spain from Bordighera to try and bully the French into making concessions in Morocco.

Given the infantile quality of diplomatic negotiations between the three fascist leaders, it is hardly surprising that relations between them were less than harmonious. In the words of a recent biographer of Ciano, discussions were conducted by a 'gaggle of ruffians, psychopaths and buffoons', and were wracked with 'petty jealousies, personal vanity and point scoring'.[7] There was therefore no shortage of malicious gossip to undermine relations. Accustomed to high levels of flattery, the Caudillo cannot have been best pleased at the continuous flow of disparaging personal comments emanating from Germany in late 1940 and early 1941. While an enraged Hitler dismissed him as 'not a sovereign but a subaltern in temperament' and 'A clown! Conceited, arrogant and stupid,'[8] Goebbels denigrated him as 'a jumped-up sergeant-major', a 'conceited loud mouth', a 'pompous ass [who] puffs himself out like anything when the moment seems favourable' and an 'inflated peacock ... sitting on his pretender's throne'.[9] (The fact that Hitler reiterated this exact phrase in the *bunker* reveals that denigration of the Caudillo was common currency within the German high command.) One German diplomat records that the Führer's outbursts about Franco flew through party offices and ministries 'like the wind'.[10] These indiscretions inevitably seeped back to Madrid. Franco, who appeared to idealise the Führer as some sort of abusive father-figure – in much the same way as Hitler himself revered Mussolini – was somewhat more circumspect in his own observations. Unlike the tempestuous Führer, he was, in any case, much too inhibited and uptight to engage in venomous gossip with his subordinates. Wary of open confrontation with even his most abject of minions, Franco was unlikely to risk Hitler's rage by openly criticising him. However, his resentments seeped into his stubborn negotiating style and implacable insistence upon his value.

An increasingly irritated Führer, reluctant to concede any such thing, dispatched a sanguine letter to Mussolini in which he philosophically concluded that 'the gist of the long Spanish speeches and written explanations is that Spain does not want to enter the war and will not do so either'.[11]

Although he viewed this as 'very regrettable', Hitler's desire to bring Spain into the war was more than balanced by a profound reluctance to acknowledge any military dependency upon Franco. Even during his last days in the bunker, Hitler was keen to establish that, despite Franco's burning desire to 'join the victor's club', Spanish intervention was at no stage deemed either necessary or desirable, observing that, 'by ensuring that the Iberian peninsula remained neutral', Franco had already extended the one service he had it in his power to give.[12] By 1941 Hitler was in any case more preoccupied with rescuing Italy from its disastrous involvement in the Balkans, and with preparations for a spring offensive to the east and the war against the Soviet Union, than with dealing with Franco. The German ambassador was directed to be 'cool and reserved with respect to the question of Spain's participation in the war'.[13]

With his beloved *Patria* reduced to starvation and penury, forced to accept food aid from the Allies and redundant in the war in Europe, Franco withdrew into an emotional fortress of his own. Even the German ambassador, von Stohrer, noticed that 'Franco, isolated and undecided, can only with difficulty be moved to make decisions ... sees fewer and fewer people and does not allow himself to be advised even by old friends.'[14] The death of Alfonso XIII on 6 March 1941 did not bring the Caudillo peace of mind. Despite vigorous attempts to suppress spontaneous expressions of grief, the King's demise resulted in a surge in monarchist sympathies. All over Madrid, houses were shrouded with black hangings.[15] When he was not working himself into a frenzy about Masonic plots, an increasingly paranoid and jealous Franco was nursing his suspicions of his elegant, sensual and popular brother-in-law. It was not just the Germans who were irritated by Franco's long-winded disquisitions. His wife's persistent interruptions of his rambling political analyses in wide-eyed deference to Serrano Suñer, and constant directives at the dinner table to 'shut up and listen to what Ramón is saying', did not go down well with the Caudillo. His fifteen-year-old daughter's question, 'Who's in charge here? Papa or Uncle Ramón?' did not help matters.[16]

Although Franco possibly depended upon Serrano Suñer for the paternal and fraternal acknowledgement he craved, and relied upon his political expertise, he was highly suspicious of his ambitions. Bitterly jealous of the Cuñadísimo's prowess at diplomatic functions, Franco must have festered at the fact that the Italians, so disparaging about him, were charmed by Serrano Suñer's wit and intelligence, while even the British ambassador, Sir Samuel Hoare, noted the striking disparity between the 'slow thinking and slow moving' Caudillo and his brother-in-law, who was 'quick as a knife in word and deed'.[17] As Serrano Suñer himself put it to the Italian ambassador: 'the Generalísimo is a simple man. It is just as well he didn't speak much with Hitler.'[18] On the other hand, in November 1941 Ciano, the Italian Foreign Minister, commented to Mussolini that 'Serrano has not yet discovered the proper tone for speaking to the Germans ... He says things with a brutality that makes one jump in one's chair.'[19] Certainly Goebbels viewed him as 'the real fly in the ointment.'[20]

The publication of a book by one of the Cuñadísimo's acolytes, suggesting that only Serrano Suñer could implement the legacy of José Antonio Primo de Rivera, was the last straw. Ignoring his brother-in-law's advice to appoint a much more vigorously Falange cabinet, on 5 May 1941 a peevish Franco brought in the fiercely anti-Falangist Colonel Valentín Galarza (who had played a pivotal role in organising the 1936 uprising) as Minister of the Interior. He was replaced as under-secretary to the Presidency with the drab and servile 36-year-old naval officer, Captain Luis Carrero Blanco. Different from Serrano Suñer in every respect, Carrero Blanco would, in due course, become Franco's right-hand man. As a sop to the monarchists, Kindelán was named Captain-General of Catalonia and his predecessor, Orgaz, was made High Commissioner in Morocco.

Galarza immediately set about curbing the power of the Falange in general, and of Serrano Suñer in particular. Removing two of the Cunadísimo's cronies from positions of power, he began the process of wresting control of the press from the Falange, thereby provoking the resignation of a number of high-ranking Falangists – including Serrano Suñer himself – on the assumption that they would be instantly recalled. Fully aware that the high-ranking Falangists who had resigned were driven more by naked ambition than by any real commitment to their party or Serrano Suñer, Franco easily bought them off with offers of senior posts. Among those drawn back were José Luis de Arrese (of dolphin sandwich fame) and the recently appointed Minister of Labour, José Antonio Giron de Velasco. When Serrano Suñer realised that all his 'friends' had slunk back to high office, he too withdrew his resignation as Foreign Minister. Although for the moment Franco still needed Serrano Suñer to balance the monarchist generals, the political clock was ticking.

The tensions between Franco and his brother-in-law echoed wider tensions between the military and the Falange, which now exploded into the open. When clashes between party members and the police resulted in some deaths in Leon, the Falangist press blamed British anti-military machinations. Franco, seemingly concerned more that the new Minister of the Interior had used his control of the press to issue an over-the-top eulogy to General Orgaz upon his departure for Morocco than about the eruption of political violence back home, was easily persuaded by the Germans to move Press and Propaganda back to the Falange. Although it was renamed the Vice-Secretariat for Popular Culture to try and give it a more civilian image, an immediate outburst of pro-German fervour indicated that little had changed. Its slogan 'One, Great, Free Spain' had a particularly hollow ring to it in a fragmented Spain that was torn between the victors and the vanquished and subject to the political restrictions and harsh censorship characteristic of totalitarian states.

Given that Franco's life was a fantasy in which he played ever-changing roles, it is not surprising that he should have been both fascinated by, and wary of, the power of cinema. Throughout the 1940s, the Compañia Industrial Film Español (Cifesa) ensured that Spanish films were imbued with dogmatic Catholic notions of morality and the sanctity of the Spanish race. In keeping with the regime's militaristic origins, sex (and not violence) was seen as the problem. A profound prurience – the product of apparently endlessly dirty minds – dominated film censorship. The titillating exposure of a cleavage, thigh or midriff was painted over. Kissing and cuddling were kept to a minimum. Unable to accept that these took place at all between anyone other than husbands and wives, an element of incest would seep into films when canoodling couples who clearly were not married were presented as brother and sister.

The censors – keen to earn the approval of their leader – tried to out-do each other to prove their ideological or sexual purity, with Church censors frequently banning authorised films, while the military confiscated approved materials. Determined to out-do the Falange and the military on the morality front, the Church adopted a particularly vigilant attitude to films, which, in due course, a particularly zealous priest would designate 'the greatest calamity that has befallen since Adam – a greater calamity than the flood, two world wars or the atomic bomb'.[21] When, despite the Church's rigour, a suspect film still managed to slip through, Church activists would place a plaque outside the cinema advising the public that 'those who watch today's programme are committing a mortal sin'. Anyone who ignored this warning was then subjected to frenzied religious tirades from pious ladies from Acción Católica, who would lurk in the entrance to cinemas and shriek 'Say an Our Father for the soul of this sinner', while others fell to their knees in prayer.[22]

Despite all these restrictions, the regime depended upon movies to take the Spanish people's minds off the appalling reality of their daily lives. With every element of their lives circumscribed, it is not surprising that the Spanish people – Franco included – developed a passion for the glamour and excitement of films. Paradoxically, this resulted in an influx of films from abroad, particularly from Hollywood, which seriously undermined the xenophobia that Franco was seeking to impose upon the Spanish people. In the late 1940s it was, perhaps, a metaphor for the Franco regime that Madrid, which had relatively few churches, had over seventy film theatres.[23]

Made to feel like a recalcitrant little boy by the Axis powers, and full of suspicions about Serrano Suñer, Franco decided to write a film of his own. It was during this time that he immersed himself in his fictionalised autobiographical film-script, which – in deference to Hitler – he entitled *Raza* (Race). It is, perhaps, no coincidence that he wrote this 'Oedipal narrative'[24] just before he mustered up the courage to topple the Cunadísimo from power. *Raza*, a simple tale of social aspiration, shrouded by noble rhetoric about Spain's glorious past, provides a clear insight into Franco's political, and psychological, priorities at that time. Possibly keen to compete with his elegant brother-in-law, Franco shunts his family up the social scale. Although the urbane Pedro is – as discussed in Chapter 1 – closely based on Franco's brother Ramón, as a lawyer, a civilian and a womaniser he also contains elements of Serrano Suñer. Keen to snatch a virile and masculine image for himself, Franco selected the charismatic romantic actor Alfredo Mayo to play José. When the film was made, Franco watched it repeatedly, weeping throughout.

Franco was not unusual in transposing his personal and psychological dilemma into the world of politics and film at that time. According to the film historian Marsha Kinder, during the Francoist era Spanish cinema was particularly keen on using 'Oedipal conflicts within the family . . . to speak about political issues and historical events'.[25] For Franco, *Raza* had political as well as psychological benefits. Not only did he use it to emphasise the official version of the Spanish civil war as a Holy Crusade, displacing 'patricide onto fratricide', but it helped his supporters gloss over the ideological contradictions inherent within his regime, supposedly in the interest of safeguarding 'the patriarchal family'.[26]

It was not just Franco's own psycho-pathology that was captured on film at this time. A number of Moroccan war films produced by the regime's propaganda machinery exposed the sort of attitudes that underpinned the Nationalist cause. *Harka*, a film about a young officer who arrives in Africa having recently left the academy (clearly based on the Generalísimo himself) was particularly revealing. According to the critic Peter Evans, this romanticised portrayal of the Moroccan venture 'unwittingly exposes the dismissive, castration-anxiety trivialisations of the female characters' and 'highlights the latent, repressed homosexuality of the group . . . seemingly arising naturally from an ideology at once marginalizing women and celebrating the triumphant independence of heroic masculinity'.[27]

Although Franco's fantasised resolution of his childhood difficulties and social shortcomings did little to resolve the reality of Spain's economic situation, it helped to clarify his attitude to the war – albeit briefly. When, on 22 June 1941, the Germans invaded the Soviet Union, Franco's awkward support for the Nazi–Soviet Pact dissolved in a cloud-burst of anti-communist enthusiasm for the Axis powers. An emotional Franco communicated his 'satisfaction at the beginning of the struggle against Bolshevist Russia'. To the horror of his senior generals, he was encouraged by Serrano Suñer to offer volunteer units of Falangists to fight 'against the common foe . . . independently of the full and complete entry of Spain into the war beside the Axis which would take place at the appropriate moment'.[28] A speech by the Cuñadísimo claiming that 'History and the future of Spain require the extermination of Russia' worked Falangists into such a frenzy of hate that they attacked the British Embassy with stones thoughtfully delivered in lorries by the authorities. (When Serrano Suñer contacted the beleaguered ambassador, Sir Samuel Hoare, to ask if he would like more police to be sent in to control the situation, he retorted 'No, but I could do with fewer students!')[29] Given Spain's military shortcomings, Franco was extremely fortunate that Stalin did not respond to the arrival of the Blue Division (laden with holy pictures and medallions illustrating the Assumption of Mary to Heaven)[30] by declaring war on him.

Despite all of this sabre rattling and Franco's provocative decision to transform non-belligerency into 'moral belligerency', Spain was still not equipped to enter the war. While Serrano Suñer patiently explained to the Germans that Spain could not survive an Allied blockade, which would undoubtedly be triggered if it joined the war, Franco blithely dismissed British objections to the dispatch of the Blue Division on the convoluted grounds that there were in fact two wars going on: a completely pointless one between Britain and the Germans, in which he had no part, and a crucial anti-communist one, in which he had a direct stake.

Franco soon tired of this delicate political balancing act. On 17 July 1941, the fifth anniversary of the outbreak of the Spanish civil war, attired in the full white summer regalia of the Jefe Nacional of the Falange, he attempted a Führer-style address to party members, during which much high-pitched shouting and aggressive gesticulation took place. While an astonished Serrano Suñer muttered, 'Is this a bull fight?', a near-hysterical Franco triumphantly linked Spain's destiny directly with that of the victorious Germans. After a slavish account of the Nazis' military triumphs, he bitterly denounced the Soviet Union and spoke with withering contempt of the 'plutocratic democracies'. This astounding lack of political circumspection horrified Vigón and other senior generals. 'It would', the British ambassador

observed, 'be hard to imagine a more provocative speech.'[31] Even the Cunadísimo advised him to leave such outbursts to his underlings, who could
then be blamed if there was adverse political fall-out. Fearing that his
disastrous political *faux pas* might trigger open rebellion among his generals, or even an Allied invasion of Spain, Franco fled to the mountains to
kill ibex, leaving others, his brother Nicolás included, to persuade the Allies
that they should not draw any conclusions from a speech designed for a
domestic audience. Nevertheless, Franco had earned himself the outright
hostility of the British Foreign Secretary, Anthony Eden, and of the American Secretary of State, who snapped that 'the only dignified course for this
country is to withhold further shipments of food and medical supplies to
Spain.'[32]

As aid from Britain and the United States diminished to a dribble, major
shortages of fuel and metals took Spanish industry to the brink of collapse.
On 1 August, General Orgaz – who was seriously considering a military
uprising against Franco – crisply demanded that the Caudillo desist from
making pronouncements on foreign issues without first consulting him
and other senior generals, and called for the immediate dismissal of Serrano
Suñer. Although Franco was not averse to dispensing with his brother-in-
law, he was not going to be told what to do by the military. Frustrated by
his prevarications, the generals began to forge links with civilian monarchists, and to make political provisions should they have to be evacuated
in the event of a German invasion of Spain.

Franco, torn between the side he hoped would win and the side he
feared would win, succeeded in offending both. After brusquely curtailing
refuelling facilities to the Germans in Las Palmas, he warned the Americans
that the imposition of 'economic thumbscrews' might drive Spain into the
war, and then firmly rejected American offers of loans and raw materials
in return for his neutrality.[33] Having thereby succeeded in arousing strong
suspicions about his overall intentions in both camps, in the late autumn
of 1941 he turned his mind back to the sordid business of consolidating his
powers at home. The crushed and starving Spanish public were pummelled
with a tidal wave of bullying propaganda, claiming that if Franco fell, Spain
would go with him, irrespective of who won the war. Franco then used the
obsequious Arrese to purge the Falange of anybody who seemed opposed
to him, and to bring the party firmly to heel.

By the time the Anti-Comintern Pact powers met in Berlin in November
1941, it was becoming clear that Hitler was running into serious trouble on
the eastern front. Although the Japanese attack on Pearl Harbor on 7
December cheered up the pro-Axis brigade, unexpected British victories in
north Africa sent hopes tumbling once more. Franco continued to be a

passive spectator when, on 11 December 1941, Hitler declared war on the United States and thereby threw away 'finally and irrevocably all hope of winning the war against the Soviet Union'. It was as though the Führer, recognising that victory was no longer possible, had set his heart on what would prove to be 'a catastrophic defeat worthy of his historic greatness'.[34]

General Kindelán clearly considered this an opportune moment to air his grievances about the corrupt inefficiency of the Falange bureaucracy and the damaging consequences to the army of its continued involvement in the ruthless repression of Republican civilians. He then demanded that Franco sever his links with the Falange and separate the posts of Head of State and Head of Government. During a public speech in Barcelona, he passionately proclaimed that the restoration of the monarchy was the only way to achieve the necessary 'conciliation and solidarity among Spaniards'.[35] Little did he know how low Franco rated such aspirations.

Aware that a timely reminder of Franco's mighty victory in the civil war was called for, at the beginning of 1942 an ingratiating Arrese organised a particularly slavish reception for the Caudillo during a tour of Catalonia to celebrate the third anniversary of the fall of Barcelona. Franco's arrival was celebrated by artillery salutes, massive processions, the release of 3000 doves and a fly-past of aircraft (hopefully not at the same time). This confusing and highly revealing gesture encapsulates the sheer hypocrisy of the Nationalists, and unwittingly illustrates the disturbed ambivalence of their leader. The doves were not so much a symbol of peace as representatives of the vanquished Republicans, driven from the air by Nationalist military might. Nevertheless, Franco's speeches – 50,000 copies of which were distributed among the vast Falangist crowd who greeted him upon his return to Madrid – hinted that some sort of healing could now take place. Always happy to associate himself with potent masculine images, the Caudillo conceded that anarchist violence in the past was 'the virile expression of our race: explosions of rebellion against a decadent fatherland', but made it clear that under his robust leadership this was no longer called for. He urged warring army officers and Falangists 'to leave behind the petty resentments' and unite within 'a single command, a single discipline, a single obedience' to him. Happy for competing groups to fight with each other, he would not have them challenging him.

Although the British disaster at Singapore on 14 February 1942 induced euphoric predictions about an imminent Axis victory, the closure of the Spanish oil refinery at Tenerife due to a shortage of fuel forced Franco to agree that henceforth oil shipments from the United States would be subject to close inspection. The Americans were justifiably suspicious about Spain's role as a blockade breaker for Germany. An aggrieved Caudillo tried to get his own back at a meeting with Salazar on 13 February, during which he did his best to poison relations between the Portuguese dictator and Britain. To his chagrin, despite his noble efforts on their behalf, the Germans were taking with ever-larger doses of salt the Caudillo's lofty assurance that 'if the road to Berlin were open, then it would not merely be one division of Spanish volunteers but one million Spaniards who would be offered to help'.[36]

On 24 February 1942, Franco learned of the death of his father, aged eighty-four. Tensions between the two men had not eased after the death of Doña Pilar. Trapped in El Ferrol throughout the civil war, Don Nicolás had been appalled at the harshness of the Nationalist repression against people he knew. Franco's niece Pilar (his sister's daughter), a constant visitor to her grandfather's Madrid home, testified that Don Nicolás became virulently anti-Francoist in the aftermath of the war and absolutely loathed Hitler. According to Pacón's wife, Pilar de la Rocha, 'He used to say terrible things in the bars he used to frequent. He used to say that he [Franco] wasn't intelligent, and after the civil war he was worse. He would shout criticisms of him in the street, and on more than one occasion, he was stopped by the police.'[37] On one occasion Don Nicolás's told his friends, 'My son considered himself a statesman and a politician of the first class because that is what his adulators have made him believe, but it is just laughable.' On another, he commented, 'What could my son know of Freemasonry? It is an association of illustrious and honourable men clearly superior to him in knowledge and openness of spirit. He does nothing but pile up against them anathemas and imaginary blame. Could it be to hide his own?'[38]

These observations did little to improve relations between the two men. Unlike his brother Nicolás or his sister's family, Franco refused to visit his father, even during his painful final illness. He did, however, ask his brother Nicolás to send a priest to take his father's confession: Don Nicolás, 'who never wanted anything to do with priests ... sent him away'. Padre José María Bulart was then dispatched to dissuade Don Nicolás from undertaking an *in articulo mortis* (death-bed) marriage with Agustina. The padre, who received a less than cordial welcome, recalled Franco's father as being 'an extremely disagreeable man. A terrible temper, he tried to throw me out.'[39] In the wake of his father's death, a vengeful Franco directed Pacón to take the body to El Pardo. When the judge refused to allow this because of Agustina's objections, the Civil Guard was sent instead and wrested Don Nicolás's body from a sobbing, hysterical Agustina. Although Franco, desperate to salvage something of his *Raza*-style fantasy, accorded his father a military funeral fit for a hero, he could not bring himself to attend. Nevertheless, he spitefully excluded both Agustina and their daughter from the occasion. According to Salóm, the moment Don Nicolás died, Agustina's possessions were removed from the house in El Ferrol.

The psychiatrist Enrique González Duro considers it significant that after his father's death Franco was desperate to get Don Nicolás's admiral's baton for himself. Instead it was given to Nicolás, a state of affairs his sister, Pilar, stubbornly insisted was appropriate 'because Paco was not a naval officer, and in any case Nicolás was the eldest in the family'. Franco's nephew Nicolás Franco de Pobil would recall that 'my uncle's single obsession was that [my father] should give it to him. This was the baton that is given to naval officers when they're promoted. It's funny because [my father] also inherited his sabre, but this was of no interest to him.'[40] Duro concludes that 'the Generalísimo failed to inherit the baton-phallus and symbolically would therefore remain castrated for ever'.[41]

Hoping to gain potency in other ways, Franco now renewed his attempts to associate himself with the macho fascist powers. Having displayed unseemly enthusiasm about the Japanese assault on the Americans at Pearl Harbor, Franco staunchly reaffirmed Spain's determination to stand alongside Germany in the fight against communism. His brother-in-law was more circumspect. Aware that the entry of the United States into the war did not bode well for the Axis, Serrano Suñer delivered surprisingly vigorous assurances to the Americans that Spain would keep out of the war, albeit with the languid proviso that it would not be judicious 'if Spain should begin to make faces at Germany at this precise stage in human history'.[42] With the American and British embassies in Madrid implementing a policy that allowed for Britain and America's 'preclusive' purchase of Spanish wolfram and other metals from Spain, which up to now had formed an important part of German war supplies, Franco was forced to divert the anger and vengefulness inflamed by his father's death a bit closer to home. In mid-April he dealt with simmering military discontent in an uncharacteristically forthright manner, sacking the monarchist General Espinosa de los Monteros – whom he suspected was involved in preparations for an anti-Franco coup alongside Kindelán and Orgaz – allegedly for his inflammatory speech against 'the disloyalty and limitless ambition' of Serrano Suñer. Lest his brother-in-law get the wrong idea, Franco swiftly dismissed the Cuñadisímo's political secretary for alleged homosexuality.

Latent tensions between Franco and his brother-in-law burst into the open when army officers and Falangist students clashed on the streets of Pamplona, Burgos and Seville. While the Minister for the Army, General Varela, complained bitterly about the damaging ineptitude of Falange officials, the Falangist poet Dionisio Ridruejo, invalided out of the Blue Division at the end of May, expressed to the Caudillo his dismay at the high levels of corruption within the regime. Franco, however, had other things on his mind.

It is perhaps significant that, after the death of his father, Franco's behaviour should trigger rumours that he was about to proclaim himself king. At the end of May 1942, Franco escaped to the Castle of Isabel la Católica – whose 'totalitarian and fascist policy' he so admired – in Medina del Campo, to inaugurate the training school of the Sección Femenina of the Falange. With the Caudillo's idealised, Madonna-like mother being projected by the Sección Femenina as a role-model for Spanish womanhood, it was a small step for her son, 'the saviour of Spain', to be presented as having rights to kingship exceeding 'rights accruing from imperial bed-chambers'.[43]

In Germany, however, the Falangist general and commander of the Blue Division, Augustín Muñoz Grandes, was openly blaming the chaotic situation in Spain on the incompetence of the Caudillo. The Germans, concerned at 'the antagonism between Franco and the military men who ... are demanding the dismissal of Serrano Suñer', thought that a *coup d'état* in the form of an ultimatum to Franco' was imminent.[44] Worried that the Nazis might back Muñoz Grandes in a military uprising against him, Franco immediately replaced him with General Emilio Estéban Infantes. Muñoz Grandes was brought back to Spain, where Franco heaped prestige and favours upon him. His 'agile left hand', as the Catalan notable Francesc Cambó described such political ploys, proved highly effective over years.

He toys with men – especially his generals – with consummate skill: now he puts the most brilliant of his aides into the shade, without anyone saying a word; now he plucks a prestigious prize out of nowhere and brings him back from the shadows into the light. And all these games he plays with such dexterity that they affect only the person concerned, thereby avoiding any joint action against himself.[45]

A disorientated Muñoz Grandes would, in due course, become one of Franco's most loyal, if difficult, supporters.

Nevertheless, Franco realised the time had come to shore up his regime and pacify his critics. During his annual speech to the Consejo Nacional on 17 July 1942, after customary complaints about 'tense vigils in which a suffocating responsibility weighs on lonely shoulders', he indignantly protested that the Francoist coalition was absolutely solid. That he was, in fact, seriously worried about conflict within the regime was exposed when he hinted that he would create a non-representative Cortes to encompass 'the contrasting of opinions ... the airing of aspirations', albeit within extremely tight guidelines. He rather spoilt the effect by concluding with the rallying cry that 'little will be saved of the liberal democratic system'

and protesting that 'the totalitarian regime has fully demonstrated its superiority . . . it is the only one which is capable of saving a nation from ruin'.[46]

That this erratic homily was hardly the best way to reconcile opposing
camps within the regime soon became clear. In mid-August 1942, a militant
Falangist threw a bomb into the predominantly Carlist crowd that had
gathered at the Sanctuary of the Virgin of Begoña near Bilbao to pray for
members of the Carlist militias killed during the war. General Varela, the
Minister of War – a Carlist sympathiser and virulent opponent of the
Falange – was presiding over the ceremony. Backed by the Minister of the
Interior, Colonel Valentín Galarza, he angrily denounced the incident as
an attempt on his own life and a flagrant attack on the army by the Falange.
He threatened to resign his position unless Franco curbed the Falange's
powers. Assuming, rightly, that the other generals would be unlikely to
rebel because they had too much to lose, Franco simply accepted Varela's
resignation and dismissed Galarza.

Despite this brisk and effective move, the poisonous whisperings of
Franco's two Iago-like advisers, Arrese and Carrero Blanco, continued to
fan Franco's jealousies of his brother-in-law, who did not help his cause by
speaking openly about Franco 'as one speaks of a moronic servant'[47] during
a visit to Italy. Even the Germans were concerned about 'the feeling of the
military men and other circles against Serrano Suñer, which can actually
be characterised as hatred'.[48]

However, although an aggrieved Franco bitterly complained that Serrano
Suñer 'only does what he feels like',[49] he only succeeded in mustering up
sufficient moral indignation to deal with him when news that he was having
an affair with the wife of Lieutenant-Colonel Diez de Rivera, the Marqués
de Llanzol, was leaked to Doña Carmen by his malicious sister-in-law, her
great crony, Pura Huétor. Enraged that Serrano Suñer was behaving like
his father, Franco summoned him to his office and dismissed him as Foreign
Minister because of his shortcomings during the Begoña crisis. When an
insouciant Serrano Suñer presented him with some papers to sign prior
to leaving, Franco childishly snapped, 'I would prefer the new minister
presented them to me.' Serrano Suñer was replaced by the elderly general
Count Francisco Gómez Jordana, whose monarchist credentials mollified
the generals, while his military background and minuscule stature soothed
the Caudillo. The pro-Axis General Carlos Asensio Cabanillas replaced
Varela as Minister of the Army. The Falange fell under Franco's direct
control when he took over the presidency of the Junta Política himself.

The fall from favour of the 'evil and disloyal' Serrano Suñer did little to
reassure the Caudillo, who would henceforth claim that his brother-in-law
was 'the only one to blame for all the evils that take place in Spain'.[50] As

always, Franco's personal and emotional impulses were inextricably linked with his ruthless political agenda. His instinct for survival enabled him to resolve a seriously dangerous crisis and come out on top. He allowed the army to gain political ground over the Falange – but only after removing his most virulent military opponents – and brought the party firmly under his own control.

In the aftermath of the rampantly pro-Axis Serrano Suñer's fall from power, Franco dispatched a fulsome letter to Mussolini emphasising the continuity of Spanish foreign policy. He need not have worried. The Führer, uncharacteristically impressed with Franco's handling of the crisis, warmly commended him for terminating Serrano Suñer's 'game of passing himself off as a friend of the Axis while preventing Spain joining the Axis coalition'. With the army now firmly under Franco's control, the Germans viewed Muñoz Grandes' plans to overthrow him as little short of a 'fantasy'.

However, the vigour with which the regime's official film company, NO-DO, established in September 1942 under the auspices of the FET y de las JONS, monitored domestic and foreign news reflected his regime's continuing, deep-rooted paranoia. Although foreign news was restricted to 'the purely frivolous (new hairstyles from Paris) and the conflictive (strikes in France and Britain) there was one constant feature: anti-communism'.[51] The female form was, inevitably, considered to be particularly dangerous. Photos of women with cleavages on display or raised hem-lines were removed or touched up, while news coverage of boxing events was banned altogether, presumably for fear that boxers' naked torsos would unleash a 'premature outburst of sexual bestiality'[52] in repressed Spanish women.

The Caudillo's undiluted enthusiasm for the Führer – who, he assured the Americans, was 'an honourable gentleman'[53] – was about to be put seriously to the test. In November 1942, thousands of Allied troops and tons of equipment were assembled in Gibraltar ready to be shipped through the Straits, right under Spanish guns, over to north Africa in Operation Torch, the objective of which was shrouded in secrecy. Although initially Franco directed Jordana to notify the Allies that an invasion of French north Africa would trigger Spain to enter the war on Germany's side, it suddenly occurred to him that these military preparations might presage an Allied attack on Spanish territory. His fears were not allayed when the Allies notified him that, if he remained out of the conflict, Spanish interests would be fully respected and economic assistance would flow, but if he allowed the Germans passage through Spain, they would not hesitate to take action against him. Face to face with the possibility of his own political, and possibly physical, demise, a traumatised Franco rushed hotfoot to the mountains, where he vented his anxieties in the frenzied slaughter of animals, leaving his extremely anxious Foreign Minister to monitor developments from Madrid. Jordana was hugely relieved when news of a massive British and American landing along the coast of Morocco and Algeria indicated that they were not about to invade Spain. Franco returned to the capital only after a cordial letter was handed over from Roosevelt reassuring him that 'Spain had nothing to fear from the United Nations'. Almost hysterical with relief, Franco slavishly assured the Allies of his heartfelt 'intention of avoiding anything which might disturb our relations in any of their aspects'.

His gratitude was short-lived. When, in November 1942, General Kindelán, articulating the disquiet of monarchist generals, demanded the Caudillo's unequivocal commitment to the Allies, the reinstatement of the monarchy – with Franco as regent – and a categoric statement of neutrality in the war, Franco was furious. With his back to the wall and his instinct for survival honed by his recent flirtation with disaster, Franco played his hand with a mixture of peasant cunning and cynical skill that helped consolidate his power and confuse friends and foes alike. He sat tight for three months, then quietly replaced Kindelán as Captain-General of Catalonia with the pro-Falangist General Moscardó. On 12 November, he reinstated the pro-German Yagüe as commander of the Spanish forces in Melilla. This had the duel benefit of neutralising German overtures to Yagüe as a potential replacement for Franco, and counterbalancing the rampantly monarchist, pro-Allied High Commissioner in Morocco, General Orgaz. The Americans, fearing that this provocative appointment was the first step towards an attack on French Morocco, assigned large numbers of troops to the border. Franco pounced upon this as an excuse to renew his pleas to the Germans for sufficient war materials to enable Spain to resist Allied incursions into Spanish Morocco. The Germans failed to meet his demands.

The German occupation of Vichy on 11 November convinced the pro-Allied camp that an Axis invasion of Spain was imminent, and Hitler enthusiasts – including Generals Asensio, Girón and Arrese – that now was the time to join the war on the German side. Franco maintained an enigmatic silence throughout this impassioned debate. Determined to keep his options open, he turned down the Germans' request to use the Balearics as a base from which to rescue airmen shot down in the sea, and then sought to improve relations with the Allies by clinching the Bloque Ibérico with Portugal on 20 December 1942. His sense of balance soon evaporated, however. After receiving greetings from Hitler, King Vittorio Emanuele III and Mussolini on his fiftieth birthday, an emotional Caudillo telegraphed the Führer his 'best wishes that victory accompanies your armies in the glorious enterprise of freeing Europe from Bolshevik terror'. On 7 December 1942 he delivered a rambling and incoherent speech to the Consejo Nacional, reaffirming his belief that 'the liberal world is crumbling' and firmly associating his regime with the 'youthful rebellion against the hypocrisy and inefficacy of the old liberal systems'. An uncharacteristically friendly Franco then attempted to explain his volatile behaviour to a bewildered and sceptical Sir Samuel Hoare in terms of his famous 'two-war' theory. Mussolini was clearly as unimpressed with Franco's attempts at obfuscation as the British Ambassador. In January 1943, to celebrate Goebbels's fiftieth birthday, he sent him 'a sword carved by Messina' originally intended for Franco but, as Ciano noted in his diary, 'times have changed.'[54]

A temporary blip also occurred in Hispano-German relations when the new German ambassador, Hans Adolf von Moltke, notified Berlin, quite wrongly, that Franco had flown to Lisbon to meet Churchill in order to negotiate Spanish entry in the war on the Allied side. Undaunted by this setback, Franco renewed his pleas to Berlin for a massive arms delivery to prevent incursions by the Allies into the Iberian Peninsula. This resulted in the signing of a secret protocol with the Germans in early February 1943 (which was never activated). It was not an auspicious moment to forge closer links with Berlin. Montgomery's success against German and Italian forces at El Alamein in October 1942, the Allied landing in north Africa soon after, and the German defeat at Stalingrad on 6 February 1943 marked a definitive turning point in the war. Although Franco was undoubtedly aware of this state of affairs, he found it hard to relinquish his pro-Axis emotions. After assuring the Allies that 'Spain will not even discuss possible military concessions to the Axis', he dispatched Arrese to Berlin, where his unfettered enthusiasm for the Nazis so enraged the Anglophile Jordana that he immediately tendered his resignation. Franco neither accepted Jordana's resignation nor reprimanded Arrese. Instead, he allowed the two men to vocalise his conflicting and differing approaches to the war, using Jordana in negotiations with the Allies, and Arrese in discussions with the Axis.

Even so, on 17 March 1943, during Franco's inaugural address to the newly created and carefully selected Cortes, he recognised that it might be wise to emphasise his authoritarian tendency in terms of Spain's glorious past and connections with the Catholic Church rather than his enthusiasm for fascism. Mistakenly encouraged by this apparent shift in emphasis, twenty-seven senior parliamentary deputies or *Procuradores*, including army officers, bankers, monarchists and even Falangists, signed a document pointing out that the traditional Spanish Catholic monarchy should be reinstated before an Axis defeat to avoid Allied retaliation against Spain because of Franco's flirtation with Germany and Italy. An enraged Caudillo immediately arrested the ringleaders and dismissed the rest of the signatories from office. Full of dark anxieties, he alleged that his security forces had exposed an international Masonic plot, the intention of which was to drive a wedge between him and the army, and impose a liberal monarchy in order to destabilise Spain and facilitate a communist take-over.

These fears provoked a surge in Franco's fascist fervour. During his civil war anniversary speech on 17 July, he worked the Falangist crowds into a frenzy. Giving them a fascist salute, he denounced the faint-hearted bourgeois and conservatives who did not understand 'our revolution', and cited communism as a justification for rejecting the chaos of democracy and maintaining the integrity of the Falange. These pro-Axis protestations could hardly have been more inappropriately timed. On 25 July 1943, Mussolini was arrested and replaced by Marshal Pietro Badoglio, triggering a powerful anti-fascist backlash in Italy. Although a sobbing Franco recounted this news to the cabinet, secretly he must have been deeply gratified at the fall from power of the Duce, whom the Führer – in marked contrast with the sort of thing he said about Franco – had once emotionally described as 'my equal – perhaps in some respects – even my superior'.[55] Maybe now Franco would become Hitler's favourite.

Any such hopes were short-lived. After invading northern Italy, the Nazis would establish Mussolini at the head of a puppet government, thereby unleashing a terrible civil war within Italy itself. For the moment, however, Franco, clearly smug at his own political survival and the Führer's omnipotence, nonchalantly assured the American ambassador, Carlton Hayes, that Germany had the power to continue the war without Italy. He then blamed insubordinate underlings for the rampantly pro-Axis propaganda being generated by the Falange press, but could not prevent himself adding that 'democratic propaganda was sometimes objectionable because it criticised the internal system in Spain'. Franco then expanded his theories about the various wars taking place, to incorporate the complex notion that Spain was entirely neutral in the Allied–Axis war, was on the side of the Americans in the war against the Japanese, and was with the Germans in the war against the Bolsheviks. When an incredulous Hayes pointed out the diplomatic discrepancies of this stance, Franco retreated into a sulky silence. Reluctant to relinquish his chosen role as the champion of anti-Bolshevism, but sensing an eventual Allied victory, Franco reluctantly directed that the Spanish press, radio and newsreel services be placed on a more impartial basis.

Meanwhile, the Americans spent as much time as possible driving around in the large limousines they had brought over from the United States with them. This strategy was designed to impress upon the Spanish government the efficacy of associating with a wealthy country that had unlimited access to gasoline. Hayes' brand new, red Buick convertible 'caused eyes to pop in every corner of Spain'. The American diplomat William Beaulac was convinced that the importation of several Packard limousines for use by Spanish ministers was a definitive factor in shifting attitudes towards the Americans. As he points out, 'Even a Falangist must have been hard put to be anti-American while he rode through Madrid's streets in a Packard limousine.'[56]

It was not just the communist threat that was worrying Franco. In December 1943, his security services discovered that the heir to the throne was urging his supporters to oppose the regime. Feeling hurt and betrayed, Franco dispatched an aggrieved and convoluted letter to Don Juan. In it, he claimed that, as Caudillo, his right to rule Spain was superior to that of the Borbóns, because it was based upon 'the rights of occupation and conquest, not to mention that which is engendered by saving an entire society'. Lest the Pretender imagine that he was enjoying himself, he hastened to point out that he had adopted power out of a commendable sense of duty, insisted that the rising of 1936 was not monarchist as much as 'Spanish and Catholic', and suggested that the exiled King's subversive attempts to return to Spain were undermining his careful preparations for a restoration. Don Juan's sharp denunciation of the 'ominous risk' of having power 'concentrated exclusively in a single person, unsanctioned by any statute enacted in a lawfully constituted institution' did not go down well with the Caudillo. Nor did he take kindly to a naïve if polite petition from General Orgaz and other members of the military High Command delicately drawing his attention to the fact that he had been in power for 'longer than the term originally foreseen' and asking 'with loyalty, respect and affection' whether 'the time had come to give Spain a monarchy'. A deeply scornful Franco had no difficulty dealing with the 'rebels' individually, most of whom then withdrew their signatures.

Always happy to jettison hard-held beliefs if they impinged upon his hold on power, in a cabinet meeting on 26 September 1943 Franco agreed to recall the Blue Division – many of whom now joined the German SS – and delivered his first public referral to Spain's 'vigilant neutrality'. Keen to avoid the pro-Allied, monarchical block drawing too many conclusions from this, he awarded a number of military medals and promotions to pro-Axis officers, including General Yagüe. This dextrous political footwork did not fool the British ambassador, who complained that 'Franco's obvious sympathies with the Axis and the impervious complacency with which he behaved towards the Allies were daily becoming more difficult to endure.'[57] American demands for a more vigorous display of neutrality, including the cessation of military and economic aid to Germany, continued to fall on deaf ears. This is not surprising, given that Franco suspected that an Allied victory 'would mean his own annihilation'.[58] The situation in Europe was, therefore, less than reassuring. With the Allies advancing on Germany from the east and west, Germany's defeat now seemed inevitable.

This alarming prospect induced the contradictory aspects of Franco's personality to spiral in opposing directions. On the one hand, he sought to persuade the Führer that 'a neutral Spain which was furnishing Germany with wolfram and other products is of greater value to Germany than a Spain which would be drawn into the war'. On the other, he tried to reassure the Allies that Spain 'had done a great service to the Allies by not entering the war'. This view was not widely shared in Washington, where the Secretary of State, Cordell Hull, considered it extraordinary 'for a country to assume it is rendering a great service to its neighbours by not attacking them'. Under pressure from Hoare and Hayes, Franco reluctantly agreed to 'take the step entirely compatible with Spanish neutrality of declaring a permanent embargo on the exportation of wolfram' to Germany.[59] When he failed to implement this, an oil embargo was imposed upon Spain from 29 January 1944.

Although, with ill-informed bravado, Franco reassured the Spanish people that the oil embargo would have little impact upon them because Spain would soon find a way of producing synthetic gasoline, the embargo was an economic disaster. When, despite his omnipotent pretensions, the victory parade of 1 April 1944 took place without tanks or armoured cars, Franco was forced to strike a deal with the Allies. On 2 May 1944, an agreement was signed between Spain, the United States and Britain whereby petroleum exports to Spain were resumed on the condition that Spanish exports of wolfram to Germany were reduced, the German Consulate in Tangier closed down, all remaining Spanish units withdrawn from the Soviet Union, and all German spies and saboteurs expelled from Spain. Although it was his own intransigence that had plunged Spain into economic and social chaos in the first place, a strident Caudillo attempted to convince himself and the Spanish people that this was a major diplomatic triumph. Construing the Allies' willingness to negotiate with him at all as a sign of their weakness, he was beginning to wonder whether they might, after all, tolerate his regime after the fall of fascism. This hope seemed vindicated when, on 24 May 1944, Winston Churchill, keen to neutralise Franco during the forthcoming Normandy landings and, as he later explained to Roosevelt, anxious to prevent 'the Iberian Peninsula [being] hostile to the British after the war',[60] disingenuously commended Franco's 'resolve to keep out of the war'.[61]

With one eye firmly to the post-war world, on 17 July 1944 Franco delivered a speech to the Consejo Nacional in which he emphasised his healing, peaceful role in Europe and outlined his regime's great achievements in health and education within Spain. He argued that 'spontaneous' outbursts of popular enthusiasm among the people and his regime's heavy reliance upon the gospels imbued it with the highest form of democracy. Reducing the sentences for some political prisoners, he emphasised the crucial role of the Falange – whose militants, like José in *Raza*, he claimed were 'half-monk, half-soldier' – in forging a unique third way somewhere between fascism and democracy. Reiterating his 'two war' theory, he offered to collaborate in the post-war battle against communism, just as long as this did not impinge upon his regime.

He immediately undermined these soothing tactics by replacing his Anglophile Foreign Minister Jordana, who had died on 3 August, with José Félix de Lequerica, seen by Serrano Suñer as 'the Gestapo man'. Lequerica had already acknowledged that 'after my pro-German activities in Vichy ... I am doomed to disappear from the international scene as soon as Hitler is defeated'. The British ambassador 'had expected Franco would have marked in some impressive manner the loss of his Foreign Minister. Instead, he seemed to regard it with his habitual complacency as an occurrence of no special significance.' 'Dictators', he concluded, 'are immune from the sorrows that touch ordinary mortals and the obligations that are respected in the world of smaller people.'[62] This was hardly the best moment for Franco to shift the composition of his cabinet in favour of the Axis. On 24 August, the city of Paris was liberated from the Germans by Free French Forces in which exiled Republicans had played a critical role. News of armoured cars roaring around the streets of Paris flying Spanish Republican flags bearing names like 'Guadalajara' and 'Teruel' raised the spectre of an invasion of Spain by large numbers of armed Spanish Republicans.

While the Red Army drove the fleeing German army back towards Berlin, Franco clung to the belief that the retreat was a device to lull the Allies into a false sense of security before unleashing a mighty secret weapon. However, even the Caudillo was beginning to recognise that things were not going quite as he hoped. He therefore notified the US ambassador of his huge relief at the Allied military successes in France, but outlined his concern that, with Germany defeated, there would be nothing to impede a Soviet domination of Europe. His attempts to place himself at the forefront of an anti-communist crusade after the war were greatly aided by the understandable but misguided influx of communist Spanish Republicans over the border into Spain. As the British ambassador commented at the time, 'the reckless movement of a few hundred Spanish adventurers on the frontier has given him the chance of posing as the champion of Spain against a red invasion [and the] pretext for arresting and executing a formidable number of his political opponents'.[63] Not only did their arrival seem to vindicate Franco's anti-communist fervour, but it kept a potentially restive army happily occupied in a guerrilla war along the border with France. It also created a sufficient surge in the hatreds and fears of the civil war to bring the monarchists in the military rallying to his support. Most unfortunate of all, it convinced an increasingly anti-communist Churchill of the efficacy of believing the Caudillo's protestations that his pro-Axis activities were 'a series of small incidents'.

In an interview with the director of the United Press Foreign Service on 7 November 1944, Franco reiterated his conviction that his regime's strong Catholic principles gave it an 'organic democracy' and a 'spirit of justice'. Echoing colonial rhetoric, he hinted that elections would take place as and when the Spanish people had grown out of the 'egoism and anarchy' which, for the moment, rendered them incapable of handling the responsibility. Having implied that the installation of a new monarchy was nigh, he suggested that his 'serene and dispassionate understanding of what is and is not just' rendered him an essential participant in the post-war peace negotiations. The near-hysterical adulation with which this interview was greeted in the Spanish press was not replicated in Europe. Franco therefore dispatched a letter to Churchill via the Spanish ambassador in London, suggesting the formation of an Anglo-Spanish anti-Bolshevik alliance to help Germany resist the Soviet Union. In London, however, a government spokesman told the House of Commons that there was no reason 'why any country which has not made a positive contribution to the United Nations' war effort should be represented at the peace conference.' Although the British Prime Minister feared that any encouragement of the opposition to Franco was tantamount 'to stirring up a [communist] revolution in Spain', he was persuaded to draft a stiff letter of reply to Franco by the Foreign Minister, Anthony Eden. In this letter – rather startlingly, given his subsequent behaviour – Churchill crisply disabused Franco of his hope that 'His Majesty's Government would be ready to consider any *bloc* of Powers based on hostility to our Russian allies, or any assumed need of defence against them'.[64] A sulky Franco had to content himself with striving to sow discord between the Allies by heaping favours on the newly arrived American ambassador, Norman Armour, while remaining snootily aloof from Victor Mallet, who replaced Sir Samuel Hoare as British ambassador.

On the night of 23 December 1944, in a gesture of a grandiloquent defiance towards everyone, Franco organised a party fit for a young princess to celebrate the coming of age of his daughter 'Nenuca'. The message of this lavish occasion was quite clear. Franco would not be making way for anyone. The old aristocracy boycotted the event, and the entire diplomatic corps – apart from the American ambassador – were excluded. That night a godfather-like Caudillo responded with characteristic ruthlessness to a rumour that the Allies were planning to replace him with a government headed by the conservative Republican, Miguel Maura. While his guests danced in sumptuous surroundings, he directed his secret police to burst into the houses of those establishment figures known to have had contact with either Maura or Gil Robles. Lequerica later bizarrely dismissed these sinister events as the work of 'communist elements' in the police force.

It was, in the circumstances, not entirely surprising that Franco would not feel remotely constrained by the requirements of the Yalta Conference, held between 4 and 11 February 1945, for free elections in the liberated countries. 'Fat, smug and self-complacent, apparently unworried by his past, undoubting as to his future, as confident of his indispensability as of his own wisdom',[65] he could afford to be dismissive. Franco's burgeoning sense of confidence was helped when, on 19 March 1945, Don Juan blighted the chances of an early restoration by issuing his premature 'Lausanne Manifesto', denouncing the totalitarian aspects of the regime and calling for the Caudillo to make way for a moderate, democratic, constitutional monarchy. Although he had the support of Kindelán and other high-ranking monarchists, without Allied support Don Juan was reliant solely upon Franco's willingness to fulfil these demands. This was unlikely to be forthcoming. As Franco tartly notified Kindelán, 'As long as I live I'll never be a Queen Mother.' A delegation was dispatched to tell the Pretender to the throne that the Church, the army and the bulk of the monarchists had remained loyal to Franco.

Despite his evident self-satisfaction, Franco's attitude to a restoration was fraught with contradictions. His political motivations were clear enough: although he did not want to share power with a potentially vengeful monarch, he needed to keep monarchist hopes alive to counterbalance the ambitions of the Falange. Emotionally, however, he was much more ambivalent. His attitude towards Don Juan exposed Franco's tortured and contradictory attitude towards authority figures. For him, Don Juan was – as the Pretender to the throne – something of a father-figure whose admiration he craved; but as Alfonso XIII's son, he was a rivalrous brother who wanted to displace him. Because of this, while Franco could not relinquish the idea of a restoration, Don Juan de Borbón was totally unacceptable to him as King of Spain. Franco's rambling, long-winded, often numbing, always self-righteous diatribes to the monarchist generals on the subject of a restoration usually succeeded in blinding both his audience and himself to his underlying motivations. His fluctuating emotional agenda helped him to convince monarchists of his total commitment to the idea of a restoration, and the Falangists that he was doing everything within his power to prevent such a possibility.

On 1 April 1945, the civil war celebrations completed the annual cleaving of the wounds. Franco reiterated his contradictory role as the facilitator of peace and the fighter of communist 'thieves' and 'assassins'. He then attempted to defuse the problem posed by Don Juan and his supporters by adopting a 'monarchical form of government', and establishing a Council of the Kingdom to designate his monarchical successor. However, he ensured that he would continue as Head of State until such time as he either died or chose to relinquish power. Feeling rather more secure, Franco then made a few conciliatory gestures towards the Allies, freeing the foreign press from censorship and (supposedly) abolishing the death penalty for offences committed during the civil war. However, in the United States the death of President Roosevelt on 12 April 1945 and his replacement by Harry S. Truman did not bring about a hoped-for improvement in relations with Spain.

Meanwhile, despite the devastating revelations of the horror of Nazi rule in Europe, the Falange press continued to commend the inspirational leadership of the Führer. Franco's own enthusiasm for Germany had not, it would seem, been dented by the devastating implementation of the 'Final Solution', which had, by the beginning of 1944, been extended to the whole of occupied Europe, and had resulted in the extermination of six million Jewish men, women and children. Although supposedly shrouded with secrecy, the Nazis' attitude to the Jews could not have been clearer. In 1939 Hitler had openly predicted a new war that would bring about 'the destruction of the Jewish race in Europe'. In the summer of 1941, Rudolf Höss – a member of the Freikorps who had become the Commandant of Auschwitz – was notified by Himmler that 'The Führer has ordered the final solution of the Jewish question and we – the SS – have to carry out this order.' On 6 October 1943, Himmler told party leaders that 'by the end of the year, the Jewish question will have been settled in all the occupied countries. Only a few individual Jews who have managed to slip through the net will be left.'[66] Whether or not Franco was privy to every detail of the Führer's murderous policy, his diplomats in Germany certainly kept him closely informed about developments there. Although he allowed Jewish refugees into Spain during the Second World War, his adoption of a strident anti-Semitism to curry favour with Hitler strongly implies that he not only had a good idea about what was going on, but also – despite (or because of) his own Jewish heritage – at some level approved of it. Indeed, many aspects of Hitler's policies echo Franco's attitude to the Republicans. Even as late as 1945, executions continued to take place on a daily basis in Spain, and Franco himself admitted that there were at least 26,000 political prisoners.

It was therefore not entirely surprising that Franco was hoping, until the very end, that Hitler would snatch victory from the jaws of defeat. Mussolini was less confident. While the Allied troops pushed towards northern Italy and the Red Army forced the German troops back to Berlin, the Duce blamed Hitler – a 'thoroughgoing authoritarian' – for everything.[67] Hitler blamed everyone and everything for impending defeat, except himself. Although in February 1945 he complained bitterly that 'Our Italian ally has been a source of embarrassment to us everywhere' and wished that 'the Italians had remained aloof from the conflict', he was reluctant to criticise Mussolini himself.[68] For Hitler, it was the German people themselves who had proved 'unworthy' of him. 'Germany', he said, 'had failed him: therefore let it be destroyed.'[69] The Führer retreated into his bunker where Goebbels soothed him with repeated readings of Carlyle's *History of Frederick the Great*, which promised a last-minute reprieve. Hitler's obsessive faith in his salvation inculcated his admirers – Franco and the Falange included – with the belief that the situation was resolvable. Even the moderately rational Albert Speer would later acknowledge that 'Strangely, this confidence [that they would win the war] existed apart from the recognition of inevitable defeat.'

It must therefore have come as a terrible shock to Franco when, on 28 April, his infallible hero and ally Mussolini was executed by communist irregulars while trying to escape from Italy. His body, and that of his lover, Claretta Petacci, were strung up in Milan for the masses to mock. On 30 April 1945, Adolf Hitler and Eva Braun took cyanide pills and then – just to make sure – he put a bullet through his own head. Determined not to suffer the same fate as Mussolini, the Führer had directed that their bodies be burnt to a cinder. Franco interpreted Hitler's suicide as evidence of his noble willingness to sacrifice himself for Europe rather than unleash his secret weapon. The death of the Führer and the end of the war in Europe was greeted in Spain with monumental eulogies to the 'Caudillo of Peace' and 'Franco's victory'. Franco did not break off diplomatic relations with the Third Reich until 8 May, 1945 – VE Day.

Although the fall of Berlin to the Red Army and the demise of Mussolini and Hitler signalled the end of many of Franco's dreams and shook his belief in totalitarian invincibility to its core, he appeared, as always, singularly unperturbed by the death of his two great heroes. Indeed, their deaths seemed to enhance his triumphant belief in his own invulnerability and providential mission. In the end, Franco would have the last laugh. Unlike either Hitler or Mussolini, his state machinery was given four decades in which to rewrite its history and create the myth of the Caudillo as the father of modernity. He would die of natural causes at the age of eighty-three.

The myth-making started the minute the war ended. On 17 September 1945 the Caudillo announced, 'It is not only our voices which rise up invoking spirituality, they are the voices of the most important men on earth, those who ask for a return to spirituality that in the middle of chaos and darkness can only be found through the light of the message of God.'[70] However, although Franco was fully aware that, in order to safeguard his power, he needed to distance himself from his fascist past and emphasise his links with God, his diplomatic path would prove far from coherent. Just as deep-rooted fears about his vulnerability repeatedly broke through his delusions of greatness, so his emotional commitment to fascism constantly undermined pragmatic attempts to emphasise the difference between his regime and the Axis powers. Oscillating wildly between attempts to per-suade the Allies that his regime was unique – not quite a democracy, but very Catholic – calm assurances that he was essential to protect Europe from communism, and outbursts of resentfulness at these bloody foreigners' presumption in dictating how he should behave, he succeeded in generating consternation and bewilderment on all sides.

Underlying his statements was a genuine sense of confusion. While the Allies condemned the Falange as fascist, for Franco they were simply 'playing ... the role of a European administration in an African colony'.[71] He could not understand how colonial powers who had long subjugated native populations could object to him doing the same with the anti-*Patria*. In any case, convinced that 'There is nothing to be gained by ceding ground and it might be taken for weakness',[72] Franco stubbornly refused to dismantle the overtly fascist Falange. Apart from anything else, he still needed them to orchestrate outbursts of popular support, to get the blame for the government's errors and to curtail the ambitions of the monarchists.

Although he was justifiably confident that the alliance between the western capitalist democracies and the Soviet Union would soon break down, the dichotomy between the Allies' hostile rhetoric and their prag-matic determination not to generate political instability in Spain would fan both his paranoia and a megalomaniacal faith in his political invul-nerability. Completely isolated within Europe, he would behave like an abusive parent, actively instigating and passively colluding in a ruthless repression and subjugation of the Spanish nation, and then insisting that it thank him. Filled with an aggrieved conviction that power had been foisted upon him by the troublesome and unappreciative Spanish people, a noble belief that he had accepted it out of an innate sense of duty and devotion, and a debilitating anxiety that his enemies were perpetually plotting to snatch it away from him, his behaviour was anything but consistent.

However, although it was Franco himself who precipitated and extended the horrors of the civil war, and then reduced Spain to a position of economic and social chaos because of his resolute commitment to fascism, it was Franco to whom an increasing percentage of the population looked to save them. Although this was partly because they needed and wanted to, and partly because of the manipulative success of his propaganda machine, writing of both past and present, he had in fact left them no alternative.

CHAPTER 8

Mirror, Mirror on the Wall

April 1945–April 1956

It is the will of almost all categories of Spaniards to avoid more bloodshed; and no single fact plays more directly into the hands of General Franco than the argument that precipitate change means another 1936.

The US Embassy in Madrid

To be a minister of Franco is to be a little king who does whatever he feels like without restraint from the Caudillo.

Lequeriqua

At the founding conference of the United Nations, held in San Francisco between 25 April and 26 June 1945, the Mexicans, encouraged by exiled Republicans, put forward a resolution that any state which had been installed with the help of the armed forces of those states that had fought against the United Nations should be excluded. This could only mean Spain. Clearly stung, Franco responded in an interview with a representative of the British United Press. With a combination of unwitting honesty and opportunistic duplicity, he urged the interviewer to 'tell the world that the Falange wields no political power in Spain', but omitted to mention that neither did anybody else. Claiming that he had purged those members of the Falange who had tried 'to identify Spain with Germany and Italy', he referred his critics to the Council of State, which 'would decide on the problems of succession as regards the throne'.[1]

While Franco was prepared to curtail the Falange's power in the interest of safeguarding his own authority, he was certainly not inclined to alienate hundreds of thousands of Falangists by disbanding their party. Nevertheless, he set about moderating some of the more superficial fascist elements of his regime and emphasising its Catholic credentials. Control of the press would pass from the Falange to the Ministry of Education, where the

Catholic Church wielded total power, and Arrese was dropped as Ministro-Secretario del Movimiento and not replaced. Alberto Martin Artajo, President of Catholic Action in Spain and a prominent member of a powerful Catholic pressure group, was made Foreign Minister. His hopes that he could exploit this position to facilitate the reinstatement of a Catholic monarchy were soon dashed. Franco simply used him to persuade many high-ranking Catholics in the western democracies and the Vatican to push for acceptance of the regime the way it was.

Just before the Potsdam Conference in early August 1945, an unusually affable and warm Franco received the new British Ambassador Sir Victor Mallet with smiling protestations 'that things would improve'. Disregarding this disingenuous *bonhomie*, the three great powers, the United States, Britain and the Soviet Union, proceeded to formalise Spain's exclusion from the United Nations, but discounted direct intervention in its 'internal affairs' for fear of provoking another civil war. (An indignant Stalin pointed out that the regime had been imposed upon the Spanish people by Hitler and Mussolini, and it was therefore hardly an internal affair.) During his annual speech to the Consejo Nacional, a petulant Franco implied that he had no desire to join anyway. Commending the skill with which he had kept Spain out of the war, he boasted that he had brought about 'order, the peace and the joy which makes Spain one of the few peoples still able to smile in this tormented Europe'. The spectre of communism was cited as his justification for standing firm. Embedded within this tirade of self-congratulation and defiance lay superficial palliatives to the Allies. A 'Spaniards' Charter of Rights' was launched, which supposedly extended civil liberties to all Spaniards. Trade unions and political parties, however, were explicitly banned.

The San Francisco and Potsdam conferences, along with the election of a new Labour government in Britain under Clement Attlee, with Ernest Bevin as Foreign Minister, induced a misplaced surge of optimism among the leaders of the Spanish left. Hopeful that the full-scale guerrilla war raging in the north and east of Spain would soon bear fruit, a government-in-exile was formed in late August under the presidency of the Republican intellectual José Giral. Exuberant monarchists assumed that the restoration of Don Juan was imminent. In fact, Franco had little to worry about. While tensions between the communist and the capitalist blocs flared, the Republican government in exile would tear itself apart with bitter disputes. As the British ambassador pointed out, 'If the strength of a government is the weakness of the opposition, the Franco regime was less precarious than many of its foreign critics and émigré opponents imagined.'[2]

An Ygor-like Carrero Blanco – ever anxious to anticipate, mirror and reinforce his master's views – confirmed this view in his report on the future of the regime, in which he directed that repression be adopted 'without fear of foreign criticisms, since it is better to punish harshly once and for all than leave the evil uncorrected'. His opinion that 'the only formula possible for us is order, unity and hang on for dear life' was entirely vindicated. With public perceptions – part despairing, part defiant and part adulatory – acknowledging that the regime was now a permanent fixture, initiatives to remove Franco looked increasingly isolated and improbable. Franco had, in large part, sapped the will for rebellion. When, on 25 August 1945, Kindelán delivered a rampantly pro-royalist speech, the Caudillo felt sufficiently secure to sack him as director of the Escuela Superior del Ejército and replace him with his crony Juan Vigón.

The ease with which Franco could dispense with passionate life-long convictions for political advantage was revealed when he bowed to British pressure to relinquish Tangier at a meeting on 7 September. As he commented, 'It's not much to lose if we can't defend it.' The fascist salute was abolished at the same meeting. Although, on the ninth anniversary of his ascendance to supreme power, Franco allowed the fascist Falange youth to march triumphantly through streets bedecked with Spanish flags, he determined to adopt 'a democratic suit as an insurance policy',[3] with a rampant cynicism that would have made Hitler proud. In early October, he agreed to hold a referendum and to announce municipal elections, which he then delayed indefinitely. The rest of the world was left in no doubt that any move to depose him would trigger a military rebellion in his support. Within Spain, the Caudillo continued to swing between the complacent conviction that 'in Spain today, one governs through the popular will' and the aggrieved belief that he was a slave to his people's whims. 'Franco', Arriba sternly reminded then, 'guides the Spanish people, but at the same time he takes his orders from them.' He can, it concluded, 'refuse them nothing'.[4]

Throughout this period, Franco continued to vent his frustration and rage on the Republicans. The huge apparatus for repression within the police, the Civil Guard and the army took up 45 per cent of the state budget for 1946. As economically counterproductive, politically pointless and – albeit on a very different scale – morally reprehensible as Hitler's 'Final Solution', it revealed much about the tortured workings of Franco's psyche. His innate vengefulness was compounded by the fact that he was by now so far removed from the people who implemented his policies – let alone those who were directly affected by them – that there was nothing to dent his innate capacity for self-delusion or to encourage his sense of responsibility. Although the Caudillo insisted that inflation was simply the invention of 'credulous simpletons in economics', and nonchalantly discounted the devastating impact the repression was having on the teetering economy, it brought the motherland to her knees.

Encased within El Pardo, nursing his bitterness at the world's unreasonable attitude to his regime, he lurched from a despairing determination to pack it all in, to robust statements that he would never 'make the same mistake as General Primo de Rivera, I don't resign. For me, it's straight from here to the cemetery.' During his rambling cabinet meetings, Franco oscillated between dark and incoherent analyses of Masonic conspiracies and cheery predictions about how he would revive the Spanish film industry with big productions of his favourite operettas. The greater his anxieties about the former became, the more he relied upon the latter to take his mind off them. Movies about Cowboys and Indians were a particular passion.

Ironically, Franco's enthusiasm for American movies expanded alongside his suspicion of foreigners. The Americans' decision in December 1945 not to replace their retiring ambassador did little for his peace of mind. When the new Spanish ambassador arrived in London, a bitter debate about Spain in the House of Commons culminated in Ernest Bevin robustly asserting that 'we detest the regime'. The British government notified Franco that British patience was 'becoming exhausted'. Although such weedy gestures were unlikely to carry much weight with the Caudillo, they confirmed his paranoid xenophobia and drove him even closer to the Falange.

In early 1946, the publication of German documents revealed the full extent of Franco's collaboration with Axis powers during the war. A United Nations investigation exposed his current policy of protecting war criminals from Germany, Italy and Vichy France, by offering them Spanish nationality. While Britain and the United States nervously debated how to handle these revelations without generating either a military or a communist uprising in Spain, Franco stormed around the country reminding the people how he had defended Spain from 'satanic machinations' during the civil war. He claimed that he was now busy defending her from 'the Masonic superstate' – from which he believed Washington and London took their orders – which was out to destroy Spain simply 'because she had carried the gospel to the world, and her men were the soldiers of God'.

Don Juan, not entirely convinced by these arguments, decided to set up residence in Portugal in February 1946 and not, as Franco had requested, move to Spain and thereby validate the regime. This greatly irritated the Caudillo and heartened the monarchists. On 13 February, 458 high-ranking members of the Spanish establishment signed an open letter to the Pretender, expressing the hope that the monarchy would be reinstated shortly. An enraged Franco resolved that 'They must be crushed like worms.' Davila managed to persuade him that imprisoning the lot without a trial would do nothing for the regime's reputation abroad. Franco had to content himself with exiling Kindelán to the Canary Islands. When Don Juan refused Franco's invitation to visit Spain for a meeting, the peeved Caudillo immediately severed all relations with him.

The monarchical rebellion and his unsatisfactory dealings with Don Juan seemed to inflame Franco's fears and his aggression. Ignoring international pleas for clemency, he directed that one of the leaders of the anti-Franco guerrilla movement, and great hero of the French resistance, Cristino Garciá, be executed alongside nine others on 21 February 1946. This point-less and provocative act of vengefulness triggered the French into closing their border and breaking off international relations with Spain. Britain and the United States were persuaded only with the greatest reluctance to sign a toothless Tripartite Declaration alongside France in the Security Council on 4 March, but firmly discounted any interference 'in the internal affairs of Spain'. Churchill's 'iron curtain' speech on 5 March confirmed Franco's belief that the western democracies feared Stalin more than they loathed him.

In a schizophrenic address to the Spanish people a few days later, Franco denounced international hostility, reiterated his determination to safeguard Spain from its enemies and reassured the western Allies of his good inten-tions. Thoroughly aggrieved at the cumbersome chores involved in being the saviour of Spain and Europe, the Caudillo complained that as 'the sentry who is never relieved ... the one who is watchful while others sleep', he deserved a bit more appreciation. Forgetting momentarily his oft-indulged enthusiasm for hunting, shooting and fishing, he grumbled about how 'as Chief of State, I see my private life and my hobbies severely limited' and boasted that 'my entire life is work and meditation'. He berated his unappreciative people for moaning about their comparatively trouble-free existences and demanded that (like his mother) they 'put a good face on bad news. The worse the news, the happier the face.' A very big smile would be needed for some time.

While the Allies bickered about Franco, the Tripartite Declaration pro-voked what proved to be the last ripple of discord in the higher echelons of the army until the mid-1950s. It was swiftly stamped out by General Varela, who replaced General Orgaz as the High Commissioner in Morocco on 12 March 1946. During the annual parade to celebrate the Nationalist victory in the civil war, on 1 April 1946, Franco was given a massive demonstra-tion of support by the Movimiento. On 6 April, 300,000 signatures were delivered to El Pardo confirming his subjects' loyalty and determination to protect him from 'the hired assassins of the forces of evil'. The Caudillo gave an unwitting insight on his tortured soul when he happily declared that the Masonic and communist plots being fabricated by evil Republican exiles to overthrow him were a clear indication that 'we exist, we are not dead and our flag flies in the wind'. Perhaps he feared that, without enemies, his tenuous sense of self would wither away completely.

Wild and unsubstantiated accusations by the Polish delegate at the Security Council on 17 April 1946, that escaped Nazis were constructing atom bombs on Spanish soil, did little to help the democratic opposition to Franco. The Caudillo responded in a robust two-hour diatribe in the Cortes, during which he denied being a dictator and insisted that the Spanish people were too wild for democracy. Conceding, in a naïve outburst of honesty, that he had been happy to be deemed Nazi-fascist and anti-democratic at a time when such regimes enjoyed great prestige in the world, he acknowledged that it was now necessary 'to underline the very different characteristics of our state'. Spitefully notifying the Spanish people that foreign ostracism was directed at them and not at him, he dismissed the help he had received from the Axis powers during the civil war as 'a drop in the ocean'. On 28 April he crisply notified the Spanish people to 'Be aware that I'm not Father Christmas [Rey Mago] who brings you things as a gift, but the Head of State.'[5]

When the Security Council recommended that the General Assembly call on all its members to break off relations with Spain, a sulky Caudillo announced the supreme indifference of 'the Spanish people' to the opinions of countries that had no right to interfere in their affairs. His affronted defiance was vindicated when Churchill delivered a blistering attack on the absurdity of the Allies telling 'the Spaniards to overthrow Franco, while, at the same time assuring them that there will be no military intervention by the Allies'.[6] Seeming to equate the political isolation into which he had plunged Spain with being ignored, humiliated and attacked by his father as a child, an aggrieved Franco immersed himself in writing virulent articles about Freemasonry, 'one of the most repugnant mysteries of the modern age'.[7] While he sought solace in Salazar's Portugal and the pro-Axis regime of Juan Domingo Perón in Argentina, his supporters continued to orchestrate massive displays of public support for their leader. On 9 December 1946, after a massive demonstration of support by Falangists, the Youth Front and civil war veterans, an exuberant and optimistic Caudillo assured them that 'the rest of the world is dangling from our feet'. He and Doña Carmen then stood for an hour, acknowledging the chants of 'Franco! Franco! Franco!'

Neither impressed nor convinced by these orchestrated displays of support for Franco, on 12 December 1946 the General Assembly agreed to a resolution excluding Spain from all its dependent bodies and directed that all its member nations withdraw their ambassadors from Spain. There were, however, no economic or military sanctions. Although an unrepentant and defiant Franco immediately ordered a new coinage to be minted, on which was engraved his bust and the words 'Caudillo by the grace of God', he was clearly hurt and bewildered by the rebuff. In February 1947 he delivered the startling but heartfelt statement to the *Washington Post* that 'I am a man who never harboured any ambitions of command or power ... If I believed that the interests of my *Patria* lay in my resigning my command, have no doubt that I would do it without hesitation and with joy since command constitutes for me both a duty and a sacrifice.'[8] Depressed by the withdrawal of ambassadors, he heaped hospitality upon any visiting foreign official, however lowly. He took considerable heart from the Truman doctrine of 12 March 1947, which pledged support for 'free peoples to work out their own destinies in their own way' in a bid to combat the expansion of communism. He suspected that the concept of 'free peoples' could be interpreted fairly loosely.

On 28 March 1947, in an attempt to address Allied disquiet about the succession, and sever links between some monarchists and exiled Republicans, Carrero Blanco drew up a working paper suggesting that the Franco regime be institutionalised as a monarchy. Franco retained control as Head of State, and the right to name his own royal successor. These ideas were formalised in the Law of Succession, upon which a referendum would be held in a bid to apply a thin veneer of 'democratic' legitimacy to the regime. Franco's hopes that Don Juan would throw himself behind this initiative were dashed when the Pretender issued the 'Estoril Manifesto' from Portugal denouncing it as illegal. He was, somewhat unoriginally, immediately dismissed in the Spanish press as being the puppet of international Freemasonry and communism.

Economically, things were still deteriorating rapidly. By May 1947, workers' wages in Spain had fallen to half their pre-civil war level, and prices had risen by more than 250 per cent. Despite the repression, the working classes were driven to organise a number of strikes across Spain. The Civil Guard and members of the Legion were ominously dispatched to Bilbao, and employers were ordered to sack workers 'without a second thought'. Those who failed to do so were imprisoned. Although the strikes were welcomed by the Basque government-in-exile as 'the greatest victory obtained by popular forces against the Franco regime', they convinced London and Washington that they needed Franco as a prop against communist subversion. Ironically, it was Franco's harsh policies themselves that were driving many workers to become communists. As an American living in Spain at the time commented to Gerald Brenan, 'They have neither bread or oil, so naturally they are all communists. If I were a working man, I would be one too.'[9]

The arrival of Eva Duarte de Perón (Evita), in Spain on a high-profile visit in June 1947 brought Franco's enthusiasm for fascism, always lurking near the surface, bubbling into the open. On 9 June, a general holiday was declared and a mass pro-Franco rally organised to celebrate Evita being awarded the Gran Cruz de Isabel la Católica, the highest possible accolade for a woman, as far as Franco was concerned. Both Franco and Evita gave fascist salutes to the chanting Falange crowd. An aggrieved Doña Carmen, sporting a hat designed to out-do Evita's in extravagance and size (as it was the hottest day of the year, she decided to bow out of the mink coat competition), looked upon Franco's simpering delight with tight-lipped disapproval. The signing of the Franco–Perón Protocol extended Argentinian aid and wheat deliveries to Spain.

The referendum on the Law of Succession took place in the wake of this public excitement. On Monday 6 July 1947, following a campaign that tainted anybody who voted 'no' as anti-Catholic, pro-Marxist and therefore intent on Spain's destruction, 93 per cent of Spaniards voted 'yes' to Franco's Succession Law. Despite a heavy police presence, intimidation and much falsification, there was no denying that Franco now enjoyed considerable popular support within Spain. Absolutely full of himself, he adopted the sovereign's right to bestow titles of nobility – a right he exploited to draw collaborators deeper into the regime. His offers of nobility placed monarchists in a difficult situation. If they accepted, they were betraying their king. If they refused, it was a public statement of opposition to Franco.

With Britain and the United States beginning to acknowledge that they had a vested interest in keeping Franco in power, while still protesting the opposite, Polish and Czech efforts to persuade the UN General Assembly to adopt full-scale economic sanctions against Spain came to nothing. The communist take-over of Czechoslovakia in February 1948 and the Berlin blockade from 24 June further consolidated Franco's position. He could – and did – congratulate himself on having survived the worst of international isolation. Berating the Americans for their misguided attitude towards Spain in the past, Franco demanded that reparation be made immediately and stubbornly resisted instigating even token gestures of liberalisation to placate the Allies. Although a move to include Spain in the programme for the economic reconstruction of Europe (the Marshall Plan) on 30 March 1948 was blocked by Truman, Franco could afford to sit tight. The Soviet Union's directive to eastern Europe to refuse any offers of aid from the West sent the post-war world spiralling into two irreconcilable blocs, with Franco firmly in the western sphere. Even moderate Spaniards were beginning to suspect that this was not an auspicious time for political change in Spain. Like a petulant child, in March 1948 Franco dispatched Lequerica, who had been rejected by the United States as ambassador in 1945, to Washington DC with the title of Inspector of Embassies and Legations. 'Greaser of Palms and Francoist Propagandist' might have been a more appropriate description.

Despite continuing British reservations about the regime – particularly in Gibraltar – the Americans were keen for relations with Spain to be normalised. Convinced that an attempt to topple the dictator would benefit the left and not the monarchists, they urged Franco to diffuse the opposition by establishing links with the popular Don Juan. Franco had already exposed his confused attitude to the monarchy when, upon showing his brother Nicolás two photographs – one of the corpses of Mussolini and Clara Petacci, the other of Alfonso XIII stepping ashore in Marseilles on the first stage of his exile – he commented that 'If things go badly I will end up like Mussolini because I will resist until I have shed my last drop of blood. I will not flee like Alfonso XIII.' Clearly equating the Spanish King's abandonment of Spain with his father's reckless flight from the family home, a self-righteous Franco notified his critics that he would never abandon his Spanish 'family' under the 'erroneous belief that they did not love him.'[10]

Despite the Caudillo's ambivalent attitude, a meeting was duly arranged with Don Juan aboard his yacht, the *Azor*, on 25 August 1948. Franco followed a well-trodden path in his dealings with the Pretender – as he persisted in calling Don Juan – lurching from an emotional hope that he had finally found a father who would acknowledge and respect him, to a venomous determination to keep him from power come what may. During the meeting, Franco wove a complex political and emotional tapestry. He wept a little, lectured a lot, and boasted that under his long-term guidance Spain would soon be the richest country in Europe. Citing the absence of popular demand – which he had himself crushed – for either a monarchy or a Republic as his justification for retaining power, Franco naïvely boasted that, if he felt like it, he could muster popular support for Don Juan within a fortnight. Having dismissed his generals as 'idiots' and 'raving lunatics', he declared that 'I do not permit my ministers to answer me back. I give them orders and they obey' and assured the Pretender that 'anyone can be bought'. Franco then insultingly claimed that the monarchy would not have the firmness of command (*mando*) necessary to rule over this malleable mob.

Gradually Franco's real agenda began to emerge. He wanted Don Juan's ten-year-old son, Juan Carlos, to complete his education in Spain under his own guidance. Politically, this arrangement would bestow a tentative validity upon Franco's role as a regent, give him considerable influence over his own succession and (or so he hoped) reconcile monarchists to his regime. Emotionally, it would enable him to fulfil the ultimate Oedipal fantasy: he would use the Prince to depose his father, Don Juan, the rightful King – who like Don Nicolás was a liberal and free-thinker – from the throne. Despite his evident unease, Don Juan recognised that the only hope for the monarchy lay in handing his son over to Franco. He would soon bitterly regret the arrangement.

In a major public relations coup for Franco, the young prince was dispatched to Spain on 9 November 1948. His arrival brought discussions between monarchists and socialists to an abrupt conclusion. It reconciled critics in the conservative establishment to his regime, and provided the paltry evidence that the Allies had been seeking that some sort of liberalisation was taking place in Spain. Furthermore, in Washington DC, Lequerica's diligent distribution of largess succeeded in establishing an increasingly powerful Spanish lobby, and generated a steady stream of high-profile American visits to Spain. On 30 September 1948, when the arrival of a US military mission coincided with *Día del Caudillo*, the Spanish press had a field day, citing the visit as American endorsement of Franco's rule.

Filled with a sense of his own omnipotence, Franco raged around Andalusia that autumn delivering customary tirades against the communists, major accolades to his own omniscience throughout the Second World War, and wild boasts about Spanish military prowess. On 12 October 1948, in a spectacular ceremony, he was invested with the title of Lord High Admiral of Castile. He and his family reviewed warships from the navies of Argentina, Brazil, Columbia, the Dominican Republic and Spain, and then gathered at the monastery of La Rábida, where Christopher Columbus had spent his last night before his famous trip. Franco had once and for all wrested his father's naval mantle and his brother Ramón's reputation as a latter-day 'Christopher Columbus' for himself. Perhaps he wished to reinforce the idea that it was only thanks to the Spanish that America had been found at all.

In Europe, efforts to draw Franco into the western sphere continued. Although public opinion in Britain and France was not shifting at quite the same speed at which their leaders' political priorities were changing – it was hard for ordinary people to accept that their wartime ally, the Soviet

Union, was now the enemy, while Hitler's great crony, Franco, was a friend – the situation was moving in the Caudillo's favour. An invitation for Spain to participate in the International Statistical Commission in November 1948 so excited Franco that he briefly forgot his contempt for the 'Masonic superstate' and the mindless materialism of the Americans, and hopefully, but vainly, offered to engage in a bilateral economic arrangement with the United States. In Britain, eminent Conservatives worked tirelessly for the resumption of diplomatic relations with Spain, while Churchill, happy as always to overlook the facts, passionately proclaimed that Franco's supportive role had greatly facilitated the Allied victory.

While Franco's self-satisfaction billowed, members of the 'other Spain' were being sucked downwards in a cycle of despair. Spain's diplomatic and economic isolation had exacted a considerable toll on Spanish working people. While the decadent beneficiaries of Franco's regime degenerated into a state of political and moral stagnation, thousands ferreted for scraps or begged in the streets. Many Spaniards were forced to live in cardboard boxes in the shanty towns that had sprung up on the outskirts of towns, or even moved into the caves in the hills. An appalled Gerald Brenan, who returned to the south of Spain in the late 1940s, describes children 'with wizened faces', women clutching their 'pinched and emaciated' babies, and 'gaunt, dejected men, standing silent against the walls and staring in front of them.' For Brenan, 'most dreadful of all are those who creep about the streets without arms or legs'. One couple bitterly complained that the Nationalists 'want to destroy our human nature. They want to turn us into animals. And meanwhile the rich ... do nothing but eat and drink, drive around in cars and seduce our women ... for them, the laws don't exist.' Others were more indulgent. A Falangist doctor insisted that Franco was a saint, who knew nothing of the activities of his entourage of 'swindlers' who were 'robbing the country'. 'Poor man,' he mused, 'he's always surrounded by his guards, has to travel in a bullet-proof car and see Spain from hoardings and balconies ... He's so unjustly blamed.'[11] As Brenan mildly comments, in a dictatorship it is hard to blame anyone else.

Franco vented his energies in crushing criticism rather than trying to address the problems arising from his policies. When Serrano Suñer wrote a blistering attack on the 'dangerous boredom' that afflicted Spain, and criticised those 'without vision', in an article published by the monarchist paper *ABC*, an incandescent Franco, promising to show him what boredom meant, threatened to close *ABC* for three months and 'exile this arrogant Serrano to the Canary Islands'. 'If it's necessary to shoot Ramón,' he added, 'he will be shot too.' But however many people Franco shot, nothing could disguise the fact that, without massive foreign aid, Spain confronted the possibility of total economic collapse within six months. With the wheat supply from Argentina declining due to unfulfilled commitments, a loan of $25 million from the United States, where the Spanish lobby was engendering great enthusiasm for military bases in Spain, came in the nick of time.

Franco had airily informed the Allies that he was not prepared to join NATO until such time as the 'advantages, guarantees, rights and obligations' of Spain had been resolved, provoking the *Daily Telegraph* to denounce his 'blunt, peevish and ill-mannered "NO" to proposals never made to him and ... bad-mannered refusal to attend a party to which he had not been invited'. Unlike Salazar's Portugal, Franco was not invited to join NATO. As a British minister put it, providing arms to him would be tantamount to 'putting a gun into the hands of a convicted murderer'. He responded to this personal slight in a passionate, self-righteous, resentful address to the nation on 31 March 1949, in which he pointed out that his neutrality had been particularly commendable as the Allies had never earned his support and his sympathies had therefore lain with the Axis powers.

His exclusion from NATO fanned his dark anxieties about democratic machinations and Masonic plots. As the First Journalist of Spain – a title he bestowed upon himself on 20 July 1949 – he decided that the time had come to publish his venomous, anti-imperial musings on Freemasonry in English. Aware that public opinion was swinging behind Franco in Britain and the United States, an appalled Lequerica frantically dissuaded him on the grounds that 'in some countries there is little taste for authentic, deep truths'.

Despite his abiding sense of injustice, there was, in fact, little during the summer of 1949 to cause the Caudillo undue concern. The guerrilla war being waged by Republicans in the Sierras was beginning to peter out, and Franco firmly rebuffed an attempt by Don Juan to remove Juan Carlos from his charge. The successful explosion of an atomic bomb in the Soviet Union announced by Truman on 23 September 1949, the establishment of Mao Tse-Tung's Chinese People's Republic at the beginning of October 1949, and a rampant anti-communist witch-hunt instigated by Senator Joseph E. McCarthy in the United States pushed the international situation further in Franco's favour. With the American public in a complete frenzy about 'Reds under the bed', the State Department began to view an alliance with Spain as essential to safeguard Iberia as 'the last foothold in continental Europe'. In a symbolic gesture, a squadron of the United States Eastern Atlantic fleet put in at El Ferrol in September 1949, and remained for five days. Franco rushed to Portugal for a high-profile meeting with Salazar to highlight the utility of the Iberian Peninsula to the western alliance.

On 18 January 1950, the US Secretary of State, Dean Acheson, wrote a widely publicised letter indicating that the United States would support Spain's inclusion within international and technical agencies, and advocating that ambassadors be reinstated in Madrid. Far from reassuring Franco, this conciliatory gesture provoked a particularly vitriolic outburst against unwarranted foreign interference, and further assaults on Britain under a thinly disguised pseudonym. He also ordered his secret police to arrest a number of prominent monarchists for the dubious infraction – in a state designated as a monarchy – of 'conspiracy to restore the monarchy'.

On 24 June 1950, the North Korean invasion of South Korea, which had been under the control of the United States since the Second World War, raised the spectre of a Third World War, with communism as the enemy. Despite Franco's ill-considered, ill-timed and ill-tempered denigration of 'the socialist imperialism of London', the General Assembly of the United Nations voted to authorise the return of ambassadors to Madrid on 4 November 1950. A scornful Franco immediately demanded substantial economic compensation for the hardship of recent years. In the wake of Egyptian calls for the withdrawal of British troops from the Suez Canal, Franco demanded the return of Gibraltar. Truman's decision, on 16 November 1950 to authorise a $62,500,000 loan to Spain for the rearmament of the Spanish military, in order to draw Franco into the anti-Soviet bloc, convinced him of the efficacy of his sabre rattling.

The appointment of an American ambassador to Madrid on 27 December 1950 inspired the Caudillo to deliver an end-of-year broadcast that was (in the words of Paul Preston) a 'virtuoso set of variations on the theme of "I told you so"'. He defiantly named the rampantly pro-Axis Lequerica ambassador to the United States and suggested Fernando María Castiella (a volunteer in the Blue Division, who had sworn allegiance to Hitler) as ambassador to Britain. When this unpalatable appointment was politely turned down, he then named Miguel, the womanising brother of José Antonio Primo de Rivera and blatant symbol of Falangism, whom the British were very reluctantly forced to accept.

Franco's instinct for divide and rule had not diminished over the years. The new American ambassador, Stanton Griffis, who arrived in Spain in early March, was referred to by Franco as 'the best ambassador imaginable',[12] while the British one -Sir John Balfour – who arrived soon after, was soon describing himself as 'an ambassador in the doghouse'.[13] Balfour concluded that his cool reception derived from the fact that 'quite a number of persons in authority, many of whom had been pro-Axis sympathisers during the war, nursed bitter feelings against a Protestant and democratic Britain'.[14]

Stanton Griffis, on the other hand, swiftly endeared himself to the Spanish people by attending a bull fight at which a demented bull, leaping the barriers, almost landed at his feet. Photos of this event received massive press coverage with the caption 'The Spanish Bull calls on the New American Ambassador.'[15] The delighted Caudillo afforded Griffis a particularly ostentatious welcome soon after.

Despite Franco's reservations, the British ambassador was, in the first instance, also received with much pageantry. Swept through the streets of Madrid in an eighteenth-century coach drawn by six plumed horses, he was accompanied by the 'Introducer of Ambassadors' along with coachmen, postilions and attendant lackeys on foot and Franco's Moorish lancers, riding horses whose hoofs had been embellished with gold. As it was feared that anti-British sentiments might explode into violence, the crowds were kept at bay by an officer of the guard riding with a drawn sabre. Balfour, however, noted 'nothing but friendliness' among the onlookers. Greeted at the palace by 'berriboned officials' and a rendition of 'God Save the King', the British entourage were ushered through 'magnificent rooms' until they reached a small reception room where the 'mild-mannered and unobtrusive' Caudillo, sporting a swallow-tailed gala uniform of a grand admiral, was waiting for them. Franco was, Balfour recalls, 'so small that when seated his feet hardly seemed to touch the ground' and his 'manner was that of a man who was eager to welcome back a friend who had repented an unjust quarrel'. Despite all this pomp and ceremony, however, Balfour considered the Spanish dictatorship to be 'a lax and amateurish affair in comparison with Stalinist Russia or Nazi Germany'.[16]

Unaware of this withering prognosis, Franco sought to impress the diplomatic corps once again at the wedding of his daughter, Nenuca, to a minor society playboy, Dr Cristóbal Martínez Bordiu, on 10 April 1950. In a minor gesture to the starving millions, the press was instructed not to report on the frenetic flow of private gifts that the occasion engendered, while officials and businesses were directed not to send any presents at all. On the wedding day, guards of honour, military bands, hundreds of guests, the full diplomatic corps and a glittering array of aristocrats were in attendance. The bride tottered under the weight of her jewellery and the groom sported the Ruritanian outfit of the Knights of the Holy Sepulchre complete with sword and crested helmet. Not to be outdone, Franco himself was dressed to the nines in the lavish uniform of the Captain-General of the Armed Forces. After emotionally escorting the bride into the chapel in El Pardo, the Caudillo recovered himself sufficiently to take his place at the side of the altar reserved for the Head of State.

Franco selected the slavering cardinal Plá y Daniel to preside over the proceedings. He did not let the Caudillo down, urging the newlyweds to take 'the family of Nazareth' and the 'exemplary Christian home of the Chief of State' as their role-models. More inclined to follow in the latter's footsteps than the former's, Nenuca's groom, the Marqués de Villaverde, was soon exploiting his family name to the full. Nicknamed Marqués de Vayavida (what a life), he lost little time in making a fortune from various business exploits, including the import of Vespa motor-scooters from Italy. (It was said that Vespa stood for *Villaverde Entra Sin Pagar Aduana* – Villaverde enters without paying customs duty.) His family acquired a huge estate just outside Madrid, and the young couple soon replaced Franco's brother Nicolás and his sister Pilar as the favourites at El Pardo. If Franco had hoped that his daughter's marriage would compensate for the marital split between his own parents or the romantic shortcomings of his marriage to Doña Carmen, he was rapidly disabused of this notion. It soon became clear that Nenuca's marriage replicated that of his own parents, something Franco found it difficult to cope with. On one occasion, when his distraught daughter attempted to discuss her husband's wayward tendencies with her father, he listened in silence and then coldly had her escorted from his presence. Nevertheless, his daughter would give him seven grandchildren on whom 'he would lavish an indulgent affection hitherto absent from his life.'[17]

The rampant acquisitiveness of her son-in-law's family further inflamed Doña Carmen's passion for antiques and jewellery, which had earned her the name 'Doña Collares' (necklaces). It had long been claimed that smaller jewellers had established an unofficial insurance syndicate to indemnify themselves against her voracious swoops. When, just before the wedding of her daughter, Doña Carmen discovered that a consortium of jewellers had dispatched a diamond tiara for the bride which had – as agreed – been returned, she sent a household servant straight to the shop to retrieve it. On another occasion she is alleged to have seized a ruby-studded belt bestowed upon Franco by a visiting Arabian potentate, and feverishly prized out the stones before handing it back to an official to be put in store.

In marked contrast with the exploits of Franco and his entourage, the 'other' Spain was suffering from a further deterioration in the economic situation. By the end of 1950, working-class wages had risen at barely half the rate of prices. Agricultural inefficiency resulted in Spain importing food with its dwindling foreign currency reserves, and power cuts left factories idle, reducing workers' wages even further. Labour militancy began to burst at the seams. On 11 March 1951, Franco appealed directly to the workers to be realistic, and to moderate their demands. Forgetting for the moment his omnipotent conviction that he presided over a land of plenty, he stated his determination to 'wipe from the conscience of the Spaniards the puerile mistake that Spain is a rich country, rich in natural products'. Understandably disinclined to heed his calls for restraint, the workers in Barcelona exploded into open revolt when the hated Civil Governor arbitrarily raised tram fares. A general strike was called on 12 March 1951. Although the unrest was blamed on communist agitators, it actually included some Falangists and members of the Catholic workers' organisation (HOAC). Despite the sinister arrival of three minesweepers off the coast of Barcelona, and the marching of marines through the streets, major bloodshed was avoided when the Captain-General of Barcelona, General Juan Bautista Sanchéz, refused to allow the army garrison out of their barracks to suppress disorder. The Civil Governor lost his job.

Unrest billowed over into the Basque country in April 1951, when 250,000 industrial workers went on strike. Once more, the leftists were joined by Falangists and members of the HOAC. Franco immediately denounced the strikers as criminals, blamed the international siege for generating economic problems within Spain, and attributed internal unrest to British and French Freemasonry. He threw in a few complaints about Gibraltar for good measure, possibly in a bid to divert attention from domestic issues, although Balfour believed that Franco was genuinely convinced that he was simply following Isabel la Católica's passionate enjoinder never to alienate Gibraltar from the Spanish Crown.[18] Barely a day went by without arrests, police beatings and courts martial. Communist and anarcho-syndicalist leaders of the strikes were imprisoned for between fifteen and twenty years, there were two death sentences and several men were shot 'trying to escape'. Some prisoners died after beatings in prison.

Despite all of this, as Franco had anticipated, the tide of history was sweeping in his favour. Within the politics of the cold war, it suited the western allies to view his repressive policies as a commendable and robust response to communism, while his oppressive labour legislation was making Spain very attractive to foreign investors. No wonder Franco felt increasingly confident about ignoring Don Juan's attempts to negotiate the installation of a monarchy for 'all Spaniards'. (Perhaps he felt that after Don Juan had handed over his son to Franco, he had no right to claim paternity to either Juan Carlos or the Spanish nation.) Although President Truman insisted that 'I don't like Franco and I never will', he was reluctant to allow his 'personal feelings override the convictions of you military men', who, convinced that Franco was not like 'typical European and Latin American dictators',[19] were prepared to pay for Spanish air bases and harbours to be adjusted to accommodate heavy American bombers and aircraft-carriers. Absolutely full of himself, the Caudillo demanded sufficient aid both to upgrade the Spanish army to help Spain protect itself from the Soviets and to reduce the food crisis.

On 18 July, Franco appointed a politically retrograde, but economically progressive new cabinet which, on the face of it, seemed to reinforce the power of the Falange. General Agustín Muñoz Grandes, who had led the Blue Division against the Soviets and been decorated by Hitler, took charge of future negotiations with the Americans as Minister of the Army. The faithful Carrero Blanco, who had been forced to resolve his marital difficulties to avoid falling out of favour with a puritanical Doña Carmen, was appointed Cabinet Secretary (effectively Franco's chief of the political general staff). Raimundo Fernández Cuesta was brought back as Minister Secretary General of the Movimiento, and José Antonio Girón remained as Minister of Labour. Joaquín Ruiz Giménez, a devout Catholic, was brought in as Minister of Education, while another Catholic and Blue Division veteran, Fernando María de Castiella, was dispatched to Rome to negotiate a Concordat with an increasingly hostile Vatican.

With the boundaries between Spain and the rest of the western world beginning to crumble, Franco acknowledged that it was both safe and advisable to concede his shortcomings as an economist, and allow the first tentative steps to be taken away from the ruinous policy of autarky. (However, although Juan Antonio Suanzes, the driving force behind autarky, was dropped from the cabinet, he continued to wield a certain amount of influence as president of the state holding company, the INI.) Meanwhile the Caudillo busied himself sowing alarm and despondency in the United States by suggesting that the British Labour Party was little short of communist, and that the French were hatching an endless array of Masonic plots. His behaviour confirmed the British and French governments' belief that by dealing with Franco the Americans were seriously undermining the integrity of the western position.

In October 1951, when the Conservatives returned to power in Britain, a delighted Franco, briefly suspending his rage at British imperialism, greeted a British emissary, the Earl of Bresborough, like a long-lost friend. Momentarily forgetting his close association with the Americans, Franco happily sneered at the United States' lack of coherent policy. The charmed Earl claimed that Franco was 'unlike ... one's idea of the typical dictator. He speaks so simply, courteously and naturally and in an unaffected and quiet voice', but conceded that 'The mind of the dictator only appears in his evidently complete conviction that every opinion he expresses is incontrovertible and the last word on the subject.'[20]

Franco was more elusive in his personal relations. Moderating distance and closeness either politically or personally was not one of his notable skills. Capable of outbursts of warmth and spontaneity with completely unknown foreign dignitaries, he did not allow any informality to creep into relations with his close friends and associates: Max Borrell, Nenuca's husband and Carrero Blanco were always required to address him as *Excelencia*. José Antonio Girón, the Falangist Minister of Labour, complained that 'he is cold, with that coldness which at times freezes the soul'. A disenchanted Pacón reflected that 'the Caudillo is effusive with those who dominate him and with the flatterers who swamp him with gifts and lavish hospitality, but as cold as an ice floe with the majority of us who are not sycophants, are serious in our conduct and speak to him loyally whether he likes it or not.'[21]

With the Americans beginning to drag their feet, Franco was greatly heartened by General Eisenhower's victory in the 1952 US presidential election. He hastened to emphasise common ground between the two countries, and between himself and the new President, primarily by wearing his own general's uniform as much as possible, and publishing photos of himself playing golf and painting at his easel improbably attired in pinstripe suits and a large fedora. With his hero-worship getting the better of him, the Caudillo slavishly commended 'the splendid sacrifice that the United States is making in Korea'. He even offered to dispatch a division of volunteers to fight in Korea under Spanish officers, until he huffily recalled that 'technically this is a war of the United Nations and the United Nations has excluded Spain'.

Franco was now confronted with the task of convincing himself and the Spanish people that the tyrannical western imperialist powers were in fact loyal friends and allies. Despite the fluidity of his sense of identity and the elasticity of his ideological convictions, this delicate process would be wracked with the usual array of digressions and political infelicities. The signing of the Concordat with the Vatican in August 1953 provided a welcome respite from the whole painful business. He was greatly cheered when, on 21 December 1953, Pius XII granted Franco, 'our beloved son', the highest Vatican decoration, the Supreme Order of Christ.

The Defence Pact with the USA, which was finally signed on 26 September 1953, gave Franco $226 million in military and technological assistance. General economic aid was limited to building projects deemed to be of military significance. In return, Franco gave up neutrality and – rather unwisely – given his conviction that the communists were poised, ready to attack at a moment's notice – permitted the construction of numerous bases next to large cities. He tried to stifle criticism of his close association with the Americans by presenting it as 'a second victory over communism'. Despite the huge economic benefits to his regime, Franco would soon regret the agreement, bitterly commenting that the 'best thing that the Americans did for us was to empty the Madrid bars and cabarets of whores, since they almost all marry American sergeants and GI's'. Although he looked upon the American agreement as the definitive consolidation of his regime, it would greatly loosen the 'unity-under-siege' that had played such a crucial political and psychological role for him and his regime.

Franco's burst of goodwill towards the West evaporated rapidly when he heard that the newly crowned Queen Elizabeth II of England would visit Gibraltar in 1954. In August 1953, his impassioned attack on Britain for 'weakening our *Patria*, creating problems for our nation, undermining and influencing the ruling classes, fermenting insurrection in the colonies and fermenting revolutionary movements from Masonic lodges and left-winger internationals' did not go down well in London or Washington.[22] Nor did his decision, early the following year, to allow Falangists – equipped, as always, with stones thoughtfully delivered in truck-loads – to demonstrate outside the British Embassy in Madrid.

Sporadic and damaging forays into international relations aside, Franco was beginning to feel that he could afford to relax – something for which he had always had a particular penchant. When he was not hunting, shooting and fishing with his friend Max Borrell, he was playing golf, watching endless westerns in the private cinema in El Pardo, or tending to his large estate at Valdefuentes. He spent considerable time indulging his stilted if accomplished skill in painting. His great obsession, however, was the crypt at the Valle de los Caidos (his 'other woman'). Completed in 1954, this was a towering monument to Franco's sense of his place in history. Although the Nationalists had directed that Spanish architecture, purged of modernist tendencies, be based on 'the essence of the glorious century of the Spanish empire, creator of states in America, and creator of that profound and perfect symbol: the Escorial',[23] the whole concept of the Valle de los Caidos was more akin to an Egyptian pyramid than anything else. The cross alone weighed 181,620 tonnes and was 150 metres high. Its arms extended 46 metres. Not only did Franco doubtless hope that this vast temple to himself would compensate for his physical and sexual shortcomings and gain him immortality, but it remained a looming and permanent reminder to the Republicans that they had been defeated and destroyed by nothing short of a demi-god. Albert Speer's comment that Hitler's passion for constructing vast and intimidating edifices was 'the very expression of a tyranny'[24] might just as well be applied to Franco.

This megalomanical sense of himself continued to hamper Franco's relations with Don Juan. When, in 1954, Juan Carlos finished the secondary education he had received at the hands of private tutors, Franco's ideas about what should happen next did not coincide with Don Juan's. The Pretender was keen for Juan Carlos to begin his university education at Louvain, but the Caudillo insisted that he attend some military, naval and air academies, do a spot of social science and engineering at Madrid University and then undertake some serious practice in the art of government 'at the side of the Caudillo'.[25] A frosty communication from Franco left Don Juan in no doubt that any interference in this process would prevent the 'installation of the monarchy in our *Patria*'.

Although Don Juan felt powerless to challenge Franco, his followers did not. There was nothing Franco could do to crush sporadic outbursts of enthusiasm for the Borbón monarchy. In the autumn of 1954, thousands of Spaniards from every walk of life flocked to Portugal to attend the coming-of age celebrations of Don Juan's daughter, the Infanta María del Pilar. Even more worrying, staunch military supporters of Franco had joined with Don Juan's followers and members of the Opus Dei – a secular Catholic pressure group – to form a so-called 'third force' (Tercera Fuerza), which was pushing for the restoration of a traditional monarchy under Don Juan, albeit within the context of the Movimiento. Although Franco had the self-appointed theorist of this group, Rafael Calvo Serer, dismissed from his post in the Higher Council of Scientific Research, the widespread appeal of the Tercera Fuerza emerged during the municipal elections held in Madrid on 21 November 1954. The first elections since the civil war, these were presented as entirely genuine because one-third of the municipal councillors would be 'elected' by 'fathers of families' and married women over the age of thirty. Blas Pérez, the Minister of the Interior, used his not inconsiderable powers to ensure a Falangist victory, resulting in the monarchist candidates being subjected to a campaign of intimidation by Falangist thugs. Despite this, monarchists claimed to have won 60 per cent of the actual votes cast. When they complained to Franco at the way the results were being presented in the press, he was stunned. He was even more appalled when General Juan Vigón, his Chief of the General Staff, told him that the bulk of the Madrid garrison had voted for the monarchy. Rather than draw any personal conclusions from monarchical successes, Franco delivered a sharp rebuke to Don Juan complaining about the behaviour of his followers.

The birth of Franco's first grandson on 9 December opened up the possibility of displacing Don Juan completely by establishing a dynasty of his own. The child's father, Cristóbal Martínez-Bordiu, who was understandably keen on this idea, persuaded the Caudillo to break with Spanish tradition and reverse the mother and father's surnames. The child thus became Francisco Franco Martínez-Bordiu. Although Franco was

momentarily engaged by the idea, he never really countenanced establishing a family dynasty. Appointing an heir at all always posed the risk of
displacement, and he was particularly mistrustful of his ruthless son-in-
law. It was clearly safer to have his 'surrogate' son, Juan Carlos – whose
rivalrous impulses would, he hoped, be directed against Don Juan and not
himself – waiting in the wings, than to unleash dangerous ambitions within
his own family. Furthermore, Franco was grasping at some tenuous form
of legality without jeopardising his own political position. He was determined to break the continuity and legitimacy of the Borbón monarchy. He
therefore determined to 'install' Juan Carlos rather than restore the rightful
heir, Don Juan, to the throne, which would render Franco's personal position untenable, and his regime an illegal and temporary aberration rather
than part of a glorious continuum from the medieval kings to a twentieth-
century monarchy. He therefore fed on people's fears that if Don Juan –
with his talk of elections, and his desire to be King of all Spaniards – was
restored to the throne, there would be another civil war.[26]

Nevertheless, keen to deflect monarchist opposition, Franco agreed to
meet up with the Pretender at the Extremaduran estate of Las Cabezas on
29 December 1954. An affable and confident Don Juan suggested to the
Caudillo that his regime would benefit from freedom of the press, an
independent judiciary, social justice, trade union freedom and political
representations. Franco's response was, as always, protracted and confusing.
Initially keen for the Pretender's approval, Franco hinted that he *might* be
prepared to separate the functions of Head of State and Head of Government, but then conceded – in an outburst of naïve frankness – that such
an arrangement would not suit him at all because 'if I remain as Head of
State, public opinion will blame me for everything bad that happens, while
everything good will be credited to the head of government'.

Gradually, his real agenda began to emerge from the foggy flow of
verbiage: he would construe Don Juan's refusal to accept that his son Juan
Carlos be educated under Franco's direct tutelage as a renunciation of
the throne. An unspoken compromise was reached whereby Franco was
allowed to educate Juan Carlos as he pleased, while Don Juan retained his
dynastic rights. When both men agreed to nominate two trustworthy
people to maintain delicate links with each other, the perpetually suspicious
Franco was astonished that Don Juan could muster so many. Nonetheless
a joint communiqué was issued implicitly recognising the rights of the
Borbón family. Juan Carlos returned to Madrid in January 1955, where he
prepared to sit the entrance examination to the Saragossa military academy
under the strict eye of his military tutors. While these events took some of
the sting out of the monarchist opposition, the young Prince's presence in

Madrid did not go down well with those members of the regime who
opposed the restoration of a monarchy. Franco, on the other hand, having
firmly reiterated his right to choose a successor who would guarantee the
continuity of his regime, was delighted to have Juan Carlos at his side. He
subjected the unfortunate young Prince to endless lectures on the dangers
of associating too closely with the aristocracy and urged him to familiarise
himself with ordinary people whom – in marked contrast with the views
he had espoused after the civil war – he claimed were 'morally healthier,
less selfish' and more genuinely patriotic than the tainted upper classes.[27]
Franco's resolute intervention in the Prince's education reaped significant
benefits. When, in the autumn of 1955, Juan Carlos started his military
training at the academy at Saragossa, he would discover that the Caudillo's
implacable opposition to reinstalling the rightful heir – his father – to the
throne was shared by many other officers, and might even trigger another
military coup.

Franco's preoccupation with the succession aside, his contribution to
government had by now subsided into receiving delegates and ambassadors
at El Pardo, and impassively presiding over interminable Friday cabinet
meetings, during which he astonished his ministers by refusing sustenance
or a lavatory break, sometimes for nine hours at a time. He sought to
impress them in other ways. Desperate to maintain contact with the Caudillo, a large band of ingratiating courtiers scrambled after him on his
extended hunting trips in quest of political preferment. They treated Franco
like a spoilt child, ruthlessly elbowing their way to his side in order to ply
him with tasty snacks, marvel at his exploits with a shotgun, and ensure
that his killings exceeded those of everybody else.

In 1954 the situation in Morocco injected a cold dose of reality into
these comforting habits. The Spanish High Commissioner, encouraged by
Franco to display an extremely uncharacteristic interest in 'the evolution
of the Moroccan people', had been actively encouraging Moroccan nationalists in the French zone with arms and money. Franco had significantly less
egalitarian notions about Spanish Morocco, which he confidently predicted
would not be ready for independence for at least twenty-five years. In
August 1955, when the French, under pressure in Vietnam and Algeria,
lifted martial law in their zone and reinstated the Sultan, Franco failed to
grasp the significance for the Spanish sector. Ignoring urgent advice to
instigate a massive programme of public spending in Morocco, he made
only the vaguest commitment to future independence. When, as predicted
by his advisers, this provoked an outburst of nationalist fervour, it was
harshly repressed. With the declaration of independence for French
Morocco on 2 March 1956, even more determined nationalist riots broke

out in the Spanish zone. On 15 March, Franco was forced to announce that Spain would relinquish its protectorate. Recognising too late that some serious-minded toadying was called for, Franco laid on a particularly lavish welcome for the Sultan, Muhammed V, when he visited Spain on 4 April. However, Franco's Rolls-Royce, a regal escort by the Caudillo's spectacularly attired horsemen from the Moorish Guard and the rapturous Spanish crowds failed to move the cold and disdainful Sultan. After an extremely tense and awkward meeting, a traumatised Franco was forced to revise his conviction that the Moroccans loved him, and that he had a very particular understanding of the Muslim mentality. The declaration of independence in the Spanish zone was signed on 7 April 1956. Apart from a few isolated outposts – Melilla, Ceuta and the region of Ifni – Spain had lost its empire in Africa.[28] This signalled the end of the imperialist dreams that had dominated Franco's thinking since he first become a soldier.

The contortions required to reconcile this major colonial setback with his internal needs and external ambitions stretched the Caudillo's elastic sense of self to its limits. Having equated the shoddy and inadequate leadership that led to Spain's imperial disasters in the past with the incompetence of civilian governments and the deficiencies of his own father, the withdrawal from Morocco challenged Franco's entire sense of identity, and his notion of himself as father to the nation. It removed at a stroke the main tenet of his regime – his determination to avenge the humiliating loss of Cuba in 1898 – and rendered those glorious battles undertaken with the Africanistas irrelevant and futile. Forced to disband his beloved Moorish Guards, the most potent symbol of his regal pretensions and the starkest reminder of the terror upon which he had established his regime, Franco's sense of himself as a latter-day El Cid leading his people to imperialist triumph was harshly exposed as futile fantasy. Pragmatic and flexible as he was, making sense of this symbolic and symbiotic loss plunged Franco into a deep depression. He could not pretend, even to himself, that it was anything other than a personal humiliation. Although he showed no overt signs of his distress in public, the crisis triggered physical symptoms – a fixed and staring expression, tremulous movements and an emotional and mental absence – that would later develop into Parkinson's disease. A concerned Pacón noted that during family meals the Caudillo would sit in total silence, staring vacantly into space, chewing distractedly on toothpicks.[29]

While a shaken and vulnerable Franco plunged into a depressed contemplation of the past, Spanish society was moving in a completely different direction. The trickle of tourism, which by the 1960s would become a veritable avalanche, was relentlessly exposing the Spanish people to foreign notions of political and sexual freedom. The emigration of Spanish workers to northern Europe in search of employment, the arrival in Spain of multi-national companies and the influence exerted by the new mass media – the cinema, the press and increasingly television – were beginning to erode the international isolation and news embargo imposed upon Spain since 1939. Although in 1951, in a superficial nod to changing times, censorship had passed from the Ministry of Education (controlled by the Catholic Church) to the new Ministry of Information and Tourism, it remained as tight as ever. Swift to recognise the potentially inflammatory nature of television (not to mention its efficacy for propaganda purposes), the regime imposed even tighter constraints than those operating for film or stage. Despite rigid controls, television would become 'a genuine window on the world'.[30]

Nothing, it seemed, could stop Spaniards coming into contact with foreigners whose views on democracy and communism differed markedly from those of the Caudillo. The oppressed Spanish people, who had been convinced by their leader that they were being treated harshly because (as a Spaniard had bitterly commented to Gerald Brenan) they were 'not like other races – we are bad, bad, bad',[31] began to suspect that it was not them to whom the western democracies objected, but the regime itself. They rejoiced 'that we were not alone, and after so many years of shame, this seemed to us like a miracle'.[32] On the other hand, as one staunch Nationalist commented to Gerald Brenan, 'between us all we have brought disgrace on Spain ... One can scarcely find a family that has not had some of its members led to death like animals.'[33] Sadly, it would take several more decades for the notion that they were innately 'evil' and deserved pun-ishment – pummelled into them for forty years by Franco's propaganda machine – to be excised from the Spanish psyche.

Given the very tight political and cultural restrictions imposed on every stratum of society, it is not surprising that the first people to rise up against the regime were students. Ironically, Falangist students, frustrated with an educational system that was entirely subordinate to the principles of Cath-olic dogma, had already burst into open discontent in the mid-1940s. Now liberal middle-class students, most of whom came from families who had been on the winning side during the civil war, but who were frustrated that they had all had to join the Falange Student Union, the SEU, began to express open discontent with the regime. Considerably less susceptible to Franco's bullying rhetoric than their traumatised parents had been, and immune to traditional religious values, young students suspected that their political choices were not necessarily confined to 'Franco or communism'.[34] However, if that was the way the Caudillo wanted it, they were more inclined to opt for the latter than for the former. The frenzied way in which the

Francoist press cited communism as the cause of all the problems had the effect – as it had done at the beginning of the civil war – of transposing paranoid predictions into self-fulfilling prophecies. Many students now turned to the far left, where the Communist Party became a focus for dissatisfied groups.

The huge divide between the day-to-day struggle for ordinary Spanish workers, and the profligacy and corruption of Francoist officials was also unacceptable to a youthful proletariat who had neither fought in the civil war nor been repressed in its aftermath. They wanted things their parents had never dreamed about. While young workers grouped in secret trade unions, or formed revolutionary groups, even Falange militants were becoming restive about the constant postponement of their 'revolution' and Franco's association with 'idiot kings'.[35] Franco was forced to respond in his end-of-year broadcast on 31 December 1955. Characteristically disinclined to heed criticism or shoulder responsibility, he blamed everything on an underlying complacency within Spanish society, which he claimed had been engendered by his successful 'captaincy' and was easy for foreigners to exploit. He denounced the liberal intelligentsia as having 'brilliance and charm, but up close [they] give off the Masonic stink and stench which characterised our sad years'. This regressive speech was a major disappointment to almost everybody. Even the newly arrived British ambassador, Sir Ivo Mallet, commented that Spaniards perceived their Caudillo as 'a complete cynic, interested only in keeping power as long as he lives, and indifferent to what may happen when he dies'.[36]

In early February 1956, progressive university students in Madrid clashed with militant Falangists and the extremist Guardia de Franco returning from a ceremony to commemorate the death of a Falangist killed during the Second Republic. While the students hurled stones at the police and shouted 'SEU no! Free unions!',[37] Falangists militants surged through the streets attacking the students and destroying university lecture rooms and offices. In the ensuing chaos, a shot was fired and a Falangist student was hit in the head. Although he survived, there were widespread fears that hot-headed party members were plotting to exact violent vengeance. The Captain-General of Madrid, accompanied by the Minister for the Army, General Muñóz Grandes, and Prince Juan Carlos's tutor, General Martínez Campos, therefore hastened to the Caudillo, to express their horror at the behaviour of the Guardia de Franco. With a 'wind of panic' blowing through the streets of Madrid,[38] Franco – predictably enough – escaped to the hills for a bout of killing. Upon his return, he was irritably persuaded to instigate a cabinet reshuffle on 13 February, in which he removed both Ruiz Giménez, whom he firmly blamed for the student unrest, and Fernández Cuesta, the Minister-Secretary of the Movimiento. The former was replaced by a conservative Falangist, Jesus Rubio García-Mina – who was of the reassuring opinion that 'students should study'[39] – and the latter by the dangerously ambitious Arrese.

With modern life becoming more complex by the minute, there were few issues upon which Franco's government was not divided. When his cabinet met on 3 March 1956, it immediately divided into two hostile camps. On the one side, José Antonio Girón supported by Arrese was pressing for a policy of massive spending; on the other, Manuel Arburúa, the Minister of Commerce, urged austerity. The Caudillo's traumatised inertia resulted in a short-lived and economically disastrous triumph for Girón, who failed to spot that huge pay increases would have an immediate impact on prices, inflation and unemployment. With supporters and opponents spiralling in different and entirely new directions, a bemused Caudillo left his ministers to squabble between themselves, clinging to the succession for solace.

His attitude on this issue was clarified somewhat when, on 29 March 1956, his protégé, Juan Carlos, managed to shoot his much loved younger brother, Alfonso, while playing with a revolver, which had, coincidentally, been given to him by the Caudillo. Alfonso was killed instantly. A devastated Juan Carlos was back in uniform within forty-eight hours.[40] Franco's feelings can only be guessed at. Perhaps he admired the Prince for keeping his emotions under such strict control. Perhaps the accident brought back memories of his stormy relationship with his own younger brother, Ramón, whom he had regularly threatened to shoot. Either way, the accident seemed to consolidate Franco's determination to secure Juan Carlos as his heir.

Although the political system in which Franco hoped to enmesh the young Prince was as politically regressive as ever, nothing it did could disguise the fact that the rigid political boundaries imposed by the Nationalists were being seriously eroded. Erstwhile pillars of Francoism, like Gil Robles, Ruiz Giménez and the Falangist poet Dionisio Ridruejo (formerly a high-ranking member of the Blue Division), were beginning to think that 'After so many years, many of us who were the victors felt ourselves defeated.'[41] New centres of opposition were emerging that spanned virtually every sector of Spanish society. Franco could no longer pretend that the clash was between the forces of good and evil, between Spain and the rest of the world, or between Nationalists and Republicans; it was between differing aspects of the regime itself. According to Gerald Brenan, even 'disillusioned and cynical' high-ranking Falangists who 'before the war had nothing, and were now rich men with houses and broad estates' were showing signs that they suffered from 'a bad conscience' and were 'very much on the defensive in Spain today'.[42] While some of his supporters sought to bury their shame in renewed ideological fervour, others would turn against the regime itself. Radical priests, convinced that the Church was betraying Christian precepts and alienating committed Catholics at a grass-roots level, joined revolutionary workers to push for social and political change. In April 1956, after a further bout of student strikes, the nephew of Frederico García Lorca, killed by the Nationalists, and the nephew of Calvo Sotelo, killed by the Republicans, stood side by side in the dock, both sworn enemies of Franco.

As Franco got older and more tired, the balance between the vengeful activist, the indolent cynic and the indecisive leader changed. With modern life too complicated to divide into traditional categories of good and evil, the Caudillo sank into a profound political torpor. As the gap between him and the real world became ever wider, he was buffeted along by political and social forces he neither understood nor controlled.

CHAPTER 9

Pandora's Box

April 1956–November 1975

It is impossible to talk to Franco about politics because he gets the impression that they are ... preparing the way for his replacement

López Rodó

the dictatorship of one man has become that of eighteen ministers

Girón[1]

As the regime lost dynamism and direction, and differing sectors fought bitterly to impose their ideas upon it, Franco himself seemed to lose his instinct for political balance. The Caudillo eagerly latched on to Arrese's mellifluent and persuasive draft *Leyes Fundamentales*, designed to impose a reassuring Nazi-style *totalitarización* upon the regime. The Falange minister's much vocalised, and to Franco highly seductive, desire to smash communism and liberalism with 'fists and guns' blinded him to the divisiveness of his self-interested plans for the future. While such sentiments may have helped take the Caudillo's mind off his humiliations at the hands of the Sultan, they engendered considerable disquiet among other members of the regime.

Blithely unaware of an impending furore within the Francoist elite, in the spring of 1956 Franco happily toured Andalusia with his minister, making speeches of 'super-falangism and aggression' to cheering crowds of delirious party members. The Church was horrified at the overt fascist overtones of Arrese's plans, which had provoked monarchist machinations to bring about an early restoration of Don Juan. Even the devoted Carrero Blanco hesitantly suggested that what Spain needed was 'a traditional monarchy for the present day'. Franco readily agreed that his wayward minister was 'a wild horse that had to be reined in', but gave few signs of wanting to do so during his speech to the Consejo Nacional de FET y de las JONS on 17 July 1956. Sucked into a time-warp by Arrese's beguiling rhetoric, a confused Franco lauded fascist Italy and Nazi Germany, and bitterly criticised the democratic systems which he believed the envious western allies had 'imposed' upon Germany and Italy to secure their economic collapse. His Foreign Minister, Alberto Martín Artajo, swiftly removed these antidemocratic musings from the published text.[2]

It was not just Franco's anachronistic fascist fervour that was generating alarm. Both Pacón and General Barroso (who replaced him as head of the Caudillo's Military Household in the summer of 1956) were worried by his increasingly lackadaisical attitude to work and the unfettered extravagance of his family. Hurt at Franco's failure to acknowledge his retirement after forty years of loyal service, Pacón was particularly disgusted by the exploits of the acquisitive and socially ambitious Doña Carmen. Franco, however, was more inclined to indulge his own extravagant passion for hunting than deal with political friction within his regime. His attempts to elude his rancorous cabinet were, however, ended in mid-September 1956 when they tracked him down in Galicia. By this stage, his ministers were bitterly divided on the Suez issue, where Colonel Nasser – a man after Franco's heart – was attempting to evict Britain from the canal as the first step in his bid to unify the 'Arabs' from Morocco to Iraq. In a characteristically quarrelsome meeting, Arrese demanded an anti-British gesture of nationalist solidarity with Colonel Nasser, while Martín Artajo heatedly argued that Spain should not diverge from its American ally on this issue. Franco went along with Martín Artajo, despite the fact that he was already secretly supplying arms to Nasser, an activity that seriously undermined his subsequent attempts to gain entry into NATO. Although Arrese scrambled back into favour soon after by organising a massive Falangist celebration of the twentieth anniversary of Franco's elevation to Head of State on 29 September – an event from which Martín Artajo unwisely absented himself – even Franco was beginning to realise just how divisive the 'golden boy of El Pardo's'[3] plans for the future were.

Monarchist hopes for the restoration of Don Juan focused upon General Juan Bautista Sánchez, the Captain-General in Barcelona. When a transport strike broke out in Barcelona, rumours that Bautista Sánchez was actively supporting the strikers prior to launching a coup sent a chill through Franco's soul. The Caudillo's uncanny luck, however, was still running strong. On 29 January 1957, Bautista Sánchez died from a heart attack. When this triggered wild rumours that he had been murdered, an inscrutable Caudillo simply commented that 'death has been kind to him ... helping him to avoid the scandal of treachery he was about to commit'.[4]

Nevertheless, Franco heeded the warning. In February 1957 he instigated a cabinet change in which Arrese – grumbling that 'Spain is once more in the hands of soldiers and priests'[5] – was moved to the Ministry of Housing for a 'cooling off' period. Franco's childhood friend, General Camilo Alonso Vega, became Minister of the Interior, and Muñoz Grandes was promoted to the symbolic rank of captain-general, previously held only by Franco. The loyal General Barroso was appointed Minister of the Army in a bid to neutralise the monarchist yearnings of the military high command. In a minor palliative to Falangist hard-liners, Alberto Martín Artajo was replaced by Fernando María de Castiella as Foreign Minister.

The most crucial change within the new cabinet was the inclusion of the so-called technocrats: Mariano Navarro Rubio as Minister of Finance and Alberto Ullastres Calvo as Minister of Commerce. A vibrant young lawyer, Laureano López Rodó – an influential member of the powerful secular Catholic pressure group, the Opus Dei, who had taken 'the three classical vows of obedience, poverty and chastity'[6] – was brought in as second-in-command to Carrero Blanco. Henceforth, strategic policy was essentially formulated by these men. Franco could no more impose balance on the conflict and confusion prevailing within his new cabinet than he could reconcile the chaos and contradictions that raged within his own psyche. He lunged back and forth between the comfortable, but economically disastrous ideology of the 1930s and an emotionally jarring, but politically pragmatic commitment to economic modernisation. Always polite and deferential with his economic advisers, the Caudillo would occasionally forget himself sufficiently to denounce the policies emanating from his own cabinet as foreign, and the equivalent of Freemasonry and communism.

Despite the determination of the technocrats to contain the dramatic overspending and rampant inflation unleashed by Girón, and to 'achieve without delay a greater degree of freedom in foreign trade',[7] the economy continued to spiral out of control. This generated a much more militant wave of strikes. While it was Franco's policies of political repression and economic autarky, his refusal to accept foreign aid in return for neutrality, and the divisiveness of his regime that had brought Spain to its knees, he immediately denounced the strikes as left-wing perversity and the work of outside agitators. He left more sophisticated economic analyses to his ministers.

That Franco was losing his political grip was made startlingly clear during a further crisis in Morocco in November 1957. Franco proved strangely disinclined to heed extensive reports about anti-Spanish activities in Ifni, one of Spain's remaining outposts on the Atlantic coast of north Africa. When these culminated in an invasion by Moroccan guerrillas, in an ironic reversal of history he hastily directed that Spanish troops be transferred to Africa in aged German planes. As his indignant generals did not hesitate to point out, this action had come much too late: Franco was ignominiously forced to accept an uneasy peace settlement in June 1958. This hammered a final, humiliating, nail into the coffin of his great imperial dreams. The traumatised Caudillo could barely muster up the energy to condemn a new wave of strikes in the Asturian coal mines and in Catalonia in the spring of 1958, which he distractedly blamed on foreign agitators and working-class laziness.

Such symptoms of Franco's political decline did little to concentrate his mind on the succession. Like Hitler, who in a moment of frank intro-spection complained that if he relinquished power 'nobody will take any notice of me any more. They'll all go running after my successor',[8] Franco was profoundly reluctant to name an heir. He was aware that people courted him for power and not friendship and was worried that once he named his successor, they would immediately try to displace him. Given his acute sensibilities, López Rodó had to move very carefully indeed when, under Carrero Blanco's guidance, he formulated his blueprint for the succession, which was unveiled in the Cortes on 17 May 1958 by Franco. Enshrined within his *Ley Orgánica del Estado*, the Declaration of the Fundamental Principles of the Movimiento created the legislative framework for the reinstatement of a Catholic monarchy with Franco as Head of State assisted by a newly created post of Prime Minister. It specifically failed to mention the Falange, but was designed to secure the survival of a rather loosely defined Movimiento and to safeguard Francoism after the death of the Caudillo. On 6 June 1958 the extremely ill Muñoz Grandes, as Chief of the General Staff, was nominated to act as regent if Franco died before the constitutional process was complete. Horrified by all this discussion about his impending death, Franco retreated to Asturias, where he engaged in a vigorous bout of salmon and trout fishing, which was, as he told Pacón, 'a great relief from my work and worries'. The greater his worries, the larger the fish had to be to compensate. In September, while on holiday in Galicia, he would – or so it was reported – catch a 20-ton whale. As his awe-struck companion Max Borrell once commented, 'to see him chase a whale is to understand all the successes of his political and military careers ... his perseverance is such that he would chase a whale to Russia'.[9]

However many animals he killed, Franco could not disguise the fact that the collapse of the Spanish economy, rocketing inflation and escalating working-class discontent were exerting considerable pressure upon the regime. Furthermore, the advent of the liberalising Pope John XXIII to the Vatican was seriously blighting the Church's pro-Francoist stance. As always, Franco blamed Don Juan for everything. During a particularly dis-jointed end-of-the-year message to the people, complex economic analyses provided by his ministers were punctuated with embittered diatribes about the 'frivolity, lack of foresight, neglect, clumsiness and blindness' of the Borbón monarchy. In a bout of flagrant projection, Franco insisted that anybody who opposed his regime was suffering from 'personal egoism and mental debility'.[10] An increasing number of people now fell into this bracket, not least erstwhile supporters of the regime filled with unease about the future. While disaffected monarchists joined the Unión Española in the hope of securing a popular monarchy and not one imposed by the dictatorship, 339 Basque priests dispatched a letter to the bishops of Spain criticising the 'lack of freedom of opinion and organisation, the methods used by the police, state control, the doctrine of the Leader's infallibility, blind conformity and the system of official trade unions'.[11] It was a devastating indictment of the regime. Even the Church hierarchy was beginning to suspect that it might be wise to distance itself from its primary position as 'the oppressive voice of the dictatorship' before Franco died.[12]

As the economy continued to spiral out of control, it was clear to the technocrats that only the intervention of the International Monetary Fund could avert total bankruptcy. This was a deeply distressing prospect for a xenophobic Caudillo. On 6 March 1959, an economic stabilisation programme was adopted by the cabinet, which, in the long run, would 'let the market rip in Spain'.[13] Although Franco would take all the credit when, in due course, this programme unleashed an 'economic miracle', his primary role was to hand responsibility over to the technocrats and go fishing. Bewildered by the sheer complexity of modern economics, upon which it was impossible to impose simplistic notions of 'good' versus 'evil', intimidated by his intellectual Opus Dei advisers and sick to death with the whole business of government, Franco detached himself from the day-to-day political process.

To begin with, the impact of the stabilisation plan on the working classes was devastating. The devaluation of the peseta and a major squeeze on public spending resulted in a wage freeze, rising unemployment, shortages of basic consumer goods and the forced closure of many businesses. In April 1959, Franco recovered his flagging sense of self when the official inauguration of the Valle de los Caidos – where he intended to be buried 'when the time comes' – coincided with the twentieth anniversary of the end of the civil war. Thousands of workers were bussed in to join the political, military and Catholic establishment in a huge ceremony in the basilica. Franco was attired in the uniform of a captain-general, Doña Carmen in black with a mantilla and high comb. They walked to their special thrones near the high altar, which the Caudillo was so reluctant to share with a monarch, under a regal canopy – a prerogative previously confined to kings and rarely used even by Alfonso XIII.[14] This was exactly the sort of ostentatious gesture that, according to the American diplomat Willard Beaulac, always provoked the nobility to 'chatter and squeal to each other and go into spasms of frustration'.[15] Invoking the divisive triumphalism of the civil war, a strident Caudillo mocked the vanquished for being forced to 'bite the dust of defeat', and heralded the heroism of 'our fallen'.[16] His less than sensitive decision to have hundreds of Nationalists exhumed in order to be reburied at the Valle de los Caidos was not popular with the bereaved families, for whom the civil war was, by now, a distant memory.

With memories of the war subsiding and papal support flagging, Franco latched on to President Eisenhower to validate his authority. On 21 December 1959, the Caudillo persuaded the President to visit Spain to discuss the practicalities of the American military bases. The President's evident distaste for Franco's obsequious and oft-repeated protestations of his humble admiration was overcome only when the two men discovered a mutual passion for shooting birds, although the President conceded that Franco's proficiency in this respect 'put him in quite another class'. Before Eisenhower returned to the United States, he embraced the Caudillo warmly. The President's visit engendered a bout of manic pro-Americanism in the Caudillo, which his sister dryly commented would make Hitler and Mussolini turn in their graves. Eisenhower himself, impressed by Franco's 'modest manners' and the fact that 'there was no discernible mannerism or characteristic that would lead an unknowing visitor to conclude that he was in the presence of a dictator' would ponder whether Franco might even win a free election should he hold one.[17] (Despite Franco's conviction that his people loved him, he never showed the slightest inclination to put such an idea to the test.) Franco's awe soon turned to derision. In his end-of-year speech, he delivered a blistering attack on Freemasonry and democracy as practised in the United States and northern Europe, laced with boastful taunts about the invulnerability of his regime. In fact, the Caudillo had never seemed more fragile. Despite muted reporting in the press, nothing could stifle speculation about Franco's declining health.

Despite his fragility, Franco continued to preside over increasingly conflictive cabinet meetings (or 'Fridays of sorrow' as Navarro Rubio called them), during which Alonso Vega raged about working-class militancy and Arrese squabbled with Navarro. When the former petulantly threatened to resign unless Franco backed him, the Caudillo – who had never put personal loyalty before political survival – blithely accepted his resignation on 17 March 1960. Two months later, Franco would readily sacrifice another of his protégés on the altar of his own survival. In Catalonia, one Sunday in

May, Luis de Galinsoga, who had been editor of the influential *La Van-guardia* in Catalonia since 1939, leaped from his pew and angrily harangued a priest who had – as was his right under new rules agreed by the government – embarked on a sermon in Catalan. When it became known that the heated discussion had culminated in the apoplectic editor roaring that 'Catalans are shits', his offended readership boycotted the paper. With public outrage at Galinsoga's outburst spilling into denunciations of the regime itself, Franco did not hesitate to sack the bemused editor, who had assumed – quite reasonably – that he was his master's voice. A lacklustre tour by the Caudillo soon after did little to conciliate the Catalans.

Galinsoga was not the only one unable to keep abreast of the times. Different elements of the regime itself were finding it difficult to span an increasingly wide spectrum between a repressive political ideology and social change associated with economic modernisation. The arrival in Spain of the SEAT 600, a small family car, refrigerators, washing machines and – most crucial of all – televisions, was changing people's lives. With the tourist trade flowering through the Costa Brava, Majorca and Torremolinos, the 'days when one had to undress at the water's edge, when Civil Guards kept stern watch on indecent exposure'[18] were going fast. Young men roared around on vespas, and girls in bikinis could be seen on the beaches. (Even so, according to John Hooper, as late as 1959 the Spanish bishops' 'Norms of Christian Decency' deemed it unacceptable for *novios* (courting couples) to walk the streets arm in arm.)[19]

For many Spaniards these changes were not exactly a dream come true. Life behind the luxurious tourist zone was as harsh as ever. Despite his determination to reimpose 'traditional Spanish values', Franco presided over a traumatic process of modernisation that drove migrants from rural areas to towns in quest of prosperity, resulting in a massive erosion of traditional rural life in Spain. Within ten years the countryside would lose nearly half of its labour force to 'the enticing shop-window of urban prosperity'.[20] Migrant workers were packed into overcrowded dormitory estates on the periphery of towns, where the shortage of services became daily more evident. Nevertheless, the vast influx of migrant workers from the countryside to towns in search of work had an enormous impact on the cultural and social changes sweeping through Spain. A complex, plural society was emerging that would in due course undermine the authoritarian nature of the regime. Thus did the economic miracle upon which the regime depended for its survival sow the seeds of its destruction.

That Franco's own finger had moved some distance from the pulse of popular thinking was amply demonstrated in late May 1960 when he arbitrarily cancelled both legs of a football match between Spain and the

Soviet Union in the quarter-finals of the first ever European Nations Cup, on the grounds that it might unleash demonstrations in support of the communists. This ideologically blinkered decision, taken at a time when Real Madrid and the Spanish national team were at the zenith of their glory, did not go down well with the Spanish fans. Forced to accept 'that it could not control outbursts of sporting fervour as easily as it could control other expressions of cultural discontent',[21] the regime henceforth exploited football to distract people from their political and social problems. As always, Franco was himself particularly susceptible to this tactic, immersing himself in football on the television.

On 19 December 1960, Navarro Rubio announced his Development Plan for the liberalisation of the Spanish economy, formulated in conjunction with the World Bank. The arrival of the World Bank mission in Spain and the advent of John Kennedy to the White House seriously unnerved Franco, who turned to Carrero Blanco for reassurance. Ever his master's shadow, Carrero Blanco produced a soothing report on 23 February 1961, assuring him that the world was still dominated by three internationals – communist, socialist and Masonic – all of which shared a determination to destroy the Franco regime. While these doom-laden prognoses satisfied the Caudillo's paranoid convictions, they failed to acknowledge that the real enemy lay within Spain itself. Working-class discontent with Franco's repressive and stifling regime was now bursting through the gaps of the repressive machinery. Even hard-line Falangists occasionally heckled the Caudillo at meetings, although they risked a heavy prison sentence by doing so. During an orchestrated tour of Andalusia in the spring of 1961, the usually deferential Alonso Vega spitefully notified the Caudillo that the cheering Falangists who had greeted him were probably paid to do so. After an uncharacteristic tour of the distressing shanty towns on the outskirts of Seville, the Caudillo was so shocked that he called upon the Andalusian rich to dig deep in their pockets to redress this situation. Clearly it did not occur to him to take any responsibility for the situation himself.

Franco's concern about social inequality and paid populism soon abated. During the twenty-fifth anniversary of the military uprising in 1961, he delivered endless eulogies to the violent inception of his regime and venomous diatribes about the vanquished in the civil war. Such sterile sentiments did little to span the widening rift in Spanish society. Nevertheless, the quarrelsome beneficiaries of his regime were decidedly unnerved at the end of 1961, when the elderly Caudillo seriously damaged his left hand after his shot-gun exploded. With the succession unresolved, the future remained an open book. Although Franco went into a soldierly stiff-upper-lip mode, even he began to suspect that the appointment of a Francoist regent to oversee the installation of an authoritarian monarchy was advisable. In fact, the only candidates he would countenance for such a task – Muñoz Grandes, Alonso Vega and Carrero Blanco – would all die before him.

Shaken by the accident, Franco readily agreed to Carrero Blanco's suggestion that the highly effective López Rodó be appointed as head of the Commissariat for the Development Plan, a central planning body proposed by the World Bank advisers. Franco's flair for bifurcating perceptions enabled him to stand by this forward-looking appointment, which ruffled feathers within his cabinet, while continuing to nurse strong suspicions about the economic motivations of the western democracies. He bitterly resented his ministers' suggestion that Spain petition to join the European Economic Community (EEC), which both he and Carrero Blanco regarded as 'a fief of Freemasons, liberals and Christian Democrats'. In fact, the EEC made it clear that, while it was prepared to discuss some form of economic agreement with Spain, it would not countenance any formal political links until major constitutional change had taken place.

It was not just the EEC that was concerned. On 12 February 1962 the Catholic journal *Ecclesia* staunchly proclaimed that 'the luxury and wastefulness of the wealthy classes are a provocation to those who lack the bare necessities to lead a life of human dignity, and they create a pathological condition within the body of society'.[22] Throughout April and May, worker-priests supported an outburst of strikes that spread rapidly from Asturian mines and Basque steelworks to Catalonia and Madrid. Horrified as messages of solidarity flowed in from other European workers, and bewildered by the support of so many priests for the unrest, Franco frantically condemned them as 'not apostolic' and as opening 'the way to communism'. Concerned that burgeoning unrest would bolster the cause of the monarchy, Franco nervously directed that publicity about Juan Carlos's marriage to Princess Sofia of Greece on 14 May 1962 be muted, and insisted that no picture of Don Juan at the wedding be published. His efforts were in vain. As the British ambassador in Madrid commented at the time, 'the wedding brought more publicity to the Spanish royal family than at any time since Franco came to power'.[23] More than 5000 Spaniards travelled to Greece to express their support for Don Juan and the Borbón dynasty.

However, Franco's attempts to sow the seeds of discord between Don Juan and Juan Carlos were beginning to bear fruit. Against the express wishes of Don Juan, the royal couple decided to move to Madrid. The Caudillo, who had long insisted that his wife be addressed as 'la Señora' and that the Royal March be played whenever she entered a room – honours hitherto reserved only for queens – vigorously encouraged the royal couple to adopt a simple lifestyle and make themselves accessible to the ordinary people.[24] Although Don Juan desperately assured the British ambassador that 'at no time has General Franco ever suggested to him or, as far as he knew, to anyone else, that Juan Carlos might ascend the throne in preference to his father', and that he was 'too good a son ever to wish to take the place of his father', he had good reason to be concerned about the future.[25]

He was not the only one. In early June 1962, a number of Spanish delegates attending the IV Congress of the European Movement in Munich – including Catholics, monarchists, exiled democrats and groups sponsored by the Church – agreed to a restrained declaration in favour of non-violent political evolution in Spain. An enraged Caudillo immediately demanded that they be imprisoned or exiled, and directed Arias Salgado, the Minister of Information, to unleash a virulent campaign in the press. This culminated in another frenzied attack on Don Juan. The Caudillo's tactless denunciation of 'the wretched ones who conspire with the reds to take their miserable complaints before foreign assemblies' did little to aid delicate negotiations with the European Community or curb the opposition.

Blaming Arias Salgado for everything, Franco agreed to a cabinet re-shuffle on 10 July which brought in more 'progressive' technocrat elements. Arias Salgado was replaced as Minister for Information by the highly intelligent and ambitious Manuel Fraga Iribarne, whose job it was to main-tain press censorship within a rapidly evolving society. The dynamic young Gregorio López Bravo, another committed member of the Opus Dei, joined the team as the Minister for Industry. Solís was kept on as Ministro del Movimiento as a sop to the Falange, and General Muñoz Grandes was appointed Vice-President of the Council of Ministers (although most of his responsibilities devolved to the increasingly powerful Carrero Blanco). To ensure that Franco was not too swamped by new faces, Alonso Vega remained as Minister of the Interior.

The more detached Franco became, the more his followers, whose sense of personal responsibility had never been nurtured, and who like him must have feared the vengeance of the vanquished, ran amok, fighting with each other for his attention, determined to safeguard their position after his death. These groups no longer divided neatly along traditional Francoist lines (Falangists, monarchists and Catholics), but diverged and conflated into new groups with extreme and incompatible aspirations for the future. The *continuista* technocrats believed that a painless transition to a Francoist monarchy under Juan Carlos could be secured only within a prosperous economy and an efficient administration. Others, *aperturistas* like Fraga, were convinced that only profound political reform would contain the billowing social unrest, while the *immovilistas* (or the *bunker* as they came to be known) advocated an immediate return to hard-line Francoism. With the different factions within his cabinet articulating the differing and contradictory aspects of his own beliefs, a bemused and ageing Caudillo tended to agree with everybody about everything. He was probably confused because his ministers, most notably Carrero Blanco, kept shunting from progressive to regressive themselves, depending upon the particular issue at stake.

Despite ill-tempered encounters between and within the differing camps, the new government did manage to generate a more dynamic, modern image. Fraga set about projecting a more mellow and subtle image of the Caudillo in the press, which was mirrored by his speech-writers. During his end-of-year broadcast on 30 December 1962, Franco diverged from his usual divisive fare. Having read out an analysis of Spain's economic 'miracle', he acknowledged that, because rapid economic growth had exacerbated social tensions, a minimum wage was necessary. However, it soon became clear that the regime was incapable of spanning the widening gap between demands for cultural freedom (Spaniards saw their first bikini-clad woman on cinema screens in 1962) and an insistence upon political repression, sometimes emanating from the same sector of society. Its internal contradictions were starkly illustrated when a Catalan anarchist kidnapped the Spanish Vice-Consul in Milan. When the Archbishop of Milan and future Pope Paul VI, Cardinal Giovanni Battista Montini, begged Franco for a merciful sentence, enraged Falangists stormed through the streets brandishing placards with half-naked women proclaiming 'Lollabrigida, yes! Fanfani and Montini, no!'[26]

When rising political expectations and social dislocation provoked a further outbreak of strikes and unrest, the regime responded with characteristic violence. In late 1962, the communist Julián Grimau was arrested, tortured and beaten so badly that his interrogators threw him out of a high window to try and disguise the injuries. Amazingly, he survived, only to face a court martial for the crime of 'military rebellion', a wide-ranging term that covered anybody who had fought for the Republicans during the civil war. He appeared in court with multiple fractures of his skull, arms and legs, still passionately protesting, 'I have already told you that I have been a communist, that I am a communist and that I shall die a communist.'[27] He was only one of more than a hundred members of the opposition tried by court martial at the beginning of 1963.

Although it would have been in the interest of the regime to be magnanimous, Franco's impulse for vengeance clouded his political judgement. Neither the condemnation of world leaders and ecclesiastical dignataries nor Castiella's impassioned pleas for clemency would move him. Nikita Khrushchev's telegram stating that 'No interest of state can justify trying a person under wartime laws twenty-five years after the end of the war'[28] clarified any remaining doubts. Grimau was executed by firing squad on 20 April 1963. This provoked an international wave of revulsion against Franco in the West. It was not, however, just Franco who had misjudged the situation; so had most of his ministers. Fraga's cynical willingness to dismiss Grimau as a 'repellant murderer' and the cabinet's wanton display of inhumanity displayed the extent to which even Franco's modernising ministers had become desensitised by years of violence. The government churlishly agreed that political infractions be designated a civilian rather than a military offence, but Franco's blood was up. A mere four months after the execution of Grimau, two anarchists were condemned to death by the barbaric method of strangulation by garrotte. This seriously undermined the credibility of the regime at a time when its survival depended on it becoming part of the capitalist world.

Franco was having difficulties enough keeping a foot in the Catholic one. Pope John XXIII's model of a just world, with its emphasis on the right of association, freedom of worship and the redistribution of wealth, had little in common with Francoist Spain.[29] The liberal ideals of the Second Vatican Council seriously undermined the Caudillo's fundamental precept that he was God's emissary on earth, who had spent his life fighting the Godless hordes. Franco lurched between the paranoid conviction that the Church had been infiltrated by communists and the complacent belief that it was not attacking him personally. In November 1965, he responded to the Second Vatican Council's denunciation of dictators by airily announcing to the cabinet that 'I do not take the reference to dictators as being directed at me, although the statement could cause problems for some countries in Latin America.' Spanish priests increasingly took a different view.

Ignoring the vocal criticism of the regime emanating from a significant number of clergymen, extensive celebrations of 'Twenty-Five Years of Peace' in 1964 orchestrated by Fraga began with a solemn *Te Deum*. They flowered into media events celebrating the spirit of the age of Franco and concluded with an adulatory film of the Caudillo's achievements, portraying Franco as the benevolent father of his people, who had heroically saved Spain from the tyranny of Nazism and the chaos of communism. Inured to adulation, a dismissive Franco's only comment on the film was 'too many parades'. Nevertheless, he confidently predicted that he was looking forward to celebrating the next twenty-five years.

The celebrations of peace were marred by outbursts of industrial unrest in Asturias. While Alonso Vega advocated harsh repression, Castiella and

Fraga persuaded Franco that, in the current circumstances, moderation would be appropriate. Nonetheless many miners were dismissed, arrested and imprisoned. On the other hand, the arrest of a communist militant who turned out to be the son of the Minister of Aviation provoked a glimmer of humanity in the Caudillo, who, recalling the antics of his brother Ramón, ruefully commented that it could happen in the best of families. He refused to dismiss the minister. That an increasingly tremulous Franco was beginning to mellow was again illustrated when, in 1964, the finals of the European football championships were scheduled to be held in Madrid, again between Spain and the Soviet Union. Far from cancelling the finals, Franco determined to attend. Despite the reservations of his ministers, who feared that he would refuse to hand over the trophy if the Soviet Union won, a delighted Caudillo was welcomed at the stadium by 120,000 fans chanting 'Franco! Franco! Franco!' Luckily for the regime, Spain beat the Soviet Union 2–1. The victory was offered up by the team's proud coach 'to the Caudillo who came to honour us this evening with his presence and to inspire the players'.[30]

In the circumstances, it was not surprising that the Spanish leader's health should be a continuous, if muted, source of anxiety. As the eminent physician Hugh L'Etaing points out, it is characteristic for the peoples of all nations to hang on to the myth of their leader's invulnerability. This was a particularly powerful issue in Spain, where Franco had long cited his superhuman physical capacity as giving him a wholly unique right to lead. Like children reluctant to countenance the human frailties of their parents, many of Franco's supporters seemed happy to collude in this fantasy. It was, however, becoming difficult to disguise the fact that the Caudillo was suffering from Parkinson's disease, a neurological disorder that may well have been exacerbated by the zealous over-prescription of drugs characteristic of dictators' doctors.[31] His alarming tendency to adopt a sudden rigid stance, an unsure walk or a vacant, open-mouthed facial expression meant that public appearances had to be intermittent and brief. Keen to associate the Caudillo with youth and virility, the Spanish people were more likely to be subjected to photos of the ageing father-figure, warmly greeting the great toreros – particularly the macho, muscular and highly popular bull-fighter, El Cordobés – than delivering diatribes about the past. The press hungrily latched on to his hunting prowess as evidence of his physical capabilities, while any mention of his physical disabilities in the press remained grounds for dismissal. Jokes about the Caudillo's immortality abounded. In one he refused the gift of a rare tortoise with a life-span of 150 years on the grounds that he would be upset when it died.

Despite such pretensions to immortality, Franco's concerned ministers –

including his old friend Camilio Alonso Vega – were desperate for him to appoint an heir. In the end, Carrero Blanco took matters into his own hands, arguing, during a cabinet meeting, that student unrest and intellectual opposition were the result of uncertainty about the succession. For once, the entire cabinet was in accord, forcing a sulky Franco to snap, 'I have undertaken to do it and I will do it.' The diagnosis of a serious illness in Muñoz Grandes, which removed him as guarantor of the post-Franco succession, did little to concentrate the Caudillo's mind. Nevertheless, in July 1965 he was persuaded by Carrero Blanco to reshuffle his cabinet. Often described as 'the last of the classic cabinet balancing acts of Franco',[32] it actually resulted in greater political power falling into the hands of Carrero Blanco and López Rodó. Although Franco continued to preside over cabinet meetings, his lack of interest was evident. Increasingly irritated by the long-winded interventions of his ministers, he waspishly commented that he was going to put an egg-timer in front of Alonso Vega. When López Rodó complained that Solís's Movimiento press was attacking the government's economic policy, Franco expressed horror but did nothing. He sometimes felt like attacking it himself.

On 13 August 1965, Franco was reluctantly persuaded to absent himself from an onerous round of hunting and fishing to attend a cabinet meeting to consider Fraga's new Press Law for liberalising censorship. Although Franco had always been a bitter opponent of press freedom, he once more found himself siding with the reformers against the hard-liners. Whether this was out of an 'anything for an easy life' mentality, complacency about the impact of a press he had long given up reading, or the realisation that the changes would have little real impact, the tired Caudillo agreed that the new law should be submitted to the Cortes in February 1966. Although Fraga's Press Law abolished advance censorship and press directives, the onus on publishers and writers to second-guess what might be considered unacceptable resulted in a great surge in Public Order Tribunals. This tentative attempt at modernisation did little to ease tensions within the cabinet. While Carrero Blanco accused Fraga of being the instigator of public immorality, a tired and tetchy Caudillo snapped, 'I am getting fed up with the fact that the press wakes up each day asking itself what shall we criticise today?' He was, however, increasingly disengaged. Even Muñoz Grandes complained that 'the Generalísimo forgets to ring me nowadays. He is in low form and lets people get away with too much.'[33]

Franco eventually gave Carrero Blanco the final draft of the Ley Orgánica del Estado on 13 June 1966, after which he went on an exhausting tour of Catalonia. Upon his return he seemed much more interested in his forthcoming summer holiday than in discussing the new 'constitution'.

His cabinet therefore submitted it straight to the Cortes without further discussion. On 22 November 1966, a feeble, bespectacled and virtually inaudible Caudillo presented it to the Cortes. Still complaining that he could 'never be relieved nor rest, but must burn himself out in finishing the task', he delivered a tremulous account of his glorious reign which had culminated in a 'rhythm of perfection and progress never equalled'. Instead of political parties, he offered 'the legitimate contrast of opinions' (although the opinions he was prepared to countenance remained very narrow indeed). The new law, which opened up representation in the Cortes under tightly controlled conditions, kept the state committed to the monarchy (but did not mention any names). It also made provision for a Prime Minister to be appointed, should Franco's health render this necessary. The Cortes accepted the text and then presented it to the Spanish people for their views. Fraga took charge of a massive media campaign, presenting a yes vote as repaying the Caudillo for his years of devoted service to the people, and a no vote as a vote for Moscow. Like a father appealing to his ungrateful children for appreciation, Franco himself delivered a stern and reproachful speech to the Spanish people. He reminded them that

I was never motivated by ambition for power. From my youngest days, they placed on my shoulders responsibilities beyond my years and rank. I would have liked to enjoy life like so many ordinary Spaniards, but the service of the *Patria* monopolised my every hour and took up my life. For thirty years, I have steered the ship of state, safeguarding the nation from the storms of the contemporary world. Yet, despite all of that, here I remain, still at my post with the same spirit of service as when I was young, employing in your service what useful life I have left. Is it too much for me in turn to ask your support for the laws which for your exclusive benefit and that of the nation are about to be submitted to a referendum?[34]

On 14 December 1966, 88 per cent of the possible electorate voted in the referendum on the *Ley Orgánica*, of which less than 2 per cent voted no. Some had voted yes in gratitude to the past and in deference to their leader, some because of the growing prosperity, and some because they hoped that it would facilitate the transition from dictatorship to monarchy. Despite intimidation and signs of electoral rigging (in some places 120 per cent of the electorate 'voted' yes), this was a massive victory for Franco – or at least a symptom that 'the years of state terror banked between 1936 and 1944 had paid off handsomely in mass political apathy'.[35] An emotional Caudillo thanked the people 'for the truly exemplary nobility with which you have consented to display, freely and wholeheartedly, your support and your trust'.[36]

In fact, Franco was much more interested in playing with his grand-children and filling in his pools coupons than in considering matters of state, particularly ones that involved the stressful consideration of his imminent demise. In May 1967 he won a million pesetas, the equivalent of £100,000 today, for a coupon that he had signed 'Francisco Franco, El Pardo, Madrid'. Unlike some of his ministers, he could barely muster up the energy to get belligerent about the United Nations' unsympathetic response to a Spanish petition on Gibraltar. Forgetting his lifetime's convictions to the contrary, he calmly stated, 'it should not be thought that we are going to get anywhere any faster by using violence' or 'trying to trip up the strong'. The only action he would countenance was the closing of the frontier with Gibraltar.

Muñoz Grandes, who had complained to Fraga in February 1967 that he and Franco 'were fed up with arguing', was finally relieved of his post as Vice-President of the Council of Ministers on 21 July. Carrero Blanco took over two months later. Franco remained President of the Council of Ministers. When the new Cortes – which had had one-third of its *Procuradores* elected by heads of families – met on 17 November 1967, Franco was swift to remind everybody that it was not sovereign: only the Caudillo could sanction laws. Refusing to name a Prime Minister on the grounds that he was not anticipating ill-health, Franco was as reluctant as ever to name a successor who might become the focus of opposition. When Queen Victoria Eugenia (widow of Alfonso XIII and mother of Don Juan) came to Spain with her son on 30 January 1968 to celebrate the birth of Juan Carlos's first son Felipe, a petty Franco refused to greet them at the airport. At the christening, when the exasperated Queen drily commented to him, 'You've got all three Borbóns in front of you. Decide!', Franco did not reply. Nor, to the exasperation of his irritable and nervy cabinet, would he name a President of the Council of Ministers.

In the spring, Franco emerged from his political torpor long enough to consolidate the hostility of the Vatican by refusing to relinquish the symbolic right to select bishops provided by Rome. He was forced to rouse himself again when the expiry of the bases agreement with the United States provoked further rancour within the cabinet. After much ill-tempered debate and misplaced posturing, the regime was forced to accept a one-year extension in return for greatly reduced aid.

On 6 December 1968 and again on 5 January 1969, Franco's much vaunted iron control of his bladder ended when he was forced to withdraw from a cabinet meeting to go to the lavatory. His ministers, who had frequently had to absent themselves for similar reasons, construed this untoward event as a worrying symptom of Franco's physical decline. In the wake of this drama, Juan Carlos decided to declare his unreserved commitment to the idea of a monarchical installation rather than restoration, and emphasised his loyalty to Franco and the Movimiento. His motives can only be guessed at. He may have feared that, if he did not stake a claim to the succession, the Borbón monarchy would be excluded from playing a stabilising role in a post-Franco Spain. He knew better than anyone that Franco would never countenance the return of his father to the throne. It was, however, a bitter medicine for Don Juan to swallow. In April, after the death of Juan Carlos's grandmother Victoria Eugenia, Don Juan had a violent row with his son during which he tried to persuade him not to accept the throne when Franco offered it.[37]

In fact, escalating unrest in the universities put further discussion about the succession firmly on the back-burner. Although, in June 1966, Franco had loftily pronounced his belief 'in the noble, generous and fair-minded youth' and insisted that 'What is needed is a dialogue',[38] his enthusiasm for discourse waned dramatically when the students burst into open rebellion once more. On 24 January 1969 the regime declared a state of emergency, despite López Rodó and Fraga's belief that this was tantamount to 'killing flies with artillery'. As instinctive supporters of repression, Carrero Blanco and Alonso Vega enthusiastically supported the action, but they rapidly changed tack when it became clear that Solís and his cronies were using the crisis to prevent Franco naming Juan Carlos, their favoured candidate, as his successor. After a particularly virulent argument between his ministers, Franco wearily agreed to lift the state of emergency and announce his support for Juan Carlos. He took care not to tell Juan Carlos about this until after he had returned from visiting his father on 12 July, on the grounds that 'I would have asked you to give me your word of honour not to reveal the secret and, if your father had asked you, you would have had to lie.'[39] Don Juan was – as Franco doubtless anticipated – deeply upset at what he construed as his son's betrayal.

Franco notified his cabinet of his decision on 21 July 1969, and despite a rearguard action by some of the hard-line Falangist opponents of Juan Carlos, presented his decision to the Cortes on the following day. Juan Carlos swore fidelity to the principles of the Movimiento in the belief that this would not prevent the possibility of democratic reform at some stage in the future. Although Juan Carlos dispatched a letter to his father reassuring him of his 'filial devotion and affection' and explaining that he was undertaking 'the biggest sacrifice of my life' to secure the return of the monarchy and secure 'many years of peace', his father was furious.[40] He immediately distanced himself from a monarchy that would be so closely linked to the dictatorship. Franco had thus succeeded in creating a rift between the Pretender and his son. Keen to establish the notion that his time in power was neither 'a parenthesis nor a dictatorship separating two epochs' but 'a true historical rectification',[41] Franco refused to designate Juan Carlos the Príncipe de Asturias, the title normally given to the heir to the throne. Juan Carlos was thus forced to collude in Franco's break with the continuity and legitimacy of the Borbón line. Accordingly, Franco had enmeshed the future of the monarchy with his own political heritage.

With the succession apparently secure, all should have been well. It was not. As he had feared, Franco's resolution of this issue signalled that his rule was, indeed, coming to an end. This realisation sent increasingly fractious competitors, desperate to stake a claim in the post-Franco era, spiralling off in differing directions. Although Franco was politically committed to the Carrero Blanco and López Rodó vision of a transition to an authoritarian monarchy, he was neurotically predisposed to heed the hysterical warnings of Solís, and the hard-line clique (camarilla) who had gathered like flies around Doña Carmen at El Pardo. This group included Nenuca's husband, Cristóbal Martínez Bordiu, old Francoists like Girón, and some deeply reactionary generals.

In 1969, Solís, desperately casting around for a way to discredit the Opus Dei technocrats, leapt upon the Matesa scandal to try and end their political predominance. This company, which manufactured textile machinery in Pamplona, was one of the flagships of the technocrats' brave new world. Persistent allegations of massive fraud in its subsidiary companies in Latin America resulted in a virulent campaign by the Movimiento press condemning 'a national disaster'. Franco, affronted more by the wanton display of press freedom than by any implication of corruption, refused to discuss the issue. (When Solís and other Falangists rushed to complain to the Caudillo about the technocrats, he allegedly snapped 'What have you got against the Opus? Because while they work you just fuck about.'[42] On 1 October 1971 he would petulantly pardon most of those on trial for the Matesa scandal.) Carrero Blanco, horrified by a campaign which implied that Spain was 'politically stagnant, economically monopolistic and socially unjust', determined that Fraga at Information and Solís as Ministro-Secretario del Movimiento be held responsible, and sacked forthwith.

He therefore persuaded the reluctant Caudillo to reshuffle his cabinet on 29 October 1969. The rakishly handsome Gregorio López Bravo took over from Castiella as Foreign Minister, while Torcuato Fernández Miranda (a member of the Opus Dei and an adviser to Juan Carlos) took over from Solís as Minister Secretary-General of the Movimiento. Camilo Alonso Vega was finally allowed to retire as Minister of the Interior. While the reshuffle seemed like a victory for the technocrats, the fact that Franco's and

Carrero Blanco's support for the *continuistas* was repeatedly undermined by their emotional commitment to the *bunker* mentality imposed a characteristically schizophrenic outlook on the new ministry. The new cabinet responded harshly to a miners' strike in Asturias and major disputes breaking out in the shipyards, construction industries and the Madrid metro. Violent police action, covert repression by semi-fascist terror squads linked to Carrero's intelligence service and the readiness of the Civil Guard to open fire on demonstrators resulted in a number of deaths of innocent bystanders. The Basque revolutionary separatist organisation Euzkadi ta Askatasuna (ETA) would pose a much more potent challenge to the regime.

Basque extremism struck a particularly neurotic chord with the Caudillo. His ruthless attitude to the Catholic Basques had already been revealed at Guernica. It was exposed again on 18 September 1970 at the World Jai-lai championships, the Hispanic version of squash. To the horror of the international press, the Caudillo looked on impassively when the man who had been in command of the only military unit in Guernica on the day it was bombed set fire to himself right in front of him, shouting 'Long live free Euzkadi!' It was therefore not hard for extreme rightists in the army to persuade Franco to instigate a highly damaging trial of sixteen Basque prisoners, including two priests.

The general furore over this decision was interrupted briefly by a high-profile visit from President Nixon – keen to compete with Eisenhower's lavish welcome in 1959 – and Henry Kissinger, to discuss the military bases. Although the President could not find fault with his ceremonial arrival, the elderly Franco and exhausted Kissinger slept soundly throughout the discussions, leaving Nixon exchanging ideas with López Bravo.[43] The American visit did little to ease tensions within Spain or assuage the sleepy Caudillo's impulse for revenge.

As the ETA trial began that December in Burgos, Franco was torn between pleas for restraint from the international press and his moderate ministers and demands for extreme measures from political hard-liners. Even his brother Nicolás frantically petitioned him not to sign the death sentences because 'It's not in your interests. I'm telling you because I love you. You are a good Christian and afterwards you will regret it.'[44] The world looked on aghast as descriptions of the tortures to which the Basque prisoners had been subjected were delivered in court. Outrage on the left that the trial had been permitted to take place at all was matched by indignation on the right that it was going on too long without exemplary punishments being administered. The trial ended with three ETA militants receiving two death sentences each. Within 'a quarter of an hour' it seemed as though Spain had 'leaped back thirty years'.[45]

After impassioned intercessions by López Rodó, Carrero Blanco and those ministers who believed that such executions were tantamount to political suicide, a reluctant Caudillo finally commuted the death penalties to thirty-year prison sentences. Despite Franco's soothing end-of-year broadcast on 30 December 1970, the Burgos trials had been a disaster for the regime, uniting the opposition in a way that had previously been impossible. When the Church begged the people to pardon its failure to be 'true ministers of reconciliation' during the civil war, the 'crusader ideology' was finally and definitively whipped from under Franco's feet.

Nervously monitoring the situation from the United States, President Nixon was increasingly convinced that only the accession of Juan Carlos to the throne before Franco's death would prevent 'a chaotic or anarchic situation developing'. He therefore dispatched General Vernon Walters on a secret mission to ascertain – from Franco himself – what plans he had made for the future. In February 1971, Walters met with an 'old and weak' Caudillo and López Bravo. After chatting briefly, an extremely tremulous Franco directed the American envoy to tell the President that 'insofar as the order and stability of Spain are concerned this will be guaranteed by the timely and orderly measures I am taking'. Vernon Walters was profoundly impressed at the 'the calm and unemotional way in which Franco had discussed the subject' of his death. When Walters sought out the opinion of some friends in the armed forces, they all discounted the possibility of Franco installing Juan Carlos on the throne before his death, but thought that he would appoint a Prime Minister. Any problems, they loftily assured him, would be 'easily' dealt with by the armed forces.[46]

Their confidence seemed entirely misplaced. The instinctive balancing act within the regime had now deteriorated into a free-for-all, into which Franco's own family had been sucked. His brother Nicolás became involved in a major scandal in which four million kilograms of olive oil went missing. Six people died in mysterious circumstances during the judicial investigation. Meanwhile on 18 March 1972 Doña Carmen's delusions of grandeur were heightened by the marriage of the highly reactionary and very ambitious Alfonso de Borbón-Dampierre (the son of Don Juan's brother, Don Jaime) to Franco's eldest granddaughter, María del Carmen Martínez Bordiu. After a characteristically excessive ceremony, at which Imelda Marcos was, symbolically, one of the few foreign guests, Doña Carmen insisted that their granddaughter be addressed as 'Your Highness' and that everybody curtsy whenever she entered a room. The union opened up yet again the possibility of a royal dynasty within the Franco family. Although this idea greatly excited Doña Carmen, and further inflamed the ambitions of the anti-Juan Carlos brigade that had gathered around her, it did not particularly engage the Caudillo. He was disinclined to have his grand-daughter's husband, over whom he had little or no influence, playing with his future. Despite Alfonso's petulant insistence that he be given a royal title on a par with that of Juan Carlos, Franco did little to further his cause.

Franco was eighty on 4 December 1972. The Spain over which he presided was spinning out of control. When, in January 1973, Spanish bishops published a long statement formally committing themselves to political neutrality, independence of the state and respect for political pluralism, the last vestiges of 'the Church–regime symbiosis of Catholic Nationalism was shattered'.[47] In fact, the regime from which the Church was seeking to detach itself was strikingly similar to the one to which the Vatican had committed its support in the 1940s. In April 1973, the police killed a striker near Barcelona. On 1 May, a policeman was stabbed to death by a member of the ultra-leftist Maoist organisation known as FRAP during a May Day demonstration. However, while right-wing officers and Falangist war veterans screamed for vengeance, a philosophical Franco discounted FRAP as 'dogs that howl . . . exiguous minorities that simply underline our vitality and prove our *Patria*'s strength and capacity to resist'.[48] Whether this insouciance was a symptom of his detachment from the real world, or an indication that he still depended upon a hostile enemy to give him a sense of identity, it did little to calm nerves on either the left or the right.

Appalled at the growing influence of the ultra-right, Tomás Garicano Goñi, who had replaced Alonso Vega as Minister of the Interior, resigned on 2 May. With ETA extremism escalating rapidly, Franco finally persuaded a reluctant seventy-year-old Carrero Blanco to become President of the Council of Ministers for a period of five years and to assemble a new cabinet. Torcuato Fernández Miranda took over as Vice-President. Apart from insisting on the inclusion of the hard-liner Carlos Arias Navarro, a prosecutor during the repression of Malaga in 1937 and a particular favourite of his wife, an exhausted and disengaged Franco simply accepted Carrero's suggestion for 'the funeral cabinet'. If Hugh L'Etaing's analysis of the physical and mental shortcomings of ageing leaders holds true, then this elderly triumvirate was not the best equipped to take the helm.[49]

With the regime's most stalwart supporters hurling themselves off a rapidly sinking ship, it lunged around without direction. Carrero Blanco's unstable amalgam of economic progression, political caution and ideological extremism had always exacerbated political instability. Now his blinkered decision to hold a show trial of ten leaders of the underground trade union, Comisiones Obreras, on 20 December 1973 proved to be a disaster. Shortly before 9.30 a.m. on the day of the trial, a squad of ETA activists detonated a bomb under his car. Carrero Blanco was killed in the explosion on his way back from daily mass. Fernández Miranda automatically took over as interim Prime Minister and managed, with the help of Arias Navarro and the senior military minister, to over-ride the wild orders issued by the Director-General of the Civil Guard to impose order 'without restricting in any way the use of firearms'.[50] It was only with the greatest difficulty that two of Carrero's ministers, the ultra-Falangists José Utrera Molina, the Minister of Housing, and Julio Rodríguez at education, were dissuaded from joining a hit squad to seek out the assassins.[51]

To begin with, a confused and disorientated Franco seemed unable to respond to this political and personal crisis. He had lost a great many friends and family over the years. This was the first time he displayed any public emotion after a major bereavement. His relationship with Carrero Blanco had, at one level, been very intimate; at another, a profoundly formal association. Muttering 'these things happen' and urging his cabinet to behave with decorum, he appeared bewildered, exhausted and red-eyed, and repeatedly broke down in tears. Unable to eat or sleep, he closeted himself in his study. Having tearfully confided in one of his aides that 'they have cut my last link with the world',[52] he wept and moaned throughout one of the masses held in Carrero's memory. Hopes that he would go on television to reassure the Spanish people were quietly abandoned. However, although, as López Rodó commented, 'Franco, without Carrero, was another Franco', he could never really change. Referring to the death of his friend during his end-of-year message to the people, Franco would spitefully comment that 'No hay mal que por bien no venga' ('Every cloud has a silver lining'). Possibly angry at being abandoned, he even began to nurse doubts about Carrero Blanco's vision of the future.

Carrero's death sent the political temperature soaring. Sensing Franco's confusion and vulnerability, Doña Carmen – apparently confusing herself with Lady Macbeth – and the El Pardo clique vigorously pushed their own political agenda. Determined to overturn the appointment of Fernández Miranda because of his (relatively) moderate views and enthusiasm for Juan Carlos, they were not particularly heartened when Franco made the emotional rather than political choice of his 75-year-old friend Admiral Pedro Nieto Antúñez for the job. Shrieking, 'They're going to kill us all like Carrero Blanco', Doña Carmen demanded 'a hard president. It has to be Arias [Navarro]. There is no one else.' Her husband finally gave in on the weary grounds that 'Pedrolo is nearly as old as I and has the same problems with his memory.'[53] On 28 December 1973, Arias Navarro – no spring chicken himself at sixty-five – became his Prime Minister.

Franco's new Prime Minister and his government reflected the same ambiguities as the old one. With the huge divisions in Franco's psyche embedded deep within the regime itself, it could not have been otherwise. While Arias tacked back and forth between displays of limited toleration and the harsh repression of labour and student unrest, it was clear that demands for change could neither be absorbed by the existing structures nor crushed by the old forces of repression. Throughout 1974, labour militancy and terrorism grew unchecked.

On 12 February 1974 Arias delivered a cautious mission statement calling for a 'controlled opening-up of the system', wider political participation within the strictest guidelines, and the introduction of political associations before January 1995. His announcement that Franco should not have to shoulder sole responsibility for political innovation horrified the *bunker* who, like playground sneaks, rushed to tell the Caudillo that some of Arias's Ministers were Freemasons. Franco was his usual volatile self. On the one hand, he welcomed the appointment of the fanatical José Utrera Molina as new head of the Movimiento and denounced 'the spirit of 12 February'. On the other, he over-ruled Arias's reactionary demands that the Bishop of Bilbao be expelled for publishing homilies objecting to the repression 'of the vitality of ethnic minorities'.[54] However, despite virulent protests from the Vatican, the EEC and several heads of state, he refused to commute the death sentences passed against a Catalan anarchist and a criminal, both of whom were executed by garrott on 2 March 1974. This provoked the European Parliament to denounce 'the Spanish government's repeated violation of basic human and civil rights [which] prevent Spain's admission to the European Community'.[55]

In Portugal, the overnight collapse of the 45-year dictatorship on 25 April sent shock waves through the El Pardo group. They were appalled that a dictatorship that had survived the physical incapacitation of Salazar in 1968 and his death, aged eighty-one, in 1970, had proved incapable of withstanding the sort of social and economic problems, and escalating left-wing guerrilla opposition, that were tearing Spain apart. Concerned that liberal members of the military had played a crucial role in bringing down the Portuguese dictatorship, the *bunker* responded viciously when young Spanish army officers – members of the clandestine Unión Militar Democrática (UDM) – published their tentative manifesto for the future calling upon 'the armed forces to defend the real interests of the entire Spanish nation and not just those of a corrupt and narrow elite'.[56] Even so, it was not until the summer of 1975 that Carrero Blanco's infamous intelligence services accumulated sufficient evidence to arrest UDM leaders.

In the wake of the Portuguese crisis, Girón – the *bunker*'s spokesman – persuaded Antonio Izquierdo Feriguela, editor of the Movimiento's mouthpiece *Arriba*, to launch a virulent attack upon Arias for opening the doors to subversion. The ultra-reactionary Blas Piñar announced that 'the hour of *caudillos* and warriors has struck'.[57] Their optimism that, if all else failed, the armed forces would intervene was not shared by right-wing generals, who set about purging the military High Command of those officers whose political views did not coincide with their own. Although Arias threatened to resign if this continued, even he accepted that it might be wise to remove the liberal General Díez Alegría from his post as Chief of the General Staff. Franco, who had been kept in the dark about all these military machinations, once more roused himself to support Arias against the *bunker*, but he was increasingly tired and distant. Fraga commented that 'he listened but heard nothing'.[58]

While the regime disintegrated alongside the infirm Caudillo, the confidence and expectations of the opposition soared. Large numbers of disaffected monarchists gathered in Estoril in Portugal, where the exiled Don Juan lived, to celebrate his saint's day on 22 June and criticise Juan Carlos's selection for the throne. The following day 20,000 Spanish workers from all over Spain gathered in Geneva to hear La Pasionaria and Santiago Carrillo, the leader of the Spanish Communist Party, promise that they would soon be in Madrid as part of a provisional government. The following month, Carrillo launched the Junta Democrática in Paris – a combination of leftists, regionalists and independents – to push for a take-over of power by a provisional government.

With hopes and fears flaring on all sides, Franco was admitted to hospital for phlebitis in the right leg. On 11 July 1974 the illness caused him to miss a cabinet meeting for only the second time in his career. On 19 July, to the fury of Doña Carmen and the Marqués de Villaverde, Arias and the President of the Cortes succeeded in persuading the Caudillo to implement Article 11 of the *Ley Orgánica del Estado*, whereby he stood down and Juan Carlos took over as interim Head of State. Juan Carlos accepted this role only with the greatest reluctance. This signified the end of Alfonso de Borbón's claims to the throne, but not the political ambitions of the El Pardo group.

Encased within the hospital, oblivious of the political storm howling outside, Franco was a strangely dependent and uncomplaining patient. Tensions in the country burst into the corridor of the hospital itself when, upon his return from a sleazy trip to the Philippines where he had been judging a Miss World competition, Franco's ambitious son-in-law, the Marqués de Villaverde, felt compelled – as the doctor in the family – to resolve medical differences with Franco's adviser Dr Gil in a vigorous bout of fisty-cuffs just outside the patient's room. Although Gil won the fight, he lost the war. His forty years of service, rewarded by Doña Carmen's grudging delivery of a television set from the large store of unwanted gifts to the Caudillo, was brought to an unceremonious conclusion.

When Franco emerged from the hospital on 24 July 1974, he looked frail, thin and bewildered. His new doctor, Dr Pozuelo, addressed Franco's Parkinson's – which had hitherto been a closely guarded secret – primarily by getting the Caudillo to fling his shoulders back and march around the room to stirring songs from the Spanish Legion. The doctor's attempts to sort out a painful abscess on his patient's foot were less successful. Franco refused to relinquish an exceptionally uncomfortable type of shoe, provided free by a servile manufacturer, on the grounds that his feet soon adjusted. When his doctor pointed out that it should be the other way around, an incredulous and weary Franco commented, 'You people like an easy life.'[59]

Although an unexpected surge of good health propelled the Caudillo back onto the golf course, his mental and physical frailty made him a susceptible target of Villaverde and Doña Carmen, who chilled his soul with dark hints about Juan Carlos and his liberal ministers' plans for the future. Thoroughly alarmed, on 2 September, Franco abruptly resumed his powers as Head of State without any prior discussion with Juan Carlos. Arias's announcement soon after that it was his firm intention to carry out the 12 February programme dispelled any satisfaction the *bunker* might have derived from Franco's renewal of power. When an ETA bomb tore apart the Cafetería Rolando next to police headquarters in Madrid, leaving eleven dead and seventy wounded, a frenzied Blas Piñar launched a bitter attack on Arias in the neo-fascist magazine *Fuerza Nueva*, accusing him of sowing 'fields of corpses'.[60] Meanwhile the El Pardo ultras, brandishing lewd photos they had themselves doctored, frantically lobbied the Caudillo to dismiss Pío Cabanillas, the new Minister for Information, on the grounds that he was peddling pornography in the press. But it was only when news of his brother Nicolás's shady dealings in 'the oil of Redondela' scandal seeped into the papers that the Caudillo was provoked into sacking the minister.

Fears that Spain was about to plunge into a blood-bath like 1936 sent the stock market plummeting. With concerned industrialists and financiers forging contacts with the opposition, Francoist figures who had been nervously testing the wind from the wings now flung themselves behind the reformists. As one monarchist commentator, Luis María Ansón, gleefully observed, 'the rats are leaving the regime's ship ... the cowardice of the Spanish ruling class is truly suffocating'.[61] A spate of resignations among Arias's more liberal ministers left him looking decidedly isolated.

Encouraged by these developments, the Junta Democrática launched a determined campaign of strikes to undermine the regime. The election of Felipe González as leader of the PSOE (the Spanish Socialist Party) in

October 1974 revived the flagging fortunes of the Socialist Party, while the erstwhile Falangist, Dionisio Ridruejo, helped form a new left-of-centre party, the USDE (Unión Social-Demócrata Española). Recognising that a peaceful transition would necessitate working with reformist elements within the regime, neither party joined the Junta Democrática.

While Arias struggled to contain the retrograde impetus of the *bunker*, Franco, mere jetsam in the political storm, was repeatedly washed against the certainties of the past. While ex-Francoists of the moderate opposition, like Dionisio Ridruejo and Joaquín Ruiz Giménez, were rounded up by the police, ETA bombs continued to explode. A further spate of strikes and renewed turmoil in the universities inflamed the sense of crisis. Arias's Statute of Associations, agreed by the Cortes on 16 December, earned hostility from both sides of the political spectrum. When, in early 1975, *Arriba* failed to note the anniversary of his 12 February speech, Arias angrily directed Utrera to dismiss its ultra-conservative editor, 'that little shit Antonio Izquierdo'.[62] Utrera immediately rushed to Franco to play him tapes of Arias saying 'Franco is old' and 'the only one with any guts here is me'.[63] Arias's behaviour seemed to come as no surprise to the tremulous dictator, who cried, 'Yes, yes, Arias is a traitor, but don't tell anyone. We must work with caution.' He nervously advised Utrera to do as he was told. (That in his declining years Franco's innate paranoia was growing uncontrollably, possibly as a result of the prescription of Diomorphine for his Parkinson's, was revealed when his doctor suggested that he dictate his memoirs into a tape-recorder prior to them being transcribed by a 'reliable typist'. The Caudillo whispered darkly, 'I don't think they'll let you.')[64]

Arias had no difficulties browbeating Franco into replacing Utrera with the more liberal Fernando Herrero Tejedor. When Utrera came to bid his farewells, he was embraced by an emotional and tearful Caudillo, who raised his arm in a tremulous fascist salute. When Arias's protégé Fernando Herrero Tejedor was killed in a car accident on 23 June 1975, Franco rallied himself sufficiently to insist that he be replaced by the hard-line spin-doctor José Solís. Such decisiveness was by now very unusual. Franco was showing distinct signs of senility. His movements were jerky and uncontrolled, his thought processes erratic and confused. His eyes, which had retained their 'keenness and vivacity'[65] long after the rest of his nondescript face had melted into his neck, were now permanently shrouded by dark glasses. He complained to Pacón that all he wanted to do was move to a monastery. Instead throughout the late winter of 1974, the El Pardo group dragged him on death-defying shooting trips. The icy winds provoked a kidney infection which, alongside his painful dental problems, seemed to mirror the inflammation and disintegration of the regime itself. Like its leader, it would, in its final death spasms, prove as repressive and violent as it had at its inception.

Perhaps – as in the past – the vengeance of the dying Franco was fanned by the death of a close member of his family. Pacón, his first cousin, constant companion and official associate since early childhood, died on 21 April 1975. Even after his retirement in 1956, Pacón had remained at the Caudillo's beck and call. It was therefore with considerable trepidation that Dr Pozuelo gently broke the news of his death to a visibly shaken Franco. Interrupting the doctor's attempts to console him, the philosophical Caudillo commented that 'in reality, doctor, this is what awaits us all', adding that his seriously ill cousin 'must have been very sad, dragging himself around this earth'.[66] He was clearly talking about himself.

Five days later, under cover of a three-month State of Exception in Vizcaya and Guipúzcoa, ultra right-wing terror squads launched a series of attacks on left-wing lawyers, clergymen and workers. Anybody suspected of being a nationalist or associating with nationalists in the Basque country was liable to be machine-gunned down, while bars, publishing houses and lawyers' offices were bombed. The feverish efforts of the intelligence services to purge the army of its democratic elements finally bore fruit on 29 July 1975. Nine leading officers of the UMD – which had been growing slowly but steadily – were arrested in a series of spectacular dawn raids more appropriate for rounding up terrorists. These same intelligence services would play a key role in a number of attempted anti-democratic coups in the post-Franco period.

That summer, the imposition of death sentences on three suspected ETA terrorists 'did as much to politicise the Basque country as the Burgos trials had done in 1970'.[67] Despite the repression, a massive solidarity demonstration took place on 11 June 1975. General strikes paralysed the region throughout August and September. A draconian new anti-terrorist law was extended to all of Spain in August. Its blanket terms resulted in a massive bout of arrests and trials in Burgos, Barcelona and Madrid. On 12 September, in addition to the three Basques condemned to death, capital sentences were imposed on three FRAP terrorists, and were extended to a further five FRAP activists six days later. Despite personal appeals for clemency from the European Parliament, the UN, the Pope, Don Juan and many bishops within Spain, mass strikes and huge demonstrations, three members of ETA and two of FRAP were shot on 27 September. Thirteen countries withdrew their ambassadors from Spain and four Spanish embassies were set on fire.[68] It would be difficult to produce a starker symptom of the regime's regressive decline.

On 1 October 1975, the thirty-ninth anniversary of his elevation to the

Headship of State, General Franco appeared before a huge crowd for the last time. Sporting his full military regalia, the shrivelled but unrepentant Caudillo was still spitting venom about the 'Masonic left-wing conspiracy' and 'communist-terrorist subversion in society'. Weeping openly, he raised his tremulous arms to the cheering crowds. On the same day, four policemen were shot, allegedly in reprisal for the executions, by a dubious new group of *agents provocateurs* calling themselves GRAPO, whom it later transpired had strange connections with the police.[69] There were fears – and hopes – that this atrocity would provoke Franco into unleashing a last frenzied outburst of right-wing brutality throughout the country.

A bout of influenza and a heart attack on 15 October hindered him from doing anything very much. Although he insisted on holding a number of formal audiences and chairing a cabinet meeting on 17 October, he worked in his study for the last time the following day. After a number of mild cardiac arrests, he received extreme unction on 25 October. By 29 October he was being given constant blood transfusions. By the night of 2–3 November, an intestinal haemorrhage had covered the bed, the carpet and a nearby wall in blood, resulting in an emergency operation being carried out there and then. It was a symbolic conclusion to a violent life.

Franco was finally taken to a properly equipped hospital where, after further surgery, he was placed on a massive array of life-support machines. Tubes and drips – as complex as the political threads plugged into his regime – emerged from his battered body. He was alive, but only just. He emerged occasionally from unconsciousness to murmur 'how hard it is to die'. It was certainly hard for his ultra supporters to let him. The El Pardo group was desperate to keep him alive until they had imposed their own candidate as President of the Consejo del Reino and of the Cortes, and so could dictate the succession. Furthermore, as Hugh L'Etaing comments, perhaps 'the protracted and tortuous medical activities around Franco's deathbed' arose from the paranoid medical staff's determination to avoid 'his or her medical skill and reputation [being] weighed in the balance and found wanting'.[70] In the end, however, Franco's daughter finally insisted that he be allowed to die in peace. At 11.15 p.m. on 19 November, the tubes and drips that had suspended Franco between life and death were removed. He died shortly afterwards. The official time of death was 5.25 a.m. on 20 November 1975. The political aspirations of the *bunker* were finally and irrevocably dashed.

Franco's political testament to the Spanish people was read out at 10.00 a.m. on 20 November. Describing himself as a 'faithful son of the Church', he begged the 'forgiveness of everyone, just as with all my heart I forgive those who declared themselves my enemy even though I never thought of them as such. I believe that I had no enemies other than the enemies of Spain.' This tentative acknowledgement of his guilt and apparent quest for conciliation was swiftly followed by a harsh admonition not to forget 'that the enemies of Spain and of Christian civilisation are on the alert'.

The response to news of General Franco's death was as contradictory and extreme as the man himself. A run on black cloth was matched by the flow of champagne. People danced wildly in the streets in some Basque towns. Between 300,000 and 500,000 people filed past Franco's body. On 23 November, while the funeral cortège was *en route* from Madrid to Cuelgamuros, a mourner fell into the grave and was rendered unconscious. It seemed symbolic of the unconsciousness that had been violently foisted on the Spanish people by years of repression. A monumental stone, matching the one that covered the grave of José Antonio Primo de Rivera, commemorated his burial place. No significant Head of State, other than General Pinochet, attended the funeral.

Epilogue

'A Sphinx without a Secret'

Tyranny is a habit, it has a capacity for development, it develops finally into a disease ... The human being and the citizen die within the tyrant for ever; return to humanity, to repentance, to regeneration becomes almost impossible.

Dostoevsky[1]

Franco's death unleashed a feverish feeding among erstwhile supporters anxious to suck the last drop of blood from their association with the Caudillo. The revelations of a number of friends, relatives and close political associates soon wrested away the fragile protective façade and exposed the man within. The mystical balloon he had inflated around himself soon popped, revealing 'a sphinx without a secret'. It had, in fact, always been that way.

Despite the grandiloquent rhetoric with which his power was shrouded, Franco's beliefs had never rested on a rigid philosophy, but were entirely opportunistic, drawing, parasitically, upon the hatreds, fears and hopes of his supporters and his opponents. The linchpin of his regime throughout his time in power was a debilitating terror that any move to dismantle it would result in another civil war. As this fear subsided after his death, so the inflated concepts of both the man and his regime were exposed as fragile figments of his demented imagination.

Franco had foisted a sense of guilty collusion or a compulsive 'culture of evasion' upon almost everyone in Spain. However, the anti-democratic and vengeful facets of his regime dissolved almost immediately in a 'pact of oblivion'. The victims of the repression, desperate to secure a bloodless transition to democracy, renounced (or denied) their desire for revenge. There were no purges of the executioners, the torturers, the gaolers, the informers or those who had accumulated such riches under the Caudillo's averted eyes. Nevertheless, in the two decades after his death, many people continued to suffer a 'profound disorientation and introspection'. In response to the right-wing refrain, 'Con Franco vivíamos mejor', democrats began to say, 'We lived better *against* Franco.'

Despite the benevolence of the Spanish people, considerable skill and delicacy was required to negotiate a path to democracy. While the start of Juan Carlos's reign was greeted with enormous goodwill both inside and outside Spain, and there was a groundswell of popular support for him to become 'King of all Spaniards', the road to democracy was fraught with hazards. He found himself bound to a backward-looking, centralist state that was still at war with communism, socialism, liberalism, democratic pluralism and regional devolution. There were still 100,000 Falangists licensed to carry guns, and the constitutional bodies established to oversee the succession were packed with hard-line Francoists, behind whom stood the Civil Guard and the army. The army, purged of its few liberal, democratic elements by Carrero's zealous intelligence services, was a constant reminder of the risks of political progress. It left the Spanish people in no doubt about what would happen if they pushed for reform or a settling of accounts. Not only would they risk another civil war, but they would have to confront their own terrible memories, and dredge up the guilt which – as has been amply demonstrated in Hitler's Germany – accompanies harsh political repression, even for the oppressed.[2]

In order to avoid a military backlash, King Juan Carlos kept Arias on as Prime Minister. While massive demonstrations and strikes in support of amnesty for political prisoners convinced the more liberal ministers of the importance of dialogue with the opposition, on 11 February 1976 Arias stubbornly announced that 'what I want to do is continue Francoism. And as long as I'm here or in political life, I'll never be anything other than a strict perpetuator of Francoism.'[3] In the Basque country, ETA, which had not laid down its arms after the death of Franco, was formulating a nationalist agenda whose ambitions went far beyond the democratic aspirations of the rest of Spain. Basque militancy did little to conciliate hard-line Francoists to political change.

The King, however, frustrated with Arias's repressive attitude and extremely limited notion of political change, demanded his resignation in early June 1976. His time in power had not been without its benefits. His rigidity succeeded in shunting many more members of the Franco elite into the reformist camp, and united the left. It took the King some time to select somebody whom he felt would be able to oversee the transition to democracy without triggering another civil war. On 3 July 1976, he made the unexpected choice of Adolfo Suárez – who had been Minister Secretary-General of the Movimiento – as his Prime Minister, in the hope that he would be uniquely placed to exploit the system's own mechanisms against itself and open the way to reform. Unlike his predecessor, Suárez swiftly recognised that profound reforms were necessary to defuse the tensions simmering in the wake of Franco's death. Having gently and skilfully nudged political reform down a mine-laden path to democracy, Suárez created an electoral coalition, the Unión de Centro Democrático. Composed of junior Francoists who had not been implicated in the regime's crimes, it swept to power in the general election of June 1977, the first to be held since 1936.

Franco's legacy – rampant inflation, unemployment, terrorism and military subversion – bedevilled the five years of Suárez's rule over the fragile new democracy. Francoist issues, like Basque and Catalan autonomy, continued to enrage right-wing generals, who were increasingly open about their readiness to take military action to prevent any weakening of the centralist state. The King was well aware of the anti-democratic elements in the army. On 5 January 1981 he warned the officer corps not to get involved 'in political activities distinct from that elevated endeavour which interests us'.[4] Under intense pressure from the military, Suárez resigned on 29 January 1981. At the investiture of his successor, Leopoldo Calvo Sotelo, on 23 February 1981 at 6.20 p.m., a group of Civil Guards under Colonel Tejero burst into the chamber of the Cortes and held the entire political class hostage. The King acted decisively. Making it quite clear that he would neither abdicate nor leave Spain, he appeared on television at 1.15 a.m. the following day to announce that the Crown would not tolerate attempts to interrupt the democratic process by force. The rebels had either to shoot him or to acknowledge defeat. They reluctantly opted for the latter. Ironically, the King – the Caudillo's protégé – had placed his personal prestige and safety at risk to safeguard democracy. Perhaps Franco should not have been surprised that, under the guidance of his 'surrogate son', Juan Carlos, the political edifices and prejudiced philosophies that underpinned his regime would crumble away. Just as he had rebelled against the Republic and disbanded everything that 'the father of the Republic' Azaña held dear, so did Juan Carlos dismantle his regime.

The coup provided a timely reminder to the Spanish people of just how precious democracy was. Franco's Spain was finally and definitively laid to rest during the trial of those who had taken part in the attempted coup, which took place in early 1982. Although the accused closely mirrored the prejudices and attitudes displayed by Franco and his supporters, they were now harshly exposed for what they had always been: 'ill mannered bullies'. Absurd caricatures, like Franco, they 'talked of nothing but patriotism and their self-appointed role as guardians of the nation's values, yet they were blind to the extent to which their actions had done nothing but bring international ridicule and shame on Spain'.[5] This was a fitting epitaph for General Franco. Although the elections of 28 October 1982 took place under the continuing shadow of military intervention, the population would no longer be intimidated. The Socialist Party, under Felipé González, received a substantial mandate from the Spanish people. The popular will had finally prevailed. The political transition was over.

In some ways, Franco's social legacy was more profound, if equally contradictory. Although the Caudillo had underpinned his regime with Catholic dogma, he had imposed a political role upon the Church which tore it apart. His vengeful policies succeeded in turning the Spanish people away from the Church, and – ultimately – the Church itself against the regime. For from bequeathing the Spanish people a Catholic state, Franco had rendered the Catholic Church less relevant in modern Spain. Determined to maintain a unified *Patria*, Franco spawned terrorist groups intent on regional independence. Despite his much vaunted determination to reimpose 'traditional Spanish values', in the 1950s and 1960s he presided over a major process of modernisation that drove migrants from rural areas to towns in quest of prosperity, resulting in a massive erosion of traditional rural life in Spain. Ironically, in a regime whose only claim to credibility was law and order, the arrival in the cities of disaffected workers resulted in an explosion in criminality.[6]

Although Franco glorified the family, his regime did more to erode the concept of 'family' and 'motherhood' than free-love among the anarchists ever did. His bequest to the Spanish people in the years leading up to his death and its aftermath would be the highest pregnancy termination rate, and the lowest birth rate in Europe. By the time of his death, three-quarters of Spaniards were in favour of divorce.[7] Although Franco's blueprint for his Spanish family was harsh, austere and religious, by denying the Spanish people any creative, political or real spiritual outlets, he foisted upon them a frivolous escapism that has proved difficult to shift. As John Hooper comments, 'Two decades after the end of Franco's dictatorship, the excesses of the Spanish people can often seem reminiscent of the archetypal convent girl, recklessly experimenting with all that was previously forbidden.' Spaniards' overall consumption of legal drugs – coffee, alcohol, cigarettes – is the highest of any nation in the European Union.[8] It is perhaps not entirely surprising that, after his death, Franco's worst fears were realised in almost every respect: a sexual revolution, democracy, and a Spain in which the vast majority can hardly muster the interest to remember him at all.

Notes

INTRODUCTION: GENERAL FRANCO – FACT AND FANTASY

1 Paul Preston, *Franco: A Biography* (London: HarperCollins, 1993), p. 572.
2 Paul Preston, *Comrades! Portraits from the Spanish Civil War* (London: HarperCollins, 1999), p. 49.
3 Javier Tusell, *Franco y los Católicos* (Madrid: Alianza, 1984), p. 116.
4 Francisco Franco, *Discursos y mesajes del Jefe del Estado, 1964–1967* (Madrid: Publicaciones Españolas, 1968), p. 469.
5 William L. Beaulac, *Career Ambassador* (New York: Macmillan, 1951), p. 179.
6 Preston, *Comrades!*, p. 48.
7 Felix Moreno de la Cova, *Mi vida y mi tiempo: la guerra que yo viví* (Seville: Gráficas Mirte, 1988), p. 165.
8 Preston, *Comrades!*, p. 71.
9 Mike Richards, *A Time of Silence: Civil War and the Culture of Repression in Franco's Spain, 1936–45* (Cambridge: Cambridge University Press, 1998), p. 9.
10 Sir Samuel Hoare, *Ambassador on Special Mission* (London: Collins, 1946), p. 287.
11 Jaime de Andrade (pseudonym of Francisco Franco), *Raza: Anecdotorio para el guión de una película* (Madrid: Ediciónes Numancia, 1942), p. 67.
12 See Erich Fromm, 'Mechanisms of Escape: Authoritarianism', in *Fear of Freedom* (London: Routledge & Kegan Paul, 1960), pp. 121–4; Norman Dixon, 'Authoritarianism', in *On The Psychology of Military Incompetence* (London: Pimlico, 1994), pp. 256–9.
13 Charles Rycroft, *A Critical Dictionary of Psychoanalysis* (London: Penguin, 2nd edn, 1995), p. 107.
14 Dixon, pp. 258–9.
15 Erich Fromm, *The Anatomy of Human Destructiveness* (London: Pimlico, 1997), p. 557.

CHAPTER 1: SMALL ACORNS

1 Joachim C. Fest, *The Face of the Third Reich* (Harmondsworth: Penguin, 1979), p. 19.
2 George Hills, *Franco: The Man and his Nation* (New York: Macmillan, 1967), p. 17.
3 Hills, p. 18.
4 Francisco Franco Salgado-Araujo (Pacón), *Mi vida junto a Franco* (Barcelona: Planeta, 1977), p. 15.
5 Franco Salgado-Araujo, p. 15.
6 See interviews with the local friends, neighbours and family (some of whom are

anonymous) compiled by Francisco Martínez López, 'Testimonios sobre Franco y su familia', *FerrolAnalysis*, no. 14, 1999, pp. 70–5.

7 Enrique González Duro, *Franco: una biografía psicológica* (Madrid: Grandes Temas, 1992), p. 19.

8 Joaquín Arrarás, *Francisco Franco* (London: Geoffrey Bles, 1938), p. 11.

9 Duro, p. 11.

10 J. W. D. Trythall, *Franco* (London: Rupert Hart-Davis, 1970), p. 22.

11 Brian Crozier, *Franco: A Biographical History* (London: Eyre and Spottiswoode, 1967), pp. 33–4.

12 Paul Preston, *Franco: A Biography* (London: HarperCollins, 1993), pp. 1–2.

13 Duro, p. 22.

14 Duro, p. 21.

15 The deeply complicated Franco family is best unravelled by looking at Francisco Franco Salgado-Araujo's *Mi vida*, pp. 8–9, and Luis Alonso Vidal y de Barnola, *Genealogia de la familia Franco* (Madrid: Editora Nacional, 1975).

16 Arrarás, p. 11.

17 Duro, p. 22.

18 Preston, p. 4.

19 Franco Salgado-Araujo, p. 14.

20 See Hills, p. 32, and also Jaime de Andrade (pseudonym Francisco Franco), *Raza: Anecdotaria para el guión de una película* (Madrid: Ediciones Numancia, 1942), pp. 58–60, 75–82.

21 Hills, pp. 20–1.

22 Franco Salgado-Araujo, p. 14.

23 Franco Salgado-Araujo, p. 15.

24 Franco Salgado-Araujo, p. 15.

25 Pilar Franco, *Nosotros los Franco* (Barcelona: Planeta, 1980), p. 27.

26 Pilar Franco, p. 72.

27 Jaime Salóm, 'The Cock's Short Flight' in Marion Peter Hold (ed.), *Drama Contemporary: Spain* (New York: Performing Arts Journal Publications, 1985), pp. 147–50, 153, 173.

28 Martínez López, pp. 70–5.

29 Hills, p. 29.

30 Salóm, pp. 146, 151.

31 Ramón Garriga, *Ramón Franco, el hermano maldito* (Barcelona: Planeta, 1978), p. 15.

32 See Martínez López, pp. 70–5.

33 Preston, p. 3.

34 Preston, p. 3.

35 Robert C. Tucker, *Stalin as Revolutionary: 1879–1929* (London: Chatto and Windus, 1974), p. 76.

36 See Martínez López's interview with someone who had known Franco in Oviedo, who commented, 'I will tell you that even Franco himself whenever he could tried to excuse himself and avoid [his sister]'.

37 Pilar Franco, p. 227.

38 Felix Moreno de la Cova, *Mi vida y mi tiempo: la guerra que yo viví* (Seville: Gráficas Mirte, 1988), p. 165.

39 From speech on 16 May 1946 (Francisco Franco, *Textos de doctrina política: Palabras y escritos de 1945 a 1950* (Madrid: Publicaciones Españolas, 1951), pp. 40–1.

40 Marsha Kinder, *Blood Cinema: The Reconstruction of National Identity in Spain* (London: University of California Press, 1993), p. 200.

41 de Andrade, p. 17.
42 de Andrade, pp. 33, 39, 40.
43 de Andrade, pp. 51–3.
44 de Andrade, p. 60.
45 Kinder, p. 200.
46 de Andrade, p. 183.
47 See Román Gubern's Adlerian analysis of Franco in 'Raza' (un ensueño del general Franco) (Madrid: Ediciones 99, 1977), p. 12.
48 José María Gironella and Rafael Borrás Betriu, 100 españoles y Franco (Barcelona: Editorial Planeta, 1979), p. 264.
49 For a discussion on the split personality, see, for example, C. G. Jung, Jung on Evil, ed. and intro. by Murray Stein (London: Routledge, 1995), pp. 174–80; Charles Rycroft, A Critical Dictionary of Psychoanalysis (London: Penguin, 2nd edn, 1995), p. 173; Melanie Klein, Love, Guilt and Reparation (London: Virago, 1988), pp. 349–53.
50 Hills, p. 29.
51 Martínez López, pp. 70–5.
52 Franco Salgado-Araujo, pp. 15–16.
53 Duro, p. 24.
54 Salóm, p. 145.
55 Martínez López, pp. 70–5.
56 See Rycroft, p. 139: 'projection of aspects of oneself is preceded by denial, i.e. one denies that one feels such and such an emotion, has such and such a wish but asserts that someone else does'.
57 Robert Waite, Adolf Hitler: The Psychopathic God (New York: Da Capo Press, 1993), p. 370.
58 Alice Miller, quoting Helm Stierlin in For Your Own Good: The Roots of Violence in Child Rearing (London: Virago, 1991), p. 189.
59 Pilar Jaraiz Franco, Historia de una disidencia (Barcelona: Planeta, 1981), p. 25; see also Duro, p. 24.
60 Franco Salgado-Araujo, p. 16.
61 Crozier, p. 35 (quoting Ramirez).
62 Franco Salgado-Araujo, p. 16.
63 Salóm, p. 151.
64 Franco discussed his experiences in Toledo with his doctor, Vicente Pozuelo, who recorded their conversations in Los ultimos 476 dís de Franco (Barcelona: Planeta, 1980), pp. 89–90, 92.
65 Franco Salgado-Araujo, p. 16.
66 Quoted in Martínez López, pp. 70–5.
67 Salóm, p. 153.
68 Jaraiz Franco, pp. 56–7.
69 Crozier, p. 34.
70 Gerald Brenan, The Face of Spain (London: Turnstile Press, 1950), p. 235.
71 de Andrade, p. 19.
72 Sebastian Balfour, 'The Loss of Empire, Regenertionism, and the Forging of a Myth of National Identity', in Helen Graham and Jo Labanyi (eds), Spanish Cultural Studies: An Introduction (Oxford: Oxford University Press, 1995), p. 25.
73 Pozuelo, p. 91.
74 Pozuelo, p. 93.
75 Crozier, p. 35; see also Pozuelo, pp. 96–8.
76 Klaus Theweleit, Male Fantasies: Volume 1: Women Floods Bodies Histories (1987)

and *Volume 2: Male Bodies: Psychoanalyzing the White Terror* (Minneapolis: University of Minnesota Press, 1989), Vol. 2, p. 144.

77 Hills, p. 62.

78 Franco Salgado-Araujo, p. 19.

79 Franco Salgado-Araujo, p. 19.

80 Pozuelo, p. 99.

81 Theweleit, Vol. 2, p. 146.

82 Hills, p. 65.

83 Stanley G. Payne, *Politics and the Military in Modern Spain* (Stanford: Stanford University Press, 1967), p. 103.

84 Payne, pp. 106–7.

85 Franco Salgado-Araujo, p. 20.

86 de Andrade, pp. 65–7.

87 Preston, *Franco*, p. 29.

88 Franco Salgado-Araujo, p. 23.

89 Salóm, p. 161.

90 Arrarás, p. 19.

91 Franco Salgado-Araujo, p. 26.

92 Theweleit, Vol. 1, p. 100.

93 Erich Fromm, *Fear of Freedom* (London: Routledge and Kegan Paul, 1960), p. 147.

94 Norman Dixon, *On the Psychology of Military Incompetence* (London: Pimlico, 1994), pp. 174, 188.

95 Alan Bullock, *Hitler and Stalin: Parallel Lives* (London: HarperCollins, 1991), p. 50.

96 Joachim Fest, *Hitler* (Harmondsworth: Penguin, 1977), p. 23.

CHAPTER 2: THE EMERGENT HERO

1 Interview with the famous journalist and biographer of Franco, Manuel Aznar, 31 December 1938: *Palabras del Caudillo, 19 abril 1937–31 diciembre 1938* (Barcelona: Ediciónes Fe, 1939), p. 314.

2 Vincente Gracia and Enrique Salgado, *Las cartas de amor de Franco* (Barcelona: Ediciones Actuales, 1978), p. 29.

3 Gracia and Salgado, pp. 57, 94.

4 Paul Preston, *Franco: A Biography* (London: HarperCollins, 1993), p. 19.

5 Román Gubern, *'Raza' (un ensueño del general Franco* (Madrid: Ediciones 99, 1977), p. 48.

6 Francisco Franco Salgado-Araujo (Pacón), *Mi vida junto a Franco* (Barcelona: Planeta, 1977), p. 30.

7 Jaime Salóm, 'The Cock's Short Flight' in Marion Peter Hold (ed.), *Drama Contemporary: Spain* (New York: Performing Arts Journal Publications, 1985), pp. 161–2.

8 Franco Salgado-Araujo, p. 30.

9 Alberto Reig Tapia, 'Historia y memoria del Franquismo' in José Luis de la Granja, Alberto Reig Tapia and Ricardo Miralles (eds), *Tuñón de Lara y la historiografía española* (Madrid: Siglo XXI, 1999), p. 196.

10 Sebastian Balfour, 'The Loss of Empire, Regenerationism, and the Forging of a Myth of National Identity', in Helen Graham and Jo Labanyi (eds), *Spanish Cultural Studies: An Introduction* (Oxford: Oxford University Press, 1995), p. 26.

11 Jo Labanyi, 'Women, Asian Hordes and the Threat of Self in Gimenez Cabellero's *Genio de España*', *BHS*, Vol. LXXIII, 1996, pp. 377–87.

12 Manuel Llaneza, *Escritos y discursos* (Oviedo: Fundación José Barreiros, 1985), p. 209.

13 *Interviu*, no. 110, 22–8 June 1978, pp. 69–70.

14 Paul Preston, *Comrades! Portraits from the Spanish Civil War* (London: HarperCollins, 1999), p. 19.

15 Preston, *Comrades!*, p. 12.

16 Joaquín Arrarás, *Francisco Franco* (London: Geoffrey Bles, 1938), p. 28.

17 Aznar, *Palabras*, p. 313.

18 Preston, *Comrades!*, pp. 14–15.

19 Preston, *Comrades!*, p. 17.

20 Preston, *Comrades!*, p. 16.

21 Franco Salgado-Araujo, p. 50.

22 Preston, *Franco*, p. 30.

23 Preston, *Franco*, p. 5.

24 Francisco Franco, Comandante, *Diario de una bandera* (Madrid: Editorial Pueyo, 1922), p. 177.

25 Erich Fromm, *Fear of Freedom* (London: Routledge & Kegan Paul, 1960), p. 140.

26 Franco Salgado-Araujo, p. 52.

27 Franco Salgado-Araujo, p. 62.

28 Franco Salgado-Araujo, pp. 61–2.

29 Franco Salgado-Araujo, p. 61.

30 Francisco Martínez López, 'Testimonios sobre Franco y su familia', *FerrolAnalysis*, no. 14, 1999, pp. 70–5.

31 Franco Salgado-Araujo, p. 62.

32 Franco Salgado-Araujo, p. 62.

33 Preston, *Franco*, pp. 199–200.

34 Klaus Theweleit, *Male Fantasies: Volume 1: Women Floods Bodies Histories* (1987) and *Volume 2: Male Bodies: Psychoanalyzing the White Terro* (Minneapolis: University of Minnesota Press, 1989), Vol. 1, pp. 86–7.

35 Francisco Franco, Comandante, p. 228.

36 Preston, *Franco*, p. 33.

37 Preston, *Franco*, p. 47.

38 Reig Tapia, p. 196.

39 Martínez López, pp. 70–5.

40 Martínez López, pp. 70–5.

41 A rumour given considerable credibility by José Luis de Vilallonga, in his fanciful account of *The Sabre of the Caudillo* (Barcelona: Plaza y Janés, 1997). One of Franco's African colleagues, Colonel Vicente Guarner, comments, 'It used to be said that the daughter was adopted' and that she was Ramón's (quoted by Francisco Martínez López in 'Testimonios').

42 de Vilallonga, p. 98.

43 Franco Salgado-Araujo, p. 71.

44 Ramón Serrano Suñer, *Política de España 1936–75* (Madrid: Editorial Complutense, 1975), p. 16.

45 Franco Salgado-Araujo, p. 81.

46 Preston, *Franco*, p. 58.

47 Peter Kemp, *Mine Were of Trouble* (London: Cassell, 1957), p. 115.

48 Preston, *Franco*, p. 59.

49 Francisco Franco, *'Apuntes' personales sobre la República y la Guerra Civil* (Madrid: Fundación Francisco Franco, 1987), p. 6.

50 Labanyi, pp. 378–9.

51 Robert Waite, *Adolf Hitler: The Psychopathic God* (New York: Da Capo Press, 1993), p. 385.

52 Franco Salgado-Araujo, p. 91.
53 Serrano Suñer, pp. 16–17, 28; Preston, *Franco*, p. 65.
54 Serrano Suñer, p. 16.
55 *ABC*, 17 April 1931.

CHAPTER 3: WILL YOU WON'T YOU JOIN THE DANCE?

1 Paul Preston, *Franco: A Biography* (London: HarperCollins, 1993), p. 72.
2 Paul Preston, 'Franco & Azana: Victor and Vanquished', *History Today*, May 1999, p. 19.
3 Paul Preston, *Comrades! Portraits from the Spanish Civil War* (London: HarperCollins, 1999), p. 205.
4 Cf. Ernesto Giménéz Caballero, *Manual Azaña (profecias españolas)* (Madrid: Ediciones Turner, 2nd edn, 1975), ch. II, pp. 41ff.
5 Preston, *Franco*, p. 75; Pilar Franco, *Nosotros los Franco* (Barcelona: Planeta, 1980), pp. 18, 24; George Hills, *Franco: The Man and his Nation* (New York: Macmillan, 1967), p. 29.
6 Ramón Garriga, *Ramón Franco, el hermano maldito* (Barcelona: Planeta, 1978), p. 232.
7 Jaime de Andrade (pseudonym Francisco Franco), *Raza: Anecdotaria para el guión de una película* (Madrid: Ediciónes Numancia, 1942), p. 82.
8 Preston, *Franco*, p. 82.
9 Mike Richards, *A Time of Silence: Civil War and the Culture of Repression in Franco's Spain, 1936–45* (Cambridge: Cambridge University Press, 1998), p. 3.
10 Preston, *Franco*, p. 84.
11 Preston, *Franco*, p. 85.
12 Jo Labanyi, 'Women, Asian Hordes and the Threat of Self in Gimenez Cabellero's *Genio de España*', *BHS*, Vol. LXXIII, 1996, p. 380.
13 Labanyi, p. 380.
14 Paul Preston, *TLS*, 3 April 1991.
15 Preston, *Comrades!*, p. 54.
16 Preston, *Franco*, p. 89.
17 Preston, *Franco*, p. 89.
18 Francisco Franco Salgado-Araujo (Pacón), *Mi vida junto a Franco* (Barcelona: Planeta, 1977), p. 108.
19 Franco Salgado-Araujo, p. 108.
20 Franco Salgado-Araujo, pp. 108–9.
21 Preston, *Franco*, p. 90.
22 Manuel Azaña, *Diarios, 1932–1933 'Los cuadernos robados'* (Barcelona: Crítica, 1997), p. 53.
23 Preston, *Franco*, pp. 91–2.
24 Paul Preston, 'Franco & Azana' (quoting Alvarez de Vayo, *Freedom's Battle*).
25 Franco Salgado-Araujo, pp. 112–13.
26 Enrique González Duro, *Franco: una biografía psicológica* (Madrid: Grandes Temas, 1992), p. 33.
27 Franco Salgado-Araujo, pp. 113–14.
28 Rafael Abella, 'Nicolas Franco Salgado-Araujo y su tiempo: esbozo biográfico', intro. to Jaime Salóm, *El corto vuelo del gallo* (Barcelona, Grijalbo, 1981), p. 67.
29 Duro, pp. 33–5.
30 Preston, *Franco*, p. 103.
31 Preston, *Franco*, p. 104.

32 Claude Martin, *Franco, soldado y estadista* (Madrid: Fermín Uriarte, 2nd edn, 1965), pp. 129–30.

33 Franco Salgado-Araujo, pp. 115–16.

34 Franco Salgado-Araujo, p. 116.

35 Franco Salgado-Araujo, pp. 115–16.

36 Martin, p. 130.

37 Diego Hidalgo, *¿Por qué fui lanzado del Ministerio de la Guerra? Diez meses de actuación ministerial* (Madrid: Espasa-Calpe, 1934), p. 81.

38 Preston, *Franco*, p. 106.

39 Preston, *Franco*, p. 109.

40 José María Gil Robles, 'Mi Relación con el General Franco' (unpublished manuscript).

41 Javier Tusell and José Calvo, *Giménez Fernández: Precursor de la democracia española* (Seville: Mondadori and Diputación, 1990), p. 155.

42 Preston, *Franco*, p. 109.

43 Preston, *Franco*, p. 110.

44 Preston, *Franco*, p. 115.

45 Franco Salgado-Araujo, p. 132.

46 Preston, *Franco*, p. 123.

47 Franco Salgado-Araujo, p. 144.

48 Preston, *Franco*, p. 127.

49 Preston, *Comrades!*, p. 222.

50 Franco Salgado-Araujo, p. 139.

51 Franco Salgado-Araujo, p. 239.

52 Franco Salgado-Araujo, p. 139.

53 Preston, *Franco*, p. 130.

54 Preston, *Franco*, p. 134.

55 Preston, *Franco*, p. 134.

56 Joaquín Arrarás, *Historia de la cruzada española*, 8 vols, 36 tomos (Madrid: Ediciónes España, 1939–43), Vol. III, tomo 10, p. 71.

57 de Andrade, pp. 83–4.

58 Robert Waite, *Adolf Hitler: The Psychopathic God* (New York: Da Capo Press, 1993), p. 386.

CHAPTER 4: MINE ALL MINE

1 C. G. Jung, *Jung on Evil*, ed. and intro. by Murray Stein (London: Routledge, 1995), p. 175, para. 449.

2 Preston, *Franco: A Biography* (London: HarperCollins, 1993), p. 146.

3 Raymond Carr, *The Spanish Tragedy: The Civil War in Perspective* (London: Weidenfeld & Nicolson, 1977), p. 88.

4 Carr, p. 80.

5 Ronald Fraser, *Blood of Spain: The Experience of Civil War 1936–1939* (London: Allen Lane, 1979), p. 106.

6 Preston, *Franco*, p. 151.

7 Mike Richards, *A Time of Silence: Civil War and the Culture of Repression in Franco's Spain, 1936–45* (Cambridge: Cambridge University Press, 1998), p. 39.

8 Fraser, p. 137.

9 John T. Whitaker, *We Cannot Escape History* (New York: Macmillan, 1943), p. 106.

10 Hugh Thomas, *The Spanish Civil War* (London: Hamish Hamilton, 3rd edn, 1977), p. 254.

11 Mike Richards, ' "Terror and Progress": Industrialization, Modernity and the Making of Francoism', in Helen Graham and Jo Labanyi (eds), *Spanish Cultural Studies: An Introduction* (Oxford: Oxford University Press, 1995), p. 178.

12 Thomas, p. 265.

13 Thomas, p. 260.

14 Thomas, p. 260.

15 José Maria Iribarren, *Con el General Mola: escenas y aspectos inéditos de la guerra civil* (Zaragoza: Liberia General, 1937), pp. 168–9.

16 Thomas, p. 359.

17 Preston, *Franco*, p. 153.

18 Carr, p. 87.

19 Whitaker, *We Cannot Escape History*, p. 105.

20 John T. Whitaker, 'Prelude to World War: A Witness from Spain', *Foreign Affairs*, Vol. 21, October 1942–July 1943, p. 107.

21 Robert A. Friedlander, 'Holy Crusade or Unholy Alliance? Franco's "National Revolution" and the Moors', *Southwest Social Science Quarterly*, no. 44, March 1964, pp. 346–55.

22 Carr, p. 135.

23 Whitaker, *We Cannot Escape History*, p. 113.

24 Galeazzo Ciano, *Diary: 1939–43* (London: Heinemann, 1947), p. 34.

25 Richards, *A Time of Silence*, p. 35.

26 Paul Preston, *Traiciones y tragedias: las tres Españas del 36* (Barcelona: Plaza y Janés, forthcoming).

27 Whitaker, *We Cannot Escape History*, p. 111.

28 Peter Kemp, *Mine Were of Trouble* (London: Cassell, 1957), p. 50.

29 Robert Waite writes that Hitler's 'conception of masculinity condemned him constantly to take the offensive because to assume a defensive posture was feminine': *Adolf Hitler: The Psychopathic God* (New York: Da Capo Press, 1993), p. 382.

30 Whitaker, *We Cannot Escape History*, p. 112.

31 Kemp, p. 41.

32 Kemp, p. 46.

33 Klaus Theweleit, *Male Fantasies: Volume 1: Women Floods Bodies Histories* (1987) and *Volume 2: Male Bodies: Psychoanalyzing the White Terror* (Minneapolis: University of Minnesota Press, 1989), Vol. 1, p. 86.

34 Jaime de Andrade (pseudonym Francisco Franco), *Raza: Anecdotaria para el guión de una película* (Madrid: Ediciónes Numancia, 1942), p. 65.

35 Whitaker, *We Cannot Escape History*, p. 113.

36 Webb Miller, *I Found No Peace* (London: The Book Club, 1937), p. 344.

37 Preston, *Franco*, p. 175.

38 Preston, *Franco*, p. 183.

39 Preston, *Franco*, p. 184.

40 Norman Dixon, *On the Psychology of Military Incompetence* (London: Pimlico, 1994), p. 254.

41 Or 'Hitler's Pope', in John Cornwell, *Hitler's Pope: The Secret History of Pius XII* (London, Viking, 1999).

42 Cornwell, *Hitler's Pope*, p. 175.

43 Carr, p. 126.

44 See Bruno Bettelheim, *The Informed Heart* (Harmondsworth: Penguin, 1988), pp. 290–3.

45 Robert C. Tucker, *Stalin as Revolutionary: 1879–1919* (London: Chatto and Windus, 1974), p. 454.
46 Preston, *Comrades! Portraits from the Spanish Civil War* (London: HarperCollins, 1999), pp. 20–31.
47 Whitaker, *We Cannot Escape History*, p. 114.
48 Preston, *Traíciones*.
49 Whitaker, *We Cannot Escape History*, pp. 108–9.
50 Preston, *Comrades!*, p. 27.
51 Preston, *Comrades!*, p. 29.
52 Knickerbocker, *Washington Times*, 10 May 1937, quoted in Herbert Southworth, *Guernica! Guernica!: A Study of Journalism, Diplomacy, Propaganda and History* (Berkeley, University of California Press, 1977), p. 52.
53 Gerald Howson, *Arms for Sale: The Untold History of the Spanish Civil War* (London: John Murray, 1998), pp. 146–52.
54 Whitaker, *We Cannot Escape History*, p. 102.
55 Whitaker, *We Cannot Escape History*, p. 103.
56 Thomas, p. 588.
57 Preston, *Franco*, p. 225.
58 Dixon, pp. 264–72.
59 Whitaker, *We Cannot Escape History*, p. 106.
60 Noel Monks, *Eyewitness* (London: Frederick Muller, 1955), pp. 80–3.
61 Southworth, *Guernica!*, pp. 12–13.
62 Galeazzo Ciano, *Diary: 1937–8* (London: Methuen, 1952), p. 91.
63 Thomas, p. 612.

CHAPTER 5: MENTAL FRAGMENTATION, PHYSICAL ANNIHILATION, POLITICAL UNIFICATION

1 *Documents on German Foreign Policy* (hereafter referred to as *DGFP*) (London: HMSO, 1949–64; Series D, 13 vols, Vol. III, 1951, p. 294.
2 Hugh Thomas, *The Spanish Civil War* (London: Hamish Hamilton, 3rd edn, 1977), p. 616.
3 Paul Preston, *Traíciones y tragedias: las tres Españas del 36* (Barcelona: Plaza y Janés, forthcoming).
4 Preston, *Franco: A Biography* (London: HarperCollins, 1993), p. 242.
5 Robert Waite, *Adolf Hitler: The Psychopathic God* (New York: Da Capo Press, 1993), p. 360.
6 Ernesto Gimenéz Caballero, *España y Franco* (Cegama: Ediciónes los Combatientes, 1938), p. 31.
7 Giménez Caballero, pp. 30–1.
8 Preston, *Franco*, p. 271.
9 Preston, *Franco*, p. 267.
10 Preston, *Franco*, p. 269.
11 Paul Preston, *Comrades! Portraits from the Spanish Civil War* (London: HarperCollins, 1999), p. 55.
12 See 'Narcissim and Group Psychology', chapter 6 in Jannine Chasseguet-Snürgal, *Creativity and Peversion* (London: Free Association Books, 1985).
13 Quotes assembled by Paul Preston in his unpublished article, 'Margarita Nelken'.
14 Preston, *Comrades!*, p. 277.

15 *Palabras de Caudillo, 19 abril 1937–19 abril 1938* (Ediciónes Fe 1938), pp. 178–9.
16 Arthur Koestler, *Spanish Testament* (London: Victor Gollancz, 1937), p. 34.
17 Koestler, p. 34.
18 Preston, *Franco*, p. 279.
19 *Palabras del Caudillo, 19 abril 1937–19 abril 1938*, pp. 72, 73.
20 Preston, *Franco*, p. 281.
21 Manuel Azaña, *Obras completas*, 4 vols (Mexico D.F.: Oasis, 1966–8).
22 Galeazzo Ciano, *Diary 1937–1938* (London: Methuen, 1952), p. 17; John Coverdale, *Italian Intervention in the Spanish Civil War* (Princeton: Princeton University Press, 1975), p. 318.
23 *DGFP*, D, Vol. III, p. 576.
24 Waite, p 383.
25 Norman Dixon, *The Psychology of Military Incompetence* (London: Pimlico, 1994), p. 275.
26 Ciano, p. 94.
27 Jo Labanyi, 'Censorship or the Fear of Mass Culture', in Helen Graham and Jo Labanyi (eds), *Spanish Cultural Studies: An Introduction* (Oxford: Oxford University Press, 1995), pp. 207–8.
28 Robert Waite, on Hitler: 'he appeared as a very different person to a great range of people; he impressed almost all of them', p. 375; see also Erich Fromm, *The Anatomy of Human Destructiveness* (London: Pimlico, 1997), p. 534.
29 John T. Whitaker, *We Cannot Escape History* (New York: Macmillan, 1943), p. 105.
30 Waite, p. 375.
31 Sir Robert Hodgson, *Spain Resurgent* (London: Hutchison, 1953), p. 102.
32 Erich Fromm, p. 550.
33 Preston, *Franco*, p. 305.
34 Preston, *Franco*, p. 309.
35 Ciano, p. 148.
36 Pilar Franco, *Nosotros los Franco* (Barcelona: Planeta, 1980), pp. 197–9.
37 Melanie Klein, 'Mourning and its Relation to Manic-Depressive States', in *Love, Guilt and Reparation* (London: Virago, 1988), p. 368.
38 7 November 1938, Franco makes a Declaration to an envoy of the United Press, *Palabras del Caudillo, 19 abril 1937–31 diciembre 1938* (Barcelona: Ediciónes Fe, 1939), p. 284.
39 Preston, *Franco*, p. 315.
40 Pilar Jaraiz Franco, *Historia de una disidencia* (Barcelona: Planeta, 1981), p. 143.
41 *Palabras del Caudillo, 19 abril–31 diciembre 1938*, pp. 295–315.
42 *Palabras del Caudillo, 19 abril–31 diciembre 1938*, p. 302.
43 Kemp, pp. 200–1.
44 Luis Bolin, *Spain, The Vital Years* (Philadelphia: Lippincott, 1967), p. 318.
45 Jo Labanyi, 'Women, Asian Hordes and the Threat of Self in Gimenéz Caballero's *Genio de España*', *BHS*, Vol. LXIII, 1996, p. 382.
46 Labanyi, 'Asian Hordes', p. 381.
47 Mike Richards, *A Time of Silence: Civil War and the Culture of Repression in Franco's Spain, 1936–45* (Cambridge: Cambridge University Press, 1998), p. 31.
48 Luis Bolin, pp. 323–4.
49 Ciano, *Diary 1939–1943* (London: Heinemann, 1947), p. 57.
50 Whitaker, p. 106.
51 Gustav Regler, *The Owl of Minerva* (London: Rupert Hart-Davis, 1959), pp. 322–3.
52 Preston, *Comrades!*, pp. 291, 298.

CHAPTER 6: DO YOU WANNA BE IN MY GANG?

1 Uxio Valentín, 'Franco Jokes: The Spaniards are Still Getting Even', *Journal of Popular Culture*, Vol. 20, spring 1987, p. 84.
2 *El pequeño libro pardo del general* (Paris: Ruedo Ibérico, 1972), p. 33.
3 Paul Preston, 'Franco and Azaña: Victor and Vanquished', *History Today*, May 1999, p. 22.
4 Mike Richards, *A Time of Silence: Civil War and the Culture of Repression in Franco's Spain, 1936–45* (Cambridge: Cambridge University Press, 1998), p. 9.
5 Richards, *A Time of Silence*, p. 34.
6 Madrid: Editorial Redención (redemption), 1940.
7 Robert Waite, *Adolf Hitler: The Psychopathic God* (New York: Da Capo Press, 1993), p. 370.
8 Paul Preston, in his forthcoming biography *Mussolini*.
9 Franco published his paranoid views on Freemasonry in *Masonería* (Madrid: Gráficas Valera, 1952) under the pseudonym 'Jakim Boor', the names of the two pillars of the Masonic Temple.
10 Francisco Franco, *Franco ha dicho . . . recopilación de las más importantes declaraciones del Caudillo desde la iniciacion del Alzamiento Nacional hasta el 31 de diciembre de 1946* (Madrid: Editorial Carlos Jaime, 1947), pp. 174–5.
11 *El pequeño libro pardo*, p. 175.
12 John Cornwell, *Hitler's Pope: The Secret History of Pius XII* (London: Viking, 1999), p. 344.
13 Klaus Theweleit, 'The Mass as Embodiment of a Specific Unconscious', in *Male Fantasies Volume 2: Male Bodies: Psychoanalyzing the White Terror*, p. 3.
14 Richards, *A Time of Silence*, p. 7.
15 Richards, *A Time of Silence*, p. 52.
16 John Hooper, *The New Spaniards* (London: Penguin, 1987), p. 167.
17 Jaime Salóm, 'The Cock's Short Flight', in Marion Peter Hold (ed.), *Drama Contemporary: Spain* (New York: Performing Arts Journal Publications, 1985), p. 169.
18 Helen Graham, 'Gender and the State: Women in the 1940s', in Helen Graham and Jo Labanyi (eds), *Spanish Cultural Studies: An Introduction* (Oxford: Oxford University Press, 1995), p. 192.
19 Gerald Brenan, *The Face of Spain* (London: Turnstile Press, 1950), p. 73.
20 Galinsoga, cited in *El pequeño libro pardo*, p. 181.
21 Preston, *Franco: A Biography* (London: HarperCollins, 1994), pp. 324–5.
22 Preston, *Franco*, p. 329.
23 Salóm, pp. 143, 154.
24 *Documents on German Foreign Policy (DGFP)* (London: HMSO, 1949–64; Series D, 13 vols), Vol. VI, 1956, p. 831.
25 *DGFP*, D, Vol. VI, p. 831.
26 Preston, *Franco*, p. 334.
27 Ciano, *Diary 1939–1943* (London: Heinemann, 1947), p. 119.
28 Preston, *Franco*, p. 337.
29 Waite, p. 385.
30 Waite, p. 385.
31 Sir Samuel Hoare, Viscount Templewood, *Ambassador on Special Mission* (London: Collins, 1946), pp. 56–7.
32 See Jo Labanyi, 'Censorship or the Fear of Mass Culture', in Graham and Labanyi (eds), *Spanish Cultural Studies*, pp. 207–14.

33 Preston, *Franco*, p. 341.

34 Hoare, p. 287.

35 Ramon Serrano Suñer, *Politica de España, 1936–75* (Madrid: Editorial Complutense, 1975), p. 30.

36 Preston, *Comrades! Portraits from the Spanish Civil War* (London: HarperCollins, 1999), p. 73.

37 Suñer, p. 30.

38 Waite, citing Dr Otto Kernberg, pp. 356–59.

39 *DGFP*, D, Vol. VIII, p. 181.

40 Brenan, pp. 99–100.

41 See Richards, *A Time of Silence*, pp. 127–46, and Stanley G. Payne, *The Franco Regime 1936–1975* (Madison: Wisconsin University Press, 1987).

42 John T. Whitaker, *We Cannot Escape History* (New York: Macmillan, 1943), p. 108.

43 See Bruno Bettelheim, *The Informed Heart* (Harmondsworth: Penguin, 1988): 'the most frequent topic of conversation ... was food – recollections of good food they had eaten before imprisonment and daydreams about what they would eat after liberation' (p. 233) and 'the omnipotent parent' (p. 297).

44 Alan Bullock, *Hitler: A Study in Tyranny* (New York: Smithmark, 1995), p. 35.

45 *The Goebbels Diaries 1939–41*, ed. by Fred Taylor and intro. by John Keegan (London: Hamish Hamilton, 1982), p. 85.

46 Hoare, pp. 45, 113.

47 Hoare, pp. 47–8.

48 Preston, *Franco*, pp. 357–8.

49 Hoare, p. 48.

50 *DGFP*, D, Vol. IX, pp. 585–8.

51 *DGFP*, D, Vol. IX, p. 587.

52 Hoare, p. 48.

53 Denis Smyth, 'Franco and World War Two', *History Today*, November 1985, p. 12.

54 Preston, *Franco*, pp. 368–70.

55 *DGFP*, D, Vol. X, p. 396.

56 Preston, *Franco*, p. 372.

57 *DGFP*, D, Vol. X, p. 443.

58 *DGFP*, D, Vol. X, p. 443.

59 Preston, *Franco*, p. 373.

60 *DGFP*, D, Vol. X, p. 463.

61 *DGFP*, D, Vol. IX, p. 88.

62 *DGFP*, D, Vol. XI, p. 85.

63 Preston, *Franco*, p. 380.

64 Preston, *Franco*, p. 381.

65 *DGFP*, D, Vol. XI, p. 213.

66 Ciano, p. 294.

67 *DGFP*, D, Vol. XI, p. 213.

68 *DGFP*, D, Vol. XI, p. 184.

69 Rosalinda Powell Fox, *The Grass and the Asphalt* (Cadiz: J. S. Harter and Associates, 1997), pp. 74–210.

70 *The Testament of Adolf Hitler: The Hitler–Bormann Documents*, intro. by Hugh Trevor-Roper (London: Cassell, 1959), p. 13.

71 Paul Schmidt, *Hitler's Interpreter: The Secret History of German Diplomacy 1935–1945* (London: Heinemann, 1951), pp. 193–6.

72 Bullock, p. 605; Trevor-Roper, p. 13.

73 Preston, *Franco*, p. 399.
74 Preston, *Franco*, p. 399.
75 Trevor-Roper, p. 14.
76 Preston, *Comrades!*, p. 60.
77 *DGFP*, D, Vol. XI, p. 467.
78 *DGFP*, D, Vol. IX, pp. 574–6.
79 *The Goebbels Diaries*, p. 159.
80 David Eccles (ed.), *By Safe Hand: Letters of Sybil and David Eccles 1939–1942* (London: Bodley Head, 1983), pp. 180, 206.
81 Preston, *Franco*, p. 406.
82 *DGFP*, D, Vol. XI, pp. 842–3.
83 Trevor-Roper, p. 21.
84 Preston, *Franco*, p. 416.
85 *DGFP*, D, Vol. XI, p. 1056.
86 Trevor-Roper, p. 49.
87 *DGFP*, D, Vol. XI, p. 1174.

CHAPTER 7: FRANCO FOR SALE

1 *Documents on German Foreign Policy* (*DGFP*) (London: HMSO, 1949–64; Series D, 13 vols), Vol. XII, 1964, p. 41.
2 *DGFP*, D, Vol. XI, p. 1141.
3 *DGFP*, D, Vol. XI, p. 1142.
4 *DGFP*, D, Vol. XI, p. 1218.
5 Paul Preston, *Franco: A Biography* (London: HarperCollins, 1993), p. 422.
6 Preston, *Franco*, p. 423.
7 Ray Moseley, *Mussolini's Shadow: The Double Life of Count Galeazzo Ciano* (New Haven and London: Yale University Press, 1999), p. 3.
8 Preston, *Franco*, p. 416.
9 *The Goebbels Diaries, January 1942–December 1943*, ed. by Louis P. Lochner (London: Hamish Hamilton, 1948), pp. 257, 323, 331; *The Diaries of Joseph Goebbels: Final Entries, 1945* ed. and intro. by Hugh Trevor-Roper (New York: G. P. Putnam's Sons, 1978), p. 17.
10 Ernst von Weisacker, John Andrews (trans.) *Memoirs* (London: Victor Gollancz, 1951), p. 164.
11 *DGFP*, D, Vol. XII, p. 197.
12 *The Testament of Adolf Hitler: The Hitler–Bormann Documents*, intro. by Hugh Trevor-Roper (London: Cassell, 1959), pp. 47–9.
13 *DGFP*, D, Vol. XII, p. 132.
14 *DGFP*, D, Vol. XII, p. 612.
15 Sir Samuel Hoare, Viscount Tempewood, *Ambassador on a Special Mission* (London: Collins, 1946), p. 292.
16 Preston, *Franco*, pp. 431–2.
17 Hoare, p. 56.
18 Preston, *Comrades! Portraits of the Spanish Civil War* (London: HarperCollins, 1999), p. 60.
19 Preston, *Franco*, p. 448.
20 *Goebbels Diaries, January 1942–December 1943*, p. 373.
21 John Hooper, *The New Spaniards* (London: Penguin, 1987), p. 153.
22 Hooper, *The New Spaniards*, p. 153.

23 Gerald Brenan, *The Face of Spain* (London: Turnstile Press, 1950), p. 33.

24 Marsha Kinder, *Blood Cinema: The Reconstruction of National Identity in Spain* (London: University of California Press, 1993), p. 198.

25 Kinder, p. 197.

26 Cf. Kinder, p. 198.

27 Peter Evans, 'Cifesa: Cinema and Authoritarian Aesthetics', in Helen Graham and Jo Labanyi (eds), *Spanish Cultural Studies: An Introduction* (Oxford: Oxford University Press, 1995), pp. 218–19.

28 *DGFP*, D, Vol. XII, p. 1080–1.

29 John Balfour, *Not Too Correct an Aureole: The Recollections of a Diplomat* (Salisbury: Michael Russell, 1983), p. 162.

30 John Cornwell, *Hitler's Pope: The Secret History of Piux XII* (London: Viking, 1999), p. 344.

31 Hoare, p. 113.

32 Preston, *Franco*, p. 442.

33 Preston, *Franco*, p. 446.

34 Robert Waite, *Adolf Hitler: The Psychopathic God* (New York: Da Capo Press, 1993), pp. 404, 409.

35 Preston, *Franco*, p. 450.

36 *Palabras del Caudillo, 19 abril 1937–7 diciembre 1942* (Madrid: Ediciónes de la Vice-secretará de Educación Popular, 1943), p. 204.

37 Francisco Martínez López, 'Testimonios sobre Franco y su familia', *FerrolAnalysis*, no. 14, pp. 70–5.

38 Enriquez González Duro, *Franco: Una biografía psicológica* (Madrid: Grandes Temas, 1992), pp. 34–5.

39 Martínez López, pp. 70–5.

40 Martínez López, pp. 70–5.

41 Duro, p. 39.

42 Preston, *Franco*, p. 458.

43 Preston, *Franco*, p. 459.

44 *DGFP*, D, Vol. XII, p. 612.

45 Preston, *Comrades!*, pp. 59–60.

46 Preston, *Franco*, p. 464.

47 Galeazzo Ciano, *Diary 1939–1943* (London: Heinemann, 1947), p. 501.

48 *DGFP*, D, Vol. XII, p. 612.

49 Preston, *Franco*, p. 462.

50 José María Toquero, *Franco y Don Juan: la oposición monárquica al franquismo* (Barcelona: Plaza y Janés, 1989), p. 55.

51 Sheelagh Ellwood, 'The Moving Image of the Franco Regime: Noticiarios y Documentles 1943–1975' in Helen Graham and Jo Labanyi (eds), *Spanish Cultural Studies: An Introduction* (Oxford: Oxford University Press, 1995), p. 202.

52 Mike Richards, *A Time of Silence: Civil War and the Culture of Repression in Franco's Spain, 1936–45* (Cambridge: Cambridge University Press, 1998), p. 65.

53 Preston, *Franco*, p. 473.

54 Ciano, p. 542.

55 *The Testament of Adolf Hitler: The Hitler–Bormann Documents*, intro. by Hugh Trevor-Roper (London: Cassell, 1959), p. 12.

56 William L. Beaulac, *Career Ambassador* (New York: Macmillan, 1951), pp. 193–4.

57 Hoare, p. 239.

58 Preston, *Franco*, p. 503.

59 Preston, *Franco*, p. 510.

60 Warren F. Kimball (ed.), *Churchill & Roosevelt: The Complete Correspondence*, Vol. III (London: Collins, 1984), pp. 162–3.

61 Preston, *Franco*, p. 512.

62 Hoare, p. 272.

63 Preston, *Franco*, p. 518.

64 Hoare, p. 306.

65 Hoare, p. 288.

66 Alan Bullock, *Hitler and Stalin* (London: HarperCollins, 1991), pp. 837, 841, 893.

67 Dennis Mack Smith, *Mussolini* (London: Weidenfeld and Nicolson, 1981), p. 315.

68 Trevor-Roper, pp. 69–75.

69 Trevor-Roper, p. 24.

70 Francisco Franco, *Textos de doctrina política. Palabras y escribos de 1945 a 1950* (Madrid: Publicationes Españolas, 1951), p. 617.

71 Richards, *A Time of Silence*, pp. 27–8.

72 Preston, *Franco*, p. 533.

CHAPTER 8: MIRROR, MIRROR ON THE WALL

1 Paul Preston, *Franco: A Biography* (London: HarperCollins, 1993), p. 536.

2 Sir Samuel Hoare, Viscount Templewood, *Ambassador on Special Mission* (London: Collins, 1946), p. 293.

3 Preston, *Franco*, p. 546.

4 Max Gallo, *Spain Under Franco: A History* (London: George Allen & Unwin, 1973), p. 291.

5 *El pequeño libro pardo del general* (Paris: Ruedo Ibérico, 1972), p. 190.

6 Preston, *Franco*, p. 559.

7 Preston, *Franco*, p. 564.

8 Preston, *Franco*, p. 567.

9 Gerald Brenan, *The Face of Spain* (London: Turnstile Press, 1950), p. 102.

10 Preston, *Franco*, p. 547.

11 Brenan, pp. 69, 73, 50–1, 163–6, 37.

12 Preston, *Franco*, p. 617.

13 Stanton Griffis, *Lying in State: The Diverting Recollections of a Self-Made Tycoon-Diplomat* (New York: Doubleday, 1952), p. 283.

14 John Balfour, *Not Too Correct an Aureole: The Recollections of a Diplomat* (Salisbury: Michael Russell, 1983), pp. 153–4.

15 Stanton Griffis, p. 283.

16 Balfour, pp. 153–6.

17 Preston, *Franco*, p. 596.

18 Balfour, p. 159.

19 Preston, *Franco*, p. 612.

20 Preston, *Franco*, p. 616.

21 Francisco Franco Salgado-Araujo, *Mis conversaciones privadas con Franco* (Barcelona: Planeta, 1976), pp. 159–60, 395.

22 Preston, *Franco*, p. 621.

23 Emma Dent Coad, 'Constructing the Nation: Francoist Architecture', in Helen Graham and Jo Labanyi (eds), *Spanish Cultural Studies: An Introduction* (Oxford: Oxford University Press, 1995), p. 224.

24 Robert G. L. Waite, *Adolf Hitler: The Psychopathic God* (New York: De Capo Press, 1993), p. 66.

25 Preston, *Franco*, p. 632.

26 Brenan, p. 37.

27 Charles Powell, *Juan Carlos of Spain: Self-Made Monarch* (London: Macmillan in association with St Antony's College, Oxford, 1996), pp. 16, 17.

28 Gallo, p. 241.

29 Franco Salgado-Araujo, p. 167.

30 Borja de Riquer I Permanyer, 'Social and Economic Change in a Climate of Political Immobilisation', in Graham and Labanyi (eds), *Spanish Cultural Studies*, pp. 265–6.

31 Brenan, p. 227.

32 Gallo, p. 253.

33 Brenan, p. 147.

34 Borja de Riquer I Permanyer, p. 267.

35 Preston, *Franco*, p. 646.

36 Preston, *Franco*, p. 648.

37 Gallo, p. 235.

38 Gallo, p. 235.

39 Preston, *Franco*, p. 651.

40 Powell, p. 17.

41 Gallo, p. 254.

42 Brenan, pp. 86, 11.

CHAPTER 9: PANDORA'S BOX

1 Paul Preston, *Franco: A Biography* (London: HarperCollins, 1993), p. 725.

2 See Preston, *Franco*, pp. 656–8.

3 Preston, *Franco*, p. 658.

4 Preston, *Franco*, p. 664.

5 Max Gallo, *Spain Under Franco: A History* (London: George Allen & Unwin, 1973), p. 248.

6 Edouard de Blaye, *Franco and the Politics of Spain* (Harmondsworth: Penguin, 1976), p. 194.

7 Gallo, p. 249.

8 Erich Fromm, *The Anatomy of Human Destructiveness* (London: Pimlico, 1997), p. 542.

9 Preston, *Franco*, p. 723.

10 Preston, *Franco*, p. 675.

11 Gallo, p. 274; see also Frances Lannon, 'Catholicism and Social Change', in Helen Graham and Jo Labanyi (eds), *Spanish Cultural Studies: An Introduction* (Oxford: Oxford University Press, 1995), p. 280.

12 Lannon, p. 277.

13 Helen Graham, 'Cracking the Fascist Carapace', *Times Higher Education Supplement*, 4 October 1996, p. 30.

14 Paul Preston, *Comrades! Portraits from the Spanish Civil War* (London: HarperCollins, 1999), p. 71.

15 Willard L. Beaulac, *Career Ambassador* (New York: Macmillan, 1951), p. 179.

16 Preston, *Franco*, p. 679.

17 Dwight D. Eisenhower, *The White House Years: Waging Peace 1956–1961* (London: Heinemann, 1965), p. 423.

18 Gallo, pp. 271–2.
19 John Hooper, *The New Spaniards* (London: Penguin, 1987), p. 152.
20 de Blaye, p. 230.
21 John London, 'The Ideology and Practice of Sport', in Graham and Labanyi (eds), *Spanish Cultural Studies*, p. 207.
22 Gallo, p. 285.
23 Charles Powell, *Juan Carlos of Spain: Self-Made Monarch* (London: Macmillan in association with St Antony's College, Oxford, 1996), p. 25.
24 Powell, p. 27.
25 Powell, p. 26.
26 de Blaye, p. 214.
27 Guy Hermet, *The Communists in Spain* (Saxon House, Lexington Books, 1971), p. 149.
28 de Blaye, p. 216.
29 Lannon, pp. 278–9.
30 Preston, *Franco*, p. 717.
31 See Hugh L'Etaing, *Fit to Lead?* (London: William Heinemann Medical Books, 1980), pp. 86–92.
32 Stanley G. Payne, *The Franco Regime 1936–1975* (Madison: Wisconsin University Press, 1987), p. 511.
33 Preston, *Franco*, pp. 727–8.
34 Francisco Franco, *Discursos y mensajes del Jefe del Estado 1964–1967* (Madrid: Publicaciones Españolas, 1968), p. 469.
35 Preston, *Franco*, p. 731.
36 Gallo, p. 343.
37 Powell, p. 37–8.
38 de Blaye, p. 247.
39 Preston, *Franco*, p. 741.
40 Powell, p. 39.
41 de Blaye, p. 226.
42 Jaime Peñafiel, *El General y su tropa: mis recuerdos de la familia Franco* (Madrid: Temas de Hoy, 1992), p. 102.
43 Henry Kissinger, *The White House Years* (London: Weidenfeld and Nicolson/Michael Joseph, 1979), p. 932.
44 Pilar Jaraiz Franco, *Historia de una disidencia* (Barcelona: Planeta, 1981), p. 203.
45 de Blaye, p. 319.
46 Vernon A. Walters, *Silent Missions* (New York: Doubleday, 1978), pp. 551–6.
47 Lannon, p. 279.
48 Francisco Franco, *Pensamiento político de Franco*, ed. by Agustín del Río Cisneros, 2 vols (Madrid: Ediciones del Movimiento, 1975), Vol. II, p. 862.
49 Hugh L'Etaing, *Ailing Leaders in Power: 1914–1994* (London: The Royal Society of Medicine Press, 1995), pp. 48–53.
50 Preston, *Franco*, p. 761.
51 Paul Preston, *The Triumph of Democracy in Spain* (London: Methuen, 1986), p. 50.
52 Preston, *Franco*, p. 762.
53 Preston, *Franco*, p. 764.
54 Preston, *Triumph of Democracy*, p. 59.
55 Preston, *Triumph of Democracy*, p. 60.
56 Paul Preston, *The Politics of Revenge: Fascism and the Military in 20th Century Spain* (London: Routledge, 1995), p. 183.
57 Preston, *Triumph of Democracy*, p. 61.

58 Preston, *Franco*, p. 767.

59 Vicente Pozuelo, *Los 476 ultimos días de Franco* (Barcelona: Planeta, 1980), p. 124.

60 Preston, *Triumph of Democracy*, p. 66.

61 Preston, *Triumph of Democracy*, p. 71.

62 José Utrera Molina, *Sin cambiar de bandera* (Barcelona: Planeta, 1989), p. 228.

63 Utrera Molina, p. 232; Javier Figuero and Luis Herrero, *La muerte de Franco jamás contada* (Barcelona: Planeta, 1985), p. 20.

64 Preston, *Comrades!*, p. 54.

65 Gallo, p. 281.

66 Pozuelo, pp. 167–8.

67 Preston, *Triumph of Democracy*, p. 73.

68 Preston, *Triumph of Democracy*, p. 74.

69 Preston, *Triumph of Democracy*, p. 75.

70 Hugh L'Etaing, *Fit to Lead*, pp. 85–6.

EPILOGUE: 'A SPHINX WITHOUT A SECRET'

1 Quoted by Alan Bullock in *Hitler and Stalin: Parallel Lives* (London: HarperCollins, 1991), p. 1075.

2 As Bruno Bettelheim points out in *The Informed Heart* (Harmondsworth: Penguin, 1988), even people who do not actively support a totalitarian regime often feel tainted by its existence and guilty at their failure to overthrow it, however impossible that would have been.

3 Paul Preston, *Triumph of Democracy in Spain* (London: Methuen, 1986), p. 80.

4 Preston, *Triumph of Democracy*, p. 187.

5 Preston, *Triumph of Democracy*, p. 218.

6 Eduard de Blaye, *Franco and the Politics of Spain* (Hardmondsworth: Penguin, 1976), p. 230.

7 John Hooper, *The New Spaniards* (Harmondsworth: Penguin, 1987), pp. 157–80.

8 Hooper, pp. 198–9.

Further Reading

Abella, Rafael, 'Nicolas Franco Salgado-Araujo y su tiempo: Esbozo biográfica', in Jaime Salóm, *El corto vuelo del gallo* (Barcelona: Grijalbo, 1981).

Adorno, T. W., Frenkel-Brunswik, Else, Levinson, Daniel J., and Nevitt Sanford, R., *The Authoritarian Personality* (New York: Harper, 1950).

Andrade, Jaime de (pseudonym Francisco Franco), *Raza: Anecdotaria para el guión de una película* (Madrid: Ediciónes Numancia, 1942).

Arrarás, Joaquín, *Francisco Franco* (London, Geoffrey Bles, 1938).

Balfour, John, *Not Too Correct an Aureole: The Recollections of a Diplomat* (Salisbury: Michael Russell, 1983).

Balfour, Sebastian, *The End of the Spanish Empire: 1898–1923* (Oxford: Clarendon Press, 1997)

Balfour, Sebastian and Preston, Paul (eds), *Spain and the Great Powers in the Twentieth Century* (London and New York: Routledge, 1999).

Beaulac, William L., *Career Ambassador* (New York, Macmillan, 1951).

Belton, Neil, *The Good Listener* (London: Phoenix, 1999).

Bettelheim, Bruno, *The Informed Heart* (London: Penguin, 1988).

Bolín, Luis, *Spain, The Vital Years* (Philadelphia: Lippincott, 1967).

Brenan, Gerald, *The Face of Spain* (London: Turnstile Press, 1950).

Brenan, Gerald, *The Spanish Labyrinth* (Cambridge: Cambridge University Press, 1943).

Bullock, Alan, *Hitler and Stalin: Parallel Lives* (London: HarperCollins, 1991).

Bullock, Alan, *Hitler: A Study in Tyranny* (Harmondsworth: Penguin, 2nd edn, 1965).

Carr, Raymond, *The Spanish Tragedy: The Civil War in Perspective* (London: Weidenfeld and Nicolson, 1977).

Carr, Raymond and Fusi, Juan Pablo, *Spain from Dictatorship to Democracy* (London: George Allen and Unwin, 1979).

Coles, S. F. A., *Franco of Spain* (London: Neville Spearman, 1955).

Cornwell, John, *Hitler's Pope: The Secret History of Pius XII* (London: Viking, 1999).

Coverdale, John, *Italian Intervention in the Spanish Civil War* (Princeton, NJ: Princeton University Press, 1975).

Crozier, Brian, *Franco: A Biographical History* (London: Eyre and Spottiswoode, 1967).

de Blaye, Eduardo, *Franco and the Politics of Spain* (Harmondsworth: Penguin, 1976).

Dixon, Norman, *On the Psychology of Military Incompetence* (London: Pimlico, 1994).

Dixon, Norman, *Our Own Worst Enemy* (London: Jonathan Cape, 1987).

Eccles, David (ed.), *By Safe Hand: Letters of Sybil and David Eccles 1939–1942* (London: Bodley Head, 1983).

Ellwood, Sheelagh, *Franco* (London: Longman, 1994).

Ellwood, Sheelagh, *The Spanish Civil War* (Oxford: Blackwell, 1991).
Erikson, Erik H., *Childhood and Society* (London: Vintage, 1995).
Fest, Joachim, *Hitler* (Harmondsworth: Penguin, 1977).
Fest, Joachim, *The Face of the Third Reich* (Harmondsworth: Penguin, 1979).
Franco, Comandante Francisco, *Diario de un bandera* (Madrid: Editorial Pueyo, 1922).
Franco, Francisco, *Palabras del Caudillo, 19 abril 1937–19 abril 1938* (Ediciónes Fe, 1938).
Franco, Francisco, *Palabras del Caudillo, 19 abril 1937–31 diciembre 1938* (Barcelona: Ediciónes Fe, 1939).
Franco, Francisco, *Textos de doctrina política: palabras y escritos de 1945–1950* (Madrid: Publicaciónes Españolas, 1951).
Franco Bahamonde, Pilar, *Nosotros los Franco* (Barcelona: Planeta, 1980).
Franco Salgado-Araujo, Francisco, *Mis conversaciónes privadas con Franco* (Barcelona: Planeta, 1976).
Franco Salgado-Araujo, Francisco, *Mi vida junto a Franco* (Barcelona: Planeta, 1977).
Fraser, Ronald, *Blood of Spain: The Experience of Civil War 1936–1939* (London: Allen Lane, 1979).
Fromm, Erich, *Fear of Freedom* (London: Routledge & Kegan Paul, 1966).
Fromm, Erich, *The Anatomy of Human Destructiveness* (London, Pimlico, 1997).
Fusi, Juan Pablo, *Franco* (London: Unwin Hyman, 1985).
Gallo, Max, *Spain Under Franco: A History* (London: George Allen & Unwin, 1973).
Garriga, Ramón, *Ramón Franco, el hermano maldito* (Barcelona, Planeta, 1978).
Gay, Peter, *Freud for Historians* (New York and Oxford: Oxford University Press, 1985).
González Duro, Enrique, *Franco: Una biografía psicológica* (Madrid: Temas de Hoy, 1992).
Gracia, Vincente, and Salgado, Enrique, *Las cartas de amor de Franco* (Barcelona: Ediciónes Actuales, 1978).
Graham, Helen, *Socialism and War: The Spanish Socialist Party in Power and Crisis: 1936–1939* (Cambridge: Cambridge University Press, 1991).
Graham, Helen, and Labanyi, Jo (eds), *Spanish Cultural Studies: An Introduction* (Oxford: Oxford University Press, 1995).
Griffis, Stanton, *Lying in State: The Diverting Recollections of a Self-Made Tycoon-Diplomat* (New York: Doubleday, 1952).
Hermet, Guy, *The Communists in Spain* (Farnborough: Lexington Books, 1971).
Hills, George, *Franco: The Man and his Nation* (New York: Macmillan, 1967).
Hoare, Sir Samuel, *Ambassador on a Special Mission* (London: Collins, 1946).
Hodgson, Sir Robert, *Spain Resurgent* (London: Hutchison, 1953).
Hooper, John, *The New Spaniards* (London: Penguin, 1987).
Jaraiz Franco, Pilar, *Historia de una disidencia* (Barcelona: Planeta, 1981).
Jung, C. G., *Jung on Evil*, ed. by Murray Stein (London: Routledge, 1995).
Kemp, Peter, *Mine were of Trouble* (London: Cassell, 1957).
Kinder, Marsha, *Blood Cinema: The Reconstruction of National Identity in Spain* (Berkeley: University of California Press, 1993).
Klein, Melanie, *Love, Guilt and Reparation* (London: Virago, 1988).
Koestler, Arthur, *Spanish Testament* (London: Victor Gollancz, 1937).
Labanyi, Jo, 'Women, Asian Hordes and the Threat of Self in Giménez Caballero's *Genio de España*', *Bulletin of Hispanic Studies*, Vol. LXXIII, 1996, pp. 377–87.
L'Etaing, Hugh, *Ailing Leaders in Power: 1914–1994* (London: The Royal Society of Medicine Press, 1995).
L'Etaing, Hugh, *Fit to Lead?* (London: William Heinemann Medical Books, 1980).
Mack Smith, Denis, *Mussolini* (London: Weidenfeld & Nicolson, 1981).
Miller, Alice, *Breaking Down the Wall of Silence* (London: Virago, 1992).

Miller, Alice, *For Your Own Good: The Roots of Violence in Child-Reading* (London: Virago, 1987).

Miller, Webb, *I Found No Peace* (London: The Book Club, 1937).

Monks, Neil, *Eyewitness* (London: Frederick Muller, 1955).

Moseley, Ray, *Mussolini's Shadow: The Double Life of Count Galeazzo Ciano* (New Haven and London: Yale University Press, 1999).

Payne, Stanley G., *Franco's Spain* (London: Routledge & Kegan Paul, 1968).

Payne, Stanley G., *Politics and the Military in Modern Spain* (Stanford: Stanford University Press, 1967).

Payne, Stanley G., *The Franco Regime 1936–1975* (Madison: Wisconsin University Press, 1987).

Powell, Charles, *Juan Carlos of Spain: Self-Made Monarch* (London: Macmillan, 1996).

Pozuelo, Vicente, *Los 476 últimos diás de Franco* (Barcelona: Planeta, 1980).

Preston, Paul, *A Concise History of the Spanish Civil War* (London: HarperCollins, 1996).

Preston, Paul, *Comrades! Portraits from the Spanish Civil War* (London: HarperCollins, 1999).

Preston, Paul, *Franco: A Biography* (London: HarperCollins, 1993).

Preston, Paul, *The Coming of the Spanish Civil War: Reform, Reaction and Revolution in the Second Republic* (London: Routledge, 2nd edn, 1994).

Preston, Paul, *The Politics of Revenge: Fascism and the Military in 20th Century Spain* (London: Routledge, 1995).

Preston, Paul, *The Triumph of Democracy in Spain* (London: Methuen, 1986).

Ramírez, Luis (pseudonym of Luciano Rincón), *Franco: la obsesión de ser, la obsesión de poder* (Paris: Ruedo Ibérico, 1976).

Regler, Gustav, *The Owl of Minerva* (London: Rupert Hart-Davis, 1959).

Richards, Mike, *A Time of Silence: Civil War and the Culture of Repression in Franco's Spain, 1936–45* (Cambridge: Cambridge University Press, 1998).

Salóm, Jaime, 'The Cock's Short Flight', in *Drama Contemporary: Spain* (New York: Performing Arts Journal Publications, 1985), pp. 139–90.

Schmidt, Paul, *Hitler's Interpreter: The Secret History of German Diplomacy 1935–1945* (London: Heinemann, 1951).

Serrano Suñer, Ramón, *Política de España 1936–75* (Madrid: Editorial Complutense, 1975).

Southworth, Herbert Rutledge, *Guernica! Guernica!: A Study of Journalism, Diplomacy, Propaganda and History* (Berkeley: University of California Press, 1977).

Suárez Fernández, Luis, *Francisco Franco y su tiempo*, 8 vols (Madrid: Fundación Nacional Francisco Franco, 1984).

Theweleit, Klaus, *Male Fantasies: Volume 1: Women Floods Bodies Histories* (Minneapolis: University of Minnesota Press, 1987).

Theweleit, Klaus, *Male Fantasies: Volume 2: Male bodies: Psychoanalyzing the White Terror* (Minneapolis, University of Minnesota Press, 1989).

Thomas, Hugh, *The Spanish Civil War* (London: Hamish Hamilton, 3rd edn 1977).

Trevor-Roper, H. R. (intro.), *The Testament of Adolf Hitler: The Hitler–Bormann Documents (February–April 1945)* (London: Cassell, 1959).

Trythall, J. W. D., *Franco* (London: Rupert Hart-Davis, 1970).

Tucker, Robert C., *Stalin as Revolutionary: 1879–1929* (London: Chatto & Windus, 1974).

Vilallonga, José Luis de, *El sable del Caudillo: Historia secreta del hombre que gobernó España como un cortijo* (Barcelona: Plaza y Janés, 1997).

Waite, Robert, *Adolf Hitler: The Psychopathic God* (New York: Da Capo Press, 1993).

Walters, Vernon A., *Silent Missions* (New York: Doubleday, 1978).

Whitaker, John T., *We Cannot Escape History* (New York: Macmillan, 1943).

Winnicott, D. W., *Human Nature* (London: Free Association Books, 1988).

Winnicott, D. W., *The Family and Individual Development* (London: Tavistock Publications, 1965).

Winnicott, D. W., *The Maturational Processes and the Facilitating Environment* (London: Karnac Books, 1990).

Index

Spanish civil war – *contd*
Italian/German support for, 114–15, 116–19; and threat of the monarchy, 115; and assaults on the Basques, 122–5, 134–5; political/territorial consolidations, 125–9, 135–7; collapse of Republicans, 137–9; departure of International Brigades, 144
Spanish Foreign Legion, 41, 42–3, 47, 48, 48–9, 51, 90, 98, 99, 105, 110
Sperrle, General Hugo von, 111, 113, 121, 122, 131
Stalin, Josef, 1, 54, 111–12, 202
Stohrer, Baron Eberhard von, 136, 166, 169
Strunk, Captain Roland von, 114
Suanzes, Juan Antonio, 217
Suárez, Adolfo, 258–9
Subirán, Sofia, 34–5
Suez Canal, 175, 213, 229

Talavera de la Reina, 100
Tangier, 166, 193, 203
Tejero, Colonel Antonio, 259
Tella, Lieutenant-Colonel Heli Rolando de, 98
Tercera Fuerza, 220
Tercio de Mutilados, 110
Teruel (Morocco), 137–8, 139
Tetuán (Morocco), 35, 51, 89, 92
Thomas, Hugh, 95, 117
Tifaruin (Morocco), 49
Toledo, 23–4, 25, 52, 55, 81, 93, 100, 102–4
Treaty of Friendship and Non-Aggression (1940), 168
Tripartite Pact, 170, 173, 205
Truman, Harry S., 197, 207, 209, 212, 213, 216
Tusquets, Father Juan, 151

Unamuno, Miguel de, 110
Unión General de Trabajodores (UGT), 39, 76
Unión Militar Democrática (UMD), 250, 254
Unión Militar Española, 72, 80
Unión Social-Demócrata Española (USDE), 253
United Nations, 201, 207, 208–9, 213, 218, 243
Utrera Molina, José, 249, 250, 253

Valencia, 93, 111, 135, 140, 141
Valenzuela, Colonel Rafael de, 48
Valle de los Caídos, 166, 219
Varela, General José Enrique, 54, 79, 100, 104, 113, 116, 133, 137, 185, 187, 205
Vatican, 115, 132, 153, 202, 218, 239, 243, 248, 250
Vera, General Felix de, 71
Victoria Eugenia, Queen, 243, 244
Vigón, Jorge, 78
Vigón Suerodiaz, General Juan, 120, 122, 139–40, 165, 166, 203, 220
Villaverde, Marqués de, 215, 251, 252
Viñuelas, Castle of, 162
Vittorio Emanuele III, 189

Waite, Robert, 158
Walters, Vernon, 247
Whitaker, John, 94, 97, 98, 100, 102, 104, 109, 112, 113, 120
Windsor, Duke of, 167
women, 152–4, 180, 188, 211

Yagüe, Colonel Juan, 26, 77, 87, 90, 98, 99, 102, 103, 104, 111, 140–1, 142, 167, 189, 192